Weismann, August

The Evolution Theory

Vol. 2

Weismann, August

The Evolution Theory

Vol. 2

Inktank publishing, 2018

www.inktank-publishing.com

ISBN/EAN: 9783747749906

THE

EVOLUTION THEORY

BY

DR. AUGUST WEISMANN

PROFESSOR OF ZOOLOGY IN THE UNIVERSITY OF FREIBURG IN BREISGAU

TRANSLATED WITH THE AUTHOR'S CO-OPERATION

BY

J. ARTHUR THOMSON

REGIUS PROFESSOR OF NATURAL HISTORY IN THE UNIVERSITY OF ABERDEEN

AND

MARGARET R. THOMSON

ILLUSTRATED

IN TWO VOLUMES

VOL. II

LONDON

EDWARD ARNOLD

41 & 43 MADDOX STREET, BOND STREET, W.

1904

CONTENTS

LIST OF ILLUSTRATIONS

LECTURE XX

REGENERATION

Budding and division—Every theory of regeneration in the meantime only provisional, a mere 'portmanteau theory'—Regeneration not a primary character—Volvox—Hydra—Vital affinities—Planarians—Heteromorphoses—Enemies of Hydroid-colonies—Regeneration in Plants—In Amphibians—In Earthworms—Different degrees of regenerative capacity according to the liability of the part to injury—Different results of longitudinal halving in Earthworms and in Planarians—Regeneration in Birds—The disappearance of the power of regeneration is very slow—Morgan's experiments on Hermit-crabs—Autotomy in Crustaceans and Insects—Regeneration of the lens in Triton.

We have endeavoured to explain the handing on of the complement of heritable qualities from one generation to another as due to a continuity of the germ-plasm, and we assumed that the germ-cells never arise except from cells in the 'germ-track'; that is, from cells which are equipped, from the fertilized egg-cell onwards, with a complete sample of slumbering germ-plasm, and are thereby enabled to become germ-cells, and, subsequently, new individuals, in which the aggregate of inherited primary constituents implied in the germ-plasm can again attain to development.

We have now to consider other cases of inheritance in relation to the same problem—the origin of their hereditary equipment.

We know, of course, that new individuals may arise apart from germ-cells, that, in many of the lower animals and in plants, they may arise by budding and fission.

For both these cases the germ-plasm theory will suffice, with a somewhat modified form of the same assumption which we made in regard to the formation of germ-cells. The origin of a new individual by budding seems often, indeed, to proceed from any set of somatic cells in the mother animal; but somatic cells, if they contain solely the determinants controlling themselves, cannot possibly give rise to a complete new individual, since this presupposes the presence of *all* the determinants of the species. But as these determinants cannot be formed *de novo*, the budding cells must contain, in addition to the usual controlling somatic determinants, idioplasm in a latent, inactive state, which only becomes active under certain internal or external influences, and then gives rise to the formation of a bud. The source of this accessory idioplasm must, however, be looked for only in the egg-cell.

In plants this bud-idioplasm must be complete germ-plasm, because the budding starts only from one kind of cell, the cambium-cells; but in animals in which—as it seems—it always proceeds from at least two different kinds of cells—those of the ectoderm and those of the endoderm—the matter is more complex. In this case these two kinds of cells will contain as bud-idioplasm two different groups of determinants, which mutually complete each other and form perfect germ-plasm, and only the co-operation of these two sets will give rise to the formation of a bud. I will not, however, go further into detail in regard to these relations, for the theory can do nothing more here than formulate what has been observed; it is hardly in a position to help us to a better understanding of the facts.

The case is not much clearer in regard to the processes which lead to the replacing of lost parts. The manifold phenomena of regeneration can also be brought into harmony with the theory, if we attribute to those cells from which the replacing or entire reconstruction of the lost part arises an 'accessory-idioplasm,' which, at least, contains the determinants indispensable to the building up of the part. It is possible that the assumed accessory idioplasm frequently contains a much larger complex of determinants, and that it depends on the liberating stimuli which, and how many of these, will become active.

If we take a survey of regenerative phenomena in the animal kingdom, it strikes us at once that the capacity is very different in different species, extraordinarily great in some and very slight in others. In general it is greater in lower animals than in higher, but, nevertheless, the degree of differentiation cannot be the only factor that determines the capacity for regeneration. That unicellular organisms can completely replace lost parts, that even a piece of an infusorian can reconstruct the whole animal if only the piece contain a part of the nucleus, we have already seen when discussing the significance of the nuclear substance. In this case the nucleus must contain the complete germ-plasm, that is, the collective determinants of the species, and these induce the reconstruction of the lost part, though they do so in a way that is still entirely obscure to us. In the meantime, our interpretation will not carry us further, either here or in regard to any other order of vital phenomena. To go further would be little short of propounding a causal theory of life itself; it would mean having a complete and real 'explanation' of what 'life' is. As yet no one has been able to claim this position. We can see the different stages through which every organism passes, and that they arise one out of the other; we can even penetrate down to the succession of those delicate and marvellously complex processes which effect nuclear and cell-division; but we are still far from being able to deduce, except quite empirically, from the present state of a cell what the succeeding one will be, that is, from being able to understand the succession of events as a necessary nexus which could be predicted. How a biophor comes to develop from itself the phenomena of life is quite unknown to us; we know neither the interaction of the ultimate material particles nor the forces which bring it about; we cannot tell what moves the hordes of different kinds of biophors to range themselves together in a particular order, what molecular displacements and variations arise from this, or what influence the external world has, and so forth. We see only the visible outcome of an endless number of invisible movements—growth, division, multiplication, reconstruction, and differentiation.

As long as we are so far from an understanding of life no theory of regeneration can be anything more than a 'portmanteau theory,' as Delage once expressed himself in relation to the whole theory of inheritance, a theory which is like a portmanteau in that one can only take out of it what has previously been put in. If we wish to explain the renewal of the aboral band of cilia in a Stentor, we first pack our trunk, in this case the nucleus of the Infusorian, with the determinants of the ciliated region, and then think of these as being liberated by the stimulus of wounding, and being brought to and arranged in the proper place by unknown forces to reconstruct the ciliary region in some unknown way. No one could be more clearly aware than I am that this is not an exhaustive causal explanation of the process itself. Nevertheless, it is not quite without value, inasmuch as it allows us at least to bring the facts together in rational order—in this case the dependence of the faculty of regeneration on the presence of nuclear substance—under a formula which we can use provisionally, that is, with which we can raise new questions. As soon as we ascend higher in the series of organisms the theory gains a greater value, for, while we leave altogether out of account any answer to the ultimate question, and thus renounce for the present the attempt to find out how the determinants set to work to call to life the parts which they control, we are brought face to face with other, in a sense, preliminary questions which we *can* solve, and the solution of which seems to me at least not entirely without value.

The first of these questions runs thus; Is the power of regeneration a fundamental, primary character of every living being in the sense that it is present everywhere in equal strength, independently

B 2

of external conditions, and thus is an inevitable outcome of the primary characters of the living substance? Or is it, though primaeval in its beginnings, a phenomenon of adaptation, which depends on a special mechanism, and does not occur everywhere in equal extent and potency?

We have already become acquainted with some facts which must incline us to the latter view. The globular Alga-colonies of *Volvox* (Fig. 63) consist of two kinds of cells, of which only one kind, the reproductive cells, possess the power of reproducing the whole, the others, the flagellate, or, as we called them, somatic cells, being only able to produce their like, but never the whole.

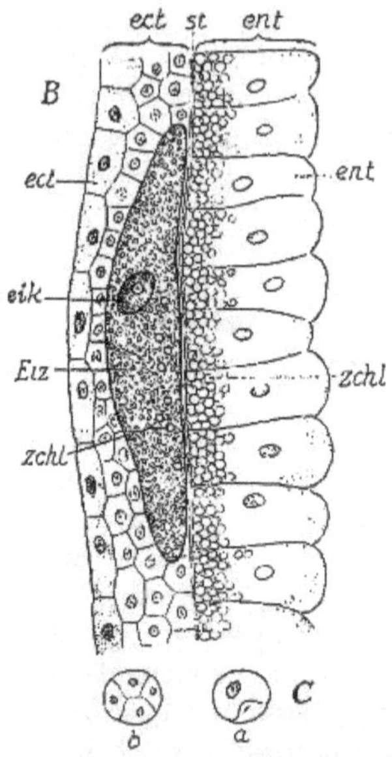

FIG. 35 *B* (repeated). *Hydra viridis*, the Green Freshwater Polyp. Section through the body-wall, somewhere in the direction of *ov* in Fig. 35 *A*. *Eiz*, the ovum lying in the ectoderm (*ect*), and including zoochlorellæ (*schl*) which have immigrated from the endoderm (*ent*) through the supporting lamella (*st*). After Hamann.

New investigations which have been carried out by Dr. Otto Hübner in my Institute have placed these facts beyond doubt. We may conclude that, in this case, a disintegration of the germ-plasm has taken place during ontogeny, by means of differential cell-division, so that only the reproductive cells receive the complete germ-plasm, while the somatic cells receive only the determinants necessary to their own specific differentiation, the somatic determinants.

In this case regeneration and reproduction coincide; there is no regeneration except the origin of a new individual from a reproductive cell.

Let us now ascend to the lowest of the Metazoa, for instance, the freshwater polyp, Hydra (Fig. 35 *A*), and we find a high degree of regenerative capacity in the restricted sense, for, in addition to the power of producing germ-cells, that is, cells which, when two combine in amphimixis, give rise again to a new animal, almost any part of the polyp can regrow a whole animal. Not only has Hydra been cut in from two to twenty different pieces, but it has even been chopped up into innumerable fragments, and yet each of these, under favourable circumstances, was able to grow again into a complete animal. Nevertheless, we are not justified in concluding that every cell possesses the power of reproducing the whole. If, with the help of a bristle, we turn one of these polyps outside in like the finger of a glove, and then prevent it turning right again by sticking the bristle transversely through it, it does not live, but soon dies, obviously because the cells of the two layers of the body, ectoderm and endoderm, cannot mutually replace each other, and cannot mutually produce each other. The inner layer, now turned outwards, cannot resist the influence of the water, and the outer layer, now turned inwards, cannot effect digestion; in short, one cannot be transformed into the other, and we must therefore conclude that both are specialized, that they no longer contain the complete germ-plasm, but only the specific determinants of ectoderm and endoderm respectively.

The animal's high regenerative capacity must therefore depend on the fact that certain cells of the ectoderm are equipped with the complete determinant-complex of the ectoderm, in the form of an inactive accessory idioplasm, which is excited to regenerative activity by the stimulus of wounding, and that, in the same way, the cells of the endoderm are equipped with the whole determinant-complex of the endoderm. It need not be decided whether all or only many of the cells, perhaps the younger ones, are thus adapted for regeneration; in any case a great many of them must be distributed throughout the whole body, with perhaps the exception of the tentacles, which are by themselves unable to reproduce the whole animal. When the animal is mutilated, the cells of both layers, equipped with their respective determinant-aggregates, co-operate in reproducing the whole from a part.

It is true that even with these assumptions we only reach the threshold of a real explanation. For, given that all the determinants of the species must be present in a fragment, we are not in a position to show how these set about reconstructing the animal in its integrity, and the most that we can say is, that it must depend on the specific kind of stimulus to which each of the cells is exposed through its direct and more remote environment, which determinants are to be first liberated, and therefore which parts are to be reconstructed.

That there are at work regulative forces, such as we were already compelled to assume in regard to the division and regeneration of unicellular organisms, as to the nature of which we cannot yet make any definite statement, but which we may call 'polarities,' or, as I prefer to say, 'affinities,' is shown by countless experiments which have been made, particularly with the freshwater polyp. Thus Rand cut off the anterior end of the polyp with its circle of tentacles, and the excised disk of living substance lengthened in a transverse direction, so that half the tentacles came to lie to the right, the other half to the left, while the body developed between these two groups, so that they became further and further separated from each other, till finally the original transverse axis of the animal became the longitudinal axis. One group of tentacles survived and surrounded the new mouth, while the other at the opposite aboral pole, the new foot, died off. This total change of structure in the polyp, as to the arrangement of its main parts, points to unknown forces, which cannot depend on the determinants as such, but on the vital characters of the living parts, and on the interactions of these with one another.

The same holds true of all the lower Metazoa that have highly

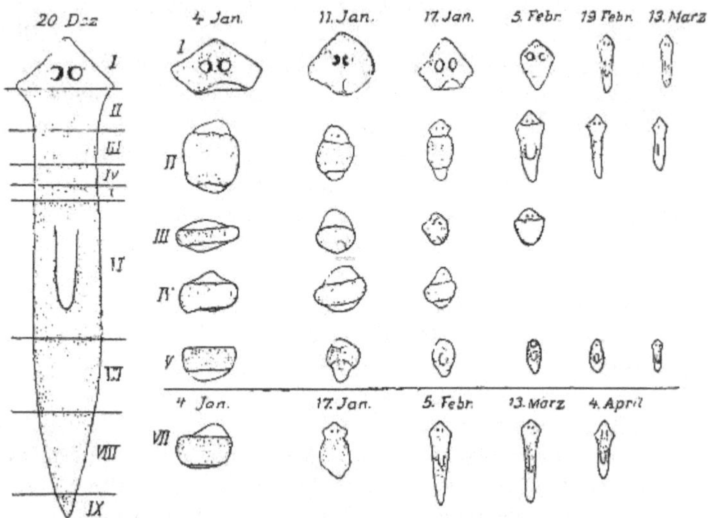

FIG. 96. A Planarian cut transversely into nine pieces. The regeneration of seven of these into entire animals is shown. After Morgan.

developed regenerative capacity, not only of polyps, but of worms such as the Planarians. Through the experiments of Loeb, Morgan, Voigt, Bickford, and others, we know that these animals respond to almost every mutilation by complete reconstruction, that they may, for instance, as is indicated in Fig. 96, be cut transversely into nine or ten pieces with the result that each of these pieces grows again to a whole animal, unless external influences are unfavourable and prevent it.

Something similar happens if the head be cut off a Tubularia-polyp, it forms a new head with proboscis and tentacles. It does so, at least, if the stalk of the polyp be left in the normal position; but if it be stuck into the sand in the reverse position a head arises at the end which is uppermost, where the roots arose previously, and the previous head-end now sends out roots. By suspending a beheaded stalk horizontally in the water a head can be caused to develop at each end of the stalk, so that we must assume that every part of the polyp is, under some circumstances, capable of developing a head, and that it must be 'circumstances'—in this case gravity, contact with earth or with water, and the mutual influence of the parts of the animal upon each other—which decide what is to be produced. Loeb, who was the first to observe this form of regeneration, called it heteromorphosis, to express the fact that particular parts of the animal might be produced at quite different places from those originally intended for them.

It would certainly be erroneous to range these cases of heteromorphosis against the determinant theory, but they certainly do not afford any special evidence of its validity as an interpretation, for all that we can say here again is that all, or at least many, cells of the animal must contain the full determinant-complex of the ectoderm, and others those of the endoderm, and that particular groups of determinants become active when they are affected by certain external or internal liberating stimuli. In regard to such animals the theory is hardly more convincing than the rival theory, that the faculty of regeneration is a general property of living substance, which does not attain to equally full expression everywhere, because it is met by ever-increasing difficulties involved in the increasing complexity of structure. The validity of the theory only begins to be seen when we deal with cases where it is demonstrable that every part cannot bring forth every other, where the power of regeneration is limited, and occurs only in definite parts in a definite degree, and can only start from particular parts. Here the assumption of a general and primary regenerative capacity fails. Any one who insists, as O. Hertwig does, that the idioplasm in all cells of the body is the same, can always plead that, in the cases in which regeneration does not occur, the fault lies, not in the regenerative capacity, but in the absence of the adequate liberating stimuli, and at first sight it does seem as if this position were unassailable. We shall find, however, that there are facts which make Hertwig's interpretation quite untenable.

My own view is that the regenerative capacity is not something primary, but rather an adaptation to the organism's susceptibility to injury, that is, a power which occurs in organisms in varying degrees, proportionate to the degree and frequency of their liability to injury. Regeneration prevents the injured animal from perishing, or from living on in a mutilated state, and in this lies an advantage for the maintenance of the species, which is the greater the more frequently injuries occur in the species, and the more they menace its life directly or indirectly. A certain degree of regenerative capacity is thus indispensable to all multicellular animals, even to the highest among them. We ourselves, for instance, could not escape the numerous dangers of infection by bacilli and other micro-organisms if our protective outer skin did not possess the faculty of regeneration, at least so far that it can close up a wound and fill up with cicatrice-tissue a place where a piece of skin has been excised. Obviously, then, the mechanism which evokes regeneration must have been preserved in some degree and in some parts at every stage of the phyletic development, and must have been strengthened or weakened according to the needs of the relevant organism, being concentrated in certain parts which were much exposed to injury and withdrawn from other rarely threatened parts. Thus the great diversity which we can now observe in the strength and localization of the regenerative capacity has been brought about. But all this can only be regarded as adaptation.

I should like to submit a few examples to show that the regenerative capacity is by no means uniformly distributed, and that, as far as we can see, it is greater or less in correspondence with the needs of the animal, both in regard to the whole and to particular parts.

It must first be pointed out that those lower Metazoa, like the Hydroid polyps in particular, which are endowed with such a high and general power of regeneration, do actually require this for their safety; they are not only soft, easily injured and torn, but they are most severely decimated by many enemies. In the beginning of May I found on the walls of the harbour at Marseilles whole forests of polyp-stocks of the genera *Campanularia*, *Gonothyræa*, and *Obelia*, all large and splendidly developed, with thousands of individual polyps and medusoids, but in a very short time the great majority of the polyps were eaten up by little spectre-shrimps (Caprellids) and other crustaceans, worms, and numerous other enemies, and towards the end of May it was no longer possible to find a fine well-grown colony. It must therefore be of decisive importance for these species if the stems and branches, which are spared because protected by horny tubes, possess the faculty of transforming their simple soft parts into polyp-heads, or of giving off buds which become polyps, or even of growing a new stock from the twigs which have been half-eaten and bitten loose from the stock and have fallen to the ground. If, finally, a torn-off polyp-stalk (of *Tubularia*) falls to the ground with the wrong side up, the end which is now the lower will send out roots, and the end now uppermost will give off a new head. This also appears to us adaptive, and does not surprise us, since we have been long accustomed to recognize that what is adapted to an end will realize this if it be possible at all. Think again of the innumerable adaptations in colour and form which we discussed in the earlier lectures. I hope later to be able to show in more detail how it comes to pass that necessity gives rise to adaptation. In regard to the case of the polyps, we can understand that, as far as a high degree of regeneration and budding was possible in these animals at all, it could not but be developed. Regeneration and budding complete each other in this case, for the former brings about in the individual 'person' what the latter does in the colony, namely, a *Restitutio in integrum*. It is readily intelligible that the former was not difficult to establish where the latter—the capacity of budding—was already in existence.

It seems at first sight very striking that the higher plants, which all depend upon budding, and which form plant-colonies (corms) in the same sense as the polyps form animal-colonies, only possess the faculty of true regeneration in a very low degree, although they are extremely liable to injury.

We see from this that the two capacities are not co-extensive, that germ-plasm may be contained in numerous cells of the body in a latent state, and yet that regeneration of each and every detailed defect may not be possible. This is the case in the higher plants in regard to most of their parts. A leaf in which a hole has been cut does not close the hole with new cell-material; a fern frond from which some of the pinnules have been cut off does not grow new ones, but remains mutilated. Even leaves which, if laid on damp earth, readily give off buds which grow to new plants, as the Begonias do, do not replace a piece cut out of the leaf; they are not at all adapted to regeneration.

From the standpoint of utility this is readily intelligible. It was, so to speak, not worth Nature's while to make such adaptations in the case of leaves or blossoms, partly because these are very transient structures, and partly because they are rapidly and easily replaceable by the development of others of the same kind. Moreover, the leaf in which we have cut a hole continues to function, but the polyp whose mouth and tentacles we have cut off could no longer take nourishment unless it were adapted for regeneration. But that this adaptation *could* have been made in the case of plants is proved by the root-tips which are formed anew when they are injured, and the closing of wounds on the stem by a 'callus.'

I shall return to plants when we are dealing with the mechanism of regeneration, but I must now direct more attention to animals, inquiring further into the question as to whether the faculty of regeneration is correlated with the degree of liability to injury to which the animal is exposed, and with the biological importance of the injured part, for this must be the case if regeneration be really regulated by adaptation.

Hardly any other vertebrate has attained such celebrity on account of its high regenerative capacity as the water-newt, species of the genus *Triton*. It can regrow not only its tail, but the legs and their parts if they are cut off. Spallanzani saw the legs grow six times, after he had cut them off six times. In the blind newt (*Proteus*) of the Krainer caves, a near relative of the common newt, the leg regenerated only after a year and a half, although the animal stands on a lower stage of organization than the newt, and thus should rather replace lost parts more easily. But Proteus lives sheltered from danger in dark, still caves, while Triton is exposed to numerous enemies which bite off pieces from its tail or legs; and the legs are its chief means of locomotion, without which it would have difficulty in procuring food. It is different with the elongated eel-like newt of the marshes of South Carolina, *Siren lacertina*. This animal moves by wriggling its very muscular trunk, after the manner of an eel, and in consequence of the disuse of its hind legs it has almost completely lost them. Even the fore-legs have become small and weak, and possess only two toes, and these do not regrow if they are bitten off, or only do so very slowly.

Earthworms are exposed to much persecution; not only birds, such as blackbirds and some woodpeckers, but, above all, the moles prey upon them, and Dahl has shown that moles often lay up stores of worms in winter which they have half crippled by a bite, while even Réaumur knew that moles frequently only half devoured earthworms. It was thus an obvious advantage to earthworms that a part of the animal should be able to regrow a whole, and accordingly we find a fairly well-developed regenerative capacity among them. But it varies greatly in the different species, and it would be interesting if we knew the conditions of life well enough to be able to decide whether the faculty of regeneration rises and falls in proportion to the dangers to which the species is exposed. Unfortunately we are far from this as yet; we only know that, in the common earthworms of the genera *Lumbricus* and *Allolobophora*, the faculty of regeneration is still very limited, for at most two worms, and sometimes only one, can develop from an animal cut into two pieces. Cutting into a greater number of pieces does not yield a larger number of worms, but usually only one, and often none at all.

This corresponds to the behaviour of their enemies, which may often bite off a piece or tear it away when the worm attempts to escape, but never cut it up into pieces. The regenerative capacity is more highly developed in the genus *Allurus*, more highly still in the worms of the genus *Criodrilus* which lives in the mud at the bottom of lakes, and most highly of all in the genus *Lumbriculus* which lives at the bottom of small ponds. Long ago Bonnet cut up a specimen of *Lumbriculus* into twenty-six pieces, of about two millimetres in length, and he observed most of these grow to complete worms again. His experiments have often been repeated in recent times, and have been extended and made more precise in many ways. Von Bülow was able to get whole animals from pieces consisting of from four to five somatic segments, and with eight or nine segments he almost invariably succeeded. A *Lumbriculus* which he had cut into fourteen pieces, one of which only measured 3.5 mm. in length, gave rise to thirteen complete worms with head and tail; only one piece perished.

These worms have little enemies with sharp jaws which may gnaw at them behind or before but cannot swallow them whole. Lyonet, famous for his analytic dissection of the wood-caterpillar (*Cossus ligniperda*), observed when he was feeding the larvæ of dragon-flies with these Lumbriculid worms that 'the anterior end of some whose posterior end had been gnawed away by the larvæ continued to live on the ground.' We can thus understand why a high power of regeneration is of use to these worms, and at the same time why it is advantageous to them to contract so that they break in pieces on very slight irritation, but to this we shall refer again.

The very diverse potency of the faculty of regeneration in animals belonging to the same small group, and nearly, if not quite, at the same level of organization, seems to show clearly that we have here to do with adaptation to different conditions of life, although we cannot demonstrate this in detail. It would certainly be erroneous to regard the conditions of life as uniform, since the worms in question not only live in different places—in the earth, in mud, or in water—and are thus exposed to different enemies, and since they may also be quite different in regard to size and speed, in means of defence, and possibly also of defiance, as is indeed in some measure demonstrable.

We meet with the same thing in a group of still smaller worms, Rösel's 'water-snakelets,' species of the genus *Nais*. These, too, behave in a variety of ways in the matter of regeneration, for while many species, such as *Nais proboscidea* and *Nais serpentina* will, if cut into two or three pieces, become two or three worms respectively, Bonnet expressly mentions an unnamed species of *Nais* which does not bear cutting up at all, and even dies if its head be cut off.

Thus neither the degree of organization nor the relationship alone determines the strength of the regenerative capacity. And as nearly related species may behave quite differently in this respect, so also do the different parts of one and the same animal; and here, too, the strength of the capacity seems to depend on the more frequent or rarer injury of the relevant part and on its importance in the maintenance of life. Let us take a few examples.

Parts which, in the natural life of the animal, are never injured, show in many cases no power of regeneration. This is so in regard to the internal parts of the newt, whose regenerative capacity is otherwise so high. I cut half or nearly the whole of a lung away from newts anæsthetized with ether; the wound closed, *but no renewal of the organ took place.* The same thing happened when a piece of the spermatic duct or of the oviduct was cut away. It is true that the kidney enlarges in higher animals when a piece has been cut out, by the proliferation of the remaining tissues, but that is a mere physiological substitution, evoked by the increased functional stimulus, due to the accumulation in the blood of the constituents of the urine. Such substitution depends on the growth of parts already existing, and it occurs in man when one kidney is removed, for the other, as is well known, may then grow to double its normal size. This is mere hypertrophy of the part that is left, it is not regeneration in the morphological sense, and it is not comparable to the re-formation of a cut-off leg in the salamander, or of a head in the worm, where the growth is not a mere increase of the remaining stump, but a new formation. It would be regeneration if a new kidney developed from the remnants of the kidney-tissue, or, in the liver, if new lobes grew in place of those which were cut off. But neither of these things happens, and, as far as I am aware, nothing of the kind has ever been observed, nothing more than new formation of liver-cells through increase of existing ones; that, however, is not regeneration in the morphological sense.

I have referred to the slight power of regeneration possessed by the blind Proteus in regard to its legs or tail, and I connected this with the absence of enemies in its thinly peopled cave-habitat. But the same animal can regenerate its gills when these are bitten off, and this is probably associated with the habit that Proteus has, in common with other newts with external gills, of nibbling at its neighbour's gills. Thus, the power of regenerating the gills was retained even when the animals migrated to the quiet caves of Krain, and were thus secured from the attacks of other enemies.

In lizards, a leg which has been cut off does not grow again, but an amputated tail does, and this has quite a definite biological reason, since the active little animal will seldom be caught by the foot by any pursuer, but may easily be caught by the tail, which is far behind. Thus the tail is adapted not only for regeneration, but also for 'autotomy,' that is, for breaking off easily when it is caught hold of.

We have already seen that some segmented worms have a very high regenerative capacity; yet every part cannot produce every other, and while, in *Lumbriculus*, any piece of from five to nine segments is able to grow a new head or tail, neither ten nor twenty nor all the segments together, if they are *halved longitudinally*, can reproduce the other half, and the cause of this inability does not lie in the fact that the animal is thereby hindered from taking food, for even the transversely cut pieces do not feed until they have grown a new head and tail. The reason must lie in the fact that the primary constituents for this kind of regeneration are wanting, and they are so because a longitudinal splitting of this cylindrical and relatively thin animal never occurs under natural conditions, and thus could not be provided against by Nature[1].

That regeneration of this kind could have been arranged for if it had been useful we learn from the Planarians among the flat worms, in which every piece cut out of the body, large or very small, from the middle, from the left side, or from the right side of the animal, grows into a complete Planarian. The animal can be halved longitudinally, as in Fig. 97, and each half will grow to a whole. This again is quite intelligible from the biological point of view, for these flat, soft,

[1] Morgan maintains that this statement is incorrect, and that *Lumbriculus* is capable of lateral regeneration. But if we look into the matter more closely we find that all he says is, that small gaps made by cutting a piece out of one side are filled up again, while the cut pieces perish. If the whole animal be halved, according to Morgan, both halves die, or if a 'very long piece' be cut out of one side, not only this piece dies, but also 'the remaining piece.' There is thus, as I have said, an essential difference between the regenerative capacity of *Lumbriculus* and that of *Planaria*.

and easily torn animals are exposed to all sorts of injuries, and are, in point of fact, frequently mutilated by enemies which are unable to swallow them whole. Von Graaf not infrequently found examples of marine Planarians (*Macrostomum*) which lacked 'a part of the posterior end or the whole tail region as far as the food-canal,' and of species of *Monotus* he found 'very often' in May specimens with the posterior end split or broken off. Probably the persecutors of these flat-worms are some species of Crustacean, but, at any rate, so much is proved, that the Planarians have abundant opportunities of making use of their faculty of regeneration, and that the species gains an advantage from it in respect to its preservation.

In contrast to this, worms which live within other animals, and are thus secure from mutilation, such as the familiar round-worms (*Nematodes*), have no power of regeneration at all, and do not survive either longitudinal or transverse division.

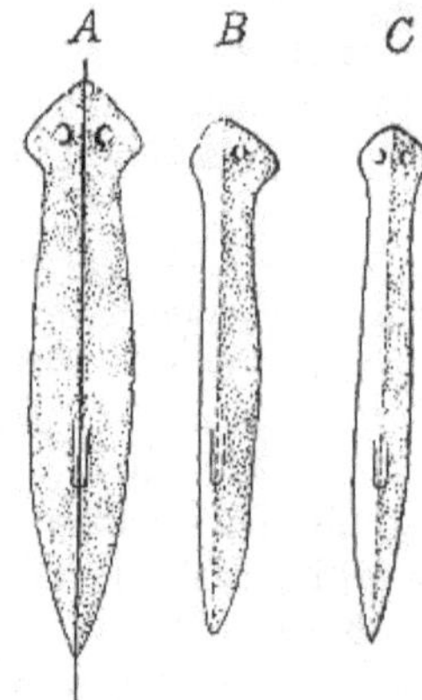

FIG. 97. *A*, a Planarian, which has been divided into two by a longitudinal cut. Each half can grow into an entire animal. *B*, the left half at the beginning of the regenerative process. *C*, the same completed. After Morgan.

Until recently birds were regarded as possessing a very low degree of regenerative capacity, and, as a matter of fact, they cannot replace a leg or a wing wholly or in part; but, what is otherwise unheard of among higher vertebrates, they can renew the whole anterior portion of the skeleton of the face, the bill, and can indeed almost reconstruct it with new bones and horny parts. Von Kennel communicated a case of this kind in regard to a stork, and for a long time this remained an isolated case, but a few years ago Bordage showed that, in the cocks which are used in the Island of Bourbon for the favourite sport of cock-fighting, the bill is regularly renewed when it has been broken off or shattered. Quite recently Barfurth gave an account of a case of complete renewal of a broken bill in a parrot. Yet it should not astonish us that the bill in birds has such a high regenerative power, for of all parts in a bird it is the one that is most readily injured; with it the bird defends itself against its enemies and its rivals, masters its prey, and tears it to pieces, pecks holes in trees (woodpecker), or climbs (parrot), or digs and burrows in the ground, or builds its nest, and so on. That the faculty of regeneration could be developed to so high a degree in relation to this particular part of the body, while the rest of the very important but rarely injured parts do not possess it at all, again points to the conclusion that the faculty of regeneration has an adaptive character.

It does not affect matters to discover cases in which we cannot recognize this relation between the regenerative capacity of a part and its importance or its liability to injury. Such instances do not lessen the convincingness of the positive cases, since we do not know the exact conditions which may lead to the increase of regenerative capacity in a part, and, above all, since we do not know the rate at which such an increase may take place. If adaptation in general depends upon processes of selection, these processes must also be able to give rise to an increase in the power of regeneration. On the other hand, it by no means follows that the disappearance of a faculty of regeneration which was once present in a part, but which has become superfluous in the course of time, must take place immediately through natural selection. For it is the very essence of natural selection that it only furthers what is useful, and only removes what is injurious; over what is indifferent it has no power at all. Thus it follows that the faculty of regeneration, when it has once been present in a part, cannot be set aside by natural selection (personal selection), for it is in no way injurious to its possessor. If it gradually decreases and becomes extinct notwithstanding this, when it is of no further use, as seems to be to some extent the case in regard to the legs and tail of the blind Proteus, that must depend on other processes, on those which generally bring about the gradual disappearance of disused parts or capacities. We shall attempt to probe to the roots of these processes later on; for the present let it suffice us to know that, according to our experience, they go on with exceeding slowness, and that it has taken whole geological periods to eliminate the legs of the snake-ancestors so completely as has been done from the structure of most of our modern snakes, while the Proteus which migrated into the caves of Krain as far back as the Cretaceous period is indeed blind, but still retains its eyes under the skin, though in a degenerate condition.

Since the degeneration of disused parts and capacities goes on so slowly it need not surprise us that we meet many parts which still possess regenerative capacity, although they are protected from injury. Thus Morgan found that, in the hermit-crab, the limbs which are protected within the mollusc shell were quite as ready to regrow as those which are actually used for walking, and thus are exposed to possibility of attack, but this proves nothing against the conclusion we drew from the facts cited above, according to which the faculty of regeneration comes under the law of adaptation. For the disappearance of this faculty must take place very much more *slowly than its growth.* For instance, the development of the tail-fin of the whale has long been an accomplished fact, while the hind-legs of this colossal mammal, which were rendered useless by the development of the tail-fin, still lie concealed in a rudimentary state within the muscles of the trunk. Yet these limbs must have lost their significance for the animal exactly at the time that the tail-fin became more powerful. Thus the retrogression must have taken place more slowly than the progressive transformation.

It is clear, then, that the faculty of regeneration is not a primary character of living beings occurring uniformly in all species of equally high organization and in all parts of an animal in the same degree; it is a power which occurs in animals of equal complexity in as varying degrees as in their parts, and which is manifestly regulated by adaptation. Between parts with the faculty of regeneration and parts without it there must be an essential difference; there must be present in the former something that is wanting in the latter, and, according to our theory, this is the equipment with regeneration-determinants, that is, with the determinants of the parts which are to be reconstructed.

If this be really so it should be capable of proof, at least in so far that we should be able to establish that the power of completing or re-forming a damaged or lost part is a limited one, localized in certain parts and cell-layers. This can be actually proved, as may be seen from numerous cases in which the faculty of regeneration is associated with autotomy, that is, with the power of breaking off or dropping off a part of the body. Even in worms we find this power, as we mentioned before in speaking of the high regenerative capacity of *Lumbriculus.* This worm reproduces in summer by what is called 'schizogony,' that is, by breaking into two, three, or more pieces, and it does not seem to require a very strong stimulus, such as pressure of the end of the worm by the jaws of an insect larva, to start this rupture; it often follows from quite insignificant friction on the ground. Certainly the power of regeneration is so great in this animal that it is out of the question to talk of localizing the primary constituents of regeneration; almost every broken surface is capable of regeneration.

But this localization is well illustrated in Insects and Crustaceans, which possess the power of self-amputation in their appendages, especially in their legs. As far back as 1826 MacCullock observed this remarkable power in crabs, and described the mechanism on which it depends. When the leg is irritated, for instance when it is pinched at the tip and held fast, it breaks off at a particular place. This line of breakage lies in the middle of the short second joint (Fig. 98, *A* and *B*, *s*), just between the insertions of the muscles (*me*, *mf*, *m*) which extend from this line towards the extremity of the limb and in the opposite direction towards the body-wall. Between these musclo-attachments the external skeleton is thin and brittle, and forms a suture, *s*, which breaks through when the animal contracts the muscles of the leg convulsively, and thus presses the lower protuberance (*a*) against a projection (*b*) of the first upper joint. Crabs require to make a very considerable muscular exertion before they can throw off the limb, and therefore they can only do it when they are in full vigour.

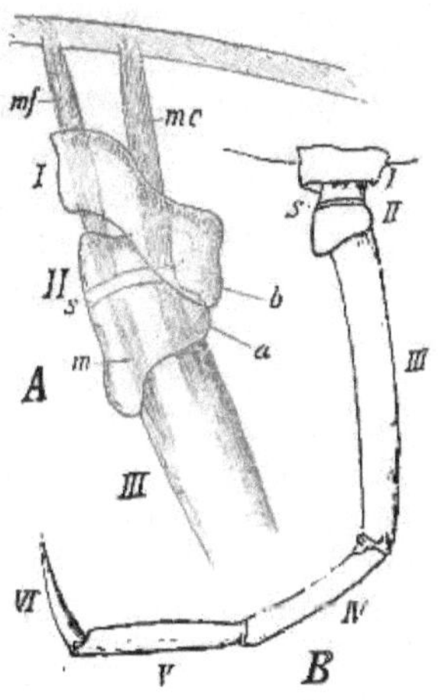

FIG. 98. The leg of a Crab, adapted for self-mutilation or autotomy. *A*, the first three joints of the limb, *I*, *II*, *III*. *s*, the suture, that is, a thin area on the second joint which is predisposed to breakage. *mf*, flexor muscle, *me*, extensor muscle, both inserted at the suture. *B* the entire leg with its six joints and with the suture (*s*). Slightly enlarged. After MacCulloch.

We have here a quite definite structural adaptation of the parts to a danger which often recurs—that of falling entirely into the power of an enemy which has seized the leg. By a sudden violent throwing-off of the leg the crab escapes from this danger. Quite similar adaptations are found among certain insects, such as the walking-stick insects or Phasmids, in which the mechanism is much the same, and lies at an almost exactly corresponding place, namely, at the line where the second and third joints of the leg, the 'trochanter' and the 'femur,' meet. In this case the advantage of the arrangement is not merely that the animals are thus enabled to escape from enemies; it is useful in another connexion, for a knowledge of which we have to thank Bordage. This naturalist observed that the Phasmids not infrequently perished at one of their numerous moultings, by remaining partially fixed in the discarded husk. Of 100 Phasmids nine died in this way, twenty-two got free with the loss of one or more legs, and only sixty-nine survived the moult without any loss at all.

That the moulting or ecdysis of insects is often hazardous may be observed in our own country, and it is familiar to every one who has reared caterpillars. These, too, often fail to get clear of their 'cast' cuticle, and they perish unless artificial aid is given to them. I have never observed any autotomy in them, but in the Phasmids it seems to be a much-used 'device,' and is therefore of great importance in the persistence of the species.

Limbs which are thus thrown off by autotomy regenerate again from the place at which they broke off, that is from the 'suture.' It had been noticed even by the earlier observers (e.g. Goodsir) that there was a jelly-like mass of cells within the joint, and that the development of the new limb started from this. It might be supposed that the regeneration-primordium is present in the rest of the leg also, but that is not the case, for the animal responds to the tearing off of one joint or of a smaller number than to the suture, not by regenerating the torn part directly, but by amputating the whole of the leg up to the suture, and then from this the regeneration of the whole leg takes place. In the Phasmids the case is similar, but with the difference that regeneration is possible from three places, from the tarsal joints, from the lower third of the tibia, and finally, from the suture between the femur and the trochanter. There is thus a regeneration-primordium (*Anlage*) at the beginning of the tarsal joints, another in the tibia, and a third in the 'suture,' and the first must be equipped, as we should express it, with the determinants of the five tarsal joints, the second with those for the lower end of the tibia as well, and the third with all the determinants of the whole leg, from the 'suture' downwards.

In any case, regeneration is here associated with definite localized pieces of tissue, and is not a general character of all the cells of the leg, and, as it obviously runs parallel at the same time with another adaptation—that of autotomy—there can be no doubt that it too is dominated by the principle of selection, and that it can not only be increased, but that it can be concentrated at particular places and removed from others. But this is only possible if it be bound up with material particles which may be present in or absent from a tissue, and which are therefore a supplement to the ordinary essential constituents of the living cells, although they do not themselves belong to the essential organization.

I might cite many more examples of localization of regenerative capacity, but will confine myself to one other, which seems to me particularly instructive, because it was first interpreted as an indication of the existence of an adaptive principle in the organism, a principle which always creates what is useful. I refer to the regeneration of the lens in the newt's larva.

G. Wolff, an obstinate opponent of the theory of selection, attempted to solve the same problem as I had before me in my experiments on the regeneration of the internal organs of newts, that is, he tried to answer the question whether organs which are never exposed to injury or to complete removal in the conditions of natural life, and which could not therefore have been influenced in this direction by the processes of selection, are nevertheless capable of regeneration. He extirpated the lens from the eye of Triton larvæ, and saw that in a short time it was formed anew, and from this he concluded that there was here 'a new adaptiveness appearing for the first time,' and that therefore adaptive forces must be dominant within the organism. The current theory of the 'mechanical' origin of vital adjustments seemed to some to be shaken by this, and the proclamation of the old 'vital force' seemed imminent. And in truth, if the body were really able to replace, after artificial injury, parts which are never liable to injury in natural conditions, and to do so in a most beautiful and appropriate manner, then there would be nothing for it but at least to regard the faculty of regeneration as a primary power of living creatures, and to think of the organism as like a crystal, which invariably completes itself if it be damaged in any part. But we have to ask whether this is really the case.

What makes the regeneration of the lens seem particularly surprising is the fact that in the fully formed animal it must arise in a manner different from that in which it develops in the embryo, that is, it must be formed from different cell-material. In the embryo it arises by the proliferation and invagination of the epidermic layer of cells to meet the so-called 'primary' optic vesicle growing out from the brain—a mode of development which cannot of course be repeated under the altered conditions in the fully developed animal. The reconstruction of the organ must therefore take place in a different way, and if the organism were really able, the very first time the lens was removed, to react in a manner so perfectly adapted to the end, and so to inspire certain cells, which had till then had a different function, that they could put together a lens of flawless beauty and transparency, we should have reason to suspect that nearly all our previous conceptions were erroneous, and to fall back upon a belief in a *spiritus rector* in the organism.

But the excision of the lens in these experiments was not by any means an unprecedented occurrence! It is true enough that newts in their pools are not liable to an operation for cataract, but it does not follow that the lens is never liable to injury, and could not therefore be adapted for regeneration. It can be bitten out along with the rest of the eye by water-beetles or other enemies, and as far back as the time of Bonnet and Blumenbach (1781) it was known that the eye of the newt would renew itself if it were cut out, given that a small portion of the bulb was left. But if this were removed the possibility of regeneration was at an end. Thus, before the first artificial excision of the lens, a regeneration-mechanism must have existed, by means of which the eye with its lens was reconstructed, and this depends on the characters of the cells of the eye itself—it is localized in the eye, and without the presence of a piece of eye-tissue no regeneration can take place. Is it then so especially remarkable that the lens should be renewed when it is artificially removed without the rest of the eye? The mechanism for its renewal is there, and is roused to activity whether the lens alone or other parts of the eye also be removed. We do not need, therefore, to assume the existence of a purposeful or adaptive force; it is more to the point to inquire where the regeneration-mechanism which suggests this inference is to be found.

A definite answer to this is given in a detailed experimental work recently published by Fischel. It corroborates what Wolff had already found, that the substance of the new lens develops from cells which cover the posterior surface of the iris, that is, from cells of the retinal layer of the eye. First, the margin of the pupil begins to react to the stimulus of the injury (extraction of the lens); its cells enlarge, become clear, while previously they were filled with dark pigment, and finally they proliferate. They thus form a cell-vesicle similar to the ectoderm-vesicle from which the lens arises in the embryo, and into this the already mentioned retina-cells from the posterior wall of the iris grow, elongate, and arrange themselves to form the so-called 'lens-fibres,' on whose form, arrangement, and transparency the function of the lens depends. This is marvellous enough, but not more marvellous than that a whole foot should grow on the cut stump of a newt's leg, or that a whole eye should arise from a residual fragment. Here, again, we do not know the processes which cause the arrangement of the cells and their often manifold locally-conditioned differentiations, in short, we do not know the *essential nature of regeneration.* But, in the meantime, we can endeavour to find out which cell-groups regeneration is bound up with in particular cases, so as to know where the vital particles, the 'determinants,' which condition regeneration, are placed by nature.

In this case there can be no doubt on that point: they are the cells on the posterior wall and the margin of the iris. And it is certainly not the *absence* of the lens which gives rise to its renewal, as would necessarily be the case if it were due to the dominance of an adaptive force. If the lens, instead of being excised, be simply pressed back into the vitreous humour occupying the cavity of the eye, a new lens is developed all the same from the irritated margin of the pupil. And if by chance this margin has been irritated in two places while extraction of the lens was being performed, then two small lenses will develop (Fig. 99, *B*). Indeed, several may begin to develop at the posterior wall of the iris, although they do not attain to full development; mechanical irritation of any part of this cell-layer is responded to by the formation of lenses. This surely disposes of the 'mystical nimbus' which would dazzle us with a new force of

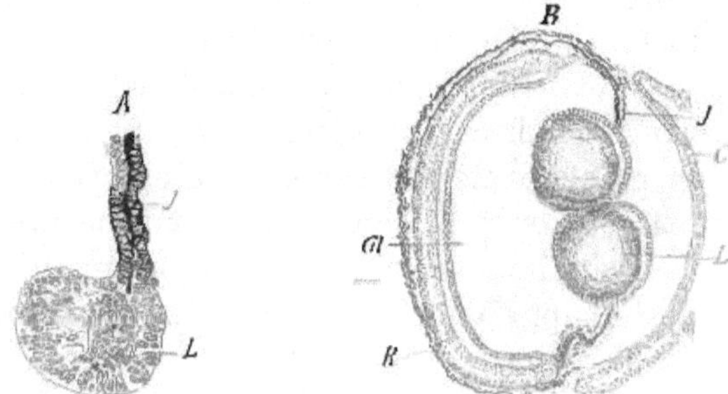

Fig. 99. Regeneration of the lens in the Newt's eye. *A*, section through the iris (*J*); from its margin and posterior (retinal) surface the primordium of a new lens (*L*) has developed after the artificial removal of the old one. *B*, section through the eye after duplicated regeneration of the lens (*L*) from two areas of the iris. *Gl*, vitreous humour. *J*, iris. *C*, cornea. *R*, retina. After Fischel.

life, always creating what is appropriate. We have before us an adaptation to the liability of newts' eyes to injury, which, like all adaptations, is only relatively perfect, since under the usual conditions of eye injury it gives rise to a useable lens, but under unusual conditions to unsuitable structures. It is exactly the same as in the case of animal instincts, which are all 'calculated' for the *ordinary* conditions of life, but, under unusual conditions, may operate in a manner quite unsuited to the necessary end. The ant-lion has the instinct to bore backwards into the sand, and he makes the same backward-pressing movements when placed on a glass plate into which he cannot force the tip of the abdomen. The same is true of the mole-cricket, which makes its usual digging movements with the forelegs even on a plate of glass. The wall-bee roofs over her cell when she has laid an egg in it, but she does so even if the egg be taken out beforehand, or if a hole be made in the bottom of the cell, so that the honey which is to serve the larva for food when it emerges from the egg runs out (Fabre). Her instinct is calculated for filling the cell *once* with honey, and *once* laying an egg in it, because such disturbances as we may cause artificially do not occur or occur very rarely in natural conditions. There are countless facts of this kind, for every instinct and every adaptation can, in certain circumstances, go astray and become inappropriate. This should be considered by those who still persist in opposing the theory of selection, for herein lies one of the most convincing proofs of its correctness. Adaptations can only arise in reference to the majority of occurrences, and variations which are only useful in an individual case must, according to the principle, disappear again. Adaptation always means the establishment of what is appropriate in an average number of cases.

Therefore the inappropriate reaction of the margin of the iris to an artificial double stimulus affords additional reason for regarding regeneration as an adaptive phenomenon. If it were the outcome of an adaptive force it could never be inappropriate; and if it were the operation of a general and primary power of the organism it would be exhibited by the nearly-related frog as well as by the newt. But, in the frog, extraction of the lens gives rise only to a sac-like proliferation of the cells of the iris margin, which form no transparent lens, but an opaque cluster of cells, which destroys vision altogether. It appears, therefore, that the frog no longer requires the power its ancestors possessed of regenerating a lost lens.

LECTURE XXI

REGENERATION (*continued*)

Phyletic origin of the regenerative capacity—The liberating stimuli of regeneration —Production of extra heads and tails in Planarians (Voigt)· Regeneration in the Starfish—Atavistic regeneration in Insects and Crustaceans—Progressive regeneration —Regeneration has its roots in the differentiation of organisms—The nuclear substance of unicellular organisms is the first organ for regeneration—The ultimate roots of regeneration.

In the previous lecture we have considered many different forms of regeneration, and have recognized them as adaptive phenomena; we have now to inquire how such regeneration-adaptations have arisen, and this is a very difficult question even in general, while in particular cases it is often quite unanswerable at present. In regard to the case last discussed, the regeneration of the lens in the eye of Triton, our hypotheses would require to reach back to the time of the primitive vertebrates with an unpaired eye, for the lens of the paired vertebrate eye, from Mammals down to the lowest Fishes, does not arise in embryonic development from the retinal cells, but always from the corneal epithelium, as the elaborate researches of Rabl have recently shown. It is true that the unpaired parietal eye of some reptiles forms its lens from the cells of the retinal layer, but it would be difficult to demonstrate the possibility of a genetic connexion between it and paired eyes, and in the meantime we must refrain from elaborating a hypothesis as to the origin of the marvellous faculty the retinal cells possess of transforming themselves into lens-fibres.

But it is easier to form some sort of picture of the origin and adaptation of the faculty of regeneration in general.

We saw that the power of regenerating a part can be localized, and that it does not belong to all the cells of the body, but only to some of them, and we have to ask how and by what steps it has been imparted to these. The faculty depends on the possession of a regeneration-primordium (*Anlage*), and this again, in our mode of expression, consists of a definite complex of determinants, and as determinants are the products of an evolution, and thus are vital units which have arisen historically, they can nowhere suddenly originate anew in a species, but must be derived directly or indirectly from the sole basis which, in each species, forms the starting-point of the individual—that is to say, in the Metazoa, from the germ-plasm of the ovum. From it the determinant-complex of every regeneration-rudiment must in the ultimate instance be derived.

We may think of the matter thus: all the determinants of the germ-plasm vary, grow slowly or quickly, and in certain circumstances may be doubled. In this way there arise what we may call 'supernumerary' determinants, which are not required in the primary building up of the body from the ovum, and which may remain in an inactive state in the nuclei of certain cells, ready to become active under certain circumstances and to produce anew the part which they control. Such regeneration-idioplasm will at first come to lie in the younger cells of the determinate organ, but it is conceivable that under the influence of selection it may be gradually shifted to other cells of a later developmental origin, or, conversely, to others in a less external position, so that, for instance, the regeneration-rudiment for the finger of a newt may be contained not merely in the cells of the hand, but in those of the fore-arm or even of the upper arm.

But all such segregation of determinant-groups cannot have taken place, as we might perhaps be inclined to think, at the periphery in the organ itself during its development; it must take place in the germ-plasm of the ovum, for otherwise it could not be transmissible, and could not be directed and modified by the processes of selection, as is actually the case, as I shall show in more detail later on.

I have already pointed out the importance of the rôle played by liberating stimuli in regeneration, and not only of extra-organismal stimuli, such as gravity, but above all of intra-organismal stimuli that is, the influences exerted in a mysterious manner by other parts of the animal on the parts which are in process of regeneration. It is a great merit of the modern tendency in evolution theory that it has demonstrated the importance of such internal influences. Although we are still far from being able to define the manner in which these influences operate, we may say so much, that it depends essentially on the nature and extent of the loss which parts are reproduced by the regenerating cells, and, also, on the position and direction of the injured surface from which the regeneration starts. The influences, still quite beyond our comprehension, which are exerted on the regenerating part by the uninjured parts constitute the liberating stimuli, which evoke the activity of one or other of the determinants contained in the regeneration-idioplasm.

Walter Voigt has shown, by a series of most interesting experiments, that it is possible not only to cause the development of a new head in Planarians by cutting them, in which case a tail may grow from the anterior portion and a head from the posterior portion, but it is also possible in an intact animal, that is, one with both head and tail, to cause the production of a second head, or a second tail, or both at once, at any part of the body margin at will, according to the direction of the cut. If the margin of the body be cut obliquely forwards (Fig. 100, *A*) a supernumerary tail arises (*C*, *s*), if it be cut obliquely backwards a supernumerary head arises (*C*, *k*), and in this way several heads and several tails may be produced in the same

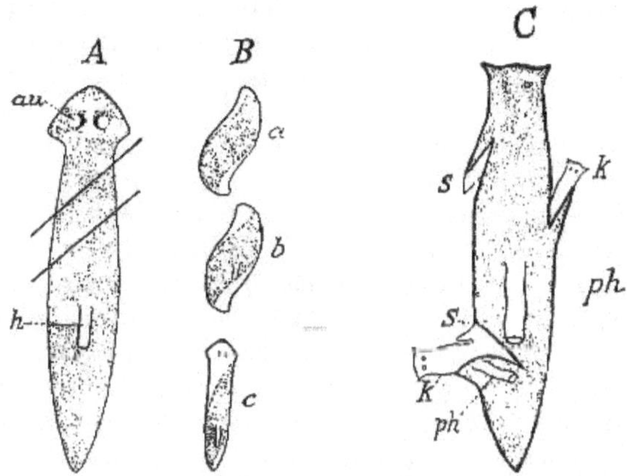

FIG. 100. Regeneration of Planarians. *A*, an animal divided into three parts by two oblique cuts. *B*, the fragments (*a*, *b*, *c*) in process of regeneration. *C*, an animal with various oblique incisions in the margin of the body, which have induced the new formation of heads (*k*), of tails (*s*), and pharynx (*ph*). *A* and *B* after Morgan; *C* after Walter Voigt.

animal. It is obvious, then, that the interaction, in the first place, of the cells of the cut surface, but probably also of the deeper-lying cells, decides which determinants are to come into action, those of the head or those of the tail, but both must be present at every part of the cut. How far below the cut surface the cells take part in this determination we cannot make out, but that it cannot be due to the co-operation of all parts is clear in this case at least, since the animal still possesses its original head and tail. The extra heads and tails thus produced prove, at any rate, that there can be no question here of the expression of an adaptive principle, a *spiritus rector*, or a vital force, which always creates what is good, but that it is rather a purely mechanical process, which takes its course quite independently of what is useful or disadvantageous, and that it must take this course according to the given regeneration-mechanism and the stimulus supplied in the special case. It cannot be supposed that these supernumerary heads and tails are purposeful, but who would expect an adaptive reaction from the animal in a case like this, since cuts of the kind which we make artificially, and *must keep open artificially* if the deformities are to develop, hardly occur in nature, and, if they did occur, would very quickly close up again? Adaptations can only develop in response to conditions which occur and recur in a majority of cases, and when they have a useful, that is, species-preserving result. The adaptiveness of the organism is blind, it does not see the individual case, it only takes into account the cases in the mass, and acts as it must after the mechanism has once been evolved. The case is the same as that of 'aberrant' or mistaken instincts, whose origin by means of selection is the more clearly proved, since we must recognize such an instinct as a pure mechanism and not as the outcome of purposeful forces.

In the regeneration of Planarians we must think of the regeneration-idioplasm as containing the full complex of the collective determinants of the three germinal layers, and possibly we must add to this cells with the complete germ-plasm for giving rise to the reproductive cells. But when the amputated tail of the newt is regenerated, or its leg, or the arm of a starfish, or the bill of a bird, we have no ground for assuming that the cells, from which regeneration starts, contain the whole germ-plasm, since the determinants of the replaceable parts suffice to explain the facts. We must even dispute the possibility of the presence of the whole germ-plasm in this case, because the faculty of regeneration of the relevant cells is really no longer a general one, but is limited to the reproduction of a particular part. This is seen in the fact that, in the starfish, whose high regenerative capacity is well known, the central disk of the body may indeed give rise to new arms[1]; but an excised arm, to which no part of the disk adheres, is in most starfishes unable to give rise to the body. Thus the arm does not contain in its cells the determinants of the disk, but the latter contains those of the arm. We are not surprised that the amputated tail of the salamander does not reproduce

[1] I see now that there are contradictory statements in regard to this case. Possibly these depend on the different behaviour of different species, and this on the varying frequency of mutilation. Starfishes which live on the shore between the rocks, for instance on the movable stones of a breakwater, are very frequently mutilated; in some places it is rare to find a specimen without traces of former wounds. H. D. King counted among 1,914 specimens of *Asterias vulgaris* 206 in the act of regenerating a part, that is, 10·76 per cent. In the case of the starfishes from deep water this cause of injury does not of course exist.

the whole animal, but this can only be because the impelling forces to the regeneration of the whole animal are wanting, that is, that the cut surface only contains the determinants of the tail and not the complete germ-plasm. It might be objected here that the tail-piece is too small to give rise to the whole body, but in *Planaria* it is only very diminutive heads and tails which grow from the artificial incisions, and the same is true of starfishes when only a single arm and a small piece of the disk have been left. Notwithstanding the small amount of living substance at their disposal, and although they are at first unable to take nourishment, they send out very small new arms (Fig. 101), close up the wounded surface, and, after reconstruction of the mouth and stomach, begin to feed anew. The new arms may then grow to the normal size.

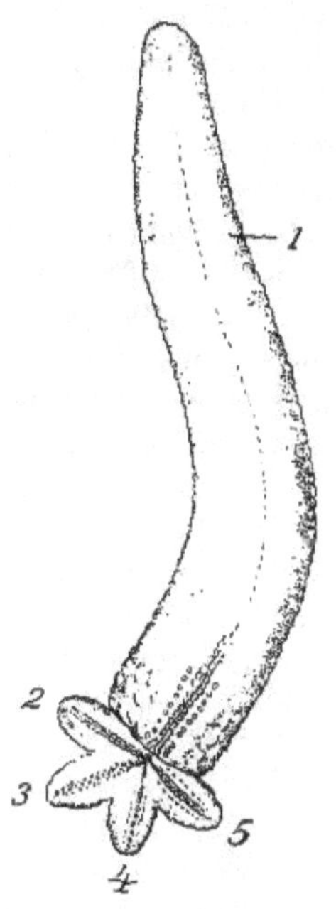

Fig. 101. A Starfish arm, growing four new arms; the so-called 'comet-form.' After Haeckel.

We must therefore assume that, in many cases, the regeneration-primordium consists of cells which only contain a definite complex of determinants in the form of latent regeneration-idioplasm, as, for instance, certain cells of the tail of Triton contain the determinants of the tail, certain cells of its leg the determinants of the leg, and so on. In many cases we can speak even more precisely, and determine from which cells the nerve-centres, from which the muscles, and from which the missing section of the food-canal will be formed, as was recently shown by Franz von Wagner in regard to the worm *Lumbriculus*, whose regenerative capacity is so extraordinarily high. We must then attribute to each of the relevant cells an equipment of regeneration-idioplasm, which includes only the relevant complex of determinants.

I need not here go further into detail, but I should still like to show that, in reality, as I assumed in regard to the regenerative capacity of a part, the root of the regeneration-idioplasm lies in the germ-plasm, that it is present there as an independent determinant-group, and, like every other bodily rudiment (*Anlage*), must be handed on from generation to generation. This assumption is necessary, as has been already indicated, on the ground that the faculty of regeneration is hereditary, and hereditarily variable, on the same ground, therefore, as that on which the whole determinant theory is based. The regeneration-determinants must be contained *as such* in the germ-plasm, otherwise a twofold phyletic development could not have occurred, as it actually has, in many parts. The tail of the lizard is adapted for autotomy; it breaks off when it is held by the tip, and this depends on a special adaptation of the vertebræ, which are very brittle in a definite plane from the seventh onwards. This is thus a very effective adaptation to persecution by enemies. The tail which has been seized remains with the pursuer, but the lizard itself escapes, and the tail grows again. But this regeneration does not take place in the same way as in the embryo; no new vertebræ are formed, but only a 'cartilaginous-tube,' a new structure, a substitute for the vertebral column; the spinal cord with its nerves is not regenerated either, and the arrangement of the scales is somewhat different.

This last point, in particular, indicates that the determinants of the regeneration-rudiment may pursue an independent phylogenetic path of their own, for this scale arrangement of the regenerated tail is an atavistic one, that is, it corresponds to a more primitive mode of scale arrangement in these Saurians. We know quite a number of cases similar to this. It not infrequently happens that cut-off parts regenerate, but that they do so not in the modern form, but in one that is in all probability phyletically older. Thus the legs of various Orthoptera, as of the cockroaches and grasshoppers, regenerate readily, but with a tarsus composed of four joints instead of five[1], and the long-fingered claws of a shrimp (*Atyoida potimirim*) is replaced by the older short-fingered type of claw, while in the Axolotl an atavistic five-fingered hand grows instead of the amputated four-fingered one.

This last case shows that it is not merely a lesser power of growth that accounts for the difference between the regenerated part and the original, for here more is regenerated than was previously present. There remains nothing for it but the assumption that the regeneration-determinants have remained at a lower phyletic level, while the determinants which direct embryogenesis have varied, and either developed further or retrogressed. It is easy to understand that the regeneration-rudiment must vary phyletically much

[1] New investigations, specially directed to this point, by R. Godelmann, have shown that 'in the great majority of cases' the regenerated legs of a Phasmid (*Bacillus rossii*) exhibit a four-jointed tarsus; but the regeneration of five joints also occurs, though only after autotomy, and only in seven out of fifty cases (*Archiv für Entwicklungsmechanik*, Bd. xii, Heft 2, July 1901). The regeneration-rudiment in this species seems to be in process of advancing slowly to the five-jointed type.

more slowly than the parts which evolved in the ordinary way and much more slowly than the determinants of these parts, for natural selection means a selection of the fittest, and the speed with which the establishment of a variation is attained depends, *cœteris paribus*, on the number of individuals that are exposed to selection with respect to the varying part. If in a species of a million living at the same time nine-tenths perish by accident, there will remain only 100,000 from which to select the 1,000 which we will assume constitute the normal number of the species. The more of those 100,000 which possess the useful variation the higher will be the percentage of the normally surviving 1,000 possessing it, and the more rapidly will the useful variation increase. But when it is a question of the variation of the regeneration-primordium, the selection will take place not among all the 100,000 individuals which chance has spared, but only among those of them which have lost a limb by accident, and thus are in a position to regenerate it more or less completely. If we assume that this takes place in 10 per cent. of cases, then selection for the improvement of the regeneration-apparatus will only take place among 1,000 individuals, and thus the process of modification of the regeneration-primordium must go on very much more slowly than that of the limb itself.

I do not see how the opponents of the germ-plasm theory can explain these facts at all, for the appeal to external influences is here entirely futile, and that to internal liberating stimuli does not suffice, since these must be different after a part has been cut off from what they were when the limb developed normally, and also different from those which prevailed at the normal origin of the limb in ancestral forms. The four-jointed tarsus of the ancestors of our cockroaches did not arise as a result of amputation. We cannot therefore avoid referring the processes of regeneration to particular 'regeneration-determinants,' which are contained in the germ-plasm and are handed on in ontogeny with the other determinants from cell-division to cell-division, till ultimately they reach the cells which are to respond, or may have to respond, to the stimulus of injury by some expression of their regenerative capacity. As these determinants, as has been shown, can often only be very slightly subject to the influence of selection processes, they will, in many respects, lag behind in the phyletic development, and will tend to belong to an ancestral type of the relevant part. They will often remain for a long time at this ancestral level, and they will always adapt themselves to new requirements more slowly than the parts which arise in the normal way, and the determinants representing these in the germ.

But the regeneration-determinants *are* variable, and, indeed, are so hereditarily, and independently of the structure of the normal parts. They thus follow their own path of phyletic development, and this one fact is enough to secure a preference for the germ-plasm theory above others that have hitherto been suggested. None of these has even attempted an explanation of this fact; the tendency has rather been to call it in question. This, however, can be done at most only in regard to the explanation of the regenerations as atavistic, certainly not in regard to the progressive variations of the regenerated part, such as have been established by Leydig and Fraisse in regard to the lizard's tail. It may be doubted whether the most primitive insects had only four tarsal joints, but there is no disputing the kainogenetic deviation of the lizard's-tail.

I have interpreted the regenerative capacity as secondary and acquired, not as a primary power of all living substance, and I should like to substantiate this in another way.

Let us go back to the simplest organism conceivable, which must have represented the beginning of life on our earth, and we see that this need not have possessed any special power of regeneration, because, for an organism without differentiation of parts, growth is equivalent to regeneration. But growth is the direct outcome of one of the primary characters of the living substance, the capacity of assimilation. This cannot be an adaptive phenomenon, nor can it have arisen through selection, because selection presupposes reproduction, and reproduction is only a periodic form of growth; but growth follows directly from assimilation. The fundamental characters of the living substance, above all the dissimilation and assimilation which condition metabolism, must have been in existence from the first when living substance arose, and must depend on its unique chemico-physical composition. But the faculty of regeneration could only be acquired when organisms became qualitatively differentiated, so that each part was no longer like every other part or like the whole. As soon as this stage was reached the faculty of regeneration would necessarily be developed, if further multiplication was to take place. For when each fragment could no longer become a whole by simply growing, some arrangement had to be made by which each fragment should receive, in the form of primary constituents, what it lacked to make up the whole. We do not know the first beginning of this adaptation, but, in its further development, it appears in the form of 'nuclear substance,' enclosed in the nucleus of the cell, and, as is well known, it is now to be found in all unicellular organisms. That the nucleus there precedes regeneration in the sense that without a piece of it the cell-soma is not able to complete itself alone, we have already seen, and the explanation of this fact has always seemed to me to be that invisibly minute vital units relating to the regeneration of the injured part leave the nucleus and evoke the development of the missing parts by laws and forces still unknown to us. Loeb has recently claimed that the nucleus is the cell's organ of oxidation; but if that be true it would still not exclude the possibility that the nucleus is also and primarily a storehouse of the material bearers of the primary constituents of a species. It must be regarded as such when we call to mind the phenomena of amphimixis in its twofold aspects as conjugation and as fertilization, and its obvious outcome among higher organisms where it implies the mingling of the parental qualities.

Thus the 'nuclear substance' of unicellular organisms is for us the first demonstrable organ of regeneration, and first of all for normal regeneration, which takes place at every reproduction, for instance, of an Infusorian. For we have already seen that, in the transverse division of a trumpet animalcule (*Stentor*), the anterior part must develop the posterior half anew, while the posterior half must develop the much more complex anterior half, with mouth region and spiral bands of cilia. But as soon as the arrangement for normal reproduction was elaborated, as soon as the nucleus was present, as a depôt of 'primary constituents,' this implied the possibility of regeneration in exceptional cases, that is, after injury. The mechanism was already there, and it came into operation as soon as a part of the animal was missing.

It is in the first nucleus, therefore, that we have to look for the source of all regenerative capacity, both in unicellular and multicellular organisms. But with the origin of the latter a limitation took place, either quite at the beginning or a little later, for each nucleus of the cell-colony no longer contained the whole complex of 'primary constituents' or determinants of the species, but, in many cases, only the reproductive cell possessed them. As soon as this began to develop into a whole by cell-division the determinant-complex was segregated. Thus the first cell-colonies with two kinds of cells arose, as we have seen in the care of *Volvox*—the reproductive cells with a complete equipment for regeneration in their nucleus, and the somatic cells with a limited equipment for regeneration in their nuclei. The somatic cell could no longer give rise anew to the whole organism, but could only reproduce itself or its like.

But as many of the lower Metazoa and Metaphyta possess *the power of budding*, that is, are able not only to produce a new individual from definite cells—the reproductive cells—with or without sexual differentiation, but from other cell-groups also, these must contain the whole complex of determinants appertaining to the reconstruction of the organism, and we have to ask how this is reconcilable with the differentiation of a multicellular organism, whose different kinds of cells depend, according to our interpretation, on the fact that they are controlled by different determinants.

Obviously, there is only one way out of this difficulty, and it is the one we have already indicated, that although the diffuse regenerative capacity which we have just alluded to occurs in species which exhibit gemmation, this does not exclude the control of a cell by a specific determinant; other determinants may be contained in the cell, in a state, however, in which they do not affect it, that is, in an inactive or latent state.

Thus we arrive in this way also at our earlier assumption that an inactive accessory-idioplasm is given to all, or at least to many cell-generations. Only among plants must this necessarily be complete germ-plasm, and among the lower plant-forms, as in *Caulerpa* among the Algæ, in *Marchantia* among Liverworts, it must be assumed to be present in nearly all the cells, according to the experiments in regeneration made by Reinke and Vöchting. But in multicellular animals which develop from two different germinal layers equipped with a different complex of determinants budding arises from a combination of at least two different kinds of cells, and we must only ascribe to each of these its own peculiar determinant-complex as regeneration-idioplasm. Higher plants show us that well-marked power of budding is not necessarily associated with a high regenerative capacity, the histologically specialized cells among them will contain no inactive germ-plasm, because they do not need it. But in animals the power of budding is probably always combined with high regenerative capacity, as is shown by the Polyps and Medusoids above all, and in a different way by the Ctenophores, which exhibit no budding and at the same time a very slight regenerative capacity, although they possess an organization scarcely higher than that of the Hydromedusæ. In the Ctenophores each of the first segmentation-cells, when artificially separated, yields only a half-embryo, and we may conclude from this that it contains no complete germ-plasm in an inactive state, or at least very little, and certainly not a sufficient quantity to make it readily regenerative.

Undoubtedly, however, the regenerative capacity occurs apart from the capacity for budding, yet this in no way contradicts the theory. As we have seen, a high regenerative capacity is to be found among many animals which occur only as 'persons' and not as colonies or stocks, but only in those which are readily liable to injury, and only in the manner conditioned by their injury. In the higher Metazoa the regenerative power becomes more and more limited, and in the Mammals it sinks to a mere closing up of wounds.

If we take a survey of the assumptions we have been compelled to make from the standpoint of the theory to explain the development of germ-cells, budding, and regeneration, it would seem as if it were contradictory to assume that, on the one hand, complete germ-plasm should be given to certain cell-series as inactive accessory idioplasm, and, on the other, that very numerous cells, at least in the lower Metazoa, should have received the idioplasm of budding, and still more numerous cells that of regeneration. But it is obvious that among the lower Metazoa the idioplasm of budding and the idioplasm of regeneration are equivalent; the same idioplasm, which, when liberated by stimuli unknown to us, co-operates from two or three germinal layers in the formation of a bud, effects, in response to the known stimulus of injury, the regeneration of the mutilated part. But germ-cells can never arise in the Metazoa from the partial budding-idioplasm or regeneration-idioplasm, because this is not complete germ-plasm, and because it can only give rise to budding or regeneration through the co-operation of two or more kinds of cells, while germ-cells always originate from *one* cell and never arise from the fusion of cells. Germ-cells can thus only arise from the cells of the germ-track, and in no other way, no matter whether the germ-track lie in the ectoderm, as in the Hydromedusæ, or in the endoderm, as in true jellyfishes (Acalephæ) and the Ctenophores, or in the mesoderm, as in many higher groups of animals. It is only apparently that these cells belong to one particular layer, for in reality they are unique in kind, and they are simply assisted in their development by one or other cell-layer, from which they not infrequently emancipate themselves, as happens so notably in the Hydromedusæ. As we have already said, it is only among plants that we must think of budding as arising from cells which contain complete germ-plasm, for here there are no 'germinal layers' corresponding to those of animal development, and the cells of 'the growing point' must be equipped with the complete germ-plasm. The plant, like the Hydroid stock and the Siphonophore colony, is saved from death, in spite of the frequent loss of its members, mainly by the fact that it is capable of producing, at almost any part above the ground, buds which develop into new shoots, with leaves and the like. This makes a power of regeneration on the part of the individual leaves and flower-parts superfluous, but at the same time it implies that an enormous number of cells must be distributed over the whole surface of the plant, each of which can in certain circumstances become the starting-point of a bud. That is to say, each must contain, in a latent state, the complete germ-plasm which is necessary for the production of an entire plant.

We must therefore assume that, in the higher colony-forming plants, germ-plasm is contained in a great many cells, perhaps in all which are not histologically differentiated, and sometimes even in those which are so, as, for instance, in the leaves of Begonias. I suppose, therefore, that in the higher plants the process of development implies a segregation of the determinant-complexes of the germ-plasm, but that this takes place at a late stage, and that in a much higher degree than among animals the individual or the 'person' carries with it germ-plasm in a latent state. To this must be attributed the fact that the plant is not only able to make good its losses in twigs and branches by sending out new shoots, but that cuttings, that is, detached shoots, are also able to take root, and in general to give rise to what is necessary to complete themselves according to the position of the part in question. In the ontogeny of animals, too, we must assume that it requires a liberating stimulus to rouse the determinants to activity, that this stimulus is to be sought for in the influence exercised by the constitution of the cell on the idioplasm contained within it, and that this constitution in its turn is subject to influences from external conditions, including the cell-soma itself. We may therefore suppose that, among plants also, the germ-plasm latent in numerous cells only becomes active in whole or in part according to the influences exerted on it by the state of the cell at the moment; but this varies with external circumstances, according to whether the cell is exposed to light or lies under ground, according as it is influenced by gravity, by moisture, chemical stimuli, and so on.

It might be objected to this that it would be simpler not to assume a segregation of the germ-plasm into determinant-complexes at all in order to explain the process of development, but rather to credit each cell with a complete equipment of germ-plasm from the beginning to the end of the ontogeny, and to attribute the differences in the cells, which condition the structure of the plant and its differentiation, solely to the different influences, external and internal, to which the cell is exposed, and which rouse some determinants to activity at one part and others at another. Perhaps the botanists would be more readily reconciled to this idea, but it seems to me that there are two points which tell against the possibility of its being correct. In the first place, it is far from being established that every cell in the higher plants is capable of giving rise, under favourable conditions, to a whole new plant; every tree and every higher plant has a multitude of cells in its leaves, its flowers, and so on, which cannot do this, which are in fact differentiated in one particular direction, that is, they contain only one kind of determinants, like the histologically differentiated cells of the tissues of the human body. Secondly, there are other organisms besides plants, and a theory of development cannot be based on the phenomena to be observed among plants alone, any more than a theory of heredity can. There are obvious differences in the processes of life among plants as contrasted with those among animals, but it is improbable that there is any thoroughly fundamental difference. It is, however, indubitable that the cells forming the tissues of higher animals, the nerve, muscle, and glandular cells, are really differentiated in one direction, and are quite incapable, under any circumstances whatever, of growing into an entire organism, and even from this alone we might conclude that they contain only one primordium or determinant. Are we then to assume that the vascular cells, epidermis-cells, wood-cells, and so on, of the higher plants, which are also differentiated in one direction, do nevertheless contain the complete germ-plasm? I do not see any ground for such an assumption.

To conclude what can be said on the subject of regeneration we must return to the question of an ultimate explanation of this marvellous phenomenon. I have declined to attempt any explanation at all, because I do not consider it possible to give a sufficient one as yet, but I should like at least to give an indication as to the direction in which we must look for it.

We assumed that there is a regeneration-idioplasm, and therefore that there are 'primary constituents' at certain positions in the body, but how does it happen that these are able to build up the lost parts in the proper situation and detail? A theoretical formula might well be thought out, according to which the determinants of successive parts would become active successively, and would thus liberate one another in an appropriate order of sequence, but there would not be much gained by this, especially as what we already know in regard to the regrowth of the legs and toes in Triton does not harmonize with such an assumption. It appears to me more important—though even here we must still be very vague as to details—to recognize that, in all vital units, there are forces at work which we do not yet know clearly, which bind the parts of each unit to one another in a particular order and relation. We were obliged to assume such forces even in regard to the lowest units, the biophors, since otherwise they could not be capable of multiplication by

D 2

division, on which all organic growth depends, unless we are to assume, as Nägeli did, a continual *generatio æquivoca* of the specific kinds of biophors (his 'micellæ'). But we shall see later, when we come to speak of spontaneous generation, that we cannot acquiesce in such an assumption. If, then, we cannot conceive of a power of division arising from within and depending solely on growth by means of assimilation, without such attractive and repellent forces or 'vital affinities' the internal parts would necessarily fall into disorder at every division. It seems to me therefore that such 'affinities' must be operative at *all stages* in the life of the vital units, not only in biophors, but also in the cell, and in the 'person' as well as in determinant and id. It is true that 'persons' no longer generally possess the power of multiplying by division, but in plants and lower animals many do possess it; and the power of giving rise anew to certain parts is obviously a part of that power of doubling the whole by division. The ultimate roots of regeneration, then, must lie in these 'affinities' between the parts, which preside over their arrangement and are able to maintain it and to give rise to it anew. In this respect the organism appears to us like a crystal whose broken points always complete themselves again from the mother-lye after the same system of crystallization, obviously in this case too as a result of certain internal directive forces, polarities, which here again we are unable precisely to define. But the difference between the organism and the crystal does not—as people have been hitherto inclined to believe—lie only in the fact that the crystal requires the mother-lye to complete itself, while the vital unit itself procures the material for its further growth; it lies also in the fact that such regeneration is not possible in every organism and at every place, but that *special* 'primary constituents' are necessary, without which the relevant part cannot arise. The indispensableness of these primary constituents, the determinants, seems to me to depend on the fact that the new structure cannot be built up simply by procuring organic material, but *that specially hewn stones, different in every case, are necessary*, which can only be supplied in virtue of an historical transmission, or, to abandon the metaphor, because the vital units of which the organ is to be reconstructed possess a specific character and have a long history behind them; thus they can only arise from such vital units as have been handed on through generations, that is, from the determinants. But these primary constituents are given to the different forms of life in very varying degrees and in very unequal distribution, and as far as we can see according to their suitability to an end.

LECTURE XXII

SHARE OF THE PARENTS IN THE BUILDING UP OF THE OFFSPRING

The ids are 'ancestral plasms'—The reducing division brings about a diversity of germ-plasm in the germ-cells—Bolles Lee's 'Neotaxis' even in the primordial germ-cells—Häcker's observations on the persistent distinctness of the maternal and paternal chromosomes—Identical twins—The individuality is determined at fertilization—Unequal share of the ids in the determination of the offspring—Preponderance of one parent in the composition of the offspring—Certain ids of the ancestors remain unchanged in the germ-plasm of the descendants—Struggle of the Biophors—Alternation of the hereditary sequences in the parts of the child—Reversion—Datura-hybrids—Zebra-striping in the horse—Three-toed horses—New experiments in hybridization among plants by Correns and De Vries—Xenia.

As far as the phenomena of regeneration and budding are concerned, we have not been able to do much more than bring them under a formula, which harmonizes with the germ-plasm theory. But the case is different with the actual phenomena of inheritance in the restricted sense, for instance, with regard to the transmission of individual peculiarities *from parent to child.* Here the theory really increases our insight and lets us penetrate deeper into the causes of the phenomena; it is here no longer a mere 'portmanteau-theory.'

We are well aware, especially from observation on ourselves, that is, on Man, that the children of a pair often resemble one another but are never alike, and that one child frequently resembles one parent, another the other, while a third may exhibit a mingling of both parents. How does this come about? Since the germinal substance of both parents is derived from that of the ovum, from which they themselves have arisen—and must therefore be the same in all the germ-cells to which they give rise—new determinants cannot be added, and old ones cannot be dropped out, and variation of the determinants, the possibility of which is granted, would still not directly bring about the familiar mingling of resemblances to the two parents, but would at most give rise to something new and strange.

Here the theory helps to elucidate matters. We found ourselves obliged to assume that the germ-plasm is composed of ids, that is, of equivalent portions of germ-plasm, each of which contains all the kinds of determinants appertaining to the building up of an individual, but each of these kinds in a particular individual form. I have already called these ids 'ancestral plasms,' and the term is appropriate, in so far that in every fertilization an equal number of ids from the father and from the mother are united in the ovum, so that the child is built up of the ids of his two nearest 'ancestors.' But as the ids of the parents are derived from those of the grandparents, and these again from those of the great-grandparents, the ids are in truth the idioplasm of the ancestors.

The expression, however, has been very frequently misunderstood, as if it were intended to mean that the ids retained *unchanged* for all time the character of their respective ancestors, and I have even been credited with supposing that our own ids still consist of the determinant-complexes of our fish-like or even Amœba-like ancestors. But in reality no id exactly or completely corresponds to the type, that is, to the whole being of any one of the ancestors in whose germ-plasm it was formerly contained, for each of the ancestors had many ids in his germ-plasm, and his entire constitution was not determined by any one of these alone, but by the co-operation of them all. The individual arising from a germ-cell must necessarily be the result of all the ids which make up his germ-plasm, but undoubtedly the share taken by some of them may be much stronger than that taken by others. It is also clear that, if we leave out of account any possible variation on the part of the ids, each of them belongs, not to one ancestor only, but to a whole series of ancestors, and must have taken part in their development, so that it is not the idioplasm of any particular ancestor, but only ancestral plasm in the general sense. In this sense we may quite well retain the designation, 'ancestral plasm,' for the id.

Thus, according to our view, the germ-plasm consists of ids, each of which contains all the determinants of the whole ontogeny, but usually in individually different quality.

Returning for a moment to the processes by which the reduction of the chromosomes, that is, of the nuclear rods of germ-plasm in the ovum and sperm-cell is brought about, we recall the fact that this happens at the last two divisions of the germ-cell, the so-called 'maturing divisions.' In these the nuclear substance, as we have seen, is divided between the two daughter-nuclei in a manner quite different from the usual one, for a longitudinal splitting of the rods, bands, or spheres in the equatorial plane of the nucleus does not take place, but half the number of rods move into the right and half into the left daughter-nucleus without previous division, so that in each daughter-nucleus the number of rods is reduced to half (Fig. 76).

Although the distribution of the rods in this manner takes place twice in succession, the normal number is not, as we have already seen, reduced to a quarter, because, long before the occurrence

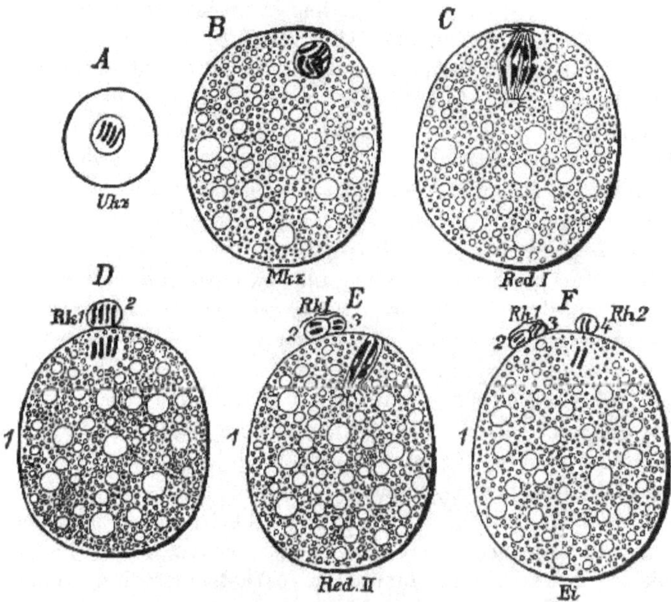

FIG. 76. Diagram of the maturation divisions of the ovum. *A*, primitive germ-cell. *B*, mother-egg-cell, which has grown and has doubled the number of its chromosomes. *C*, first maturation division. *D*, immediately thereafter; *Rk* 1, the first directive cell or polar body. *E*, the second maturation spindle has been formed; the first polar body has divided into two (2 and 3); the four chromosomes remaining in the ovum lie in the second directive spindle. *F*, immediately after the second maturation division; 1, the mature ovum; 2, 3, and 4, the three polar cells, each of these four cells containing two chromosomes.

of the first maturing division, a duplication of the rods by means of longitudinal division had taken place, and thus the first division differs from an ordinary division in that the splitting of the rods does not take place during the process of dividing but long beforehand. Only the second maturing division differs from all other nuclear divisions known to us, since it is not associated with any splitting of the rods at all, but conveys half of the existing rods into each daughter-nucleus. It is the true reducing division, through which the number of the rods is reduced to one half[1].

This numerical reduction must, however, have other consequences; it must make the germ-cells of the same individual qualitatively unlike, that is, in relation to their value in inheritance. Let us assume only four chromosomes of the rod-form ('idants') as the nuclear elements of a species, two of which, *A* and *B*, come from the mother, and other two, *C* and *D*, from the father, the last maturing division may, as far as we can see, result either in removing the combination *A* and *B* from *C* and *D*, or *A* and *C* from *B* and *D*, or *A* and *D* from *B* and *C*; there is thus a possibility of one of six different combinations of rods in any one germ-cell. What is the same thing, six different kinds of germ-cells differing in their hereditary primary constituents may *be developed in the same* individual. As this new combination, or, as we may call it, neotaxis of the germ-plasm elements, takes place in female as well as in male individuals, there is a possibility that, in fertilization, $6 \times 6 = 36$ individuals with different primary constituents may arise from the germ-cells of the same two parents. Of course the number of possible combinations increases very considerably in proportion to the normal number of rods, for with eight of these it comes up to 70, and with sixteen to 12,870; the number of individuals differing in their inherited primary constituents would thus be enormous, for each of the 70 or of the 12,870 different hereditary minglings of the ovum could combine in amphimixis with 70 or 12,870 different sperm-cells, so that 70×70 and $12{,}870 \times 12{,}870$ offspring individually different in their primary constituents might arise from the same two parents. In Man there are said to be sixteen nuclear rods; so that in his case the last-mentioned number of parental hereditary minglings might occur. This may seem a disproportionately high number as compared with the small number of children of a human pair, but we must not judge from the case of Man alone, and in plants and animals, which we have already discussed, the number of descendants is very much larger, and is often enormous. We saw what significance this apparent extravagance on the part of nature has, for without it adaptation to changed conditions of life would not be possible, since, if only so many were born as could attain to reproduction, no selection of the fittest could take place. The same would be the case if all the young of a species were alike, and even if all the descendants of a single pair

[1] Recent investigations have shown that the reduction of the chromosomes does not always take place exactly in accordance with the scheme here indicated, but that it differs from it in many cases. But as investigations on this point are as yet by no means complete, I need not go into the question further; the ultimate result is the same in any case.

were alike, effective selection would be excluded, since only as many individualities could be selected as there were pairs of parents. It is easy to understand that selection works more effectively the larger the number of descendants of a species and the more they differ from each other. The chance that the best possible combination of characters will occur is thereby increased.

Although we cannot calculate how many individuals of different combinations of characters natural selection requires to work upon in order to direct the evolution of the species [1], we can understand that only as large a choice as possible can secure that the best possible adaptations of all parts and organs are brought about and maintained. Precisely in the fact that in every generation such an enormous superfluity of individuals is produced lies the possibility of such intensive processes of selection as must continually take place, if the adaptation of all parts is to be explained. For if among the thousands of descendants of a fertile species each hundred were alike among themselves, these hundreds would have, as far as natural selection was concerned, only the value of a single variant. But such an all-round adaptation as actually exists in the structure of species requires as many variants as possible; it requires that each individual should be a *peculiar complex of hereditary characters*; that is, that all the fertilized germ-cells of a pair should possess an individually well-marked character.

The justification of this postulate becomes all the clearer if we take into consideration the male germ-cells as well as the female. Let us think of the enormous number of sperm-cells which are produced by many animals, and indeed by the highest of them—an almost incalculably large number which certainly goes far beyond millions. Let us assume that in Man there may be 12,870 million spermatozoa, then, with sixteen ids, and with an equally frequent occurrence of all possible combinations of germ-plasm—there would be 12,870—there would be a million of each type containing identical germ-plasm. The danger that several ova would be fertilized by identical sperm-cells would be by no means small.

It cannot, therefore, surprise us that other means have been employed by Nature to secure re-groupings of the ids. The simplest means would be, if before each division of the primitive germ-cells the nuclear rods were to divide, and if the split halves were

[1] For this reason I have left the number of id-combinations given above unaltered, though, according to the most recent researches into the processes of maturation, they are probably too high, since every conceivable combination does not actually occur. We are here concerned less with the exact number than with the principle.

irregularly intermingled, then at the formation of the next nuclear spindle an entirely new arrangement of the halves would result. But in animals, at least, this is certainly not the case; the processes of reduction are restricted to the maturing divisions.

Years ago Ischikawa observed that, in the conjugation of *Noctiluca*, the nuclei of the two animals become closely apposed, but that they do not fuse, although they behave like a single nucleus in the division which follows. In this case *paternal and maternal nuclear substances remain separate* (Fig. 83, vol. i. p. 317). The same phenomenon has since been repeatedly observed in many-celled animals, first by Häcker, then by Rückert in the Copepods, and afterwards by Conklin in the eggs of a Gastropod (*Crepidula*). But all these observations referred only to the earlier stages of ovum-segmentation up to twenty-nine cells, and it could not be affirmed that the distinctiveness of the paternal and maternal chromosomes lasted till farther on into the ontogeny. Professor Häcker now informs me, however, that he has been able to trace this separateness in a Copepod (*Canthocamptus*) not only from the beginning of segmentation on to the primitive genital cell, but also through the divisions of this up to the mother-egg-cell [1]. Thus we may now assume that the paternal and maternal hereditary bodies remain distinct, not only for a time, but throughout the whole development, a fact which confirms our assumption of the independence of the nuclear rods, notwithstanding their apparent breaking-up in the nuclear reticulum of the 'resting' nucleus. This new knowledge throws fresh light in another direction; it proves to us that the remarkable and complicated processes which go on in the nucleus during the maturing divisions have really the significance which I long ago ascribed to them [2], that of effecting the maximum diversity of intermingling of the paternal and maternal hereditary elements. For Häcker has shown that during the second maturation-division the paternal and maternal chromosomes are no longer united each in a special group, but occur scattered about in the nucleus, and subsequently come together again to form two differently combined groups.

If this were not so, if the maternal and paternal chromosomes remained separate, then the reducing division would cause only one of these groups to reach each of the germ-cells, and thus each mature ovum or sperm-cell would contain either only paternal or only maternal hereditary bodies. But this would make a reversion to

[1] Since this was written Häcker has published his results. See *Anatom. Anzeiger* xv (1902), p. 440.

[2] See my essay, *Amphimixis*, Jena, 1891.

more than three generations back impossible, and as such reversions undoubtedly occur, we must conclude that manifold new combinations of the paternal and maternal chromosomes take place. This obviously happens during the maturation-divisions, at least in the Metazoa.

The more numerous the rods or the free individual ids in a species are, the more numerous are the possible combinations. Whether all the mathematically possible combinations actually occur is a different question, which I should not like to answer in the affirmative just yet; but in any case the *actual* number of combinations in a species with many nuclear elements will be greater than in one with few, and in this respect those species in which the ids occur as independent granules will have an advantage over those in which they are combined into rods or bands (idants). These latter, however, afford us a better possibility of deducing the new combinations of the ids, although the idants themselves are not outwardly distinguishable from each other.

I must refrain from going into these highly interesting processes in more detail just now. So much is certain, that Nature makes use of *various means* to bring about the re-combination, and at the same time the reduction of the ids during the two 'reducing divisions.' This is proved by the fact recently established by Montgomery, that in many animal groups reduction results from the *first* maturing division. Whether it operates at this stage with rings, bands, double rods, X-shaped structures, groups of four (tetrads), and so on, all this serves the same end, the more or less thoroughgoing re-arrangement of the hereditary vital units. I am convinced that new investigations into these processes, if they were undertaken from this point of view, would lead to very important results [1]. It would be important to find out how great the variations are which thus arise, for it is very probable that they differ in degree in the different animal-groups. Even the combination of the ids into rods (idants) indicates that some species may be more conservative than others in maintaining their id-combinations, and that there will be among them a greater tenacity in the hereditary combinations of characters (i.e. of the 'type' of the

[1] Since this was written for the first edition observations of this process have been considerably increased, and discussions as to the exact interpretation of these are in full tide; we are surrounded by a wealth of new observations, facts, and explanations, without having attained to a consistent and unified theory. Several naturalists, such as Boveri, Häcker, Wilson, and others, have attempted interpretations, but these are in many points contradictory to one another. It is therefore impossible to enter into the question in detail here; further light from new observations must be awaited. So much we may say, however, that it is not chance alone which presides over the re-arrangement of the chromosomes during the reducing divisions; *affinities* play a part also; there are stronger or weaker attractions between the chromosomes, which aid in determining their relative position to one another.

parents). If we should succeed in penetrating more deeply into these processes we should probably also understand why in certain human families the hereditary characters are transmitted more purely and more tenaciously than those of other families with which they have mingled, and so on. It may well be that the persistence of character is due to the fact that ids which have once combined into rods hold firmly together, for it seems to me in no way impossible that individual differences should occur even in these most delicate processes.

But let us leave these more intimate questions out of account altogether, and turn our attention to the more obvious and less delicate phenomena, and we find that the re-arrangement of ids (Neotaxis) which we have just discussed affords a simple explanation of the generally observed phenomenon of the differences between individuals! Each individual is different from every other, not in the case of Man alone, but in all species in which we can judge of differences, and this is true not only of descendants of different parents, but even of those of the same parents.

Of course the differences between two brothers or two sisters do not depend entirely on the hereditary basis, but in part also on external conditions which have affected them from embryonic development onwards. Let us suppose that of two brothers who have sprung from identical germ-cells one becomes a sailor, the other a tailor; it would not surprise us to find them very different in their fiftieth year, one weather-beaten and tanned, the other pale; one muscular, straight, and vigorous, the other weakly and of bent carriage. The same primary constituents develop differently according to the conditions to which they are exposed. But the two brothers will still resemble each other in the features of the face, colour of hair, form of eyes, stature and proportion of limbs, perhaps even in a birth-mark, more than any other human beings of their own or any other family, and this resemblance will depend upon the identity of the hereditary primary constituents, on the similar id-combination of the germ-plasm.

Man himself affords a particularly good example in favour of this interpretation in the case of so-called 'identical twins.' It is well known that there are two kinds of twins, those that are not strikingly alike, and often very different, and those that are alike to the extent of being mistakable for one another. Among the latter the resemblance may go so far that the parents find it necessary to mark the children by some outward sign, so that they may not be continually confused. We have now every reason to believe that twins of the former kind are derived from two different ova, and that those of the latter kind arise from a single ovum, which, after fertilization, has divided into two ova. This not infrequently occurs in fishes and other animals, and we can bring it about artificially in a number of species by experimentally separating the two first blastomeres.

We have here, then, a case of absolute identity of the germ-plasm in two individuals, for the id-combination of the two ova derived from the same process of fertilization must be exactly the same. That in such a case, notwithstanding the inevitable differences of external influences to which the twins are exposed from intra-uterine life onwards, such a high degree of resemblance should arise is a fact of great theoretical importance. From the basis of the germ-plasm theory we can very well understand it, for, according to the theory, only precisely similar combinations of ids can give rise to identical individuals.

But we learn more than this from the occurrence of identical twins. They prove above all that the whole future individual is determined at fertilization, or, to express it theoretically, that the id-composition of the germ-plasm is decisive for the whole ontogeny. It might have been supposed that the combination of ids could change again during development, and that a greater multiplication of some than of others might take place at certain stages of development, or through certain chance external influences. It might have been thought that there was a struggle among the ids in the sense that some of them were suppressed and set aside. All such suppositions break down in face of the fact of identical twins, which teaches us that identical germ-plasm evokes an ontogeny which runs its course as regularly as two chronometers, which are constructed and regulated alike.

But when I say that a struggle of the ids, in the sense of a material setting aside of some of them, cannot take place, I by no means intend to maintain that the influence which each individual id exerts on the course of development may not be disproportionate to that exerted by others, and, under some circumstances, very disproportionate indeed. I must refrain from entering into this subject in detail now, but I should like to give at least an indication of what I mean.

If the germ-plasm consists of ids, these ids collectively must determine the structure, the whole individuality — let us say, briefly, the 'type' of the offspring; it is the resultant of all the different impelling forces which are contained in the different ids. If these were all equally strong, and all operating in the same direction, they would necessarily all have the same share in the resultant of development, the 'type' of the child. But this is not the case.

Numerous experiments on the hybridization of two species of plant have taught us that the descendants of such hybridization usually maintain a medium between the ancestral species; but it is not always the case, for in many hybrids the character of one species, whether paternal or maternal, preponderates in the young plant.

We recognize the same thing still more clearly in Man, whose children by no means always maintain a medium between the characters of the two parents, but frequently resemble one—the father or the mother—much more strongly than the other.

How can this fact be theoretically explained? Must we ascribe to the ids of the father or of the mother a greater determining power? Without excluding such an assumption as on *a priori* grounds inadmissible, I am inclined to believe that we do not require it to explain *this* phenomenon. For, if we take our stand simply on the fact of the preponderance of one parent, it follows directly from this that not all the ids control the type of the child, let the cause of the non-co-operation of some of them be what it may. But if in this case only a portion of the ids contained in the germ-plasm controls the type, this combination of ids suffices to make the child resemble one parent, the father, for instance, and consequently half the number of ids is sufficient in some circumstances to determine the child—taking for granted that the one-sidedness of the inheritance is complete, which never actually happens. But the half number of ids can only suffice if it includes the same combinations of ids which have determined the type in the case of the father; as soon as one or more ids of this particular combination are replaced by others the paternal germ-plasm alone is not enough to call forth complete resemblance in the child.

But, at the reduction, a change of arrangement of ids takes place, and a new combination arises, and thus each germ-cell receives its particular group of ids. It may thus happen that, in one particular sperm-cell, exactly the same group of ids is contained as that which determined the type of the father, and that the same is true of a particular egg-cell in regard to the type of the mother. Let us now assume that a sperm-cell and an egg-cell meet, which contain both those groups of ids which had determined the type of the father and of the mother; if the determining power of the maternal and paternal ids were equal a child would result which would maintain the medium between father and mother.

As is well known this does happen not infrequently, although it is difficult or impossible to demonstrate it precisely. In plant-hybrids proof is easier, and it has been established that by far the greater number of hybrids maintain a medium between the characters of the two ancestral species. This proves that our assumption of equal strength of the ids of both species must be correct in general, for we know definitely in this case, as I shall show later, that the paternal and the maternal ids are equivalent as regards the characters of the species. This is the case, for instance, with the hybrids between the two species of tobacco-plant, *Nicotiana rustica* and *N. paniculata*, which were reared by Kölreuter as far back as the eighteenth century, and which then, as now, maintained a fairly exact medium between the two ancestral species, and did so in all the individuals. Both species thus strive to stamp their own character on the young plant, and in both the hereditary power is equally great; in both it is contained in the same number of ids, that is, in the half, for both kinds of sex-cell have undergone reducing division. We have here, then, strict proof that the half number of ids suffices to reproduce in the offspring the type of the species, or, more generally, of the parents.

If we apply these results to the inheritance of individual differences in Man, we may say, that those germ-cells, to which at the reducing division the same combination of ids has been handed on as that which already determined the type of the parent, will endeavour to impress this image again on the child. If a female cell of this kind combine with a male which likewise contains the facies-combination of the parent, in this case the father, the same thing will happen which we described in the case of the plant-hybrids, that is, a medium form between the type of the two parents will arise.

Not infrequently, however, there is a marked preponderance of the one parent in the type of the child, and we have to inquire whether the theory gives us any help with regard to such a case.

One might be inclined to assume a difference in the determining power of the paternal and maternal ids, but if we cannot show to what extent and for what reason this power may be different such an assumption remains rather an evasion than an explanation. Moreover, it would not always apply to the conditions in Man, for if, for instance, the ids of a particular mother were in general stronger than those of the father, all the children of the pair in question would necessarily take after the mother; but it happens not infrequently that one child resembles the father preponderantly, and another the mother. Moreover, the ids pass continually from the male to the female individual, and conversely, by virtue of the continuity of the germ-plasm, so that the idea that sex can have anything to do with the relative strength of the ids is altogether erroneous.

But, as I have already said, unilateral inheritance occurs even in the mingling of species-characters, and most clearly in the case of plant-hybrids. Thus, for instance, hybrids between the two species of pink, *Dianthus barbatus* and *Dianthus deltoides*, resemble the latter species much more closely than the former, and the hybrid between the two species of foxglove which are wild in Germany, *Digitalis purpurea* and *Digitalis lutea*, is much more like the latter than like the former.

It might be reasonably asked whether, in these crossings, the normal number of ids in one species is not greater than in the other. We know that, among animals at least, differences in the normal number of chromosomes occur even in very nearly related species. It is not impossible that this, in many cases, is really the cause of the diversity of transmitting power in different species. Nevertheless, we cannot rest satisfied with this, for, in the first place, this cause could not apply to the apparent unilateral inheritance from one parent in Man, since the normal number of ids, as far as we know, is strictly maintained in the same species, and second, this would not explain certain phenomena of inheritance in plant-hybrids.

It happens not only frequently, but usually, that the different parts of the hybrid take after one or other parent in different degree, and this is the case also with children. In the hybrid between the two species of tobacco-plant, *Nicotiana rustica* and *N. paniculata*, which I have already given as an example of a medium form between the two parents, such diversities occur regularly in all the hybrid individuals. Thus the corolla-tube of the hybrid is nearer *N. paniculata* in regard to its length, but nearer *N. rustica* in regard to its breadth. Many hybrids suggest one parent-form in the leaves, the other in the blossoms. In the same way in the child the form of eye may be that of the father, the colour of the iris that of the mother, the nose maternal, the mouth paternal—in short, the preponderance in heredity swings hither and thither from part to part, from organ to organ, from character to character, and this is even the rule though the oscillations may not always be apparent and are often invisible.

If we think of the proposition we arrived at earlier, and which was proved chiefly by the case of identical twins, that the facies or 'type' of the descendant is determined at fertilization, we may be inclined to regard such an oscillation of the hereditary tendencies as almost impossible, for it means that, with the given mingling of parental germ-plasms, the potency of inheritance from the two parents in every part of the offspring is determined once for all in advance. But the case of identical twins corroborates these oscillations, for in them, too, the father predominates in one part, the mother in another, and it proves, at the same time, that these oscillations do not depend on any chances whatever in development, but that they are exactly predetermined in the mingling of the hereditary substances in the germ-plasm of the fertilized ovum, and are strictly adhered to throughout development.

This fact can only be explained thus: the primary constituents of the different parts and characters of the body are contained in the parental germ-plasm in varying degrees of hereditary or transmissive strength, and this can be understood very well from our point of view without putting anything new into the 'portmanteau' of our theory (Delage).

But I must digress a little in order to make this plain.

When, in speaking of plant-hybrids, I said that the collective ids of the germ-plasm of a species must be equivalent in regard to the characters of the species, I did not speak quite precisely; in the majority of ids, in many cases in an overwhelming majority, this must be the case, but not actually in all, at least not on the assumption we make that the transformation of species is accomplished under the control of natural selection.

Let us recall what we have already established in regard to the evolutionary power of natural selection, namely, that the changes which it controls can never transcend the range of their utility, and it will be clear to us that, of the many ids which make up the germ-plasm of the species, only so many will be modified as are necessary to evoke the character which has varied. Just as the protective resemblance of an insect to a leaf may be raised to a very high pitch, but can never become perfect, because an imperfect resemblance is already sufficient to deceive the persecutor, and the selective process comes to a standstill because individuals which possessed a still greater resemblance to a leaf would be no better protected from destruction than the others, so in the modification of a species the whole of the ids need not at once be modified, if a majority is sufficient to stamp the great majority of individuals with the desired variation. But it may happen that, at the reduction of ids during the development of the germ-cells, an id-combination with wholly or almost wholly unchanged ids may come together in one germ-cell, and if another sperm-cell of this kind meets with an egg-cell similarly constituted, an individual of the old species must arise. But this must—on our assumption—be at a disadvantage as compared with the transformed individuals in the struggle for existence, and will perish in it, and therefore the number of unmodified ids in the germ-plasm of the species will gradually diminish. It is obvious, however, that this will take place very slowly, as we may conclude from the phenomena of reversion, of which I shall have to speak later on.

But what is true of the ids is true also of their constituent parts, the determinants, and that—if I mistake not—is fundamental in the interpretation of the alternation of hereditary succession in the parts of the child.

According to our theory, the ids do not collectively exert a controlling influence on the cells, not even on the germ-cells, whose histological differentiation into spermatic or egg-cells can only depend on control through specific sex-cell determinants. It is the different determinants of the ids that control; transformations of the species will, it is true, depend on transformations of the ids, but this need not necessarily consist in a variation of *all* the determinants of the id. If, for instance, two species of butterfly, *Lycæna agestis* in Germany and *Lycæna artaxerxes* in Scotland, only differ from each other in that the black spot in the middle of the wing in *L. agestis* is milk-white in *L. artaxerxes*, no other determinants in the id of the germ-plasm can be different except those which control this particular spot. In a majority of the ids in *L. artaxerxes* the determinants of this spot must have been modified, let us say, to the production of 'milk-white.' This majority will increase very slowly if the white colour has no pronounced advantage for the persistence of the species, but it will increase gradually, as we have already seen, though extremely slowly, through the elimination of those individuals whose germ-plasm at the reducing division has chanced to receive a majority of ids with the old, unmodified determinants, and which have therefore reverted to the ancestral form. This will happen whenever the new character has any use, however small, in maintaining the species.

But in most modifications of species quite a number of parts and characters have undergone variation either simultaneously or in rapid succession; in many cases nearly all the details of structure, and therefore almost all the determinants of the germ-plasm, must have varied. We must not, however, assume that all the equivalent determinants, for instance, all the determinants K in all the ids, have varied[1], and above all we must not take for granted that the determinants of different characters or parts of the body, for instance, the determinants *L*, *M*, or *N*, must all undergo variation in an equal number of ids. It will depend on two factors whether a new character is implicit, in the form of varied determinants, in a small or in a very large majority of ids: first, on the relative age of the character, and, secondly, on its value in relation to the persistence of the species. The more important a character is for the species the more frequently is it decisive for the life or death of the individual, and the more sharply will individuals not possessing it be eliminated, and the more rapidly, therefore, will those whose germ-plasm still contains a majority of the unvaried determinants of this character tend to disappear. In this way these determinants will tend to sink down from generation to generation to an ever smaller minority in the germ-plasm of those that survive.

Thus in the ids of any species which has been in some way transformed—and that is as much as to say, in every species—the equivalent or homologous determinants are modified in a very varied percentage. A very modern and at the same time not very important character *K′* will only be contained in a small majority of ids, while in the remainder the original homologous ancestral determinant *K* is contained; an older but not very much more important character *M′* must have its determinants in a larger majority in the ids, while a character *V′* of decisive importance for the preservation of the species, if it has been in existence long enough, must be represented in almost all the ids, so that the homologous unvaried determinants of the ancestral species *V* can only have persisted in an id here and there.

If this argument be correct, many phenomena of inheritance become intelligible, especially the variability in the expression of the inheritance in the parts of the offspring, which is more or less rigidly predetermined at fertilization. For the germ-plasm thus contains in advance every kind of determinant in diverse *nuances*, and in definite numerical proportions. In a plant *N′*, for instance, *Ba′* may be the determinant of the modern leaf-form, and may occur in twenty-two out of twenty-four ids of the germ-plasm, while the two remaining ids still contain unmodified the old leaf-form determinants *Ba*, which the ancestral form *N* possessed. But the flower of *N′* may be of still more recent origin, and contain the

[1] By equivalent or homologous determinants I mean the determinants of different ids which determine *similar parts*, e.g. the scales of that wing-spot in *Lycæna agestis* which is alluded to above, and to which we must refer again in more detail.

E 2

modern flower determinants *Bl'* only in sixteen out of twenty-four ids, while in the other eight the old flower-determinant *Bl* of the ancestral form has persisted. Let us now suppose that another nearly related species *P'* has, conversely, a recently changed leaf-form but a very ancient form of flower, so that the former is represented only in sixteen ids by the determinants of the leaf *ba'*, and the latter in twenty-two ids by the flower-determinants *bl'*: it is obvious that when the two species are crossed, notwithstanding the equal number of ids in the germ-plasm, the leaves of the hybrid will resemble more closely those of the ancestral form *N*, and the flowers those of the form *P*; it is even conceivable that in such a case the numerically preponderating leaf-determinants *N*, and the equally preponderating flower-determinants of *P* may form a close phalanx, so to speak, against the much less numerous homologous determinants of the other species, and that against this power working in a definite direction the others can make no headway and are simply condemned to inaction.

How we may or can picture this as occurring is a question which of course admits only of being answered very hypothetically, and it leads us, moreover, into the region of the fundamental phenomena of life, with the interpretation of which we are not here concerned. For the present we have assumed that life is a chemico-physical phenomenon, and we have postponed the deeper explanation of it to the remote future, that we may confine ourselves in the meantime to the solution of the problem of inheritance on the basis of the forces resident in the vital elements. But we may, nevertheless, make the supposition that a kind of struggle between the different kinds of biophors may take place within the cell, if the homologous determinants of all the ids for the control of the cell have entered into it.

In many cases this struggle will be decided by the numerical preponderance of one kind of determinant over the other, but it is certainly conceivable that dynamic differences may also have something to do with it.

Let us, however, abstain from trying to penetrate further into the obscurity of these processes, and let us content ourselves with establishing that the preponderance of one parent in some or many parts of the child may be almost if not quite complete, and that this compels us to assume that the hereditary substance of the other parent is in such cases rendered inoperative—for we know it is present—since the ids of both parents all go through the whole ontogeny, and are contained in every somatic cell.

Upon this struggle between homologous determinants depends the possibility of the entire suppression or inhibition of the influence of one parent, the whole diversity in the mingling of paternal and maternal character in the body of the offspring. It is in this that we must seek the explanation of the fact that not only whole bodily parts of the child, such as arms, legs, the nature of the skin, the form of the skull, may take after sometimes the father, sometimes the mother wholly or predominantly, but that the small separate subdivisions of a complex organ may sometimes turn out more maternal, sometimes more paternal. Thus intelligence from the mother and will from the father, musical talent from the father and a talent for drawing from the mother, may be inherited by the same child. I do not doubt that genius depends in great part on a happy combination of such mental endowments of the ancestors in one child. Of course something more is necessary, namely, the strengthening of certain of these hereditary endowments, but of this we shall speak later.

It is, however, not only the immediate ancestors, that is to say, the parents, that have to be taken account of in this mingling of hereditary contributions, but also those more remote. Not a few characters in the child do not occur in either parent, but were present in the grandparents, and their reappearance is called 'atavism' or 'reversion.' Let us consider this phenomenon in more detail, and try to find out whether and how far it can be interpreted by means of our theory.

The simplest and clearest cases are again found among plant-hybrids. It may happen, for instance, that a hybrid between two species, when dusted with its own pollen, gives rise to descendants, some of which resemble only one of the ancestral forms: thus we have reversion to one of the grandparents. The explanation of this lies in the different modes in which the reducing divisions are effected; if they take place in such a manner that all the paternal ids of the hybrid are separated from the maternal ids, then the result is germ-cells which are like those of the grandparents, that is, those of the parent species, and these, if they happen to combine in amphimixis, must give rise to a pure seedling of one or other of the two ancestral species. This case occurs less rarely than was formerly supposed, and than it could do if absolutely free combination of the idants took place at reduction. If combination were quite unrestricted, all other possible combinations would be likely to occur as frequently as these. But recent experiments have shown that, in many plant-hybrids, the germ-cells of the hybrids which are fertilized by their own pollen are either purely paternal or purely maternal. There cannot, therefore, be free combination of the idants at the reducing divisions; the idants of the two parent-forms separate from one another and do not combine. It is doubtful, however, whether the same thing occurs within a race, for instance, in the case of reproduction within a human race.

In Man reversion to a grandparent occurs not infrequently, and we may explain it thus: the id-group which controlled the type of the grandfather was also contained in the germ-cell which gave rise to the existence of the father, but it did not dominate the type in that case because a more powerful id-group was opposed to it in the germ-cell of the grandmother. When, later on, at the reducing divisions of the germ-cells of the father, this id-group again arrived in the sperm-cells of the father, it would predominately control the type of the child, that is, of the third generation, provided that the egg-cell with which it combined contained a weaker id-group.

In the case of ordinary plant-hybrids what are designated reversions can only be called so in a wide sense, for the ancestral characters are contained *visibly* in the parent, although mingled with those of the other parent. In human families, however, there are undoubted cases in which one or more characters of the grandparent reappear in the child which were not in any visible way expressed in the parent, and must therefore have been contained in the parent's germ-plasm in a latent state. And there are both in animals and plants reversions to ancestors lying much further back, to characters and groups of characters which have not been visible for many generations, and the occurrence of these can only be explained on the assumption that certain groups of ancestral determinants have been carried on in the germ-plasm in too small a number to be able to give rise ordinarily to the relevant character. Such isolated determinants may, however, in certain circumstances be strengthened by the amphimixis of two germ-cells both containing small groups of them, and thus augmented they may gain a controlling influence. In this case the chances of the reducing divisions have a part to play, since they bring together the old unvaried ancestral determinants which, as we have seen, may persist in the germ-plasm of any species through a long series of generations. This would, of course, only suffice to bring about a reversion if the determinants of the ancestral species were still contained in the germ-plasm in comparative abundance. If this is no longer the case, something more is necessary, and that is the relative weakness of the more modern determinants.

If two white-flowered species of thorn-apple, *Datura ferox* and *Datura lævis*, be crossed, there arises a hybrid with bluish violet flowers and brown stalks instead of green. This was interpreted by Darwin as a reversion to violet-flowering ancestral species on both sides, for there are even now a great number of species of *Datura* with violet flowers and brown stalks. When the two white forms are crossed the reversion takes place every time, not merely in some cases, and we may conclude from this that in both these species there is still such a strong admixture of the same unvaried ancestral ids that they always excel the ids of the two modern species crossed, in strength though certainly not in number. And this superiority must again depend on the fact that similar determinants of the same part are cumulative in their effect, while dissimilars are not.

For this reason reversions to remote ancestors occur readily when species and breeds are crossed, while they are rare in the normal in-breeding of a species. The reversions of the breeds of pigeon to their wild ancestral form, the slaty-blue rock-pigeon, never result, as Darwin showed, and as we have already noticed, from pure breeding of one race, but only when two or more breeds are repeatedly crossed with one another. Even then it occurs by no means always, but only now and again. The germ-plasm of the breeds must therefore still contain ids of the rock-pigeon, but in a small number, varying from individual to individual. If by fortunate reducing divisions and the meeting together of a sperm-cell rich in ancestral ids with a similarly endowed egg-cell the number of ancestral ids be raised to such a point that it exceeds the number of modern-breed ids contained in each one of the conjugating germ-cells, the ancestral ids control the development and reversion occurs, for the ancestral ids together have a cumulative effect while the ids of the two parent breeds are different and therefore, as far as they are so, cannot be co-operative in their influence. But it must be understood that they need not be different as far as *all* their determinants are concerned, but usually only as regards some groups, and thus it happens that reversion does not occur in regard to all, but only in regard to particular characters—thus in the *Datura* hybrids, chiefly in regard to the colour of the flowers and the stem, and in the hybrids between different breeds of pigeon mainly in regard to the colour and marking of the plumage.

The reversions of the horse and ass to striped ancestors, which Darwin has made famous, go much further back into the ancestral history of the species, for while we know the ancestral form of the domestic pigeon in the still living rock-dove (*Columba livia*), the ancestral form common to the horse and the ass is extinct, and we can only suppose that it was striped like a zebra, because such striping occasionally occurs in pure horses and pure asses, at least in their youth, although now only on the legs, and because this striping is often more marked in the hybrid between the horse and the ass, the mule. In Italy, where one sees hundreds of mules, the striping is not exactly frequent, but it may occur in about two per cent., while in America it is said to be much more frequent. The germ-plasm of the horse and the ass must therefore contain, in varying numbers, ids whose skin-colour determinants represent in part still unmodified ancestral characters. When two germ-cells chance to meet in fertilization, both of which have received, through a favourable reducing division, a relatively large number of such ids, a relative majority of these in the fertilized ovum is opposed to the dissimilar and therefore mutually neutralizing homologous determinants of horse and ass, and reversion to the ancestral form occurs.

These cases of reversion are enough to show us that the old unmodified ancestral determinants may persist in the germ-plasm through long series of generations. But an even deeper glimpse into the dim ancient history of our modern species of horses is afforded by the occurrence of three-toed horses, references to a small number of which the palæontologist Marsh was able to discover in literature, and one of which he was able to observe in life. Julius Caesar possessed a horse whose three-toed feet represented a reversion to the horses of Tertiary times, *Mesohippus*, *Miohippus*, and *Protohippus* or *Hipparion*; for all these genera possessed, in addition to the strong middle toe, two weaker and shorter lateral toes.

In the germ-plasm of our modern horses there must still persist in certain ids the determinants of the ancestral foot, which, after a long succession of favourable reducing divisions combined with favourable chances of fertilization, may come to be in a majority, and may thus be able to induce a reappearance of a character which has long been hidden under the surface of the present-day type of the species.

I do not propose to enter further on the discussion of the phenomena of inheritance. A more detailed investigation of the phenomena of reversion is to be found in '*The Germ-plasm*,' published ten years ago; and the discussion could not be resumed here without a critical consideration of a relatively large series of newly acquired facts not always harmonizing, and, as yet, not even fully available. The year 1900 has given us the investigations of three botanists, De Vries, Correns, and Tschermak, who have sought by experiments in hybridization between different sorts of peas, beans, maize, and other plants, to throw light on the phenomena of inheritance, and thus on the actual processes which occur in the germ-plasm at the reducing division. This led to the discovery that similar experiments had been published as far back as 1866 by the Abbot of Brünn, Gregor Mendel, and that these had been formulated as a law which is now called Mendel's law. Correns showed, however, that this law, though correct in certain cases, did not by any means hold good in all, and we must thus postpone the working of this new material into our theory until a very much wider basis of facts has been supplied by the botanists. There is less to be hoped for from the zoologists in regard to this problem owing to the almost insuperable difficulties in the way of a long series of experiments in hybridization in animals. I myself have repeatedly attempted experiments in this direction, and have always had to abandon them, either because the crossing succeeded too rarely, or because the hybrids did not reproduce among themselves, or did so defectively, or because the distinguishing characters of the crossed breeds proved insufficiently tenacious or diagnostic. But it would be a fine task for zoological gardens to undertake such experiments from the point of view of the germ-plasm theory, and their success would afford material for the criticism of the theory, the more valuable because it is apparent from the experiments on plants that the processes of heredity are manifold, and are far from being uniform in different domains [1].

I have assumed for my theory that the reducing division took place according to the laws of chance, and that thus every combination of ids occurred with equal frequency. This assumption seems to be confirmed, by the experiments of the botanists I have mentioned, only in so far that in the crossing of hybrids with one another every combination of distinctive characters occurred with equal frequency. But, on the other hand, the splitting of the germ-plasm at the reducing division seems, as I said before, in many cases to take place in such a way that the id-groups of the two parents are discretely separated from one another; this was so in the stocks, peas, beans, and other hybrids. But even if this were always the case in these, we could hardly infer that it must be the same everywhere; we should rather expect that the relationship of the two parents and their ids would bring into play the finer attractions and repulsions between the ids of the germ-plasm, and would thus determine their arrangement and grouping. Further investigations may clear up this

[1] Castle and Allen have recently published the results of experiments in crossing white mice with grey, and these confirm Mendel's Law.

point; in the meantime we can only say that already—even among hybrids—many deviations from Mendel's Law have been established, for instance, by Bateson and Saunders (1902).

Before I conclude this lecture I should like to refer briefly to a phenomenon which Darwin was acquainted with and sought to explain through his theory of Pangenesis, but which at a later date was regarded as not sufficiently authenticated to justify any attempt at a theoretical explanation, since it seemed to contradict all our conceptions of hereditary substance and its operations. I refer to the phenomenon to which the botanists have given the pretty name of Xenia (guest-gifts), and which consists in the fact that in crosses of two different plants the characters of the male may appear not only in the young plant but even in the seed, so that a transference of paternal characters seems to take place from the pollen-tube to the mother, to the 'tissue of the maternal ovary.' In heads of yellow-grained maize (*Zea*) it is said that, after dusting with pollen from a blue-seeded variety, blue seeds appear among the yellow, and similar observations on other cultivated plants have been on record for more than half a century. Thus dusting the stigma of green varieties of grape with the pollen of a dark blue kind is said frequently to give rise to dark blue fruits.

Darwin accepted these observations as correct, and endeavoured to explain them as due to a migration of his 'gemmules' from the fertilized ovum into the surrounding tissue of the mother-plant. His explanation was not correct, we can say with confidence now, but he was right so far, for the phenomena of Xenia do occur; they are not illusory as most modern botanists seem inclined to believe. I myself was at first inclined to wait for further facts in proof that the phenomena of Xenia really occurred before attempting to bring them into harmony with my theory, and this will not be found fault with when it is remembered that these cases of Xenia seem to stand in direct contradiction to the fundamental postulates of the germ-plasm theory. For this depends essentially on a definite stable structure of the germ-substance, which lies within the nucleus in the form of chromosomes, and which cannot pass from one cell to another in any other way than by cell-division and division of the nucleus; how then could it pass from the fertilized ovum to the cells of the endosperm which do not derive their origin from it at all, but from other cells of the embryo-sac? In point of fact some of my opponents have cited Xenia as an actual refutation of my theory.

That cases of Xenia really do occur is now established by the comprehensive and at the same time exceedingly careful experiments recently made by C. Correns with *Zea Mais*; it is only necessary to look through the beautiful figures with which his work is adorned to be convinced that heads of maize whose blossoms have been dusted with the pollen of a different kind produce more or less numerous seeds of the paternal kind, usually mingled with those of the maternal. Thus heads of the variety *Zea alba* resulting from fertilization with *Z. cyanea* exhibited a majority of white grains, but among them a smaller number of blue; and the converse experiment, of dusting *Z. cyanea* with the pollen of *Z. alba*, yielded heads in which a minority of white grains appears among a majority of blue. But it is always

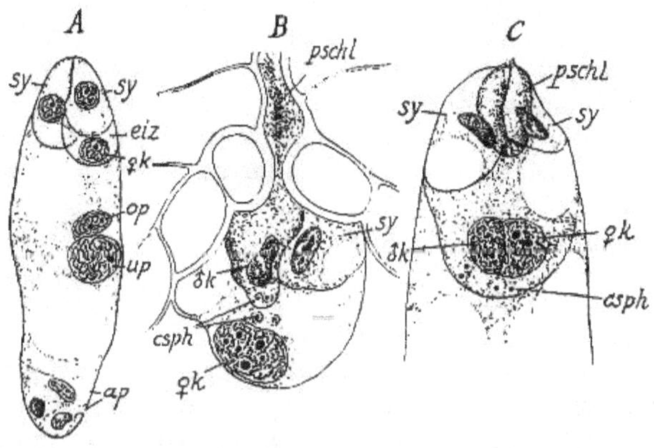

Fig. 82. Fertilization in the Lily (*Lilium martagon*), after Guignard. *A*, the embryo-sac before fertilization; *sy*, synergidæ; *eiz*, ovum; *op* and *up*, upper and lower 'polar nuclei'; *ap*, antipodal cells. *B*, the upper part of the embryo-sac, into which the pollen-tube (*pschl*) has penetrated with the male sex-nucleus (♂*k*) and its centrosphere; below that is the ovum-nucleus (♀*k*) with its (also doubled) centrosphere (*csph*). *C*, remains of the pollen-tube (*pschl*); the two sex-nuclei are closely apposed. Highly magnified.

only the nutritive layer surrounding the embryo—the endosperm—which exhibits the character of the paternal species, and even the capsule surrounding the seed shows nothing of it, but is purely maternal. Thus the heads of different species with pale-yellow capsule, when dusted with the pollen of *Z. rubra*, never have red seeds like those of *Z. rubra*, but always seeds with a pale-yellow skin, while, in the converse experiment, dusting of the red-skinned species *Z. rubra* with pollen from *Z. vulgata*, all the seeds are red, like those of the maternal species, and the influence of the paternal species only shows when the strong red skin has been removed, so that the intense yellow colour of the endosperm, which in the pure maternal species is white, is exposed to view. Thus the mysterious influence of the pollen never goes beyond the endosperm, and the riddle of this influence is solved in the most unexpected manner, indeed was solved even before Correns had securely established the genuine occurrence of Xenia. The explanation is due to recent disclosures in regard to the processes of fertilization in flowering plants.

It had long been known that the pollen-tube contains not merely one generative nucleus but two, which arise from one by division. But what had till recently remained unknown was that not only one of these penetrated into the embryo-sac to enter into amphimixis with the egg-cell, but that the other also makes its way in, and there fuses with the two nuclei which had long been designated the upper and lower polar-nuclei (Fig. 82, op. cit.). Nawaschin and Guignard demonstrated that these two nuclei fuse *with the second male* nucleus; thus two acts of fertilization are accomplished in the embryo-sac, and one of these gives rise to the embryo, while the second becomes nothing less than the endosperm, the nutritive layer which surrounds the embryo, whose origin from the polar nuclei had been previously recognized.

Thus the riddle of Xenia is essentially solved. We understand how paternal primary constituents may find their way into the endosperm, and indeed must do so regularly; we understand also how the paternal influence never goes beyond the endosperm. The riddle is thus not only solved, but at the same time the view which assumes a fixed germ-plasm, and believes it to lie in the nuclear substance of the germ-cells, receives further confirmation, if it should need any, for if facts which are apparently contradictory to a theory can be naturally brought into harmony with it, this affords a stronger argument for the correctness of the theory than the power of explaining the facts which were used in building it up.

There is much more to be said in regard to Xenia, and I am sure that much that is of interest will be brought to light by deeper investigation; theoretical difficulties will still have to be overcome, and I have already pointed out one of these in my '*Germ-plasm*,' but I must here rest satisfied with what has been already said.

We have now passed in review and attempted to fit into the theory a sufficiently large number of the phenomena of heredity for the purpose of these lectures. Although, as is natural, much of this must remain hypothetical, we may accept the following series of propositions as well founded: there is a hereditary substance, the germ-plasm; it is contained in very minimal quantity in the germ-cells, and there in the chromosomes of the nucleus; it consists of primary constituents or determinants, which in their diverse arrangement beside or upon one another form an extremely complex structure, the id. Ids and determinants are living vital unities. Each nucleus contains several, often many, ids, and the number of ids varies with the species and is constant for each. The ids of the germ-plasm of each species have had a historical development, and are derived from the germ-plasm of the preceding lineage of species; therefore ids can never arise anew but only through multiplication of already existing ids.

And now, equipped with this knowledge, let us return to the point from which we started, and inquire whether the Lamarckian principle of evolution, the inheritance of functional modifications, must be accepted or rejected.

LECTURE XXIII

EXAMINATION OF THE HYPOTHESIS OF THE TRANSMISSIBILITY OF FUNCTIONAL MODIFICATIONS

Darwin's Pangenesis—Alleged proofs of functional inheritance—Mutilations not transmissible—Brown-Séquard's experiments on Epilepsy in guinea-pigs—Confusion of infection of the germ with inheritance, Pebrine, Syphilis, and Alcoholism—Does the interpretation of the facts require the assumption of the transmission of functional modifications?—Origin of instincts—The untaught pointer—Vom Rath's and Morgan's views—Attachment of the dog to his master—Fearlessness of sea-birds and seals on lonely islands—Flies and butterflies—Instincts exercised only once in the course of a lifetime.

As I have already said in an earlier lecture, Darwin adhered to Lamarck's assumption of the transmission of functional adaptations, and perhaps the easiest way to make clear the theoretical difficulties which stand in the way of such an assumption is to show how Darwin sought to present this principle as theoretically conceivable and possible.

Darwin was the first to think out a theory of heredity which was worthy of the name of theory, for it was not merely an idea hastily suggested, but an attempt, though only in outline, at elaborating a definite hypothesis. His theory of 'Pangenesis' assumes that cells give rise to special gemmules which are infinitesimally minute, and of which each cell brings forth countless hosts in the course of its existence. Each of these gemmules can give rise to a cell similar to the one in which it was itself produced, but it cannot do this at all times, but only under definite circumstances, namely, when it reaches 'those cells which precede in order of development' those that it has to give rise to. Darwin calls this the 'elective affinity' of each gemmule for this particular kind of cell. Thus, from the beginning of development there arises in every cell a host of gemmules, each of which virtually represents a specific cell. These gemmules, however, do not remain where they originated, but migrate from their place of origin into the blood-stream, and are carried by it in myriads to all parts of the body. Thus they reach also the ovaries and testes and the germ-cells lying within these, penetrate into them, and there accumulate, so that the germ-cells, in the course of life, come to contain gemmules from all the kinds of cells which have appeared in the organism, and, at the same time, all the variations which any part may have undergone, whether due to external or internal influences, or through use and disuse.

In this manner Darwin sought to attribute to the germ-cells the power of giving rise, in the course of their development, to the same variations as the individual had acquired during its lifetime in consequence of external conditions or functional influences.

I abstain from analysing the assumptions here made; their improbability and their contradictions to established facts are so great that it is not necessary to emphasize them; the theory shows plainly that it is necessary to have recourse to very improbable assumptions, if an attempt is to be made to find a theoretical basis for the transmission of acquired (somatogenic) characters. Even when Darwin formulated his theory of Pangenesis his assumptions were hardly reconcileable with what was known of cell-multiplication: now they are above all irreconcileable with the fact that the germ-substance never arises anew, but is always derived from the preceding generation—that is, with the continuity of the germ-plasm.

If we were now to try to think out a theoretical justification we should require to assume that the conditions of all the parts of the body at every moment, or at least at every period of life, were reflected in the corresponding primary constituents of the germ-plasm and thus in the germ-cells. But, as these primary constituents are quite different from the parts themselves, they would require to vary in quite a different way from that in which the finished parts had varied; which is very like supposing that an English telegram to China is there received in the Chinese language.

In spite of this almost insuperable theoretical obstacle, various authors have worked out the idea that the nervous system, which connects all parts of the body with the brain and thus also with each other, communicates these conditions to the reproductive organs, and that thus variations may arise in the germ-cells corresponding to those which have taken place in remote parts of the body.

Even supposing it were proved that every germ-cell in ovary or testis was associated with a nerve-fibre, what could be transmitted to it by the nerves, except a stronger or weaker nerve-current? There is no such thing as *qualitative* differences in the current; how then could the primary constituents of the germ be influenced by the nerve-current, either individually or in groups, in harmony with the organs and parts of the body corresponding to them, much less be caused to vary in a similar manner? Or are we to imagine that a particular nerve-path leads to every one of the countless primary constituents? Or does it make matters more intelligible if we assume that the germ-plasm is without primary constituents, and suppose that, after each functional variation of a part, telegraphic notice is sent to the germ-plasm by way of the brain as to how it has to alter its 'physico-chemical constitution,' so that the descendants may receive some benefit from the acquired improvement?

I am not of the number of those who believe that we already know all, or at least nearly all, that is essential, but am rather convinced that whole regions of phenomena are still sealed to us, and I consider it probable that the nervous system in particular is not yet exhaustively known to us, either in regard to its functioning or in regard to its finest structural architecture, although I gratefully recognize the advances in this domain that the last decades have brought about. In any case, such assumptions as I have just indicated, or similar ones, seem to me quite too improbable to furnish any foothold for progress. Yet we must always remain conscious that we cannot decide as to the possibility or impossibility of any biological process whatever from a purely theoretical standpoint, because we can only guess at, not discern, the fundamental nature of biological processes. At the close of this lecture I shall return to the question of the theoretical conceivability of an inheritance of functional adaptations; but first of all we must consider the facts and be guided by them alone. If they prove, or even make it seem probable, that such inheritance exists, then it must be possible, and our task is no longer to deny it, but to find out how it can come about.

Let us therefore investigate the question whether an inheritance of acquired characters, that is, in the first place, of functional adaptations, is demonstrable from experience. We shall speak later on of the effect of climatic and similar influences in causing variation; the case in regard to them is quite different, because they undoubtedly affect not only the parts of the body but the germ-cells as well.

When we inquire into the facts which have been brought forward by the modern adherents of the Lamarckian principle as proofs of the inheritance of acquired characters in this restricted sense, we shall find that none of them can withstand criticism.

First, there are the numerous reputed cases of the inheritance of mutilations and losses of whole parts of the body.

It is not without interest to note here how opinion in regard to this point has altered in the course of the debate.

At the beginning of the discussion they were all brought forward as evidence of undoubted value for the Lamarckian principle.

At the Naturalists' Congress in Wiesbaden in 1887, kittens with only stumps of tails were exhibited, and they were said to have inherited this peculiarity from their mother, whose tail, it was asserted, had been accidentally amputated. The newspapers reported that the case excited great interest, and biologists of the standing of Rudolf Virchow declared it to be noteworthy, and regarded it as a proof, if all the details of it were correct. From many sides similar cases were brought forward, intended to prove that the amputation of the tail in cats and dogs could give rise to hereditary degeneration of this part; even students' fencing-scars were said to have been occasionally transmitted to their sons (happily not to the daughters); a mutilated or torn ear-lobe in the mother was said to have given rise to deformity of the ear in a son; an injury to a father's eye was said to have caused complete degeneration of the eyes in his children; and deformity of a father's thumb, due to frost-bite, was said to have produced misshapen thumbs in the children and grandchildren. A multitude of cases of this kind are to be found in the older textbooks of physiology by Burdach, and above all by Blumenbach, and the majority have no more than an anecdotal value, for they are not only related without any adequate guarantee, but even without the details indispensable to criticism.

As far back as the eighteenth century the great philosopher Kant, and in our own day the anatomist Wilhelm His, gave their verdict decidedly against such allegations, and absolutely denied any inheritance of mutilations; and now, after a decade or more of lively debate over the pros and cons, combined with detailed anatomical investigations, careful testing of individual cases, and experiment, we are in a position to give a decided negative and say *there is no inheritance of mutilations.*

Let me briefly explain how this result has been reached.

In the first place, the assertion that congenital stump-tails in dogs and cats depended on inherited mutilation proved to be unfounded. In none of the cases of stump-tails brought forward could it even be proved that the tail of the relevant parent had been torn or cut off, much less that the occurrence, in parents or grandparents, of short tails from internal causes was excluded. At the same time anatomical investigation of such stump-tails as occur in cats in the Isle of Man, and in many Japanese cats, and are frequently found in the most diverse breeds of dogs, showed that these had, in their structure, nothing in common with the remains of a tail that had been cut off, but were spontaneous degenerations of the whole tail, and are thus deformed tails, not shortened ones (Bonnet).

Experiments on mice also showed that the cutting off of the tail, even when performed on both parents, does not bring about the slightest diminution in the length of tail in the descendants. I have myself instituted experiments of this kind, and carried them out through twenty-two successive generations, without any positive result. Corroborative results of these experiments on mice have been communicated by Ritzema Bos and, independently, by Rosenthal, and a corresponding series of experiments on rats, which these two investigators carried out, yielded the same negative results.

When we remember that all the cases which have been brought forward in support of an inheritance of mutilations refer to a *single* injury to one parent, while, in the experiments, the same mutilation was inflicted on both parents through numerous generations, we must regard these experiments as a proof that all earlier statements were based either on a fallacy or on fortuitous coincidence. This conclusion is confirmed by all that we know otherwise of the effects of oft-repeated mutilations, as for instance the well-known mutilations and distortions which many peoples have practised for long, sometimes inconceivably long, ages on their children, especially circumcision, the breaking of the incisors, the boring of holes in lip, ear, or nose, and so forth. No child of any of these races has ever been brought into the world with one of these marks: they have to be re-impressed on every generation.

The experience of breeders agrees with this, and they therefore, as Wilckens remarks, have long regarded the non-inheritance of mutilations as an established fact. Thus there are breeds of sheep in which, for purely practical reasons, the tails have been curtailed quite regularly for about a century (Kühn); but no sheep with a stump-tail has ever been born in this breed. This is all the more important because there are other breeds of sheep (fat-rumped sheep) in which the lack of the tail is a breed character; it is thus not the case that there is anything in the intrinsic nature of the tail of the sheep to prevent it becoming rudimentary. The artificially rounded ear of fox-terriers, too, though cut for generations, never occurs hereditarily. Mr. Postans of Eastbourne informs me that the cocks which are to be used for cock-fighting are docked of their combs and wattles beforehand, and that this had been done for at least a century, but that no fighting cock without comb and wattles has been reared. In the same way various breeds of dog, such as the spaniels, have had their tails cut to half their length regularly and in both sexes for more than a century, yet in this case there is no hereditary diminution of the length of tail. Deformed stump-tails do indeed occur in most breeds of dog, but, as I said before, their anatomical character is quite different from that of artificially shortened tails, moreover they may occur in breeds whose tails have not suffered from the fashion of docking, as, for instance, in the Dachshund.

We may therefore affirm that an inheritance of artificially produced defects and mutilations is quite unproved, and in no way bears out the supposed inheritance of functional changes.

This is now admitted by the great majority of the adherents of the Lamarckian principle, and we may now regard this kind of 'proof' as disposed of.

In addition to the above, various sets of facts have been brought forward as proofs, and in particular the much discussed experiments of Brown-Séquard on guinea-pigs, from which it was inferred that epilepsy artificially induced could be transmitted. But these experiments do not really prove anything in regard to the question at issue, because epileptic-like convulsions may have very various causes, and these are, for the most part, quite unknown. Since artificial epilepsy can be induced in guinea-pigs by the most diverse injuries to the central or peripheral parts of the nervous system, this of itself points to the fact that it is not a question of the mere lesion of anatomical structure, I mean, of the breaking of the continuity of a definite part, and of its transmission. The result would, in any case, differ according to whether certain centres of the brain, or half the spinal cord, or the main nerve-trunks were cut through. There must, therefore, be something more needed to produce the appearance of epilepsy—some morbid process which may arise at different parts of the nervous system, and be continued from them to the brain-centres. This is corroborated by the fact that it takes at least fourteen days, and often from six to eight weeks, for epilepsy to develop after the operation, and that in many cases it does not develop at all. I have made the suggestion that, during or after the operation, some kind of pathogenic micro-organism might easily reach the wounded parts, and there excite inflammation, which may extend centripetally to the brain. Similar processes have been observed in connexion with lymph-vessels, and why should they not occur in connexion with nerves?

It has been objected to this that the guinea-pig's epilepsy may be produced by blows on the skull, and also by a destructive compression of the *nervus ischiadicus* through the skin, and that in both cases the epilepsy may reappear in the following generation; and this, it is supposed, shows that the intrusion of microbes is excluded. If this were so beyond a doubt, and if we could exclude the possibility that there were previously various microbes within the body, which could only penetrate into the nervous substance after the cutting or destruction of the neurilemma, nothing would be gained that would in any way

F 2

support the Lamarckian principle. One could only say: Certain injuries to the nervous system give rise secondarily in guinea-pigs to morbid phenomena like epilepsy, and all sorts of functional disturbances of the nervous system often appear in the next generation, including in rare cases even the phenomena of epileptic convulsions. That this is a case of the transmission of an acquired anatomical modification brought about by the injury is not only unproved, but is decidedly negatived, for the injuries themselves are never transmitted. Thus what is transmitted must be quite different from what was acquired, for no one has ever detected in the offspring the lesion of the nerve-trunk which was cut through in the parent, or any other result except the disease to which the original injury gives rise. Moreover, the inheritance of these morbid phenomena has been again brought into dispute quite recently owing to the investigations of such experts in nervous diseases as Sommer and Binswanger, and the correctness of Brown-Séquard's results, which have dragged through the literature of the subject for so long, has been emphatically denied [1].

Clearly formulated problems, like that of the inheritance of acquired characters, should not be confused by bringing into them phenomena whose causes are quite unknown. What do we know of the real causes of those central brain-irritations which give rise to the phenomena of epilepsy? It is certain enough that there are diseases which are acquired and are yet 'inherited,' but that has nothing to do with the Lamarckian principle, because it is a question of *infection* of the germ, not of a definite variation in the constitution of the germ. We know this with certainty in regard to the so-called Pebrine, the silkworm disease which wrought such devastation in its time; the germs of the pebrine organism have been demonstrated *in the egg* of the silk-moth; they multiply, not at once but later, in the young caterpillar, and it is the half-grown caterpillar, or even the moth, that succumbs to the disease.

Whether in this case also the disease germs are transmitted through the male sex-cells is not proved, as far as I am aware, but that this can happen is shown by the transmission of syphilis from father to child. That in this case, also, the exciting cause of the disease is a micro-organism cannot be doubted, although it has not yet been proved. Thus even the minute spermatozoon of Man can contain microbes, and transmit them to the germ of a new individual.

This discussion of scientific questions ought not to be brought down to the level of a play upon words, by bringing forward cases like the above as evidence for the inheritance of 'acquired characters,'

[1] See H. E. Ziegler's report in *Zool. Centralblatt*, 1900, Nos. 12 and 13.

as was done, for instance, by M. Nussbaum, who cited as a proof of this the migration of the alga-cells which live in the endoderm of the green freshwater Hydra into the ovum, which is originally colourless, and originates in the ectoderm of the animal (Fig. 35 *B*, p. 169, vol. i). It seems to me better to make a precise distinction between the transmission of extraneous micro-organisms through the germ-cells and the handing on of the germ-plasm with the characters inherent in its structure. Only the latter is inheritance in the strict scientific sense, the former is infection of the germ.

Still less than the cases of inherited traumatic epilepsy can the morbid constitution of the children of drunkards be regarded as a proof of the inheritance of somatogenic characters, though this has often been maintained. I will not lay any stress on the fact that the allegation itself is, according to the most competent observers, such as Dr. Thomas Morton[1], far from being established. But even if it were quite certain that the numerous diseases of the nervous system, amounting sometimes to mania, which are frequently observed in the children of drunkards, were really *caused* by the drinking of the parents, it ought not to be overlooked that we have here to do not with the hereditary transmission of somatic variations, but of variations *directly* induced in the germ-plasm of the reproductive cells, for these are exposed to the influence of the alcohol circulating in the blood, just as any other part of the body is. That by this means variations in the germ-plasm can be brought about, and that these may lead to morbid conditions in the children cannot be denied, and ought not on *a priori* grounds to be called in question. For we are acquainted with many other influences—climatic, for instance—which directly affect and cause variation in the germ-plasm. Whether this is so in the case of drunkenness, and in what manner it comes about, whether through direct action of the alcohol, or through infection of the germ with some microbe, we must leave to the future to decide; the whole question is out of place here; it can in no way help us to clear up the problem with which we are now occupied.

But even if there were not a trace of proof of the transmissibility of functional modifications, that alone would not justify us in concluding that the transmission is impossible, for many things may happen that we are not in a position to prove at present. If it could be shown that there was a whole group of phenomena that could not be explained in any other way than on the hypothesis of such inheritance, then we should be obliged to assume that it really

[1] Morton, 'The Problem of Heredity in Reference to Inebriety,' Proceed. Soc. for the Study of Inebriety, No. 42, Nov. 1894.

occurred, although it was not demonstrable, and, indeed, not even theoretically conceivable. This is the standpoint of the adherents of the Lamarckian principle at present.

They say there are a great number of transformations which are simply and easily explained, if we regard them as the effects of inherited use or disuse, but which admit only of a strained explanation, and sometimes of none at all, on the basis of natural selection, and these are not a few isolated cases, but whole categories of them.

I will submit a few of these, and show at the same time why I cannot regard them as convincing, even if it be the case that we are not at present in a position to explain them without the aid of the Lamarckian principle. But let me hasten to add that it is my belief that we can do this, although certainly not without first giving a somewhat extended application to the principle of selection.

It has often been maintained that the existence of animal instincts is in itself enough to prove that the Lamarckian principle is operative. In one of the earlier lectures I showed that at least the greater number of instincts must have originated in purely reflex actions, and therefore, like these actions themselves, can only be explained through natural selection. A reflex action, such as coughing, sneezing, shutting of the eyelids, and so on, differs from an instinctive action in the lesser complexity and shorter duration of the series of movements liberated by a sense-impression, and also in that it does not require to enter into consciousness at all; but no very precise boundary can be drawn between the two, and, in any case, both depend, as we have already seen, on a quite analogous anatomical basis. It is only a difference in degree whether, at the sight of a rapidly approaching object, the muscles of the eyelids contract, and by shutting the lids, protect the eye, or whether the fly, which we intend to seize with our hand, is impelled by the sight of the rapidly approaching shadow of the hand to fly quickly up. The action of the fly may be regarded as reflex, or equally well as instinctive. But there is also only a difference in degree, not in kind, between this simple action and the complex and protracted behaviour of a mason-bee, the sight of whose colony impels her to fly out and fetch clay, with it gradually to build a neat cell, to fill this with honey, to lay an egg in it, and finally to furnish the cell with a roof of clay. Since all reflex mechanisms, and all the natural instincts of animals, contribute to the maintenance of the species, and are therefore useful, their origins must be referable to natural selection, and we have only to ask whether they must be referred to it always, and to it alone.

It cannot be doubted that, in Man, and in the higher animals voluntary actions which are often repeated gradually acquire the character of instinctive actions. The individual movements pertaining to the particular action are no longer each guided by the will, but a single exercise of will is enough to liberate the whole complex action, such as writing, speaking, walking, or the playing of a whole piece of music; frequently the will-impulse may be absent altogether, and the action be set going simply by an adequate external stimulus, as in the case of sleep-walking, which is observed in fatigued children and soldiers, and in somnambulists. The external stimulus is transmitted to the proper group of muscles as unfailingly as in the case of true instincts, and this happens not only in regard to actions which, like walking, are essential to the life of the species, but also in regard to those which have arisen from chance habits or exercises. Often a short practice is sufficient to make an action in this sense instinctive, and the complexity of the instinct-mechanism gained by such practice is often astounding. Under some circumstances a person may play a piece on the piano from the score, and yet be thinking intently of other things, and be quite unconscious of what is played. In the same way it may happen that a person dominated by violent emotion, when trying to free himself from it by reading, may read a whole page, line by line, without understanding in the least what has been read. In the last case it is not directly demonstrable that the reader has made all the complex delicate eye-movements which would be liberated by the sight of the words, but in the case of playing, the listeners can perceive that the piece is correctly played, and thus that the stimulus exercised by each note on the retina of the eye is translated into the complex muscular movement of arm and finger, corresponding both to the pitch and the duration of the note, and to the simultaneousness of several notes.

In all these cases it is probably not always quite new paths which are established in the brain, but use is made of particular tracks in the innumerable nerve-paths already existing in the nerve-cells (neurons) which are 'more thoroughly trodden' by practice, so that the distribution of the nerve-current takes place more easily along them than along others[1]. This much-used metaphor does not indicate the actual structural changes which have taken place, but it serves at least to indicate that we have to do with material changes in the ultimate living elements of the nerve-substance (nerve-biophors) whether these changes be in position or in quality. Now,

[1] This, however, is by no means intended to cast doubt on the possibility that quite new paths may arise during the individual life, as is made probable by the recent investigations of Apáthy, Bethe, and others.

if such brain-structures and mechanisms acquired through exercise in the individual life could be transmitted, new instincts would certainly arise in this way, and many naturalists hold this view still.

If the inheritance of acquired characters had already been proved in other ways, we could not refuse to admit that it might play a part in the higher animals in the modification and new formation of instincts. We should then have to admit that habits can be inherited, and that instincts actually are or may be, as they have often been said to be, inherited habits. But to make the converse conclusion, and to infer from the result of the brain-exercise in the individual life and its similarity to inborn instincts that the latter also depend on inherited exercise, and that there must therefore be inheritance of acquired characters, is hardly admissible.

It might be all very well if there were no other explanation! But as instincts depend on material brain-mechanisms which are variable, like every other part of the body, and as, furthermore, they are essential to the existence of the species, and, down to the minutest detail, are adapted to the circumstances of life, there is no obstacle in the way of referring their origin and transformation to processes of selection.

It has been asserted that the results of training, for instance in dogs, can be inherited, since the untaught young pointer points at the game, and the young sheep-dog runs round and barks at the flock of sheep without biting them. It is, however, often forgotten that, not only have these breeds arisen under the influence of artificial selection by Man, but that they are even now strictly selected. My colleague and friend, Dr. Otto vom Rath, who unhappily died all too soon for Science, and who was not only a capable investigator, but an experienced sportsman, told me that huntsmen distinguish very carefully between the better and the inferior young in a litter, and that by no means every whelp of a pair of pointers can be used for hunting game-birds. Lloyd Morgan points out the same thing, and he is undoubtedly a competent judge in the domain of instinct: he confirms the statement that the pointer 'often points at the quarry, it may be a lark's nest, without instruction,' but he says at the same time, that the power is inborn in very varying degrees, and that, in his opinion, selection undoubtedly plays a part.

It must not, therefore, be believed that the habit of the pointer depends on training; it is only strengthened in each individual by training, but it depends on an innate predisposition to creep up to the game, and is thus a form of the hunting instinct. Man has taken advantage of this, and has increased it, but has certainly not ingrafted it into the breed by whipping. And something similar will be found to be true in all cases of so-called inheritance of the effects of training. It must not be forgotten what astounding results can be achieved in the individual by training. The elephant is the best example of this, for it only exceptionally breeds in captivity, and all the thousands of 'domesticated' elephants in India are tamed wild elephants. Yet they are as gentle and docile as the horse, which has been domesticated for thousands of years; they perform all kinds of tasks with the greatest patience and carefulness, in many cases without being under constant superintendence. They are indeed animals of great intelligence; they understand what is required of them, and they accommodate themselves readily to new conditions of life.

The attachment of the dog to its master and to Man generally has often been cited as a proof of the origin of a new instinct by the inheritance of acquired habitude; but the dog is a sociable animal even in a wild state, and by living in co-operative association with Man it has transferred its sociable affections to him. We find exactly the same thing in the elephant which has been caught wild and tamed. It is particularly emphasized by those who have accompanied animal transports in Africa that the young elephants are wild and malicious towards the blacks who teased and maltreated them, but complaisant and harmless towards the whites who treated them kindly. The attachment of elephants to their keepers and to every one who shows them kindness is familiar enough; it does not depend on a newly acquired impulse, but on the sociable impulse inherent in the species, which, in the wild state, causes them to live in fairly large companies, and on their inoffensive, timid, and, we may almost say, affectionate disposition.

Of course it is easy enough to give an imaginative theoretical interpretation of the origin of a new instinct from a newly acquired habit. We have often heard that sailors have found the birds in distant uninhabited islands quite free from fear; they let themselves be struck down with cudgels without attempting to escape. The extermination of the Dodo three centuries ago is a well-known example of this. Chun, in his magnificent work on the German Deep Sea Expedition of 1898, has recently communicated numerous interesting examples of the indifference of birds towards Man when they have not learned what his presence means: thus the sea-birds of Kerguelen, penguins, cormorants, gulls, 'kelp-pigeons' (*Chionis*), and others, behaved towards Man very much like the tame geese of our poultry yards. Even enormous mammals like the 'sea-elephant,' a seal with a proboscis-like prolongation of the nose, neither attempted to escape nor showed any hostility to man, but quietly let itself be caught. Similar tales were told by Steller in 1799, after he had been obliged to pass a winter with his sailors on an island in the Behring Straits. The numerous gigantic sea-cows (*Rhytina stelleri*) which lived there were so confiding that they allowed the boat to come quite up to them, and the sailors were able to kill many of them from time to time, using their flesh for food. But towards the end of the winter the animals began to be shy, and, in the following winter, when other sailors to the polar regions endeavoured to hunt them too, it was very difficult to secure them; they had recognized man as an enemy, and fled from him when they saw him from afar. Thus the same individuals which had earlier carelessly allowed man to come up to them now avoided him as an enemy. *This was not instinct, it was a behaviour controlled by the will and founded on experience.* But it would soon become 'instinctive' if the meeting with the enemy were often repeated, just like the winding-up of a watch, which is often done at a wrong time, for instance, on changing clothes during the day, and thus without reflection. It is quite easy to conceive that if the material brain-adaptation which causes flight without reflection at the sight of man were transmissible, the flight-instinct might become a congenital instinct in the species in question. But this assumption is unfounded; for, as is shown by the case of the sea-cow, we do not require it where the animal is of sufficient intelligence to perform by its own discernment the action necessary to its existence. The action may thus become 'instinctive' through exercise and imitation in the *individual* life, without however attaining to transmissibility.

But in many cases this is not enough, namely, in all cases in which the degree of intelligence is not sufficiently high, or where the flight movement must follow so rapidly that it would be too late if it had to be regulated by the will, as, for instance, the shutting of the lids when the eye is threatened, or the flight of the fly or the butterfly when an enemy approaches. Both fly and butterfly would be lost in every case if they had voluntarily to set the flight-movement going after they became conscious of danger. If they had first of all to find out from whom danger threatened no individual would escape an early death, and the species would die out. But they possess an instinct which impels them to fly up with lightning speed, and in an opposite direction, whenever they have a visual perception of the rapid approach of any object of whatever nature. For this reason they are difficult to catch. I once watched the play of a cat, ordinarily very clever at catching, as she attempted to seize a peacock-butterfly (*Vanessa Io*), which settled several times on the ground in front of her. Quietly and slowly she crept within springing distance, but even during the spring the butterfly flew up just before her nose and escaped every time, and the cat gave it up after three attempts.

In this case the beginning of the action cannot lie in a voluntary action, for the insect cannot know what it means to be caught and killed, and the same is true of innumerable still lower animal forms, the hermit-crabs and the Serpulids, which withdraw with lightning speed into their houses, and so forth. It seems to me important theoretically, that the same action can be liberated at one time by the will, at another by the inborn instinct-mechanism. In both cases quite similar association-changes in the nerve-centres must lie at the root of the animal's action, but in the first case these are developed only in the course of the individual life by exercise, while in the second they are inborn. In the former, they are confined to the individual, and must be acquired in each generation by imitation of older individuals (tradition) and by inference from experience, in the latter they are inherited as a stable character of the species.

It has been maintained by many that the origin of instincts through processes of selection is not conceivable, because it is improbable that the appropriate variations in the nervous system, which are necessary for the selective establishment of the relevant brain-mechanism, should occur fortuitously. But this is an objection directed against the principle of selection itself, and one which points, I think, to an incompleteness in it, as it was understood by Darwin and Wallace. The same objection can be made to every adaptation of an organ through natural selection; it is always doubtful whether the useful variations will present themselves, as long as they are due solely to chance, as the discoverers of the selective principle assumed. We shall attempt later to fill up this gap in the theory, but, in the meantime, I should like to point out that the process of selection offers the only possible explanation of the origin of instincts, since their origin through modifications of voluntary actions into instinctive actions, with subsequent transmission of the instinct-mechanism due to exercise in the individual life, has been shown to be untenable.

If any one is still unconvinced of this, I can only refer to the cases we have already discussed of instincts which are only exercised once in a lifetime, since, in these, the only factor that can transform a voluntary action into an instinctive one is absent, namely, the frequent repetition of the action. In this case, if any explanation is to be attempted at all, it can only be through natural selection, and as we have assumed once for all that our world does admit of explanation, we may say, *these instincts have arisen through natural selection.*

Even though it may be difficult to think out in detail the process of the gradual origin of such an instinctive activity, exercised once in a lifetime, such as that, for instance, which impels the caterpillar to spin its intricate cocoon, which it makes only once, without ever having seen one, and thus without being able to imitate the actions which produce it, we must not push aside the only conceivable solution of the problem on that account, for then we should have to renounce all hope of a scientific interpretation of the phenomenon. We may ask, however, whether there is not something lacking in our present conception of natural selection, and how it comes about that useful variations always crop up and are able to increase.

But if we must explain, through natural selection, such complex series of actions as are necessary to the making of the cocoon of the silkworm or of the Saturnia moth (*Saturnia carpini*), what reason have we for not referring other instincts also to selection, even if they be repeated several times, or often, in the course of a lifetime? It is illogical to drag in any other factor, if this one, which has been proved to operate, is sufficient for an explanation.

Thus, as far as instincts are concerned, there is no necessity to make the assumption of an inheritance of functional changes, any more than there is in regard to any purely morphological modifications. As the instincts only exercised once show us that even very complicated impulses may arise without any inheritance of habit, that is, without inheritance of functional modification, so there are among purely morphological characters not a few which, though effective, are purely passive, which are of use to the organism only through their existence, and not through any real activity, so that they cannot be referred to exercise, and therefore cannot be due to the transmission of the results of exercise. And, if this be the case, then transformations of the most diverse parts may take place without the inheritance of acquired characters, that is, of functional modifications, and there is no reason for dragging in an unproved mode of inheritance to explain a process which can quite well be explained without it. For if any part whatever can be transformed solely through natural selection, why, since there is general variability of all parts, should this be confined to the passive organs alone, when the active ones are equally variable, and equally important in the struggle for existence?

There are, indeed, many of these passive parts among animals; I need only recall the coloration of animals, the whole set of skeletal parts, so diversely formed, of the Arthropods, the legs, wings, antennæ, spines, hairs, claws, and so on, none of which can be changed by the inherited results of exercise, because they are no longer capable of modification by exercise; they are ready before they are used; they come into use only after they have been hardened by exposure to the air, and are no longer plastic; they are at most capable of being used up or mutilated. Finally, even so convinced an advocate of the Lamarckian principle as Herbert Spencer has stated that among plants the great majority of characters and distinctive features cannot be explained by it, but only through the principle of selection; all the diverse protective arrangements of individual parts, like thorns, bristles, hairs, the felt-hairs of certain leaves, the shells of nuts, the fat and oil in seeds, the varied arrangements for the dispersal of seeds, and so on, all operate by their presence alone, not through any real activity which causes them to vary, and the results of which might be transmitted. An acacia covered all over with thorns seldom requires to use its weapons even once, and if a hungry ruminant does prick itself on the thorns it is only a few of these which are thus 'exercised,' the rest remain untouched.

But since all these parts have originated notwithstanding their passivity, there must be a principle which evokes them in relation to the necessities of the conditions of life, and this can only be natural selection, that is, the self-regulation of variations in reference to utility. And if there is this principle, we require no other to explain what is already explained.

I can quite well understand, however, that many naturalists, and especially palæontologists, find it difficult to accept this conclusion. If we think only of those parts that actively function, and thus change by reason of their function, being strengthened by use and weakened and diminished in size by disuse, and if, further, we follow these parts through the history of whole geological epochs, we may certainly get the impression that the exercise of the parts has directly caused their phyletic evolution. The direction prescribed by utility in the course of the individual life and in the phylogeny is the same, and the intra-selection, that is, the selection of tissues within the individual animal, leads towards the same improvements as the selection of 'persons.' Thus it appears as if the phyletic variations followed those of the individual life, while in reality the reverse is true; the changes arising from variations in the *germ are primary, and they determine the course of phylogenesis,* while the tissue-selection in the individual life only elaborates and improves, according to the demands made upon it, the material afforded by the primordial equipment of the germ.

The American palæontologist, Osborn, cites the case of the horse's feet as an example in support of his view that modification brought about by use in the individual life must be transmitted in order that the phyletic transformations may be brought about, but this example is perhaps the best that could be chosen to prove the contrary. He supposes that, in every young horse, the means of locomotion are improved at every step, so to speak, through the contact with the ground, and I am quite willing to admit that this is so. But that only proves that, even now, an elaboration and improvement of the equipment which the germ affords is indispensable, as it has been at all times and in all animals, and thus that, notwithstanding the enormous number of generations which our modern horse has behind it, the functional acquirements of the individual have not yet been impressed upon the germ. Why not? Because the horse becomes perfect without this, and there was no reason why personal selection should perfect the primary constituents of the germ still further, since the finishing touch of perfection through use is readily afforded by the conditions of each individual life.

Moreover, when Osborn, Cope, and other palæontologists emphasize that, in phyletic evolutionary series, *definite paths of evolutionary* change are adhered to, and are not deviated from either to right or to left, they are undoubtedly right, but the conclusion which they draw is not justifiable, whether they assume with Nägeli that there is a power of development, a principle of perfecting, or whether, as Osborn does, they assume the transmission of the modifications brought about through use in the individual life. There remains a third possibility, that the quiet and constant evolution in a definite direction is guided by selection, and as, in passively useful parts, that principle alone is admissible, I see no justification for assuming it to be inoperative in regard to those which are actively functional. All these variations which have led up, for instance, to the modern form of the horse's foot are useful; if they were not, they could not have been produced either by use or by disuse in the individual life.

At the same time, here again, we are justified in inquiring whether the assumption of 'chance' germinal variations, which we have hitherto made with Darwin and Wallace, affords a sufficient basis for selection. Osborn says very neatly in this connexion, 'We see with Weismann and Galton the element of chance; but the dice appear to be loaded, and in the long run turn "sixes" up. Here arises the question: What loads the dice?'

Until recently we might have answered, 'external conditions': it is they that load the dice one-sidedly, and condition that the same straight path of phylogenesis is adhered to, and exactly the same direction of variations is preferred and maintained. It has to be asked, however, whether this answer, which is certainly not absolutely incorrect, is sufficient by itself, whether the dice are not falsified and one-sidedly loaded in another sense, so that they always throw a preponderating number of the useful variations. We shall attempt very soon to solve this problem, but in the meantime I must refer to another argument in favour of assuming the Lamarckian principle, perhaps the most important and it may be thought the most difficult of all to refute, the so-called co-adaptation of the parts of an organism, that is, the fitting together of many individual organs for a common purposeful functioning.

LECTURE XXIV

OBJECTIONS TO THE THESIS THAT FUNCTIONAL MODIFICATIONS ARE NOT TRANSMITTED

Giant stag as an example of co-adaptation or 'harmonious adaptation'—This occurs even in passively functioning parts—Skeleton of Arthropods—Stridulating organ of ants and crickets—Limbs of the mole-cricket—Wing-venation—Colorations which form mimetic pictures—Harmonious adaptations in worker-bees and ants—Degeneration of their wings and ovaries—The quality of food acts as a liberating stimulus—Vom Rath's case of drones fed with royal food—Transition-forms between females and workers—Wasmann's explanation of these—The Amazon ants—Two kinds of workers—Appendix: Zehnder on the case of ants—On the skeleton of Arthropods—Hering's interpretation of Ehrlich's Ricin experiments—Hering's position in regard to the transmission of functional modifications.

It was Herbert Spencer, the English philosopher, who first brought the argument of co-adaptation into the field against my view of the non-inheritance of functionally acquired modifications. He pointed out that many, if not, indeed, most modifications of bodily parts, to be effective, implied further changes, often very numerous, in other parts, and these latter must therefore have changed *simultaneously* with the part which was being changed under the control of natural selection; this, however, is only conceivable as due to an inheritance of the changes caused by use, since a simultaneous alteration of so many parts through natural selection would be impossible. If, for instance, the antlers of our modern stag were to grow to the size of those of the Giant Stag of the Irish peat-bogs, which measured over ten feet across from tip to tip, this would mean—as has already been shown—a simultaneous thickening of the skull, and to bear the heavy burden, a strengthening of the *ligamentum nuchæ*, of the muscles of the neck and back, of the bones of the legs and their muscles, and, finally, of all the nerves supplying the muscles; and how could all this happen simultaneously with, and in exact proportion to the growth of the antlers, if it depended—as natural selection assumes—on chance variations of all these parts? What if the appropriately favourable variation in one of these organs did not occur? A harmonious variation of all the parts—bones, muscles, nerves, ligaments—which unite in a common activity, is an inadmissible assumption, because, in many cases, such co-operating groups of organs have in the course of evolution developed in opposite directions. In the giraffe, for instance, the fore-legs are longer than the hind-legs, which is the reverse of what obtains in the majority of ruminants; in the kangaroo the hind-legs, on the contrary, have developed to a disproportionate size, while the fore-legs have degenerated into relatively small grasping arms. Co-operating parts, like the fore and hind limbs, may thus follow opposite paths of evolution; their variations need not always be directed to the same end.

The difficulty presented by these so-called co-adaptations or harmonious correlations cannot be denied, and we must also admit that, if the results of exercise were inherited, the explanation of the phenomenon would, in many cases—but not, indeed, in all—be easy, because the adaptation of the secondarily varying parts in each individual life would correspond exactly to the altered function of the part, and would be transmitted to the descendants, and in them would again be subject to such a degree of variation, according to the principle of histonal selection, as might be conditioned by the further progress of the primary variation. The simplicity of the explanation is striking, if only it were at the same time correct! But there are whole series of facts, or rather of groups of facts, which prove that the causes of co-adaptation do not lie in the inheritance of functional modifications, and this must be recognized, even though we may not yet be in a position to state the causes of co-adaptation, and to say whether natural selection suffices to explain it or not.

I must first point out that co-adaptations occur not only in *actively, but also in passively functioning parts.* Very numerous instructive examples are to be found among the Arthropods, whose whole skeleton belongs to this category. It has been objected that this is not wholly passive, but that, like the bones of vertebrates, it is stimulated by the contraction of the muscles and incited to functional reaction, and that it thickens at places where strong muscles are inserted, and becomes or remains thin where it is not exposed to any strain from the muscles. But this is not the case, for the chitinous skeleton can only offer resistance to the muscular contractions when it is no longer soft, as it is immediately after it is secreted. As soon as it has become hard, it can no longer be altered, and can at most be worn away externally by long use. The proof of this lies in the necessity for moulting, which is indispensable to all Arthropods as long as they continue to grow, but does not occur later. Every one who has followed the growth of an insect or a crustacean knows well that the moultings or ecdyses are often accompanied by great changes, and hardly ever occur without some slight changes in the form of the body, especially of the limbs, with their teeth, bristles, spines, and so on. These new or transformed parts are formed before the throwing-off of the old chitinous shell, and under its protection, and they are brought about by an elaboration or transformation of the living soft matrix of the skeleton, the hypodermis, which consists of cells, and is the true skin. They must thus have arisen in the ancestors of our modern Arthropods in the same way, that is, not by a gradual modification *during* use, but by a slight sudden transformation before use. The steps in the transformation may have been very small, a bristle may have become a little longer in the second stage of life than it was in the first, or instead of five bristles a particular spot may bear six in the second or third stage of life; but the variations in the phyletic development must always be caused by germ-variations which effect from within the variation in the relevant stage of development. But the part which has varied can only function after it has become firm and immodifiable.

If these circumstances be kept clearly in mind, they furnish a quite overwhelming mass of proof against the views of the Lamarckians.

Furthermore, it is not even true that the thickest parts of the external skeleton are those at which the muscles are inserted. The wing-covers of beetles offer the best proof to the contrary, for there are no muscles at all in them, yet they are, in many species, the hardest and thickest part of the whole chitinous coat of mail. The reason is not far to seek; they protect the wings and the soft skin of the back, which lies concealed beneath them, and the muscles are inserted in this!—a relation which can be explained only by its suitability to the end, and not as due to any direct effect.

When we remember the origin—which we have just described—of the external skeleton from the soft layer of cells underneath it, the thickness of the chitinous skeleton, which is very different at different places in the same animal, but always adapted to its end, furnishes a case of co-adaptation in parts which have a purely passive function. The thickened part cannot be due to the insertion of a muscle, but it is always there in advance, from internal causes, so that the muscle finds sufficient resistance. Close to it there may lie, perhaps, the edge of a segment, and at this spot the chitinous skeleton becomes almost suddenly thinned to a joint membrane capable of being bent or folded, not *because* there was no pull from the muscles at this spot, but in order that the two segments may be connected movably. Thus, nowhere in the whole body of the Arthropod can the adaptation of the skeleton, in regard to thickness and power of resistance, be regulated by function itself, but only by processes of selection which imparted to each spot the thickness it required, in order to be effective in its function, whether that be offering resistance to the strain of the muscles, or giving suppleness to a joint, or affording the necessary hardness for biting the prey, or for boring into wood or earth, or merely for protecting the animal from external injuries.

There are, however, many individual functions of the Arthropods the exercise of which depends on the simultaneous change of several skeletal parts; as, for instance, many of the 'singing' or vocal apparatuses in insects. In quite recent times such vocal organs have been discovered in ants, in which they consist of a small striated region on the surface of the third abdominal segment, and a sharp ridge on the segment in front; the latter is rubbed against the former by the movements of the two segments. Quite a similar 'stridulating organ' has long been known in the bee-ant (*Mutilla*), and the whistling sound produced by it is easily heard by our ears; moreover August Forel has heard it in the large wood-ant (*Campnotus ligniperdus*), and has described it as an 'alarm-signal,' which the animals give each other on the approach of danger—an observation which has recently been confirmed by Wasmann and extended by Robert Wroughton in regard to Indian ants. All these arrangements for producing sound depend always on two organs, of which one resembles the bow, the other the strings of a violin; the one is of no value without the other, and they must therefore have developed simultaneously, yet they cannot have arisen through use, and the inheritance of the results of use, because they are both dead chitinous parts, which are never strengthened by rubbing against each other with the movements of the abdomen, but are rather worn away.

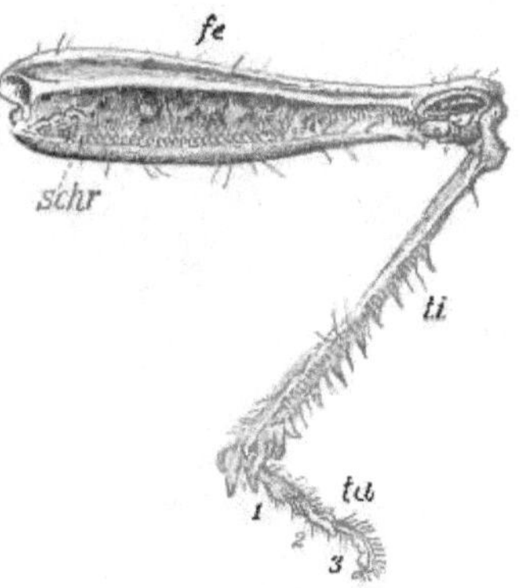

FIG. 91 (repeated). Hind-leg of a Grasshopper (*Stenobothrus protorma*), after Graber. *fe*, femur. *ti*, tibia. *ta*, tarsal joints. *schr*, the stridulating ridge.

The same is true of the chirping organs of grasshoppers, beetles, and crickets; in all cases they consist of two different parts, which together produce a sound, and which therefore must have arisen simultaneously, and the origin of which cannot be referred to the inheritance of the results of exercise, but rather to selection. It

G 2

is thus possible that co-adaptation of at least two parts may take place even when the hypothetical Lamarckian principle is altogether excluded.

When I say that we have here a case of two parts adapted to each other, that is, strictly speaking, understating the case, for, in the crickets and locusts, for instance, there is a whole series of peg-like chitinous papillæ (Fig. 86), the so-called 'bridge,' each of which must have arisen by itself through variation of the corresponding spot of skin. At least I can see no ground for the assumption that the chitinous surfaces on which the 'bridge' is now placed would necessarily, from internal reasons, have varied precisely in the line of the bridge as it has done.

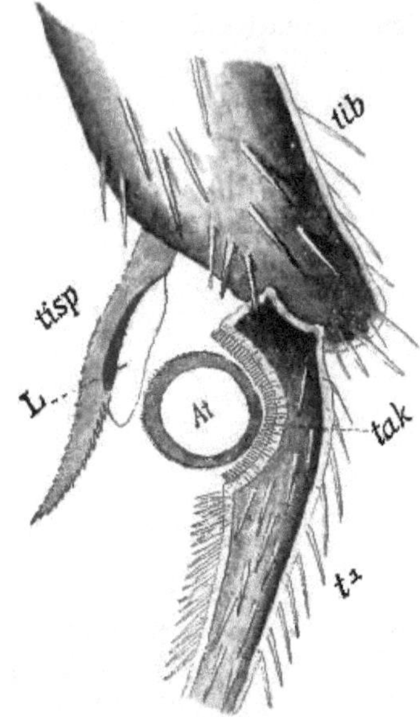

Fig. 102. Brush and comb on the leg of a Bee (*Nomada*). *tib*, end of the tibia. t^1, first tarsal joint with the brush and its comb (*tak*). Between these and the tibial spine (*tisp*) with its lappet (*L*) the cross-section of an antenna (*At*) is indicated. Drawn from a preparation by Dr. Petrunkewitsch.

Instructive examples of the co-adaptation of several parts to a common action in organs which are not subject to the Lamarckian principle are afforded by the diverse arrangements for cleaning the antennæ, the bearers of the smelling-organ which are so important to the life of insects (Fig. 102). Here even the adaptation of an indented area on the tibia of the anterior leg to the cylindrical form of the antenna which passes through it, is sometimes so striking (Fig. 102, *tak*) that it might be thought that it must have arisen through a gradual wearing out; yet this is impossible, since we have to do with hard dead chitinous surfaces, and moreover not with a solid mass, like a hone, which is worn down by the knife, but with a hollow, thin-walled tube. In ants, bees, and ichneumon-flies this minute, semi-circular indentation contains small, pointed, triangular saw-teeth, closely set like those of a comb (*tak*), and the apparatus is made usable by the fact that a firm spine (*tisp*), fused to the end of the tibia, overhangs the notch and presses the antenna towards it. In many species this spine is double, or it is furnished with a thin comb or lappet (Fig. 102, *L*), or with rows of teeth, or with short bristles; in short, it may be equipped in the most different ways. Not infrequently, as in wasps of the genera *Sphex*, *Scolia*, *Ammophila*, the spine itself is also bent in a semicircle on the surface directed towards the notch, and this may be effected in very different ways, either by a bending of the whole thickness of the spine, or by the presence of a comb which is concave on its inner surface. I should never come to an end if I were to enumerate all the remarkable details which may be found in the two main parts of this apparatus, and which show very clearly how essential a co-operation of the two is in fulfilling the function of cleaning the antennæ. This fitting together of the two main parts cannot have been brought about in accordance with the Lamarckian principle; the adaptation must therefore have come about in some other way.

The same thing is shown by the legs and other appendages of insects and crustaceans, which are adapted for the most diverse functions, and the individual sections of which must be correlated if the function is to be possible. Let us consider only the claw structures in crustaceans and scorpions. Here, too, it seems as if the outgrowth of the last joint of the leg, which functions as the arm of the claw, must have arisen as a direct effect of use, through the pressure of an object held fast by the last joint, the movable half of the claw. Frequently, moreover, tooth-like protuberances occur on the fixed blade of the claw (Fig. 103). But how could these have arisen as a direct effect of pressure, since they are always preformed during the soft state of the appendage *before use*, and are only made use of after it is fully hardened. The soft crustaceans, the so-called 'butter-crabs' which have just cast their shells, creep carefully away and avoid using their limbs until they have become hard again. Here, too, we have the co-adaptation of two parts which vary independently, and which cannot be affected by the Lamarckian principle.

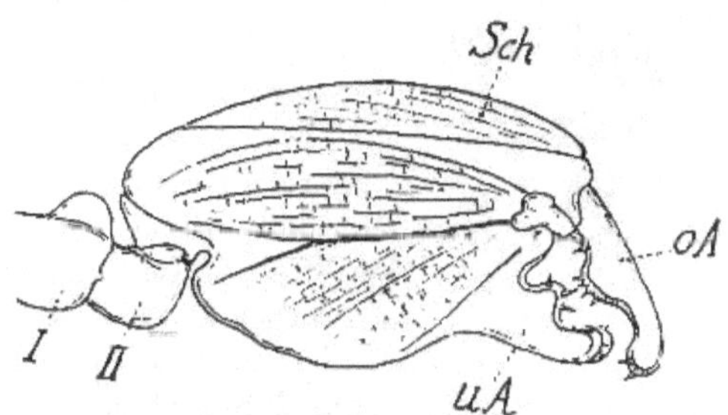

Fig. 103. Claw (*Sch*) on the leg of a 'Beach-fly,' an Amphipod Crustacean (*Orchestia*). *I*, *II*, the two first joints. *uA*, the lower blade of the claw, a non-mobile prolongation of the penultimate joint. *oA*, the upper blade of the claw, the movable last joint; the tubercles and indentations of the two blades fit one another. After F. Müller.

But the appendages furnish more complex examples of mutual adaptation. Thus the individual sections of the anterior leg of the mole-cricket (*Gryllotalpa*) have varied greatly, yet quite differently, and the whole together forms a most effective digging-tool. With it the animal digs out the earth before it to right and to left, and to do this it makes with both legs simultaneous outward movements, which are otherwise quite unusual among insects, and does so with such strength that Rösel von Rosenhof saw two bodies each weighing three pounds pushed away in this manner. In this case four chief parts of the leg (Fig. 104), the coxa (*cox*), the femur (*fe*), the tibia (*tib*), and the tarsi (*tars*) are so adapted to each other in form, joints, thickness of skeleton, and size, that they cannot have varied otherwise than in relation to each other, but each piece has done so in an individual manner. Most remarkable of all is the short broad tibia, equipped with four large, hard teeth, which has to perform the digging in the ground after the manner of a spade, while the disproportionately thin and weak tarsal joints, the last of which bears two perfectly straight spines instead of claws, are directed upwards, and do not touch the ground, being no longer used for walking. Rösel supposed, probably correctly, that they are used for cleaning the spade when it becomes clogged up with earth, since the animal cannot clean it with its mouth. These quite unusually formed parts of the limb cannot have become what they are as the direct results of use, because, for one thing, it would have been not their broad surfaces, but their narrow edges, which would most easily cut through the earth, that would have been directed outwards. The peculiar curving, first concave, then convex, of the outer surface of the digging foot is exactly what is best adapted for cutting into the earth and for the pushing aside which follows, but it is not what it would have become if the chitin-wall had yielded to the pressure of the earth and adapted itself to it. But, as we are again dealing with the chitinous skeleton, there can be no question of the direct effect of use, and, it seems to me, it must be admitted that here we have a case of co-adaptation of at least seven different parts, which have varied independently of each other, without any assistance from the Lamarckian principle.

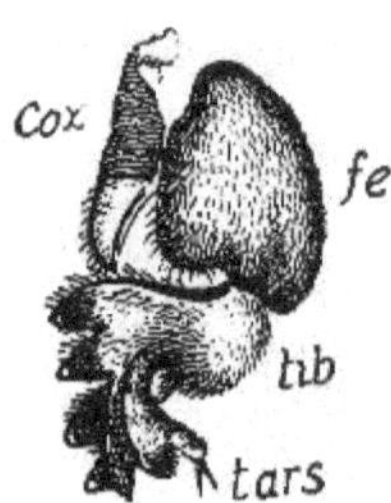

FIG. 104. Digging leg of the Mole-cricket (*Gryllotalpa*). *cox*, coxa attaching the limb to the thorax. *fe*, the short broad femur. *tib*, the tibia forming a broad spade with six large sharp teeth. *tars*, the tarsal joints, which are turned upwards and cannot be used in locomotion. After Rösel.

But much more complicated cases than this might be cited, if we were in a position to estimate exactly the functional value of the individual parts of the wing-venation in the different insects, for it is well known that this venation serves the systematist as a basis for the definition of genera, especially in Lepidoptera and Hymenoptera. That is to say, it varies from genus to genus in a characteristic manner, obviously corresponding to the differences in the wing-form, and in the flight itself. But, unfortunately, we are still far from being able to make more than quite general hypotheses as to the meaning of the lengthening and strengthening, or conversely, the degeneration or elimination, of this or that vein. From extreme cases, however, as for instance the rich venation in good fliers with large wings, and the scanty venation in poor fliers with small wings, we learn at least so much, that the degree and even the manner of venation bears a definite relation to the function of the wing, and this we might have assumed. But these wing-veins, in as far as they serve as a support for the weak wing-membrane, are purely chitinous structures, skeletal parts which are not even renewed from time to time like the skeletal parts of the leg and many other parts of the insect. As they are laid down at first in the pupa as soft strings of cells, so they remain, and they only begin to be used when they are completely hardened. *They can therefore never have been caused to vary through use in the course of the phyletic development of species and genera*, and the Lamarckian principle can have no part in their transformations. But if they follow the most subtle changes, which we cannot precisely demonstrate, of the whole wing-surface and in the mode of flight, as a man is followed by his shadow, there must be some other principle which adapts the organ to its function, and which is able continually to adapt the large number of individual wing-veins in the manner most advantageous for the general function. Here, therefore, we have a state of matters exactly corresponding to that obtaining in the transformation of actively functioning parts which form a system with common co-operative action, as, for instance, in the case we first discussed, that of the stag's antlers.

Other even more complicated examples of harmonious adaptation of passively functioning parts are afforded by the markings of animals, such as those of the butterfly's wing. The colours have only a passive rôle, whether they be due to pigments alone, or to structure, or to both combined. When the coloration of a surface undergoes adaptive variation, this cannot be due to any action of the colour, but must depend on adaptation through selection. Yet it is well known that there are many butterfly-wings whose surfaces exhibit different colours and different shades of colour on their different parts, and that in such a way that together they form a picture, that of a leaf, a piece of bark, a stone overgrown with lichen, an eye, and so on. In such a case the individual colour-spots stand in a particular, indirect relation to each other; although they are independent of each other in their variation, they are not indifferent and due to chance, for together they produce a common picture; this is harmonious adaptation of many parts, where the Lamarckian principle is absolutely excluded.

It may, perhaps, be objected that this mimetic picture does not arise all at once, but very slowly in the course of long series of generations, and, indeed, of species. This must of course be so; the simple beginnings are complicated and perfected through the course of long ages. This is implied in the principle of selection as we understand it. But does any one suppose that the gigantic antlers of the giant-stag were developed in a few generations? In this case, too, must not numerous races have succeeded each other before the primitive antlers attained this enormous size? If this must be assumed there was abundance of time for the adaptation, through *germinal* variations, of the secondarily varying parts, the muscles, tendons, nerves, and bones, for all these parts function actively, and can without difficulty meet, in the individual life, the increased claims made upon them by a slight increase in the size of the antlers. For the certain and indubitable consequence of exercise, of increased use, is the strengthening of the functioning parts.

Thus the appropriate germinal variation of the secondarily varying parts may be delayed for a little without the individual being any the less effective, or being obliged to succumb in the struggle for existence. I do not, however, assert for a moment that the whole explanation of the phenomena of co-adaptation is included in this; on the contrary, I hope soon to be able to show that we may in such cases assume a preponderance of variational tendencies in a favourable direction, and that there is thus an indirect connexion between the utility of a variation and its actual occurrence. In the first place, however, I must refer to the other group of facts which I have indicated, which show, likewise, that the simultaneous co-adaptation of different parts may arise in certain circumstances, although the Lamarckian principle be excluded. These are the facts presented to us by the sterile forms of those insects, which, like bees, termites, and ants, live together in large societies.

Ants and bees are of special interest to us in this connexion, because they have long been carefully watched by a number of distinguished naturalists, and most of their vital functions have been precisely studied. Ever since the days of 'Old Peter Huber' in Geneva there have again and again been excellent observers who have devoted almost the whole of their life-work and talents to the more complete study of these wonderful animals. These insects are of interest to us here, because, in the course of the social life, a type of individual has arisen which diverges in structure in many parts of the body from both the male and the female, although it is sterile and does not reproduce, or does so in so few instances that the fact is of no moment in considering the origin of the present bodily structure. As is well known, these neuters, or better, workers, are, among ants and bees, females which differ from the true females not only in their smaller size and their infertility, but in many other points as well. Among ants, for instance, they are absolutely wingless, and at the same time they have a much smaller and differently formed thorax and a larger head. But the most striking point is the difference in their instincts, for while the females, concerned only with reproduction, pair and lay eggs, it is the workers who feed and clean the helpless emerging larvæ, and put them in places of safety, who carry the pupæ into the warm sunshine, and afterwards back again to the sheltered nest, who make this nest itself, and keep it in order, after having collected or prepared the material for it; it is they alone who defend the colony against the attacks of enemies, who undertake predatory expeditions, attacking the nests of other ants, and engaging in obstinate combats with them.

How can all these peculiarities have arisen, since the workers do not reproduce, or do so only exceptionally, and, in any case, are incapable of pairing, and therefore—among bees at least—only produce male offspring? Obviously it cannot have been through the transmission of the effects of use and disuse, since they leave no offspring to which anything could be transmitted.

Herbert Spencer has attempted to maintain the position that the characters of the workers of to-day already existed in the pre-social state, that is, before the ants began to form colonies, and that, therefore, they have not been newly evolved but only preserved. But, even if this be conceded in regard to the care of the brood and the building instinct, so much remains that could not have existed at that stage, that the problem of the origin of these new characters remains unsolved. The wings, for instance, among ants, can only have been lost when females appeared which did not reproduce, for the pairing of ants is associated with a nuptial flight high in the air. The wings are not merely absent in the workers, they do not even develop in the pupæ; they are, as Dewitz showed, present even now in the larva in the form of imaginal disks, but from the pupa-stage onwards they degenerate, and the segments of the thorax to which they are attached likewise appear small and modified. A variation of the germ-plasm must therefore have taken place, and to this is due the fact that the wing-primordia no longer develop, and that the thorax has a different development from what it had at the time when the animals were still fertile.

It has indeed been said that there is no need for assuming a variation of the germ-plasm, since the degeneration of the wing might be produced by inferior nourishment. This opinion is based on the fact that, among bees, the workers do actually arise from female larvæ which have received a meagre diet poor in nitrogenous elements, while the same female larvæ supplied with an abundant diet rich in nitrogen develop into queens.

But even though we may assume that there is a similar difference in the mode of feeding among most ants, because the workers are considerably smaller than the fertile females, it would be quite erroneous to conclude that the difference between the two types rests solely on the effect of differences in diet. The elimination of an individual organ has never yet been determined by bad and scanty nourishment; it is the whole animal with all its parts that degenerates and becomes small and weakly. Often as caterpillars of different species have been placed on starvation diet, whether for experimental purposes or to procure very small butterflies, it has never yet happened that a single organ, such as antenna, leg, or wing, has thereby been eliminated or caused to degenerate. I have myself instituted many such experiments with the maggots of the blue-bottle fly, by supplying them from their earliest youth with just as little food as possible without actually starving them to death, yet never have these larvæ given rise to flies in which the wings were absent or rudimentary.

Nor did these starved flies ever exhibit degenerate ovaries; they were always completely developed and equipped with the full number of ovarian-tubes. It was to decide this particular point that these experiments were instituted, for my opponents maintained that degeneration of the ovaries was a direct result of inferior nourishment. But that is not the case. Special investigations in regard to ants, undertaken at my request by Miss Elizabeth Bickford, showed that the anatomical results reached by earlier investigators, like Adlerz and Lespès, in regard to the degeneration of the ovaries in workers, were absolutely correct, and that the 'degeneration' consists not merely in the fact that the ovarian-tubes and ovum-primordia remain small, but also in a diminution of the *number* of ovarian-tubes (Fig. 105); the workers have always fewer ovarian-tubes than the females of the same species, and—what is of especial importance—the reduction in the number of ovarian-tubes has been effected to a different extent in different species of ants. In the red wood-ant (*Formica rufa*) the workers still possess from twelve to sixteen ovarian-tubes; in the meadow-ant (*Formica pratensis*) only eight, six, or four; in *Lasius fuliginosus* there are usually only two (one on either side); and in the little turf-ant (*Tetramorium caespitum*) there are none at all. We have here, therefore, a phylogenetic process of degeneration, which has reached different degrees in the different species, and has only been completed in one (*Tetramorium*). The case stands as I previously stated it: 'The elimination of a typical organ is not an ontogenetic process, but a phylogenetic one,' it depends not upon 'the mere influences of nutrition which affect the development of the individual, but always on variations in the germ-plasm, which, to all appearance, can only come about in the course of a long series of generations[1].

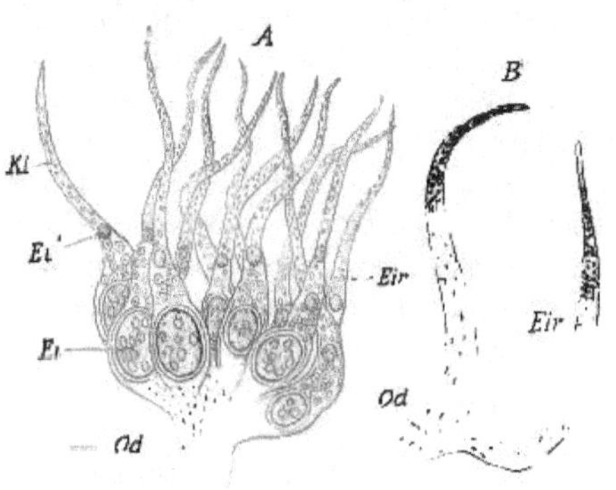

Fig. 105. Ovary of a fertile Queen-Ant and ovaries of a Worker. *Od*, oviduct. *A*, one ovary of *Myrmica laevinodis* with many ovarian-tubes, in each of which there is an almost ripe egg (*Ei*) and a younger egg (*Ei'*). *B*, the ovaries of a Worker of *Lasius fuliginosus*; each ovary has only one ovarian-tube, and no ripening egg-cells. After Elizabeth Bickford.

Against this proposition an observation by O. vom Rath has been cited. According to it, three drone larvæ which had been accidentally fed by the workers with royal food exhibited striking retrogressive peculiarities in their sexual organs. The testes contained only immature sperms (just before emergence from the pupa), and the copulatory organ was entirely wanting. That a certain degree of fatty degeneration of the testes should be caused by the 'unusual fattening' is not surprising, but it seems to me very questionable whether the absence of the copulatory organ can be referred to the abnormal diet; it ought to be definitely decided, by the investiga-

[1] *Aeussere Einflüsse als Entwickelungsreize*, Jena, 1894.

tion of numerous cases, whether some abnormal peculiarity in the constitution of the germ-plasm in these eggs was not the true cause. Hitherto, unfortunately, I have not been able to procure the fresh material necessary to decide this point[1]. From all this it must be evident that we are not justified in regarding either the absence of wings or the degeneration of the ovaries as a direct result of the inferior nourishment supplied to the workers in the larval state: but should any one still have doubt on this point I may mention that, among our indigenous ants, there are two species in which the workers are just as large as the fertile females, and that in tropical America a species (*Myrmecocystus megalocola*) occurs in which the workers are larger than the true females; this must mean that they have received more food than the females, though perhaps not the same mixture of food.

From all the facts we have discussed we can confidently conclude that the differences in structure, which distinguish the workers from the true females, do not depend upon the influence, in the individual lifetime, of a poorer diet, but upon variation in the primary constituents of the germ; we must conceive of the germ-plasm of ants as containing, in addition to male and female ids, special ids of workers, in which the determinants of wing and ovary are degenerate in some degree, while the determinants of other parts, such as the brain, are more highly developed. The manner of feeding, however, and perhaps the mingling with the food of a special secretion of the salivary glands, acts as a stimulus which determines whether one kind of id or another is to be liberated, that is, to become active and to enter on the path of development.

A proof of this view is to be found, it seems to me, in the existence of transition forms between workers and true females, which was first brought to general knowledge by Forel. Perhaps it would be better to call these 'mongrel forms,' for their various parts do not maintain a medium between the two types, but many parts follow the type of the worker, and others that of the true female. Thus Forel twice found a nest of the red wood-ant which contained a large number of these mixed forms, all of which possessed the small head and large curved thorax of the queen, but otherwise resembled the workers in size and appearance, and also in the

[1] Since completing my manuscript I note that the point was settled three years ago, when Koshewnikow had the opportunity of investigating drone-pupæ which were abnormally reared in royal cells, and therefore fed with royal food. He found their sexual organs perfectly normal, and agrees with me that the abnormalities in Vom Rath's case must have been due to some other cause. (See the report by Von Adelung on the Russian paper in *Zool. Centralblatt*, Sept. 10, 1901.)

degeneration of the ovaries. Many of them were very small, only 5 mm. in length, and had probably received very little food, and, according to the theory of direct influence, these should have been pure workers. That they possessed the head and thorax of a queen is a proof that the characters of both forms of individual were present in the germ-plasm as primary constituents, or indeed entire ids. In normal circumstances only one kind of these ids would have become active, either the worker-id or the queen-id, but in abnormal circumstances they might both be liberated to activity simultaneously, and then they would stamp one part of the body with the character of a queen, another with that of a worker. Forel observed one of these nests in two successive years, and both times found the mixed forms in large numbers [1]. In the second year he found a great number of newly-emerged individuals of this type. I have already inferred from this observation that the mixed forms were probably in both years the offspring of the same mother, and this may well have been the case. My further conclusion, that the mixed forms must be due to some abnormality in the constitution of the germ-plasm of the maternal eggs, no longer appears to me so convincing as it did formerly, because, in the interval, we have learnt, through that indefatigable investigator of ants, Pater Wasmann, that there is another possible explanation of these mixed forms; it, too, is based upon a hypothesis, but it is so interesting that I must briefly outline it to you.

Like Forel and myself, Pater Wasmann had supposed that the reason of this kind of mixed form (the so-called pseudogynous worker) lay in an abnormality of the constitution of the germ-plasm, but he now regards it as the result of a change in the mode of rearing instituted by the workers with respect to the constitutionally female or queen larvæ, because there was a scarcity of workers. The hypothesis sounds very daring, but it is well founded, at least in so far that there really is a reason why a scarcity of females must occur at certain times in some colonies of ants, and this might certainly determine the workers in charge of the larvæ to feed females with worker food, so as to rear them to render the necessary assistance.

This reason lies in the occasional presence of a parasitic beetle, *Lomechusa strumosa*, whose larvæ, curiously enough, are cared for and fed by the ants as though they were their own, and in return they eat up the larvæ of the ants, often destroying them in large numbers.

[1] There are different kinds of 'mixed forms' among ants, which may owe their origin to a variety of conditions, as Forel, Wasmann, and Emery have shown in detail.

Wasmann informs us that the parasitic larvæ grow up just at the time at which the ants are rearing their workers, and it is these, therefore, which fall victims to the Lomechusa-larvæ, and the result is that a scarcity of young workers must soon make itself felt. The workers seek to make this good by rearing as workers all the larvæ previously destined for queens. But this only succeeds partially, because the development towards true females has already begun; thus mixed forms arise.

This explanation would be rather in the air if we did not know that, among bees, such changes in the manner of rearing are by no means uncommon. Indeed they occur regularly when the queen of a hive perishes and no more 'female' eggs are in store; young worker larvæ are then fed with royal food, and these develop into queens. There can thus be no doubt that these insects have it in their power to liberate to activity either the female ids or the worker ids by a specific mode of feeding, and there is nothing contrary to reason in admitting the possibility of an alternation of this influence in the course of development, for something analogous occurs in regard to secondary sexual characters, as, for instance, the appearance of male decorative colours in ducks that have become sterile.

But this change in the mode of rearing bee-larvæ gives rise to pure queens and not to mixed forms, and we must therefore regard it as undecided whether Wasmann's explanation is correct in this case, and whether an abnormality in the constitution of the germ-plasm may not be the true cause of this or other kinds of mixed forms among ants. In any case the 'Lomechusa hypothesis' rests upon the assumption of different kinds of ids in the germ-plasm, as Pater Wasmann expressly states, and the differences between the worker and queen-ants have their cause in this, and not directly in the kind of larval food.

If there were not different ids corresponding to the different kinds of individuals in the germ-plasm a kind of polymorphism might indeed have arisen in the colony through differences in nutrition, but it could not have been of the kind we now see—that is, a sharply defined differentiation of persons, in adaptation to their different functions. This presupposes elements in the germ which can vary slowly and consistently in a definite direction without causing any change in the rest of the germ.

This state of affairs gives to the phyletic evolution of the workers a great theoretical significance, for it proves that positive as well as negative variations of the most diverse parts of the body, that simultaneous and correlative variations of many parts, can take place in the course of the phylogeny, without the co-operation of the Lamarckian factor. I have not hitherto laid any special emphasis upon the degree of differences occurring between workers and queens; but I must now add that this may far exceed the degree that we are familiar with in our common indigenous ants, both in regard to instinct and to bodily form. Even in the red Amazon ant of Western Switzerland, *Polyergus rufescens*, we find quite a new instinct [1], that of carrying off the pupæ of other species of ants, not to devour, but to introduce them to their own nest and thus secure 'slaves.' For these workers of a strange species, which emerge in a strange nest, naturally regard the place of their birth as their home, and do there what instinct impels them, and what they would have done in the nest of their parents: they feed the larvæ, fetch food, collect building material, and so on. The domestic activity of the workers of the master-species thus becomes superfluous, and they have ceased to exercise it, and have now entirely lost the power of caring for their brood, searching for food, and keeping up the nest. They have even forgotten how to take food themselves, because they are always fed by the 'slaves.' Forel informs us—and I have myself repeated the experiment—that *Polyergus* workers, which are shut up with a drop of honey on the floor of their prison, will leave it, their favourite food, untouched, and finally starve, unless one of their 'slaves' be shut up with them. As soon as this happens, and the slave perceives the honey, it partakes of it, and then the 'mistress' comes and strokes the 'slave' with her antennæ to signify her desires, whereupon the 'slave' proceeds to feed her from its own crop.

But while the *Polyergus* workers have forgotten their domestic habits, and have even ceased to be able to recognize their food, remarkable changes have taken place in their jaws; these have lost the blunt teeth on the inner margin, which, in other species, serve for masticating the food, for seizing building material, and for other domestic occupations, and have become sharp weapons, bent in the form of a sabre, very well suited for piercing the head of an enemy, but also well adapted for carrying off the pupæ, because they can seize them without doing them any injury.

No one will doubt that the predatory expeditions of the Amazon ants, and the slave-making habit, can only have developed after the habit of living in large companies had long existed, and this case proves that variations of instinct, as well as of bodily structure, can

[1] 'New' in this sense, that the instinct is not exhibited by most worker-ants, that it did not occur in the primaeval ancestors of modern ants. It is, however, exhibited by a number of modern forms, and even by some German species.

take place even after the workers have long been sterile. The case is the more instructive that it *seems* as if it were due to the transmission of a newly acquired and inherited habit of life, while in point of fact these Amazon-workers can transmit nothing, because they bear no offspring. But if old instincts can be lost, and new ones acquired, when all possibility of inheritance is excluded, we see that Nature has no need of the Lamarckian factor of modification for her transformations and new adaptations.

If we wish to understand clearly that, in these changes, we have to do not merely with the alteration of a single part, but of many parts which all work together, we have only to think of the still more striking physical modifications which have taken place in many tropical ants, and which have lead to a dimorphism of the workers. In many species, certainly, the only difference is in size, so that one can distinguish between large workers and small, and the former are sometimes five times as big as the latter. But even in the South European *Pheidole megalocephala*, which is abundant in Italy, the larger workers are also different in structure from the smaller, for they have an enormous head with powerful jaws. They are usually known as 'soldiers,' and are entrusted with the defence of the colony. Emery directly observed in regard to *Colobopsis truncata*, an ant which lives in the trunks of trees, that the soldiers, with their enormous heads, occupied all the entrances to the nest, ready to seize any intruder with their powerful jaws. In the Sauba ant (*Œcodoma cephalotes*) Bates described three different types of worker, differing in size, and although he was not able to determine with certainty what the particular function of each was, there can be no doubt that they have special offices, and that the differences in their structure are adaptations to the differences in their functions. The same is true of the Indian ant, *Pheidologeton diversus*, depicted in Fig. 106, whose three forms of workers I owe to the kindness of Professor August Forel.

If the increase in the size of the head and jaws must bring with it an increase in the thickness of the skeleton of these parts, as well as a strengthening of the musculature of the head, it follows that the strain on the body must be greater, just as in the case of the increase in the weight of the stag's antlers, so that the skeleton of the thorax must likewise have become thicker and heavier, the muscles and nerves of the legs stronger, the articulations of the joints capable of greater resistance; in short, a whole series of variations of other parts must have taken place simultaneously, if the primary variation was to be of use, and not to lead to the destruction of its possessor. Here again we have a proof that the co-adaptation of many parts can take place without any intervention of the Lamarckian principle, and that there must be some other factor which brings this about.

Where, then, shall we look for this other factor, if not in the processes of selection, in the selecting of the most suitable variations among all those which occur? We are confronted with the alternative of either working out a sufficient explanation with this factor, or of giving up the attempt at explanation altogether. Yet the application of the principle of selection in relation to the neuters of colony-forming insects is by no means simple, for, as the workers are sterile, a modification of them through processes of breeding cannot begin directly with themselves. The workers which exhibit the most

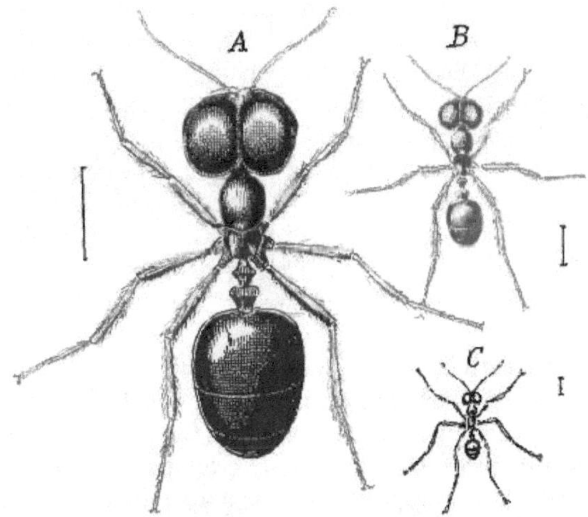

Fig. 106. Three workers of the same species of Indian Ant (*Pheidologeton diversus*), drawn from specimens supplied by Prof. August Forel. *A*, the largest, *B*, the intermediate, *C*, the smallest form.

suitable variations cannot be selected for breeding, but only their parents, the sexual animals, and these according to whether they produce better workers or worse. This is how Darwin looked at the matter, and his view receives support from one peculiarity in the composition of these animal colonies, whose significance becomes apparent in relation to this problem. It has long been known that in a bee-hive there are from 10,000 to 20,000 workers, but only one true female, the so-called queen, and the meaning of this remarkable arrangement probably is, that the adaptation of the workers through natural selection becomes much more easily possible, *since the whole number are the children of a single pair*. It is not the individual workers, but the whole colony, that is, the whole progeny of the queen, which is selected, according to the greater or less degree of effectiveness displayed by the workers. Strictly speaking, it is the single queen that is selected in relation to her power of producing superior or inferior workers. A colony whose queen was unsatisfactory in this respect could not hold its own in the struggle for existence, and only the best colonies and the best hives would survive, that is, through their descendants. If the hive contained a hundred queens instead of a single queen the process of selection would be much more complex and less clear, and it is even quite conceivable that the production of specially modified workers, adapted to their functions, or of two or three different kinds of workers, would not have been possible at all. For it would not have helped much if one out of a hundred females had produced workers of better structure; only a majority of such females could give the colony any advantage as compared with other colonies.

It has not been definitely established whether, among ants, a single female is in all cases the founder of the whole colony, but it is certain that there are only a few females. In the tropical Termites we know that the ovaries of the female attain to such a colossal size that one female must certainly suffice for the necessities of the largest colonies. Grassi has shown, indeed, that, as far as the South European Termites are concerned, not only are there several females present, but that even the workers frequently reproduce; but the Termites in general are inhabitants of warm countries, and the few European species probably hardly represent the original composition of these animal colonies. But of the tropical species, which have as yet not been sufficiently studied, we know at least the extraordinary dimensions of the body, and the corresponding fertility of the queens, and we conclude from this that only a few can be present in each termitary[1].

Now that we have discussed all these facts it will not be out of place to summarize the results, in as far as they have any relation to the acceptance or rejection of the theory of the inheritance of acquired characters.

No *direct* proof of such transmission could be found; on the contrary, it has been shown that all that has hitherto been advanced as such will not stand the test of close examination; an inheritance of wounds and mutilations does not exist, the transmission of traumatically induced epilepsy is not only doubtful as regards its causes, but

[1] Ingwe Sjostedt has recently established in Africa that it is usually a single queen and a single king that found a termitary (*Schwed. Akad. Abh.* Bd. 34, 1902).

cannot even be considered as the transmission of a particular morphological lesion.

We may regard as *indirect* proofs such facts as can only be explained on the assumption of this mode of inheritance, and in this connexion our opponents have cited especially the correspondence between modifications acquired through use in the individual lifetime, and worked out through histonal selection, with the phyletic transformations of the same parts. But it has been shown that a number of parts which do not function actively at all, but only passively, and thus cannot be caused to change through use, like the hard skeletal parts of the Arthropods, vary phyletically in the same certain and direct course as those which function actively, so that we have every ground for assuming that there are other factors operating in the transformation of the active as well as of the passive parts. Finally, we discussed the last and strongest argument which has been put forward in favour of the Lamarckian principle, that of co-adaptation, that is, the simultaneous adaptation of many parts co-operating in a common action, and we were able to contravert this altogether by showing that exactly similar phenomena of co-adaptation occur in systems of passively functioning parts, and further, that they occur also among the workers of ants and bees, that is, in animals which do not reproduce, and which, therefore, cannot transmit the acquired results of exercise during their life.

We therefore reject—and are compelled to reject—the Lamarckian principle, not only on the ground that it cannot be proved correct, but also because the phenomena, to explain which it is used, occur also under circumstances which absolutely exclude any possibility of the co-operation of this principle.

Supplementary note on the Transmissibility of Acquired Functional Modifications.

I cannot conclude this section without some reference to the utterances of some naturalists who have quite recently attempted to represent the inheritance of functional modifications as a conceivable and even a necessary assumption.

I may name first Ludwig Zehnder, a physicist who has wandered into the domain of biology. In regard to the very facts which I have adduced as evidence *against* the existence of such inheritance, he has endeavoured to show how we might conceive of them as having by this very means arisen [1].

He deals with the case of ants, that is to say, with the differen-

[1] Zehnder, *Die Entstehung des Lebens*, Freiburg-i.-Br., 1899.

H 2

tiation of the sterile workers into several castes, in the following interesting manner.

The task of the workers is to procure all the food necessary for all the individuals of the colony in quantity and quality corresponding to the demand; failing this the whole colony would perish. Now the different persons of the colony need different food, according to their constitution and their functions. Soldiers, for instance, are more powerful than ordinary workers, since they are adapted for fighting, and they therefore require a different kind of food from the weaker workers who are adapted only for other duties. Since the soldiers have evolved from the latter by selection, what we may, for the sake of brevity, call the soldier-food in the common stores of the ants would be drawn upon more lavishly than before, and would therefore disappear more quickly, and, whenever this occurred, those workers which had already brought in this kind of food would be impelled to bring more and more to satisfy the demand for it. But in order to do this they would require to exert themselves more, and would therefore require a larger quantity of food—not of course soldier-food, but the particular kind which their particular qualities demanded. Probably this second importation of food was undertaken by a second kind of worker, for, according to Zehnder, each worker does not carry all the kinds of food; they are divided into legions, each of which has its particular task of food-collecting to fulfil.

In the end the storehouse of the ant-colony must contain a provision in which the different kinds of food are in exact proportion to the necessities of the different kinds of persons in the colony. It must alter in its composition again as soon as, in the course of time, one or other kind of person acquires new characters, for these presuppose a new kind of diet

But how are these acquired characters to be transmitted since neither soldiers nor workers reproduce? Zehnder answers this by pointing out that the sexual animals eat *all* the kinds of nourishment which are accumulated in the stores, that is to say, all the different kinds of food exactly in the proportion in which they have been imported—the proportion in which the different kinds of persons are represented in the colony. Thus the kinds of nourishment which caused the appearance of the newly acquired characters in the non-sexual animals also reached the sexual animals and their sex-cells, and there gave rise to substances which evoke the relevant qualities in their descendants, for instance, in the soldiers, or in the still more modified workers, and so on; and thus we have an 'inheritance of acquired characters.'

This is certainly ingeniously and cleverly thought out, and it reads even better and more smoothly in the original than in my brief summary, but it will hardly be regarded as a refutation of my position; the hypotheses are all too daring for that. We have no knowledge that particular modifications in form can be produced and conditioned by particular kinds of food, and, indeed, the contrary has been proved, namely, that the two or three different castes of polymorphic species have precisely similar diet. I need only recall the six forms of female in *Papilio merope,* of which at least three have been obtained from the same set of eggs, and by feeding with the same plant.

It is true that there are ants which lay in stores of nourishment, but these consist, for the most part, of one kind of seeds, or of honey, not of different substances, and we have no knowledge that the different persons use different food, or even that there is any diversity in the mode of feeding the helpless larvæ. The feeding in some species takes place from mouth to mouth, and therefore cannot be precisely investigated, and we can only suppose from analogy with bees that the larvæ of the males and females frequently receive not only more abundant, but qualitatively different food. They are fed from the crop unless the food consists of the pith of a tree in which the larvæ are imbedded, as Dahl informs us is the case with some tropical ants of the Bismarck Archipelago.

But even if we assume that the soldiers take different food from the ordinary workers, and different again from that of the sexual animals, is it by virtue of the quality of their food that they have become what they are? Have our breeds of pigeons or hens been produced by different diet, or do we know anything in the whole range of animal life of such a parallelism between food and bodily structure as Zehnder here assumes? And if, in reality, let us say, the breeds of pigeon had arisen through specific dieting, and we were to feed one pair with the specific food-stuffs of three different breeds, would the descendants of this pair exhibit the form of these three breeds? Or would they exhibit them in precisely the proportion in which the food-stuffs had been mixed? It seems to me that Zehnder's assumptions diverge so far from what we are accustomed to regard as solid ground in biology that they hardly require consideration, and yet he not only uses them for the explanation of the case of the ants, but bases upon them the whole of his theory of the inheritance of acquired characters.

He considers that the results of use (that is, increased function) are generally transmitted, because the increase in the organ which is functioning more strongly changes the composition of the blood, by withdrawing from it in a greater degree the specific substances which the organ in question—a muscle, for instance—requires for its activity. All parts of the animal are thereby affected and modified, but especially those smallest vital units or 'fistellæ' (corresponding to biophors) which preside over digestion, and of which there are several sorts. Among them those work most arduously which have to produce the specific substances which serve for the nutrition of the muscles with increased function, because these are needed in larger quantities. This kind of digestive 'fistella' therefore multiplies, while other kinds, whose products are not required and therefore not used up, cease to be so active, diminish in number, and in course of time disappear. In this way the composition of the blood is altered, and with it to a greater or less degree all the characters of the whole organism. Of course the reproductive cells are also under the influence of this change in the composition of the blood, because the different nutritive substances are accumulated within them in an altered proportion corresponding to the changed composition of the blood, the nutritive substances for the muscles with increased function being contained in it in a larger quantity, and thus the greater development of the muscle will repeat itself in the progeny, that is to say, *the acquired character is transmitted.*

It is obvious that this is precisely the same line of argument as that used in reference to the origin of the worker and soldier ants. The different kinds of 'digestive fistellæ' correspond to the different food-carrying workers, and the blood to the assumed storehouse from which soldiers and workers select the food suitable for their respective needs, while the sex-cells in the one case, the sexual animals in the other, partake of all kinds exactly in the proportion in which they are stored, and thus the organ which functions most vigorously must be stronger in the offspring.

How the minute quantity of nutritive material contained in the ovum, still less in the sperm, is to effect the strengthening of the particular muscles in the descendants is not stated; moreover, such minimal quantities of food must soon be exhausted, and cannot possibly increase. It would seem as if the muscles could not even begin by being stronger, much less that they should remain so, if they were not exercised equally vigorously by the descendants. If the specific nutritive stuffs were 'fistellæ,' that is to say, were living units capable of multiplication, one could understand it. But there can, of course, be no possibility of a production of living units through digestion; that can only give rise to digested substances. Or if the alteration in the composition of the blood produced in the determinant system of the germ-plasm just those variations requisite to bring about a strengthening of the muscular system, it would remain to be shown how this could happen, for the gist of the problem lies in this. For muscles do not lie in the germ-plasm as miniature models of the subsequent muscular system, and even if they did, would not all the muscles, and not merely those which were no longer exercised, decrease hereditarily when a particular group, like the muscles of the ear in man, degenerates? Zehnder replies to this with the hypothesis that the muscles are not all chemically alike, but that each possesses a particular chemical formula, though they may all be very similar, and that, therefore, the nutritive materials required by each must be slightly different. In that case there would require to be, in the ovum and sperm of man, in order that functional modifications might be transmitted, as many special nutritive substances as there are muscles, and, in addition to these, innumerable hosts of other kinds of specific nutritive substances for all the other parts of the body, since all of them can be strengthened by exercise and weakened by disuse. And even if we suppose that all these millions of specific nutritive substances are accommodated within the germ-cells, as Zehnder's theory requires, they could not perform what Zehnder ascribes to them, for, as we have already said, they cannot multiply in the manner of living units, and so control the growing organism. The different specific nutritive materials contained in the blood are just as powerless to perform the task ascribed to them by Zehnder as the specific kinds of food in the hypothetical storehouse of the ants are to give rise to the different persons of the ant-colony.

Zehnder also attempts to overthrow the arguments against the Lamarckian principle which I based on the skeleton of Arthropods.

It does not seem to him probable that the chitinous coat of mail can be an absolutely dead structure, and he supposes that very delicate nerve-fibrils penetrate into all its most minute parts, and so are stimulated by 'every pressure and every strain' exerted on the chitinous skeleton. They 'work' when they are stimulated, and in doing so they use up 'their specific food-stuffs.' At places which are frequently stimulated the corresponding nerves develop more than elsewhere. The necessary specific food-stuffs for these particular nerves therefore increase proportionately within the body, and also in the reproductive cells. Accordingly, in the germ-cells there is an increase of the aforesaid nervous substances, which in the offspring become associated with the relevant part of the chitinous covering, and induce in development the secretion of chitin at this part. At this particular spot, then, the chitin will be specially thick.

This clearly implies that each particular part of the skin has its specific nutritive substances, necessitated by the nerves which traverse it! Thus there must be as many nerve-nutritive substances as there are skin-nerves, specific chemical combinations for every part of the body which is capable of heritable variation. This is so extraordinarily improbable that I need say nothing more about it. If the Lamarckian principle requires this kind of hypothesis to bolster it up, it is undoubtedly doomed.

If we disregard altogether the positive aspect of Zehnder's hypothesis, and assume that the skin-nerves are really stimulated through the chitin by every strain and pressure to which a spot of skin is exposed, and that they cause a correspondingly greater secretion of chitin, which would then, according to the Lamarckian principle, be hereditary, does this harmonize with what actually occurs in the development of the skeleton as we know it in the case of Insects and Crustaceans? Not at all! Can we suppose that the carapace of a crab or the enormously hard wing-covers of a water-beetle are exposed to a continual pounding and pressing and pushing? Exactly the contrary is the case. Every assailant takes care not to grasp the animal where it is so well protected, and seeks out the most vulnerable parts for its attacks. It may be answered that, while this is certainly the case now, the animals were badly protected when the ancestral forms were evolving. But that they could not have become hard by dint of being frequently bitten or otherwise wounded should be obvious from the fact that the whole of the wing-covers and the whole of the carapace is uniformly covered with thick chitin, while each wound would only stimulate particular spots; and we should also have to admit that, since these parts of the skin which are now so well protected are no longer seized and stimulated, they would long ago have become thin again, according to the principle of the degeneration of parts no longer used, or, in this case, no longer stimulated. But there is no need for wasting time over such quibbles, since there is a fact which absolutely contradicts Zehnder's hypothesis. I mean the degeneration of the chitinous skeleton in those Crustaceans and Insects which protect the abdomen within a shelter like the hermit-crabs, the caddis-flies (Phryganidæ), (Fig. 107) and the sack-carrying caterpillars of the Psychidæ among Lepidoptera. The hermit-crabs, as is well known, squeeze their abdomen into a usually spirally-coiled Gasteropod shell, and they always choose houses which are wide enough to conceal the whole body up to the hard claws when necessity arises. In this case there is surely a continual pressure on the abdomen, which, being soft, must be squeezed very tightly every time the animal retreats into its shell. One of my opponents has described the disappearance of the tough integumentary skeleton from the abdomen of these animals as an inherited result of this pressure, and another regards it as the inherited result of the degeneration of the muscles in this part of the body. But, according to Zehnder, this continuous pressure, and the frequent rubbing up and down of the abdomen on the inner surface of the Gasteropod's shell, would undoubtedly have a stimulating effect on the skin-nerves, and would therefore bring about a thickening of the chitinous cuticle. In regard to the larval Phryganidæ and Psychidæ, the case would be the same, though

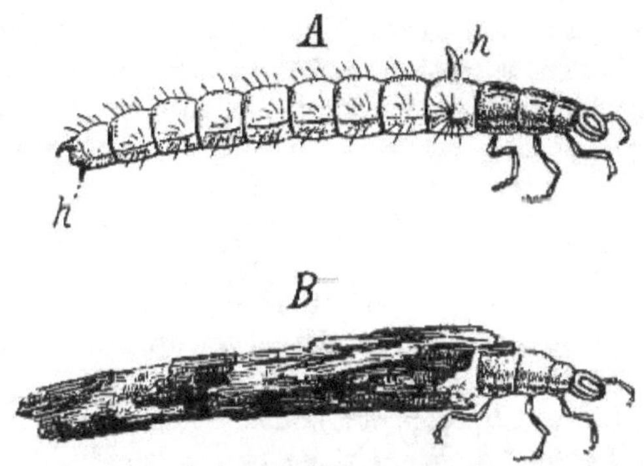

FIG. 107. Larva of a Caddis-fly, after Rösel. *A*, removed from its case, showing the hooks (*h*) which attach it thereto, and the whitish abdomen, covered only by a thin cuticle. *B*, the same larva, moving about with its case.

perhaps hardly to the same degree, for while these larvæ make their own houses, and will therefore at least make them big enough to begin with, the pressure and friction must increase with the growth of the animal.

If the regulation of the strength of the integumentary skeleton be referred to selection, we see at once why carapace and wing-covers should be of equal thickness throughout their whole extent, and why they do not disappear, although they do not function actively, and are less stimulated than any other parts of the skeleton; and we also understand why the abdomen of hermit-crabs and of larval Phryganidæ and Psychidæ has become soft, whether it be exposed to pressure or friction in a greater or a less degree. It no longer requires to be hard, because it is protected by the house, and in the case of the Pagurids it must not be hard because it could not then be readily squeezed into the hard-walled and narrow recesses of the Gasteropod shell; in this case there has therefore been positive selection. I have not yet referred to the fact that the chitinous covering is certainly not living, though it is not exactly dead; it is a secretion of the epidermic cells, not a tissue, and we cannot suppose that there are any nerve-endings in it. It is almost superfluous to say that the fact that the skin is cast is in itself enough to make such an assumption untenable, for the whole of the assumed delicate nervous network would be shed at every moult and torn away from the nerves which lead to it. As far as my knowledge goes, nothing of this kind occurs anywhere in the whole range of the animal kingdom.

Even if we assume, for the benefit of Zehnder's hypothesis, that although there are no nerves in the chitin itself yet irritations affecting the chitinous coat may be transmitted through it to the delicate nerve-endings lying beneath it, this should take place in a greater degree at the thin places of the skeleton than *at the thick parts!* But this interpretation is again fallacious, for we see that the tactile organs of Arthropods always break through the chitinous cuticle and protrude beyond it in the form of setæ.

Of the many other opponents of my views in regard to the transmissibility of acquired functional modifications, I need only deal in detail with Oscar Hertwig.

He seeks for direct proofs of an inheritance of acquired characters, and believes that he has found these in the hereditary transmission of acquired immunity from certain diseases. He reminds us of Ehrlich's well-known experiments on mice with ricin and abrin.

Even small doses of these two poisons kill mice, but they are tolerated in very minute doses, and if their administration be continued for some time in such minute doses, the animals gradually acquire a high degree of insensitiveness to these poisons; they become immune to ricin and abrin.

This immunity is transmitted from mother to young, but it only lasts for a short time, about six to eight weeks after birth. Yet this is regarded by Hertwig as an illustration of the transmission of an acquired character, as an acquired modification of the cells of the body, for he explains the immunity on the assumption that all the cells of the body undergo a particular variation due to the influence of the poison, and are thus, to a certain extent, modified in their nature, and that the ovum also undergoes this variation and transmits it to the young animal. The immunization might certainly come under the category of functional modifications, and it might be thought that we have here a case of transmission of such an acquired character.

Against this, however, we have to put the fact that *the acquired immunity is not transmitted from the father to the descendants.* Hertwig attempts to explain this by saying that the short duration of the experiments has only allowed the poison to affect the cell-substance (cytoplasm) and not the nucleus, that is, the hereditary substance of the sperm-cells, an assumption which has little probability considering the intimate nutritive relations between the cell-nucleus and the cytoplasm. I should be rather inclined to conclude from the difference in the transmitting power of the sperm and of the ovum, that this 'inheritance of immunity' does not depend, as Hertwig supposes, on a modification of the cells to 'ricin immunity,' but, as Ehrlich and the bacteriologists believe, on the production of so-called 'anti-toxins,' and that these anti-toxins are handed on to the embryo not by the ovum itself, but by the interchange of blood between mother and offspring which lasts throughout the whole embryonic period. It is then self-evident why no transmission of immunity through the father occurs.

But it would lead me too far were I to attempt to refute all the attempts that have been made to interpret individual cases as due to the inheritance of acquired characters. I should, however, like to say something as to the theoretical possibility of such an assumption.

When we try to conceive how experiences and their consequences can be entailed, how new acquirements of the 'personal part can have representative effects on the germinal part,' we find ourselves confronted with almost, if not entirely, insuperable difficulties. How could it happen that the constant exercise of memory throughout a lifetime, as, for instance, in the case of an actor, could influence the germ-cells in such a way that in the offspring the same brain-cells which preside over memory will likewise be more highly developed—that is, capable of greater functional activity? We know what Zehnder's answer to such a question would be; he would make the blood the intermediary between the brain-cells and the germ-cells, but we have seen that specific food-stuffs for each specific cell-group cannot be assumed, and that, even if they could, they would not meet the necessities of the case. Yet every one who does not regard the germ-plasm as composed of determinants is constrained to make some such assumption. But if we take our stand upon the theory of determinants, it would be necessary to a transmission of acquired strength of memory that the states of these brain-cells should be communicated by the telegraphic path of the nerve-cells to the germ-cells, and should there modify only the determinants of the brain-cells, and should do so in such a way that, in the subsequent development of an embryo from the germ-cell, the corresponding brain-cells should turn out to be capable of increased functional activity. But as the determinants are not miniature brain-cells, but only groups of biophors of unknown constitution, and are assuredly different from those cells; as they are not 'seed-grains' of the brain-cells, but only living germ-units which, in co-operation with the rest exercise a decisive influence on the memory-cells of the brain, I can only compare the assumption of the transmission of the results of memory-exercise to the telegraphing of a poem, which is handed in in German, but at the place of arrival appears on the paper translated into Chinese.

Nevertheless, as I have said before, I do not disagree with those who say, with Oscar Hertwig, that the impossibility of forming a conception of the physiological nexus involved in the assumed transmission does not *ipso facto* constrain us to conclude that the transmission does not occur. I cannot, however, agree with Hertwig that the case is exactly the same as in the 'converse process,' that is, 'in the development of the given invisible primary constituents in the inheritance of the cell into the visible characters of the personal part.' Certainly no one can state with any definiteness how the germ goes to work, so that from it there arises an eye or a brain with its millionfold intricacies of nerve-paths, but although the process cannot be understood in detail, it can in principle, and this is just what is impossible in regard to the communication of functional modifications to the germ. Moreover, in addition to this, there is the very important difference that, in the one case, we know with certainty that the process actually takes place, although we cannot understand its mechanical sequence in detail, while in the other we cannot even prove that the supposed process is a real one at all. From the fact that we are unable to form clear conceptions of a hypothetical process, we are not justified, it seems to me, in assuming it to be real, even though we are aware of many other processes in nature which we are unable to understand.

Nor does Hertwig take up this position, for he is at pains to show the mechanical possibility of the process of inheritance which he assumes, and he bases this upon the suggestions made by Hering in his famous work *Ueber das Gedächtniss als eine allgemeine Function der organisirten Materie* [*On memory as a general function of organized matter*], 1870. As this essay probably contains the best that can be said in favour of a transmission of functional modifications, and as it also includes some indisputable truths, we may consider it in some detail.

Hering is undoubtedly right in regarding 'the phenomena of consciousness as functions of the material changes of organic substance, and conversely.' That is, he believes that every sensation, every perception, every act of will arises from material changes in the relevant nerve-substances. But we know that 'whole groups of impressions, which our brain has received through the sense-organs, are stored up in it, as if resting, and below the margin of consciousness, to be reproduced when occasion arises, in correct order of space and time, and with such vividness, that we may be deceived into regarding as a present reality what has long ceased to be present.' There must therefore remain in the nerve-substance a 'material impact,' a modification of the molecular or atomic structure, which enables it 'to ring out to-day the note that it gave forth yesterday if only it be rightly struck.'

Hering attributes a similar power of memory and reproduction to the germ-substance; he believes that he is justified in making the assumption that acquired characters can be inherited, although he admits that it 'appears to him puzzling in the highest degree' how characters which developed in the most diverse organs of the mother-being can exert any influence on the germ. That he may be able to assume this he points to the interconnexion of all organs by means of the nervous system; it is this that makes it possible that 'the fate of one reverberates in the other, and that, when excitement takes place at any point, some echo of it, however dull, penetrates to the remotest parts.' To the delicate-winged communication by means of the nervous system, which unites all parts among themselves, must be added the general communication by means of the circulation of the fluids of the body. According to Hering's view, the germ experiences, in some degree, in itself all that befalls the rest of the organs and parts of the organism, and these experiences stamp themselves more or less upon its substance, just as sense-impressions or perceptions stamp themselves upon the nerve-substance of the brain, and these experiences are reproduced during the development of the germ, just as the brain brings memory-pictures back to consciousness. He says, 'If something in the mother-organism has so changed its nature, through long habit or exercise repeated a thousand times, that the germ-cell resting in it is also penetrated by it in however weakened a fashion, when the latter begins a new existence, expands, and increases to a new being whose individual parts are still itself and flesh of its flesh, it reproduces what it experienced as part of a great whole. This is just as wonderful as when an old man suddenly remembers his earliest childhood, but it is not more wonderful than this.'

But I think it is more wonderful. There exist demonstrably in the brain thousands upon thousands of nerve-elements, whose activity is a definite and limited one, because each particular visual impression, for instance, only excites to activity certain definite nerve-elements, and can leave memory-pictures in these alone. According to my conception of it, the germ-plasm is quite as complex in its composition, and does not consist of homogeneous elements, but of innumerable different kinds, which are not related to the parts of the complete organism indiscriminately, but only to particular parts. But is it allowable to assume that there are invisible nerve-connexions, not only to every germ-cell, but also within the germ-plasm, to every determinant, like the nerve-paths which lead from the eye to the nerve-cells in the optic-area of the brain? For if it were otherwise, how could we conceive of the modification of an organ—as, for instance, the ear-muscles in Man—communicating itself to the precise determinants of these muscles in the germ-plasm? I have often been met with the reproach that my conception of the composition of the germ-plasm is much too complex—but the complexity of Hering's suggestion seems to me to go a long way beyond mine.

Hering's ideas, which are not only ingenious but very stimulating, might be accepted as the first indication of an understanding of the assumed inheritance of functional modifications, if it could be proved that such inheritance is a fact; but, as we have seen, that is not the case. The assumption might be permitted, perhaps, if it could be shown that certain groups of phenomena left no other possibility of explanation open except this assumption, but that also, as far as I can see, is not the case. Of course, others hold a different opinion, but chiefly because they have rejected without much reflection the sole explanation which presents itself for numerous phenomena—I mean the processes which we are about to study under the name of 'germinal selection.' But, in any case, Hering's ideas seem to me very valuable, because they make it apparent that, however much we know of the organism, we only know it in a general way, and that numberless delicate processes go on in it which leave no trace for our microscope, and that we can only recognize the final results of numerous invisible and often, in their subtlety, also unimaginable factors. This ought to be taken to heart, especially by all those who speak of simplicity in reference to the germ-plasm. So much at least is certain: If there were any inheritance of functional modifications, we should have another proof that the germ-plasm is composed of determinants, for without them there could be no possibility that the 'experiences' of an individual organ would be transmitted to the germ in the way that the Lamarckian principle implies. Something, and that something material, must be modified in the germ-plasm if the vigorous use of a group of muscles, or of a gland, or of a nerve-cell, is to be communicated to the germ, and not to the whole germ-plasm, but only to so much of it as is necessary to cause variation in the corresponding group of cells in the child. It may perhaps be said that this still does not necessitate the assumption of special determinants for these cell-groups, and that one might, with Herbert Spencer, conceive of the germ-plasm as consisting of homogeneous units which vary in the development in accordance with the diverse regularly alternating influences to which it is exposed from step to step, and that, therefore, in each of these units of very complex structure only a single molecule, or perhaps only a single atom, would need to vary in order that, in the course of development, the resulting cell-group should appear in the rudiment in somewhat altered strength.

But I do not believe that a chemical molecule, still less an atom, is sufficient for this, for reasons which I have already stated—yet we need not go into this now, but rather deduce the consequences of this admission. It follows that the 'unit' is made up of numerous 'molecules' or 'atoms,' of which each, by dint of changes it has undergone, causes particular parts of the body to vary in a definite manner: in other words, we have here again a theory of determinants, only they are on a much smaller scale, since each invisible little vital particle or 'unit' contains all the determinants within itself, while in my theory it is only the id, that is, the visible chromosome, which includes the determinant complex. Such a theory would be far from a simplification of mine, it would rather complicate it enormously, and that without anything being gained. At most it would be made more evident how inconceivably complex the nerve-paths must be which lead from the part that has been modified by exercise to the germ-plasm, and must also lead to all the innumerable 'molecules or atoms' of the individual 'units.' But even on my theory of the composition of the ids as aggregates of living determinants, such nervous transmission of qualities would be a monstrosity which no one would accept, and I think on this account that my argument as to the impossibility of conceiving of the transmission of the modifications of the personal part to the germinal part retains its force, notwithstanding Hering's interesting analogy.

If the transmission of functional modifications were an indisputable fact, I repeat, we should have to give in, and then we might regard the 'memory of organized material' as affording a hint of the possibility of the unimaginable process. But as long as the occurrence of this transmission cannot be proved either directly or indirectly, such a vague possibility of explanation need not induce us to assume an unproved process.

LECTURE XXV

GERMINAL SELECTION

On what does disappearance after disuse depend, if not on the Lamarckian principle?—Panmixia—Romanes—Fluctuations in the determinant-system of the germ-plasm due to unequal nutrition—Persistence of germinal variations in a definite direction—The disappearance of non-functioning parts—Preponderance of minus germinal variations—Law of the retrogression of useless parts—Variation in an upward direction—Artificial selection—Influence of the multiplicity of ids and of sexual reproduction—Personal selection depends on the removal of certain id-variants—Range of influence of germinal selection—Self-regulation of the germ-plasm, which is striving towards stability—Ascending variation-tendencies may persist to excess—Origin of secondary sexual characters—Significance of purely morphological characters—The markings of butterflies.

Now that we have recognized that the assumption of a transmission of functional modifications is not justifiable, let us discuss some of the many phenomena to explain which many people believe the Lamarckian principle to be indispensable, and let us inquire whether we are in a position to give any other explanation of these. How has it come about that the effects of use and disuse *appear* to be inherited? Can we find a sufficient explanation in the principle of selection, and in the natural selection of Darwin and Wallace?

The answer to these two questions will be most quickly found if we begin by seeking for an explanation of the disappearance of a part when it ceases to be exercised.

That this cannot lie in the Lamarckian principle we have already learnt from the fact that passively functioning parts, such as superfluous wing-veins, also disappear, and that the loss of the wings and degeneration of the ovaries has taken place in worker ants, which can transmit nothing because they do not reproduce.

We might be inclined to regard this gradual disappearance and ultimate elimination of a disused organ as a direct gain, on the ground that the economy of material and space thus effected may be of decided advantage to the individual animal and thereby also for the maintenance of the species, and that those animals would have an advantage in the struggle for existence in which the superfluous organ was reduced to the smallest expression. But that would be far from supplying us with a sufficient explanation of the phenomenon; the individual variations in the size of an organ which is in

II. I

process of degenerating are, even in extreme cases, far too slight to have any selection-value, and I cannot call to mind a single case in which the contrary could be assumed with any degree of probability. What advantage can a newt or a crustacean living in darkness derive from the fact that its eye is smaller and more degenerate by one degree of variation than those of its co-partners in the struggle for existence? Or, to use Herbert Spencer's striking illustration, how could the balance between life and death, in the case of a colossus like the Greenland whale, be turned one way or another by the difference of a few inches in the length of the hind-leg, as compared with his fellows, in whom the reduction of the hind-limb may not have gone quite so far? Such a slight economy of material is as nothing compared with the thousands of hundredweights the animal weighs. As long as the limbs protrude beyond the surface of the trunk they may prove an obstacle to rapid swimming, although that could hardly make much difference, but as soon as the phyletic evolution had proceeded so far that they were reduced to the extent of sinking beneath the surface, they would no longer be a hindrance in swimming, and their further reduction to their modern state of great degeneration and absolute concealment within the flesh of the animal cannot be referred even to negative selection.

Years ago I endeavoured to explain the degeneration of disused parts in terms of a process which I called Panmixia. Natural selection not only effects adaptations, it also maintains the organ at the pitch of perfection it has reached by a continual elimination of those individuals in which the organ in question is less perfect. The longer this conservative process of selection continues, the greater must be the constancy of the organ produced by it, and deviations from the perfect organ will be of less and less frequent occurrence as time goes on.

Now if this conservative action of natural selection secures the maintenance of the parts and organs of a species at their maximum of perfection, it follows that these will *fall below this maximum as soon as the selection ceases to operate.* And it does cease as soon as an organ ceases to be of use to its species, like the eye to the species of crustacean which descends into the dark depths of our lakes, or to the abyssal zones of the ocean, or into a subterranean cave-system. In this case all selection of individuals ceases as far as the eye is concerned; it has no importance in deciding survival in the struggle for existence, because no individual is at a disadvantage through its inferior eyes, for instance, by being in any way hindered in procuring its food. Those with inferior organs of vision will, *ceteris paribus,* produce as good offspring as those with better eyes, and the consequence of this must be that there will be a general deterioration of eyes, because the bad ones can be transmitted as well as the good, and thus the selection of good eyes is made impossible.

The mixture thus arising may be compared to a fine wine to which a litre of vinegar has been added; the whole cask is ruined because the vinegar mingles with every drop of the wine. As deviations from the normal are always occurring in every part of every species, and among them some that lessen the value of the organ, rarely perhaps at first, but after a time in every generation, a sinking of the organ from the highest point of possible perfection becomes inevitable as soon as the organ becomes superfluous. The functional uselessness of the organ must go on increasing the longer it is disused, as will readily be admitted if it be remembered that only the most perfect adaptation of all the separate parts of an organ can maintain its functional capacity, that all the parts of an organ are subject to variation, and that every deviation from the optimum implies a further deterioration of the whole. An eye, for instance, can no longer vary in the direction of 'better' if it has already reached the highest possible point of perfection; every further variation must deteriorate it.

Romanes gave expression to this idea, that the cessation of natural selection alone must cause the degeneration of a part, a decade before I did, but neither he nor the scientific world of his time attached great importance to it, and it was forgotten again. This was intelligible enough, for, at that time, the validity of the Lamarckian principle had not been called in question, and therefore the need for some other principle to explain the disappearance of disused parts had not begun to be felt.

I found myself in quite a different position. As my doubts regarding the Lamarckian principle grew greater and greater, I was obliged to seek for some other factor in modification, which should be sufficient to effect the degeneration of a disused part, and for a time I thought I had found this in panmixia, that is, in the mingling of all together, well and less well equipped alike. This factor does certainly operate, but the more I thought over it the clearer it became to me that there must be some other factor at work as well, for while panmixia might explain the deterioration of an organ, it could not explain its decrease in size, its gradual wearing away, and ultimate total disappearance. Yet this is the path followed, slowly indeed, but quite surely, by all organs which have become useless. If panmixia alone guided the deterioration of the organ, and it was

I 2

thus only chance variations which were inherited through panmixia and gradually diffused over the whole species, how could it come about that all the variations were in the direction of smaller size? Yet this is obviously the case. Why should no variations in the direction of larger size occur? And if this were so, why should a useless organ not be maintained at its original size, if it be admitted that an increase in size would be prevented by natural selection? But this never occurs, and diminution in size is so absolutely the rule that the idea of a 'vestigial or rudimentary' organ suggests a 'small organ' almost more than an 'imperfect' one.

There must then be something else at work which causes the minus-variations in a disused organ to preponderate persistently and permanently over the plus-variations, and this something can lie nowhere else than where the roots of all hereditary variations are to be found—in the germ-plasm. This train of thought leads us to the discovery of a process which we must call selection between the elements of the germ-plasm, or, as I have named it shortly, *Germinal Selection.*

If the substance of the germ-plasm is—as we assumed—composed of heterogeneous living particles, which have dissimilar rôles in the building up of the organism, there must of necessity be among them a definite labile state of equilibrium, which cannot be disturbed without modifying in some way the structure of the organism itself which arises from the germ-plasm. But if our further view be correct, that these individual and different living units of the germ-plasm are 'determinants,' that is, are the primary constituents of particular parts of the organism, in the sense that these parts could not arise if their determinants were absent from the germ-plasm, and that they would be different if the determinants were differently composed, we can draw far-reaching deductions.

It is true that we cannot learn *anything directly* in regard to the intimate structure of the germ-plasm, and even in regard to the vital processes going on within it we can only guess a very little, but so much we may say—that its living parts are nourished, and that they multiply. But it follows from this that nourishment in a dissolved state must penetrate between its vital particles, and that whether the determinants grow, and at what rate they do so, depends mainly on the amount of nourishment which reaches them. As long as the germ-cells multiply by division the determinants have no other function but to grow; a part of their substance undergoes oxidation and thereby yields the supply of energy necessary to assimilation, that is, to the formation of new living substance.

If each kind of determinant always secured the same quantity of nourishment, all would grow in the same degree, that is, in exact proportion to their power of assimilation. But we know that in less minute conditions which we can observe more directly, there is nowhere absolute equality, that all vital processes are subject to fluctuations; any little obstacles in the current of the nutritive fluid, or in its composition, may cause poorer nutrition of one part, better of another. We may therefore assume that there are similar irregularities and differences in the minute and unobservable conditions of the germ-plasm likewise, and the result must be a slight shifting of the position of equilibrium as regards size and strength in the determinant system: for the less well-nourished determinants will grow more slowly, will fail to attain to the size and strength of their neighbours, and will multiply more slowly.

But the vigour of growth does not depend only on the influence of nourishment; one cell grows quickly, another slowly in the same nutritive fluid; it depends in great part on the cell's power of assimilation. In the same way the assimilating power of the determinants and their affinity for nourishment will vary with their constitution, and a weaker determinant will remain smaller than a stronger one, even when the stream of nourishment is the same.

It seems to me that it is upon the unequal nutrition of the determinants conditioned by the chances of the food-supply that individual hereditary variability ultimately depends. If, for instance, the determinant *A* receives poorer nourishment at a particular time than the determinant *B*, it will grow more slowly, remain weaker, and then, when the germ-cells develop into an animal, the part to which it gives rise will be weaker than it usually is in other individuals.

These primary inequalities in the equipment of the determinants which are caused by a passing inequality in the food-stream are, of course, so slight that we are unable to observe their consequences. They must persist for a considerable time before they become observable, but they may persist for a long time, and their effect must then mount up, because every diminution in the strength of the determinant also signifies a lessened power of assimilation, and growth becomes slower for the twofold reason that passive and active nutrition decrease at the same time. In the less minute conditions observable in the histological elements of the body we know that function strengthens the organ, and that disuse weakens it, and we are justified in applying this proposition also to these more intimate conditions and minuter vital units. Thus, in the course of the multiplication of the germ-cells, the less vigorously working determinant, A, will gradually, but very slowly, become weaker, that is, of diminished power of assimilation, presupposing of course that the intra-germinal food-stream does not become stronger again at the same place—a possibility to which I shall subsequently refer. But while one determinant may be slowly becoming weaker, its neighbour, on the other hand, may be varying on an ascending scale, just because the former is, on account of its diminished power of assimilation, no longer able to exhaust completely the food-stream which flows to it.

The determinants are thus in constant motion, here ascending, there descending, and it is in these fluctuations of the equilibrium of the determinant-system that I see the roots of all hereditary variation, while in the fact that the variation-directions of particular determinants must continue the same without limit as long as they meet with no obstacle lies the possibility of the adaptation of the organism to changing conditions, the increase and transformation of one part, the degeneration and disappearance of another, in short, the processes of natural selection. The reason why such variation movements must continue until they meet some resistance is that every chance upward or downward movement—due, that is, to mere passive fluctuation in the food-supply, at the same time strengthens or weakens the determinant, and makes it either more or less capable of attracting nourishment to itself; in the former case an increasingly strong stream of food will be directed towards it, in the latter more and more of the available food-supply will be withdrawn from it by its neighbour-determinants on all sides; in the former the determinant will go on increasing in strength as long as it can go on attracting more nourishment, in the latter it will continue to become weaker until it disappears altogether. To the ascending progression, as is evident, there are limits set, not only by the amount of food which can circulate through the whole id, but also by the neighbour determinants, which will sooner or later resist the withdrawal of nourishment from them; but for the descending progression there are no limits except total disappearance, and this is actually reached in all cases in which the determinants are related to a part which has become useless. But both these movements, the upward and the downward alike, are quite independent of natural selection, i.e. of personal selection; they are processes of a unique kind which run their course purely in accordance with intra-germinal laws. Whether a determinant 'ascends' or 'descends' depends solely upon the play of forces within the germ-plasm, not upon whether the direction of the variation in question is useful or prejudicial, or on whether the organ in question, the determinate, is of value or otherwise. In this fact lies the great importance of this play of forces within the germ-plasm, that it gives rise to variations quite independently of the relations of the organism to the external world. In many cases, of course, personal selection intervenes, but even then it cannot directly effect the rising or falling of *the individual* determinants—these are processes quite outside of its influence—but it can, by eliminating the bearers of unfavourably varying determinants, set a limit to further advance in such directions. This we shall consider in more detail later on. Personal selection operates by removing unfavourably varying individuals from the genealogical tree of the species, but at the same time the determinants which are varying unfavourably are also removed, and their variation is thus put a stop to for all time.

I have called these processes which are ceaselessly going on within the germ-plasm, Germinal Selection, because they are analogous to those processes of selection which we already know in connexion with the larger vital units, cells, cell-groups and persons. If the germ-plasm be a system of determinants, then the same laws of struggle for existence in regard to food and multiplication must hold sway among its parts which hold sway between all systems of vital units—among the biophors which form the protoplasm of the cell-body, among the cells of a tissue, among the tissues of an organ, among the organs themselves, as well as among the individuals of a species and between species which compete with one another.

If this be the case, we have here ready to hand the explanation of every heritable variation of a part, ascending and descending alike. Let us consider for a little the latter category—that is, the disappearance of functionless *or useless organs.* It is clear that, from the moment in the life of a species that an organ, *N*, becomes useless, natural selection withdraws her hand from it; individuals with better or worse organs *N* are now equally capable of life and struggle, the state of panmixia is entered upon, and the organ *N* of necessity falls somewhat below its previously attained degree of perfection.

That this must be so will be admitted when it is remembered that each organ of a species is only maintained at its highest level because personal selection keeps ceaseless watch over it, and sets aside all the less favourable variations by eliminating the individuals which exhibit them. But this is no longer the case with a useless organ. When a weaker variant of a disused organ arises through the intra-germinal fluctuations of nutrition, this is transmitted to the descendants just as well as the normally developed organ, and in the course of generations will be inherited by a greater and greater number of individuals, and must ultimately be inherited by all in some degree or other. The objection has been urged from many sides that variations upwards would be quite as likely to arise as those downwards, but this is an error. Even if, at the beginning, the minus-variations were rarer than the plus-variations, in the course of generations the minus ones would preponderate because ascending variations of disused organs are not indifferent for the organism but injurious to it. Perhaps an increase in the size of the organ itself would do no harm, but in that of its determinant it certainly would, because an ascending determinant requires more nourishment than previously, and withdraws it from its surroundings, and thus from the determinants in its immediate neighbourhood; but these are those of functioning and indispensable parts. Individuals in whose germ-plasm the determinants of disused organs ascend, and thereby depress the determinants of organs which are still active, are subject to personal selection, and are eliminated. There thus remain only those with descending determinants; in other words, the chance of variants in the direction of weakness in useless determinants far outweighs that of variants in the direction of increased strength; the latter will soon cease to occur at all, for as soon as a determinant has fallen a little below its normal level, it finds itself upon an inclined plane, along which it glides very slowly but steadily downwards. This might be disputed if it could be maintained that, at every stage of the descent, a change of direction was possible. But this probably takes place rarely and only in the case of individual ids, and will therefore not be permanent because in general the stronger neighbour determinants will possess themselves of the superfluous nourishment, and a lasting ascent will thus be impossible to the weakened determinant. This is precisely what I have called Germinal Selection. The determinant whose assimilating power is weakened by ever so little is continually being robbed by its neighbours of a part of the nourishment which flows towards it, and must consequently become further weakened. As no more help will be given to it by natural selection, since the organ is no longer of any value to the species, the better among the weakened determinants of N are never selected out, and they must gradually give way in the struggle with the neighbouring determinants which are necessary to the species, becoming gradually weaker and ultimately disappearing.

This process can, of course, no more be proved mathematically than any other biological processes. No one who is unwilling to accept germinal selection can be compelled to do so, as he might be to accept the Pythagorean propositions. It is not built up from beneath upon axioms, but is an attempt at an explanation of a fact established by observation—the disappearance of disused parts. But when once the inheritance of functional modifications has been demonstrated to be a fallacy, and when it has been shown that, even with the assumption of such inheritance, the disappearance of parts which are only *passively* useful, and of any parts whatever in sterile animal forms, remains unexplained, he who rejects germinal selection must renounce all attempt at explanation. It is the same as in the case of personal selection. No one can demonstrate mathematically that any variation possesses selection value, but whoever rejects personal selection gives up hope of explaining adaptations, for these cannot be referred to purely internal forces of development.

The total disappearance of a part which has become useless takes place with exceeding slowness; the whales, which have existed as such since the beginning of the tertiary period, have even now not completely lost their hind-limbs, but carry them about with them as rudiments in the muscular mass of the trunk, and the birds, which are even older, still show in their embryonic primordia the five fingers of their reptilian forefathers, although even their bird-ancestors of the Jurassic period, if we may argue from *Archaeopteryx*, had only three fingers like our modern birds. A long series of similar examples might be given, and modern embryology in particular has contributed much that, like this example of birds' fingers, points to a certain orderliness in the disappearance of the individual parts of an organ which has become superfluous. Parts which, in the complete animal, have disappeared without leaving a trace, appear again in each embryonic primordium, and disappear in the course of the ontogeny. Speaking metaphorically, we might express this on the basis of the determinant theory, by saying that the determinants, as they become weaker, can only control an increasingly short period of the whole ontogeny of the organ, so that ultimately nothing more than its first beginning comes into existence. But this is only a metaphor; we cannot tell what really happens as long as we are ignorant of the physiological rôle of the determinants, and even of the laws governing the degeneration of a useless organ. In respect of the latter, much might still be achieved if comparative anatomy and embryology were studied with this definite end in view, and perhaps we should even be able to draw more definite conclusions in regard to the composition and activity of the determinants in the germ.

In the meantime we must be content with the knowledge that, on the determinant hypothesis, the disappearance of organs which have become useless may be regarded as a process of intra-selection going on between the 'primary constituents' (*Anlagen*) of the germ, and depending on the same principle of the 'struggle of parts' which William Roux introduced into science with such brilliant results. If a struggle for food and space actually takes place, then every passive weakening must lead to a permanent condition of weakness and a lasting and irretrievable diminution in the size and strength of the primary constituent concerned, unless personal selection intervenes, and choosing out the strongest among these weakened primary constituents, raises them again to their former level. But this never happens when the organ has become useless.

This explains why not only parts with active function, like limbs, muscles, tendons, nerves, and glands, disappear when they cease to function, but also passive parts like the colouring of the external surfaces of animals, the lifeless skeletal parts of Arthropods and the exact adaptation of their thickness to the dwindling function, the disappearance of superfluous wing-veins, and of the hard chitinous covering of the abdomen when it is concealed in a protecting house, as in the case of hermit-crabs, Phryganidæ, and Psychidæ. Here too we find a sufficient explanation of the fact that parts which have become functionless, such as the wings of ants, can disappear even in the case of sterile workers.

The principle of germinal selection, however, can only be understood in its full significance if we take the positive aspect also into consideration. We had reached the conclusion that because of the fluctuations of the food-supply one set of the homologous determinants represented in the various ids may vary in a minus direction, and another set in a plus direction, and that this direction will be adhered to as long as no intra-germinal obstacles come in the way. As long as this does not happen the determinant concerned will pursue the path of variation it has once struck out, and indeed the tendency will be strengthened, because every passive variation, upwards or downwards, results in a strengthening or weakening of the determinant's power of assimilation.

Let us take a case of positive variation of the determinants of an organ *N*, which would be more useful to the species if it were more highly developed than it had previously been. The variation in an upward direction is at first purely passive, having arisen from fluctuations in the food-supply, but it soon becomes active, since the determinants that have become stronger will have a stronger affinity for food and will attract more and more of the available supply. The increased food-stream is thus maintained, and its gradual result is such a strengthening of the determinants in the course of generations of germ-cells, that the parts controlled by these determinants—the determinates—must enter on a path of plus-variations. If to this there be added personal selection, either natural or artificial, any fluctuations of this primary constituent towards the minus side will be effectually prevented, the direction of variation will remain positive, and the continued intervention of personal selection may raise its development to its possible maximum, that is, so far that further development in the same direction would not make for greater fitness, and personal selection must call a halt. This will always happen as soon as further increase of the organ would be prejudicial to the living power of the whole, and when the harmony of the bodily parts would thereby be permanently disturbed.

That variation in an upward direction really can persist for a long time is shown by artificial selection as practised by Man in regard to his domesticated animals and cultivated plants. At first general variability, or at least variability in many directions, sets in as a result of the greatly altered conditions of life: the ordinary fluctuations of the determinants are intensified by the greater fluctuations in the nutritive stream, and it becomes possible for Man consciously or unconsciously to select for breeding whatever he prefers among the chance variations that arise in individual parts or in whole complexes of parts, and he may thus give rise to a long-continued, often apparently unlimited, augmentation of variations in the same direction, although he cannot exercise *any direct* influence upon the germ-plasm or its determinants. When a determinant has assumed a certain variation-direction it will follow it up of itself, and selection can do nothing more than secure it a free course by setting aside variations in other directions by means of the elimination of those that exhibit them.

That artificial selection can cause the increase of a part has long been established, but in what way this is possible, and how it can be theoretically explained has hitherto been very obscure, for even if we take the favourable case that both parents possess the desired variation, it cannot be supposed that the characters of the parents are, so to speak, added together in the child; all we can say is that the probability that the children will also exhibit the character in question—for instance, a long or crooked nose—becomes greater. Certainly an increase of the character may result if in both parents the determinants K are present in excess as compared with the heterodynamous determinants K' and K'', for in that case there is an increased probability that, through reducing divisions and amphimixis, there will again be a preponderance of the determinants K composing the germ-plasm of the child, and further, that these determinants K will dominate strongly as compared with the few K's. It may thus happen that the long nose of the two parents will give rise to a still longer nose in the child, or that parents of considerable bodily size may have still bigger children, but such increase would be confined to one generation, and would not lead to a permanent increase of the character; permanent increase cannot depend merely on the number of the determinants K and on their supremacy over their converse, the determinants K'; it must also depend on their own variation, and this again can depend only on germinal selection and not upon personal selection, although the former can be materially assisted by the latter.

That inheritance from both parents is only a secondary consideration in regard to the increase of a part by artificial selection is made evident by the fact that *many secondary sexual characters* have been modified, although the breeder selected only in regard to one parent. Nevertheless in this very domain the greatest results have been achieved: witness the Japanese breed of cocks with tail-feathers six feet long. This astonishing result has been reached by the strictest selection of the cocks in which the feathers were a little longer than those of other cocks, and the increase in the length of feathers depended—according to our theory—simply on the fact that, by the selection of the determinants which were already varying in the direction of increased length, this process of increase was guarded from interruption by chance unfavourable conditions of nutrition. The continuance of variation in the upward direction in which it had already started is not effected directly by personal selection, but is so indirectly, for without this constant fresh intervention of selection the increase would be apt to come to a standstill, or the variation might even take a contrary direction. There are two other factors operative to which we have not yet given sufficient attention. They are, the multiplicity of the ids in every germ-plasm, and sexual reproduction.

If—as we must assume—each germ-plasm is made up of several or many ids, there must be several or many determinants of each part of the organism, for each id contains potentially the whole organism, though with some individuality of expression. The child is thus not determined by the determinants of a single id, but by those of many ids, and the variations of any part of the body do not depend on the variations of a single determinant *X*, but on the co-operation of all the determinants *X* which are contained in the collective ids of the relevant germ-plasm. Thus it is only when a majority of the determinants have varied upwards or downwards that they dominate collectively the development of the part *X'* and cause it to be larger or smaller.

We have assumed passive fluctuations in nutrition to be the first cause in individual variation, and it is obvious that the action of this first cause of dissimilarity must be greatly restricted by the multiplicity of the ids and the corresponding homologous determinants. For although passive fluctuations in nutrition should occur continually in the case of all determinants, this would not imply that they would follow the same direction in all the determinants *X* of all ids, for some determinants *X* might vary upwards, and others downwards, and these might counteract each other in ontogeny; so that in many cases the fluctuations of the individual determinants will not be felt in their products at all. But since there are—as we shall see later—only two directions of variation, upwards and downwards, plus and minus, it must also sometimes happen that a majority take one direction, and this affords the basis on which germinal selection can build further, and on which it is materially supported by reducing division and the subsequent amphimixis.

For reducing division removes half of the ids and thus of the determinants from the mature germ-cell, and according as chance leaves together or separates a majority of *X*-determinants varying in the same direction, this particular germ-cell will contain the primary constituents of a plus- or of a minus-variation of *X*, and it is possible that the presence of a majority or a minority may be entirely due to the reduction. The germ-plasm of the parent may contain, for instance, the determinant *X* in its twenty ids 12 times in minus-variation form, 8 times in plus-variation form: and the reducing division, according to our view, may separate these into two groups of which one contains eight plus- and two minus-variations, the other ten minus-variations, or the one six plus- and four minus-variations, the other two plus- and eight minus-variations, and so on. Now every germ-cell which contains a majority of plus- or minus-variations—and this must be the case with most of them—may unite, if it attains to amphimixis, with a germ-cell which also contains a majority of plus or minus *X*-determinants, and if similar majorities let us say plus—meet together, the plus-variation of X must be all the more sharply emphasized in the child.

Thus, although the individual determinants X may not be incited to further variation by their co-operation with others varying in the same direction, the collective effect of the plus-determinants will be greater, and adherence to the same direction of variation in the following generation will be assured, for if in the germ-plasm of the parent there be, for instance, sixteen out of twenty determinants possessing the plus-variation, a minus-majority can no longer result from reducing division.

It is upon this that the operation of natural selection, that is, personal selection, must depend--that the germ-plasms in which the favourable variation-direction is in the majority are selected for breeding, for it is this and nothing else that natural selection does when it selects the individuals which possess the preferred variations. The ascending process is thus considerably advanced, because the opposing determinants are more and more eliminated from the germ-plasm, till the preferred variations of X are left, and among these, as ascent in the direction begun continues, the opposing variations are again set aside by germinal selection, and so on. Reducing divisions and amphimixis are thus powerful factors in furthering the transformations of the forms of life, although they are not the ultimate causes of these.

Now that we have made ourselves familiar with the idea of germinal selection we shall attempt to gain clearness as to what it can do, and how far the sphere of its influence extends, and, in particular, whether it can effect lasting transformations of species without the co-operation of personal selection, and what kind of variations we may ascribe to it alone.

First, I must return for a moment to the question we have already briefly discussed- whether the variation of a determinant upwards or downwards must so continue without limit. We might be inclined to think that the great constancy which many species exhibit was a plain contradiction of this, for if every minute variation of a determinant necessarily persisted without limit in the same direction, we should expect to find all the parts of the organism in a state of continual unrest, some varying upwards, some downwards, always ready to break the type of the species. Must there not be some internal self-regulation of the germ-plasm which makes it impossible that every variation which crops up can persist unlimitedly? Must there not be some kind of automatic control on the part of the germ-plasm, which is always striving to re-establish the state of equilibrium that has once been attained by the determinant system whenever it is disturbed?

It is difficult to give any confident answer to this question. We cannot reach clearness on this point through our present knowledge of the germ-plasm, because we possess no insight into its structure: we can only draw conclusions as to the processes in the germ-plasm from the observed phenomena of variation and inheritance. But two facts stand in direct antithesis to one another, first, the high power of adaptation possessed by all species, and the undoubted occurrence of unrestricted persistence in a given direction of variation, as seen in artificial selection, and in the disappearance of parts which have ceased to function; and, secondly, t' e great constancy of old-established species which do indeed always exhibit a certain degree of individual variability, but without showing marked deviations as a frequent occurrence or in all possible directions, as they certainly would if every determinant favoured by a chance increase in the nutritive stream necessarily and irresistibly went on varying further in the same direction. Or can the constancy of such species be maintained solely by means of personal selection, which is continually setting aside all the determinants which rise above the selection-value by eliminating their possessors? I was for long satisfied that this was the true solution of the difficulty, and even now I do not doubt that personal selection does, in point of fact, maintain the constancy of the species at a certain level, but I do not believe that this is sufficient, but rather that it is necessary to recognize an equalizing influence due to germinal selection, and to attribute to this a share in maintaining the constancy of a species which has long been well adapted. I am led to this assumption chiefly by the phenomena of variation in Man, for we find in him a thousand kinds of minute hereditary individual variations, of which not one is likely to attain to selection value. Of course the constant recurrence of reducing divisions prevents any particular id which contains a varying determinant from being inherited through many generations; for so many ids are being continually removed from the genealogical tree by the constant rejection of the half of all ids of every germ-plasm, that only a small part of the ancestral id remains in the grandchild, great-grandchild, and so on. Certainly some of the ids of the ancestors compose the germ-plasm of the descendants, and if all the determinants of one of these ids had begun to vary persistently upwards or downwards in an ancestor, then all the determinants of the relative id in the descendants would possess the variation in an intensified degree; and however slowly the variation advanced it would attain selection-value in some one or other of the descendants, and would thus break the previously stable type of the most perfectly adapted species. The descendant in question would then succumb in the struggle for existence. But as the number of the determinants in the germ-plasm is probably much greater than that of the descendants of one generation, every descendant would in the course of time deviate unfavourably in some one character from the type of the species, and then either all the descendants would be eliminated or the type would become unstable. But neither of these things happens, and there are undoubtedly species which remain constant for long periods of time, therefore the assumption must be false and every variation of a determinant does not of necessity go on in the same direction without limit.

I therefore suppose that although slight variations are ceaselessly taking place upwards or downwards in all determinants, even in constant species, the majority of these turn again in the other direction before they have attained to any important degree of increase, at least in the germ-plasm of all species which have had a definitely established equilibrium for thousands of generations. In such a germ-plasm, or to speak more precisely, in the id of such a germ-plasm, marked fluctuations in the nutritive stream will not be likely to occur as long as the external conditions are unchanged, but slight fluctuations, which will not be wanting even here, may often alternate and turn in an opposite direction, and thus the upward movement of a determinant may be transformed into a downward one. Every determinant is surrounded by several others, and we can imagine that the regular nutritive stream which we have assumed may be partially dammed up by a slight enlargement of the determinant, and that this will drive the surplus back again. But however we may picture these conditions, which are for all time outside of the sphere of observation, the assumption of a self-regulation of the germ-plasm, up to a certain degree, cannot be regarded as inconceivable or unphysiological.

But there are limits to this self-regulation; as soon as the increase or decrease of a determinant attains a certain degree, as soon as it has got beyond the first slight deviation, it overcomes all obstacles, and goes on increasing in the direction in which it has started. This must happen even in the case of old and constant species, and frequently enough to admit of an apparent capacity for adaptation in all directions. Every part of a species can vary beyond the usual individual fluctuations, and as this is possible only by means of intra-germinal processes, we must assume that even in the case of germ-plasms which have long remained in a state of stable equilibrium there may occasionally be marked fluctuations in the nutritive stream, and thus more than usually pronounced variations of the determinants affected by it will occur. These yield the material for new adaptations if they are in the direction of fitness, or they are eliminated either by the chances of reducing division or by personal selection if new adaptations are not required.

The old-established hereditary equilibrium of the germ-plasm must be most easily disturbed when the species is in some way brought into new conditions of existence, as, for instance, when plants or animals are domesticated, and when in consequence, as we have already assumed, the nutritive currents within the id gradually alter, quantitatively and qualitatively; and on this account alone certain kinds of determinants are favoured, while others are at a disadvantage. In this way there arises the intensified general variability of domesticated animals and cultivated plants which has been known since the time of Darwin. Something analogous to this must occur in natural conditions, though more slowly, when a species is subjected to a change of climatic conditions, but we shall discuss this later on in more detail.

We have thus arrived at the idea that the slight variations of the determinants may be counteracted whether they be directed upwards or downwards, and that in the case of so-called constant species they do frequently equalize themselves; but that more marked variations, produced by more pronounced nutritive fluctuations, may in a sense go on without limit, and then can only be restricted and controlled by personal selection, that is, by the removal of the ids concerned from the genealogical lineage of the species.

In one direction variation can be proved to go on without limit, and that is downwards, as is proved by the fact of the disappearance of *disused organs*, for here we have a variation-direction, which has been followed to its utmost limit, and which is completely independent of personal selection; it proceeds quite *uninterfered with* by personal selection, and is left entirely to itself. It is a significant fact that the disappearance of the individual parts of a larger organ, according to all the data that are as yet available, proceeds at a very *unequal rate*, so that it evidently depends to a great extent on chance whether a disused part begins to degenerate sooner or later. Thus in one of the Crustaceans living in the darkness of the caves of North America the optic lobes and optic nerves have disappeared, while the retina of the eye, the lens, and the pigment have been retained, and in others the reverse has taken place, and the nerve-centres have persisted while the parts of the eye have been lost (Packard). Variations of the relevant determinants towards the minus direction may thus occur, sometimes sooner, sometimes later; but when once they have started they proceed irresistibly, though with exceeding slowness.

But variation in an upward direction also, when it has once been set a-going, may in many cases go on unchecked until limits are set to it by personal selection, when the excess of the organ would disturb the harmony of the parts, or in any other way lessen the individual's chances of survival in the struggle for existence. This is proved especially by the phenomena of artificial selection, for almost all the parts of fowls and pigeons have been caused to vary to excess by breeding, and must thus have been, so to speak, capable of unlimited increase; and yet, as we have seen, personal selection cannot directly cause progress in any direction of variation; it can only secure a free course by excluding from breeding the bearers of variations with an opposite tendency. The beards of hens, the tail-feathers of the long-tailed domestic cocks, the long and short, straight and curved bills of pigeons, the enormously long ruffled feathers of the Jacobin, the multiplication of the tail-feathers in the fan-tail, and innumerable other breed-characters of these playthings of the breeder, prove that when variation-tendencies of any part are once present, that is, when they have arisen through germinal selection, they apparently go on unchecked until their further development would permanently and irretrievably destroy the harmony of the parts. As soon as this is threatened the breed loses its power of survival, and Darwin in his time cited the case of many extremely short-billed breeds of pigeon, which require the aid of the breeder before they can emerge from the hard-shelled egg, because their short and soft bills no longer allow them to break their way out. Here the correlation between the hardness of the egg-shell and that of the pigeon's bill has been disturbed, and the breed can now only be kept in existence by artificial aid.

There must be a possibility of something similar occurring in natural conditions, and when it does the species concerned must die out. But in the majority of cases the self-regulation which is afforded by personal selection will be enough to force back an organ which is in the act of increasing out of due proportion to within its proper limits. The bearers of such excessively increased determinants succumb in the struggle for existence, and the determinants are thus removed from the genealogical lineage of the species.

Having now established the fact that determinants can continue their direction of variation without limit because of internal, that is intra-germinal, reasons, we have come nearer an understanding of many secondary sexual characters, whose resemblance to the excessive developments artificially produced in our domestic poultry is so very striking. Here, too, we shall have to regard germinal selection as the root of the variations of plumage and other distinguishing characters, which have evolved by intra-germinal augmentation into the magnificently coloured crests, tufts, and collars, into the long or graduated, multiplied or erectile tail-feathers of the birds of Paradise, pheasants, and humming-birds. The conception of sexual selection formulated by Darwin will be so far modified, that we are no longer compelled to regard every minute step in this cumulative process as due to the selection of the males by the females. A preference of the finest males may still take place, and is probably general, since only thus could the distinguishing male characters become common property, that is, be transmitted to all or the majority of the ids of the germ-plasm, but the increase of the individual determinants which are in the act of varying goes on in each individual id, quite independently of this personal selection.

As it is not a single id with its determinant a in ascending variation that controls the organ A, but as it always requires a majority of the ids a, this must be secured here by personal selection just as it is in ordinary natural selection. If the handsomest males are the successful competitors, then a majority of the transformed ids a' will be transmitted to a number of their descendants, and the oftener this happens the larger will the majority be, and the less becomes the danger that it will be dispersed again by reducing division and amphimixis. Personal selection is thus in no way rendered superfluous by germinal selection, only it does not produce the augmentation of the distinguishing characters, but is chiefly instrumental in fixing them in the germ-plasm; it collects, so to speak, only the favourably varying ids, and, where complex variations depending on the proper variation of many ids are concerned, it combines these. How very great the influence of personal selection may be in this case of secondary sexual characters we see clearly from the soberly coloured mates of the brilliant males, for here natural selection has been operative in conserving the coloration inherited from remote ancestry.

But if the question be asked, how *the first majority* of determinants varying in the same direction is brought about, there are two possibilities: first, by chance, and secondly, by influences which cause particular determinants of all the ids to vary in almost exactly the same manner. We shall find illustrations of the latter among climatic varieties; but the cases of the first kind are the more important, for they form the foundation and the starting-point for processes of selection of a higher order, for personal selection. It might seem perplexing that processes of such importance should depend ultimately upon chance; but when we remember that there are only two directions of variation, namely a plus direction or a minus direction, we recognize that the chance of a majority in one direction or another is much greater than that of absolute equilibrium between the two, and there is therefore a very strong probability that in many individuals of the species either the upward or the downward movement of a determinant *A* will preponderate.

Now as such variation movements, when they are of a certain strength, increase automatically, we can easily see that they must gradually attain to a level at which they acquire selection value, and how then, by personal selection, the ids with favourably varying determinants may be collected together.

Of course it is not possible to state positively the time at which in individual cases a variation acquires a biological significance, that is, selection value. We can only say in a general way that, as soon as it attains this, personal selection either in a positive or a negative sense *must* intervene; an injurious variation tends to the elimination of its possessor, a useful one increases the probability of its survival.

There must, however, be for every variation a stage of development in which it has as yet no decisive biological importance, and this stage need not by any means be so insignificant that we cannot see it, or can hardly do so: in other words, there are characters which have arisen through germinal selection, which are of purely 'morphological importance.'

It has often been disputed whether there can be any such thing as 'purely morphological characters,' which are indifferent as far as the existence of the species is concerned. This question used to be an important one, because the sphere of operation, and therefore the importance of the Darwin-Wallace selection—personal selection—depends on the answer, since this mode of selection only begins when a character has some biological importance. But as soon as we take germinal selection into consideration the question loses its importance, because we now know that every variation is indifferent to begin with, but every one can, under favourable circumstances, be increased to such a pitch that it attains biological importance, and that personal selection then takes over the task of carrying it on, either in a positive or a negative sense. We may therefore leave this disputed point alone just now, for while germinal selection seems still far from being generally recognized, we have to remember that we are not at all in a position to judge with any certainty as to the biological value of a character. What labour and painstaking investigation it has cost to give a verdict as to this even in a few instances! Innumerable characters appear indifferent, and are nevertheless adaptations. Darwin in his day pointed out the need for caution in this matter, referring to the case of animal coloration as an example; very little attention had been directed to it for a long time because it had been believed to be without significance. And how many diverse kinds of characters among animals and plants, which had likewise been regarded as 'purely morphological,' have on more careful investigation shown themselves of very great biological importance. I need only refer to the shape, position, hair-arrangement, colour, and lustre of flowers, and their relation to cross-fertilization by means of insects, or to the thickness and shape of the leaves of tropical trees with their coating of wax and their gutter-like outlets for carrying off the tropical rain which falls in terrible downpour (Haberlandt, Schimper), or to the limp, perpendicular drooping of the tufts of the young and tender

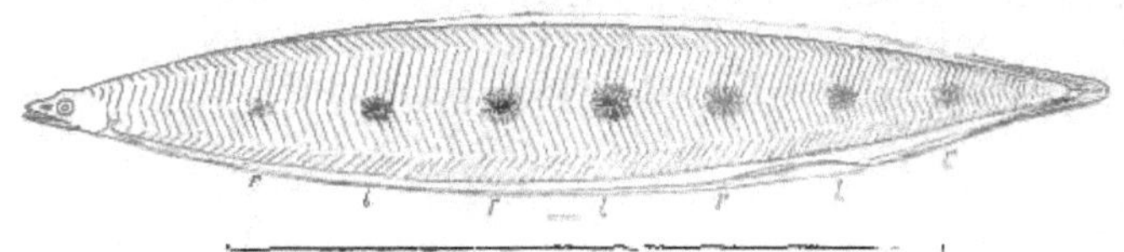

FIG. 107, *C*. Leptocephalus stage of an American Eel, with seven pigment spots, of which three are on the left (*l*) and four on the right (*r*) side. After Eigenmann.

leaves of the same trees, which also secures protection from being battered and torn by the rain.

There are even characters the biological use of which is unknown to us, but in regard to which we can affirm that they have a use. Thus Eigenmann described the larva of an American eel, which differs from other so-called 'Leptocephali' in that a row of seven black spots runs along its side. Apparently all these lie upon the side turned towards us, but in reality they are distributed on both sides, three lying on the left and four on the right, and so arranged that they look like a single row of spots at regular intervals, for the flat little fish is absolutely transparent. The habits of this larva are not yet known, but we may conclude that this appearance of a simple row of spots must have some value for the animal, for such a significant asymmetry could not have arisen for purely internal reasons (Fig. 107, *C*). It is possible that the fish is thus made to resemble parts of some marine alga, and that it is thereby protected from many enemies; that there is not a complete row upon each side may depend upon the fact that the two rows would be visible at the same time, and that they would blur each other in the eyes of the swimming enemy, and so destroy the resemblance of the picture to its unknown model.

But it cannot be denied that there are characters which have no special biological significance. There are doubtless many such characters, which stand beyond the threshold of good or bad, and which are therefore not affected by personal selection; it is difficult and often impossible to point these out with certainty. The shape of the human nose and of the human ear, the colour of the hair and of the iris, may be such indifferent characters whose peculiarities are to be referred solely to germinal selection. On the other hand, I would not venture to assert that the gay colouring and the complex markings on the wings of our modern Lepidoptera are always and in all cases unimportant, even when we cannot interpret their details either as protective, or as a sign of nauseousness, or as mimetic. The usually very exact similarity of the colour pattern in the individuals of each species seems to point to the intervention of personal selection in some form or other, for in what other way could such a large majority of variations in the same direction have developed in the germ-plasm as this constancy of the character indicates.

We know, of course, that the colours of butterflies and moths can be caused to vary through external and especially climatic influences, but this would only account for simple modifications of colour, and not for the origin of the complex colour patterns that actually occur. I therefore believe with Darwin that sexual selection has had much to do with this by giving a slight preference to the variations produced by spontaneous germinal selection, and thus preventing the majority of varied ids once acquired from being scattered again, but always collecting more of them, and so securing free play for the increase of the new character through intra-germinal processes. In this way have arisen not only the brilliance of our Lycænidæ and of the large Morphidæ of South America, but also many of the coloured spots, streaks, bands, eyes, and other components which have gradually in the course of time evolved into the complex colour pattern of many of our modern butterflies. I should like to remind any one who doubts this of a fact which corroborates the view that personal selection has co-operated in the production of these colours—I refer to the inconspicuous colouring of the females of many of these brilliant males—while in contradistinction to these cases there are other species in which both sexes are alike brilliant, so that it is impossible that mere spontaneous germinal selection can have determined that the females, because of their femaleness, should vary in a different manner from the males.

But while I believe that sexual selection in particular has had much to do with producing the colours of Lepidoptera, the basis of all these colour variations must still be looked for in germinal selection, and we shall see later on how it is possible to think of the diversified and often relatively abrupt transformations of marking as the resultant of the co-operation of climatic influences with germinal selection.

Of course there must also be unimportant changes in butterfly-markings which depend solely on the internal play of forces in the determinant system, and to this must be referred the markings of many of the 'variable' species whose variations are mere fluctuations in the details of marking, which have therefore caused much trouble to the systematists. Truly unimportant variations will rarely or never combine into a 'constant' form, and the fact that there are species which are 'variable' in such a high degree is enough to make us refer their variations to their lack of importance, for if they possessed any biological value the less valuable among them would gradually be removed by selection. Perhaps the variable species of certain moths like *Arctia caja*, and especially *Arctia plantaginis*, the little 'bear' of the Alps and Apennines, must be reckoned among these. But from the fact that there are such fluctuations in the markings of Lepidoptera, it seems to me that we must conclude that species which show a high degree of constancy in their markings have been influenced by selection, or by climatic influences which turned the play of forces within the determinant system in the same direction in all individuals. All these considerations and conclusions are quite sound and serviceable theoretically, but they are difficult to apply to individual cases, and where this is attempted it must be with the greatest caution, and, if possible, on a basis of investigations specially undertaken for the purpose; for how should we know whether a species which to-day is highly variable may not a geological epoch later become a very constant one? We must in any case assume that marked fluctuations of characters are associated with many transformations.

LECTURE XXVI

GERMINAL SELECTION (*continued*)

Germinal selection, spontaneous and induced—Climatic forms of *Polyommatus phlœas*—Deformities—Excessive augmentation of variations—Can it lead to the elimination of a species?—Saltatory variations, copper-beech, weeping trees—Origin of sexual distinguishing characters—Formation of breeds among domesticated animals—Degenerate jaws—Human teeth—Short-sightedness—Milk-glands—Small hands and feet—Ascending variation—Talents, intellect—Combination of mental endowments—The ultimate roots of heritable variation—There are only plus- and minus-variations—Relations of the determinants to their determinates—The play of forces in the determinant system of the id—Germinal selection inhibited by personal selection—Objection on the score of the minuteness of the substance of the germ-plasm.

HITHERTO we have derived the variations of the determinants of the germ-plasm, upon which we based the process of germinal selection, from *chance local* fluctuations in nutrition, such as must occur in an individual id, independently of the nutrition of the other ids of the same germ-plasm. But there are doubtless also influences which set up similar nutritive changes in *all ids,* and by which, therefore, all homologous determinants, in as far as they are sensitive to the nutritive change in question, are affected in the same manner. To this category belong changes in the external conditions of life, and particularly climatic changes. It is, then, germinal selection alone which brings about the presence of a majority of ids with determinants varying in the same direction, and personal selection has no part in the transformation of the species. Many years ago I instituted experiments with a small butterfly, *Pararga egeria,* and these showed that a heightened temperature so influenced the pupæ of this form that the butterflies emerged with a different and deeper yellow ground-colour, similar to that of the long-known southern variety *Meione.* More thoroughly decisive, however, were the experiments on *Polyommatus phlœas,* the small 'fire-butterfly,' which were carried on in the eighties by Merrifield in England and by myself almost at the same time. I shall discuss these later in more detail, and will only say here that this butterfly, whose range extends from Lapland to Sicily, occurs in two forms, the southern distinguished by a 'dusting' of deep black from the northern, in which the wing-surfaces are of a pure red-gold. The experiments showed that the southern form can be artificially produced by warmth, and the interpretation must be that the direct influence of higher temperature affects the quality of the nutritive fluids in the germ-plasm, and thereby at the same time the determinants of one or more kinds of wing-scales are caused to vary in all the ids in the same direction, in such a fashion that they give rise to black scales instead of the former red-gold ones. It is thus certain that there are external influences which cause particular determinants to vary in a particular manner. I call this form of germinal variation 'induced' germinal selection, and contrast it with 'spontaneous' selection, which is caused, not by extra-germinal influences, but by the chances of the intra-germinal nutritive conditions, and which will, therefore, not readily occur at the same time in all the ids of a germ-plasm, and so will not give rise to variation of the same kind in the homologous determinants of all the ids.

The two processes must also be distinguished from each other in their relation to personal selection, for induced germinal selection will go on increasing until the maximum of variation corresponding to the nature of the external influences and of the determinants concerned is reached. Since *all* the ids are equally affected and caused to vary in the same way, personal selection has nothing to take hold of, and the variation might go on intensifying even if it should become biologically prejudicial. But it is quite otherwise with spontaneous germinal selection, which has its roots not in all, but only in a majority of the ids. Here the variation may go on increasing by germinal selection alone, but only until it acquires a positive or negative biological value, that is, until it becomes advantageous or prejudicial to the life of the individual; then personal selection intervenes and decides whether it is to go on increasing or not. Spontaneous germinal selection can therefore only lead to the general variation of a whole species when it is supplemented by some external factor such as, especially, the utility of the variation.

This does not imply, however, that indifferent variations of large amount could not arise through spontaneous germinal selection, but they would remain confined to a small number of individuals, and would sooner or later disappear again. The congenital deformities of Man may in part fall under this category. If, for instance, certain determinants are, by reason of specially favourable local nutritive conditions, maintained for a long time in progressive variation, they will become so strong that the part which they determine will turn out excessive, perhaps double. Hereditary polydactylism in Man may perhaps be explained on this principle, and I had already referred it to the more rapid growth and duplication of certain determinants of the germ even before formulating the idea of germinal selection. In this I was at one with the pathologist Ernst Ziegler, who had designated polydactylism as a germ-variation, and in contrast to others had not interpreted it in an atavistic sense, as a reversion to unknown six-fingered ancestors. All excessive or defective hereditary malformations may be referred to germinal selection alone, that is, to the long-continued progressive or regressive variation of particular determinant-groups in a majority of ids.

The fact that, as far as our experience goes, superfluous fingers are never inherited for more than five generations may be simply explained, for there has been no reason for the intervention of personal selection, either in the negative sense, for the six-fingered state does not threaten life, nor in the positive, since it is not of advantage. The deformity depends on spontaneous germinal variation, which must have taken place in a majority of ids or it would not have become manifest. But such a majority of 'polydactylous' ids is liable to become scattered again in every new descendant, and to be reduced again into a minority which can no longer make itself felt by the chances of reducing division and the admixture of normal ids in amphimixis. A polydactylous race of men could only arise through the assistance of personal selection; in that case there would doubtless be just as much chance of success in breeding a six-fingered race as there was in breeding the crooked-legged Ancon sheep from a single ram which was malformed in this manner. Without a gradual setting aside of the germs with normal ids, that is, without personal selection, such spontaneous deformities, and indeed all *spontaneous* variations, must fail of attaining to permanent mastery.

This must frequently be the case in free nature also, but we shall have to investigate later on, in the section devoted to the formation of species, whether external circumstances (inbreeding) may not also occur which make it possible for spontaneous variations to become constant breed-characters, even although they remain neither good nor bad, and are thus not subject to the action of personal selection.

In general, however, amphigony with its reduction of the ids and its constant mingling of strange ids will form the corrective to the deviations which may arise through the processes of selection within the id, and which lead to excessive or superfluous development of certain structures, to a complete disturbance of the harmony of the parts, and ultimately to the elimination of the species.

It must be admitted, however, that Emery was probably right when he directed attention to the possibility of a 'conflict between germinal and personal selection.' It is quite conceivable that in cases of useful variations, that is, of adaptations, the processes of selection within the germ-plasm may lead to excessive developments, which personal selection cannot control, because, on account of their earlier usefulness, they have in the course of a series of generations and species become fixed not only in a majority of ids, but in almost all the ids of the collective germ-plasm of the species. In this case a reversal must be difficult and slow, for the gathering together of ids with relatively weaker determinants can only take place slowly, and it is questionable whether the species would survive long enough for the slow process to take effect. But, apart from the question of time, such a reduction of an excessive development would sometimes be quite impossible, for the simple reason that there is nothing for personal selection to take hold of.

Döderlein has pointed out that many characters go on increasing through whole series of extinct species, and ultimately grow to such excess that they bring about the destruction of the species, as, for instance, the antlers of the giant stag or the sabre-like teeth of certain carnivores in the diluvial period. I shall have to discuss this in more detail in speaking of the extinction of species; it is enough to say here that such long-continued augmentations in the same direction can never be referred *solely* to germinal selection, since it is hardly conceivable that a species—much less a whole series of species—should arise with injurious characters: they would have become extinct while they were still in process of arising. Although we see that the Irish stag, with his enormous antlers over ten feet across from tip to tip, was heavily burdened, we are hardly justified in concluding that the size and weight of the burden on his head tended to his destruction from the first—for in that case the species would never have developed at all—but it may well be that at some time or other the life-conditions of the species altered in such a manner that the heavy antlers became fatal to it. In this case the variation-direction which had gained the mastery in all ids could no longer be sufficiently held in check by personal selection, because the variations in the contrary direction would be much too slight to attain to selective value. Sudden, or at least rapidly occurring changes in the conditions of life, such as the appearance of a powerful enemy, exclude all chance of adaptation by the slow operation of personal selection.

If we look into the matter more carefully, we see that it is not strictly true to say that germinal selection alone brings about the extinction of a species by cumulative augmentation of structures which are already excessive; *it is the incapacity of personal selection to keep pace with the more rapid changes in the conditions of life and to reduce excessive developments to any considerable extent in a short time.* This would always be possible in a long time, for the determinants of the excessive organ *E* can never be equally strong in all the ids; they always fluctuate about a mean, however high this mean may be. Here again it must still be possible that reducing-divisions and amphimixis may lead to the formation of majorities of ids with weaker *E*-determinants, and if sufficient time be allowed, artificial selection could, by consistently selecting the individuals with, let us say, weaker antlers, give rise to a descending variation-movement. There are no variation-movements which cannot be checked; every direction can be reversed, but time and something to take hold of must be granted. That was wanting in the case of the giant stag, for it would not have been saved even if its antlers had at once become a couple of feet shorter, and germinal selection can hardly make so much difference as that.

Analogous to hereditary deformities, and of special interest in connexion with the processes within the germ-plasm, are '*sports*,' variations of considerable magnitude which suddenly appear without our being able to see any definite external reason for them. I have already discussed these in detail in my *Germ-plasm*, and have shown how simply these apparently capricious phenomena of heredity can be understood *in principle* from the standpoint of the germ-plasm theory.

The chances of the transmission of the saltatory variation will be greater or less according to whether the variation of the relevant determinants involves a bare majority of ids or a large majority, for the more ids that have varied, the greater is the probability that the majority will be maintained throughout the course of ensuing reducing divisions and amphimixis, that is, that the seeds of the plant will reproduce the variation, and will not revert to the ancestral form. Although one of the most satisfactory results of the id-theory lies precisely in the interpretation of these conditions, I do not wish to enter into the matter here, but will refer to the details in my *Germ-plasm*, published in 1894, which I consider valid still. At that time I had not formulated the idea of germinal selection, but the explanation of the occurrence of such sport-variations which I gave was based upon the assumption of nutritive fluctuations in the germ-plasm, which gave rise to variations in certain determinants. There was still lacking the recognition that the direction of variation once taken must be adhered to until resistance was met with, and that the determinants stand in nutritive correlation with one another, so that changes in one determinant must re-act upon the neighbouring ones, as I shall explain more fully afterwards. I also showed from definite cases that such sports, though they are sudden—'saltatory'—in their mode of occurrence, are long being prepared for by intimate processes in the germ-plasm. This 'invisible prelude' of variation depends on germinal selection. When a wild plant is sown in garden-ground it does not require to vary at once; several, even many, generations may succeed each other which show no sports; suddenly, however, sports appear, at first singly, then, perhaps, in considerable numbers. It is not, however, by any means always the case that considerable numbers occur, for some varieties of our garden flowers have arisen only once, and then have been propagated by seed; and such saltatory sports in plants which are raised from seed are usually constant in their seed, and if they are fertilized with their own pollen they breed true—a proof that the same variations must have taken place in the relevant determinants in a large majority of ids.

In animals, it would appear, such saltatory variations occur much more rarely than in plants; the case examined in detail by Darwin of the 'black-shouldered peacock' which suddenly appeared in a poultry-yard is an example of this kind. Much more numerous, however, are the instances among plants, and especially among plants which are under cultivation. This indicates that we have here to do with the effect of external conditions, of nutritive influences which cause the slow variation of certain determinants, sometimes abetting and sometimes checking. As soon as a majority of ids varied in this way comes to lie in a seed, a sport springs up suddenly and apparently discontinuously—a plant with differently coloured or shaped petals or leaves, with double flowers, with degenerate stamens, or with some other distinguishing mark, and these new characters persist if the variety is propagated without inter-crossing.

But it happens sometimes, though more rarely, that not the whole plant but individual shoots may exhibit the variation. To this class belong the 'bud-variations' of our forest trees, the copper-beeches, copper-oaks, and copper-hazels, the various fasciated varieties of oak, beech, maple, and birch, and the 'weeping trees'; also the numerous varieties of potato, plantain, and sugar-cane. It seems that only a few of these breed true when reproduced from seed, or in other words, they usually exhibit reversions to the ancestral form: on the other hand, in the weeping oak for instance, nearly all the seedlings exhibit the character of the new variety, though 'in varying degrees.' The records as to the transmissibility of bud-variations through seed are probably not all to be relied upon, and new investigations are much to be desired, but the fact that in many cases they may be propagated not only by means of layers and cuttings but by seed also, is most important in our present discussion, for it proves that here too the varied determinants must be contained in a majority of ids. As it is only a single shoot that exhibits the saltatory variation, only the germ-plasm which was contained in the cells of this one shoot can have varied, and it must have done so in so many ids that the variation prevailed and found expression. But that, in this case also, the variation does not appear in all, but only in a small majority of ids, is proved by the frequent reversion of bud-varieties to the ancestral form. I have already reported a case of this kind shown to me by Professor Strasburger in the Botanic Gardens in Bonn, where a hornbeam with deeply indented 'oak-leaves' had one branch which bore quite normal hornbeam leaves. In my own garden there is an oak shrub of the 'fern-leaved' variety, whose branches bear some leaves of the ordinary form; variegated maples with almost white leaves often exhibit in individual branches a reversion to the fresh green leaves of the ancestral form. We see from this that what is so energetically disputed by many must in reality occur—namely, differential or non-equivalent nuclear division—for otherwise it would be unintelligible how the ids of the new variety, if they once attain a majority in the tree, could give place in an individual branch to a majority of the ancestral ids. Only differential nuclear division, in the manner of a reducing division, can be the cause of this. Of course this implies only a dissimilar or differential distribution of the ids between the two daughter-nuclei, not a splitting up of the individual ids into non-equivalents.

That in free Nature bud-variations left to themselves can ever become permanent varieties is probably an unlikely assumption, because of the inconstancy of their seeds which only breed true in rare cases; nor is it likely that such variations as the copper-beech, the weeping ash, and so on could hold their own in the struggle for existence with the older species; but there is certainly nothing to prevent our assuming that, in certain circumstances, saltatory variations, when they have a germinal origin, may become persistent varieties and may even lead to a splitting of the species. This may happen, for instance, when the variations remain outside the limits of good and bad, and thus are neither of advantage to the existence of the species nor a drawback thereto. In the next chapter we shall discuss the influence of isolation upon the formation of species, and it will be seen that in certain conditions even indifferent variations may be preserved, and that saltatory variations, as for instance in the evolution of species of land-snails or butterflies, may have materially contributed to bring this about.

I should like to emphasize still more the part played by saltatory variations arising from germinal selection in the origin of secondary sexual characters. As soon as personal selection, whether sexual or ordinary, prefers as useful in any sense a saltatory variation, it is not only preserved and becomes a character of a variety, but it may increase, and we have to ask whether such sudden variations are frequently of a useful kind, especially when not individual characters alone, but whole combinations of them are implicated. If we may judge from the sports of the flowers and the leaves of plants, transformations useful to the species as a whole rarely occur suddenly, that is, they occur only in a few out of very numerous sports; they are much more frequently indifferent, although quite visible and often conspicuous variations.

For this reason I am disposed to attribute to saltatory variations a considerable share in the production of distinctive sexual characters. From saltatory variations in flowers, fruits, and leaves we know that these may be conspicuous enough even on their first appearance, and so we are justified in finding in such variations the first beginnings of many of the decorative distinguishing characters which occur in the males of so many animals, especially butterflies and birds. As soon as it is admitted that variations of considerable amount, which have been slowly prepared in the germ-plasm by means of germinal selection, can suddenly attain to expression, one of the objections against sexual selection is disposed of, for conspicuous variations are necessary for the operation of this kind of selection, since the changes in question must attract the attention of the females if they are to be preferred. Without such preference, even though it be not quite strict and consistent, a long-continued augmentation of the decorative characters is inconceivable.

But as intra-germinal disturbances of the position of equilibrium in the determinant system is at the root of the saltatory variations of our cultivated plants, it must also have played a large share in the evolution of breeds among our domesticated animals, which is therefore by no means wholly due to artificial selection operating upon the variation of individual characters. In all breeds in the formation of which the production of more than a single definite character was concerned, as, for instance, in the broad-nosed breeds of dog—bull-dog and pug-dog—we may refer the peculiar variation of many parts to disturbances of the equilibrium of the determinant system, which bring to light, not suddenly as in the case of saltatory variations, but gradually and increasingly, the curious complex of characters. Darwin referred such transformations of the whole animal facies, where a single varying character is deliberately selected, to correlation, and by this he understood the mutual influence of the parts of an animal upon one another. Such correlation certainly exists, as we have already seen in discussing histonal selection, but here we have rather to do with the correlation of the parts of the germ-plasm, with the effects of germinal selection, which, affected by the artificial selection of particular characters, gradually brings about a more marked disturbance in the whole determinant system.

In the evolution of our breeds of domesticated animals, germinal selection in the negative sense must also have played a part—I mean through the weakening and degeneration of individual determinants. Only in this way, it seems to me, can we explain the tameness of our domestic animals, dogs, cats, horses, &c., in which all the instincts of wildness, fleeing from Man, the inclination to bite, and to attack, have at least partly disappeared. It is, of course, very difficult to estimate how much of this is to be ascribed to acquired habitude during the individual lifetime. The case of the elephant might be cited in evidence of tameness which arises in the individual lifetime, for all tame elephants are caught wild, but it seems that captured young beasts of prey, such as the fox, wolf, and wild cat, not to speak of lions and tigers, never attain to the degree of tameness exhibited by many of our domesticated dogs and cats. The very considerable differences in the degree of tameness of dogs and cats go to show that the case is one of instincts varying in different degree.

If this be so, then the instinct of wildness, if I may express myself so for the sake of brevity, has degenerated in consequence of its superfluity, and through the process of germinal selection, which allowed the determinants of the brain-parts concerned to set out on a path of downward variation upon which they met with no resistance on the part of personal selection.

Herbert Spencer adduced against my position the case of the reduction in the size of the jaws in many breeds of dog, especially in pugs and other lap-dogs, which he regarded as evidence of the inheritance of acquired characters. But this and analogous cases of the degeneration of an organ during a long period in which the animal had been withdrawn from the conditions of natural life is intelligible enough on the assumption of persistent germinal selection aided by panmixia. The jaws and teeth in these spoilt pets no longer require to be maintained at the level of strength and sharpness essential to their ancestors which depended on these characters, and so they fell below it, became smaller and weaker, but could not disappear altogether, for the process of degeneration was brought, or is being brought, to a standstill by the intervention of personal selection.

Even the lower jaw in Man is declared by many authors to be degenerate. Collins found that the lower jaw of the modern Englishman was one-ninth smaller than that of the ancient Briton, and one-half smaller than that of the Australians; Flower showed that we are a microdont race like the Egyptians, while the Chinese, Indians, Malays, and Negroes are mesodont, and the Andamanese, Melanese, Australians, and Tasmanians are macrodont. This does not of itself imply that we exhibit a degeneration of dentition, though this conclusion is hinted at by other facts, such as the variability of the wisdom-teeth. It need not surprise us, indeed, that a retrogressive variation tendency should have started in this case, for, with higher culture and more refined methods of eating, the claims which personal selection was obliged to make on the dentition have been greatly diminished, and germinal selection would thus intervene.

Every one knows how the quality of human teeth has deteriorated with culture, and this not in the higher classes only, but even among the peasantry, as Ammon has observed. The time is past when raw flesh was a dainty, and when bad teeth meant poor nutrition, if not actual starvation. Even nowadays famine plays a terrible and periodically recurrent rôle as an eliminator among some negroid races.

Many other organs in man have been reduced from their former pitch of perfection through culture, and some of them are still in process of dwindling. When I formulated the idea of panmixia and applied it to explain cases which had previously been referred to the inheritance of the results of disuse, I regarded the short-sightedness of civilized Man from this point of view. My opinion aroused lively opposition at the time, especially on the part of oculists, who very emphatically referred the phenomenon to the inheritance of acquired shortsight, and indeed regarded it as a proof of the transmission of functional modifications.

But, apart from the fact that the assumption of this mode of inheritance must now be regarded not only as unproved, but as contradicted by reliable data, panmixia, in conjunction with the ceaseless fluctuations within the germ-plasm—germinal selection—affords a better explanation than the other theory was ever in a position to offer. At that time I pointed out that the survival of the individual among civilized races had not for a very long time depended on the perfection of his eyesight, as it does for instance in the case of a hunting or warlike Indian, or of a beast of prey, or of a herbivore persecuted by the beast of prey. And this is by no means due solely to the invention of spectacles, but in a much greater degree to the fact that every man no longer has to do everything, so that numerous possibilities of gaining a livelihood remain open to the less sharp-sighted; that is, the division of labour in human society has made the survival of the short-sighted quite feasible. As soon as this division of labour reached such a degree that the founding of a family offered no greater difficulty to the short-sighted individual than to one with normal sight, short-sightedness could no longer be eliminated; and partly because of the mingling with normal sight, but partly also because of the never-failing minus-fluctuations of the germ-plasm determinants concerned, a variation in a downward direction was bound to set in, and will continue until a limit is set to it by personal selection. Meantime, we are obviously still in the midst of the process of eye-deterioration; and the resistance to it is somewhat inhibited in its operation, because although individuals with extremely bad sight are for the most part hindered from gaining an independent livelihood and having a family, this is certainly, thanks to our mistaken humanity, not always the case. There are even instances of marriage between two blind persons!

As yet, however, the deterioration of eyes has not advanced very far; not nearly all families are affected by it, and even in Germany, the land of the 'longest school form' and of the greatest number of spectacle-wearers, short-sight is still usually acquired by individuals, although there must frequently be a more or less marked predisposition to it. It is a common objection to this view that in England, France, and Italy the percentage of short-sighted individuals is much lower, and, in point of fact, one sees far fewer people wearing spectacles in those countries. This, however, does not prove that a similar deterioration of eyes has not begun there also, for how could the small inherited beginnings be detected if they were not accentuated by the spoiling of the eyesight in the lifetime of the individual by much reading of bad print, and by writing with bent head, as is still too often the case in many German schools.

That our interpretation, through panmixia on a basis of germinal selection, is the correct one, we infer also from the fact that short-sightedness has been proved to be a frequent character even among our domesticated animals, such as the dog and the horse. These animals receive protection and maintenance from Man, and their survival and reproduction no longer depend on the acuteness of their sight, and thus the eye has fallen from its original perfection, just as in Man, although in this case reading and writing play no part.

A whole series of similar slight deteriorations of individual organs and systems of organs might be enumerated, all of which have appeared in consequence of long and intensive culture in Man. All these must depend upon germinal selection, on a gradually progressive weakening of the determinant-groups concerned, under the conditions of panmixia, that is, in the absence of positive selection.

To these must be added the deterioration of the mammary-glands and breasts, and the inability to suckle the offspring which results chiefly from this. Here we have a variational tendency which could not appear in a people at a lower stage of culture, and it has not become general in the lower classes of society among ourselves.

The muscular weakness of the higher classes is another case in point, and all gymnastics and sports will be of no avail as long as a relative weakness of the muscles is not a hindrance to gaining a livelihood, and having a family. Even universal conscription will do nothing to check this falling off of the bodily strength. Certainly military service strengthens thousands, and hundreds of thousands of individuals, but it does not prevent the weaklings from multiplying, and thus reproducing the race deterioration. But it would indeed be well if only those who had gone through a term of military service were allowed to beget children.

It is only among the peasantry, inasmuch as they really work and do not merely look on as proprietors of the ground, that such a deterioration of the general muscular strength could not become the permanent variational tendency of the determinants concerned, because among genuine peasants bodily strength is a condition of having and supporting a family—at least on an average.

The diminution in the firmness and thickness of the bones in the higher classes, and many another mark of civilization, must be looked at from the point of view of panmixia and germinal selection; perhaps also the smaller hands and feet which frequently occur along with a more graceful general build in the higher ranks of European peoples. It would certainly not be surprising if in families which usually intermarry, and which in no way depend for their material subsistence on the possession of large and powerful hands and feet or bones generally, a downward variation of the relevant germ-deter-

L 2

minants should have developed, but this could never overstep a certain limit, because it would then be prejudicial even in civilized life. That we must be very careful not to regard large hands and feet as the direct result of hard physical toil was brought home to me by an observation of Strasburger's. He was particularly struck by the fact that the peasants of the high Tatra (Carpathians) were distinguished by the smallness of their hands and feet.

But while civilization has excited numerous downward variations in the germ, it has, on the other hand, been the cause of numerous hereditary improvements—variations in an upward direction. This opens up new ground, for hitherto we have been confronted with the alternative of either accepting the inheritance of acquired characters, and on this basis referring the talents and mental endowments of civilized Man to exercise continued throughout many generations, or of admitting an increase of mental powers only in as far as they possess 'selection value,' that is, as they may be decisive in the struggle for existence. To these mental qualities belong cleverness and ingenuity in all directions, courage, endurance, power of combination, inventive power, with its roots in imagination and fertility of ideas, as well as desire for achievement, and industry. Throughout the long history of human civilization these mental qualities must have increased through the struggle for existence, but how have the specific talents such as those exhibited in music, painting, and mathematics come into existence? And how have the moral virtues of civilized Man been evolved, and particularly unselfishness? For it can hardly be maintained of any of these endowments that they possess selection-value for the individual.

It is not my intention to discuss these questions in detail; they are too many-sided and of too much importance to be treated of merely in passing; moreover, I gave expression years ago to my views on this subject by dealing with one example—the musical sense in Man. I do not believe that the musical sense had its beginnings in Man, or that it has materially increased since the days of primitive Man, but in conjunction with the higher psychical life of civilized peoples its expressions and applications have risen to a higher level. It is, so to speak, an instrument which has been transmitted to us from our animal ancestors, and on which we have learnt to play better the more our mind has developed; it is an unintended 'accessory effect' of the extremely fine and highly developed organs of hearing with their nerve-centres which our animal ancestors acquired in the struggle for existence, and which played a much more important rôle in the preservation of life in their case than it does in ours. The musical sense may be compared to the hand, which was developed even among the apes, but which civilized Man in modern times no longer uses merely to perform its original function, grasping, but also for many other purposes, such as writing and playing the piano. And just as the hand did not originate through the necessities of the piano, neither did the extremely delicate sense of hearing of the higher animals develop for the sake of music, but rather that they might recognize their enemies, friends, and prey, in darkness and mist, in the forest, on the heath, and at great distances.

The case is probably the same with the rest of the special psychical endowments or talents. I do not of course maintain that they, like the musical sense, did not at some time play a rôle in the struggle for existence and survival, and therefore could not increase, but the increase was certainly not continuous, but much interrupted, so that it would extend only to small groups of descendants, and therefore could only contribute very slowly to the elevation of the psychic capacities of a whole people. But in certain individuals and families such augmentations would certainly take place through germinal selection, and it seems to me probable that these would never be wholly lost again, even if they appeared to be so, but would be handed on, in id-minorities, through the chain of generations, and would slightly raise the average of the talent in question, and might even, under favourable circumstances, combine in the development of a genius. We know how strongly hereditary such specific talents are: let us suppose that the determinants of, say, the musical sense have, by the intra-germinal chances of nutrition, been started on a path of ascending variation: they will continue in this path until a halt is called from some quarter or other. This can only happen if, in the reducing division, or in amphimixis, the highly developed musical determinants are wholly or partly eliminated, or are reduced to a minority. As long as this does not happen the ascending variation will go on, and then we may have the birth of a Mozart or of a Beethoven. Personal selection will not interfere either in a positive or a negative sense, since high development of the musical sense has no effect either in advancing or retarding the struggle for existence; the increase will therefore go on until the large majority of highly developed musical determinants, which we must assume in the case of a musical genius, is reduced, or even transformed into a minority, through unfavourable reducing divisions of the germ-cells, and by association with the germ-cells of less musical mates.

The fact that highly developed specific talents have never been known to be inherited through more than seven generations is quite in keeping with this view. But even this persistence has been observed only in the case of musical talent, and the long continuance of the inherited talent may well be due, as Francis Galton suggests in his famous statistical investigations into the phenomena of inheritance, to the fact that musical men do not readily choose wives who are absolutely lacking in this talent. It would be easy to rear an exceedingly highly gifted musical group of families within the German nation, if we could secure that only the highly-gifted musically should unite in marriage—that is, if personal selection could play its part. In another more general domain of mental endowment a case of this kind has been recorded, for Galton tells us of three highly gifted English families which intermarried for ten generations, and in that time scarcely produced a descendant who did not deserve to be called a distinguished man in some direction or other.

Of course, such continued persistence, through a long series of generations, of a high general mental level is more possible than the transmission and increase of a specific talent, for in the former case it is a question of a mixture of different high mental endowments, of which not all need be developed in every individual, and yet the individual need not fall to mediocrity if he possesses a combination of other qualities. But in musical talent, on the other hand, the falling from the height once attained takes place as soon as this one character is no longer represented in a sufficiently strong majority of determinants. Of course it would be a mistake to believe that the talent of a Sebastian Bach or a Beethoven depended solely on the highly developed musical sense; in them, as in all great artists, many highly developed mental qualities must have combined with the musical sense; a simpleton could never have written the Mass in B minor or the Passion of St. Matthew even if he had possessed the musical genius of Sebastian Bach. In this fact lies a further reason why genius is seldom found at the same pitch in two successive generations; the combination of mental characters always varies from father to son, and slight displacements may give rise to very great differences in relation to the manifestations of the specific talent. Under certain circumstances, the weak development of a single trait of character, as, for instance, power of action, or the excessive development of another, such as indecision or desultoriness, may so nullify the existing favourable combinations of mental characters, such as, let us say, musical sense, inventive talent, depth of feeling, &c., that they bear no fruit worth mentioning. And since, as we have already seen, the different mental qualities of the parents are to a certain extent separately transmitted, that is, since they may appear in the children in the most diverse combinations, we should rather be surprised that pronounced talent in a specific direction can persist in a family for two and a half centuries than that it should do so very rarely. For reducing division is always combining the existing mental qualities anew, and amphimixis is adding fresh ones to them.

Thus germinal selection, that is, the free, spontaneous, but definitely directed variation of individual groups of determinants, is at the root of those striking individual peculiarities which we call specific talents; but it can attain to the highest level only rarely and in isolated cases, because these talents are not favoured by personal selection, and therefore the excessively highly developed determinants upon which they depend may be dispersed in the course of generations; they may sink to smaller majorities, or even to minorities, in which case they will no longer manifest themselves in visible mental qualities.

We deduced the process of germinal selection on the basis of the assumption that the nutrition of all the parts and particles of the body, therefore also of the determinants and biophors of the germ-plasm, is subject to fluctuations. We regarded the resulting variations of these last and smallest units of the germ-plasm as the ultimate source of all hereditary variation, and therefore the basis of all the transformations which the organic world has undergone in the course of ages and is undergoing still.

We have still to inquire whether we can give any more precise account of the nature of these units of the germ-plasm. If I mistake not, we may say at least so much, that all variations are, in ultimate instance, quantitative, and that they depend on the increase or decrease of the vital particles, or their constituents, the molecules. For this reason I have hitherto always spoken of only two directions of variation—a plus or a minus direction from the average. What appears to us a qualitative variation is, in reality, nothing more than a greater or a less, a different mingling of the constituents which make up a higher unit, an unequal increase or decrease of these constituents, the lower units. We speak of the simple growth of a cell when its mass increases without any alteration in its composition, that is, when the proportion of the component parts and chemical combinations remains unchanged; but the cell changes its *constitution* when this proportion is disturbed, when, for instance, the red pigment-granules which were formerly present but scarcely visible increase so that the cell looks red. If there had previously been no red granules present, they might have arisen through the breaking up of certain other particles of protoplasm, for instance, in the course of metabolism, so that, among other substances, red granules of uric acid or some other red stuff were produced. In this case also the qualitative change would depend on an increase or decrease of certain simpler molecules and atoms constituting the protoplasm-molecule. Thus, in ultimate instance, all variations depend upon quantitative changes of the constituents of which the varying part is composed.

It might be objected to this argument that chemistry has made us acquainted with isomeric combinations whose qualitative differences do not depend upon a different *number* of the molecules composing them, but upon their different arrangement; it might be supposed that something similar would occur also in morphological relations. And, in point of fact, this seems to be the case. We may, for instance, imagine one hundred hairs as being at one time equally distributed on the back of a beetle, and at another standing close together and forming a kind of brush, but although this brush would be a new character of the beetle, yet its development would depend upon quantitative differences, namely, on the fact that the same skin-area, which in the first case bore perhaps only one hair, had in the second case a hundred. The quantity of hair cells has notably increased upon this small area. In the same way the characteristic striping of the zebra depends not on a qualitative change in the skin as a whole, but upon an increased deposit of black pigment in particular cells of the skin, therefore on a quantitative change. In relation to the whole animal it is a qualitative variation, as contrasted, for instance, with the horse, but in respect of the constituent parts which give rise to the qualitative variation it is purely quantitative. The character of the whole edifice is changed when the proportion of the stones of which it consists are altered.

Thus the determinants of the germ may not only become larger or smaller as a whole, but some kinds of the biophors of which they are made up may increase more than others, under definite altered conditions, and in that case the determinants themselves will vary qualitatively, so that, from the changing numerical proportions of the different kinds of biophors, a variation of the characters of the determinants can arise, and consequently also qualitative variations of the organs controlled by the determinants—the determinates. But, since nothing living can be thought of as invariable, the biophors themselves may, on account of nutritive fluctuations, grow unequally, and thereby vary in their qualities. To follow this out in greater detail and attempt to guess at the play of forces within the minutest life-complexes would at present only be giving the rein to imagination, but in principle no objection can be made to the assumption that every element of life down to the very lowest and smallest can, by reason of inequalities in its nutrition, be not only started on an ascending or descending movement of uniform growth, but can also be caused to vary *qualitatively*, that is, in its characters, because its component parts change their proportions.

Of course we know nothing definite or precise with regard to the units of the germ-plasm, and we cannot tell what is necessary in order that a determinant shall determine a part of the developing body in this way or in that; thus we have no definite idea of the relations subsisting between the variations of the determinants and those of their determinates, but we know at least so much, that hereditary variation of a part is only possible when a corresponding particle in the germ-plasm varies; and we may at least assume that these correspond to each other so far, that a greater development of the one implies a greater development of the other, and that a reversal of these relations is impossible. If the determinant X disappears from the germ-plasm the determinate X' disappears from the soma. It is therefore justifiable to infer from the degree of development of an organ the strength of its determinant, and to assume that plus- and minus-variations in both are correspondingly large.

But in addition to the fluctuations in the equilibrium of the germ-plasm which lie at the root of all hereditary variation, we have to take into account something which we have already touched upon briefly—the correlation of the determinants, the influencing of one determinant by those round about it. I have spoken for the sake of brevity of 'the determinant' of a part, although all the large and more important parts must certainly be thought of as represented by several or many, if not, indeed, by whole groups of determinants. Although it is quite out of our power to follow the complex processes of the mutual influences of the determinants upon each other, we can say this at least, *that these influences must exist*, and we have here a faint indication of what must occur in the case of spontaneous variations within the germ-plasm. We must, in the first place, think of the individual determinants as arranged in groups, so that, for instance, the determinants of the right and left half of the body lie together, and therefore are frequently affected together by influences which cause variation, so that both vary in the same direction at the same time. In point of fact, analogous deformities, such as polydactylism of both right and left hands, and even of hands and feet at once, do actually occur. That the right and left hands, the fore- and hind-limbs, are represented in the germ by particular determinants, may be inferred from their frequently different phyletic evolution into different forms of hand and foot, e.g. into flipper and rudimentary hind-leg in the whale, as well as from the cases of particulate inheritance, which are rare, but which undoubtedly do occur, such as when, in Man, there is a maternal blue eye on one side of the head and a paternal brown eye on the other. But almost more striking than the differences between these homologous or homotypic parts are their points of resemblance, and these may probably be in part referred to their disposition side by side and common history in the germ-substance, although a far larger proportion of them are probably due to their adaptation to similar functions, and are therefore to be regarded as a phenomenon of convergence within the same organism.

We have already seen that the first increase in the growth of one determinant means a withdrawal of nourishment, however slight, from its neighbours; this can, of course, be equalized again if the claims on the common nutritive stream from another quarter are at the same time diminished; but it is possible that the claims from another quarter may also be increased, and the withdrawal will then be more marked, and the determinants being thus injured from two directions at once will sink downwards with greater rapidity. But it is also conceivable that the majority of determinants of a part may vary upwards, and, by their combined increased power of assimilation, direct towards themselves such a greatly increased stream of nourishment that the whole organ—for instance, a particular feather in a bird—varies in an upward direction, and becomes larger and larger, as we see in the case of many decorative feathers: or that certain determinants vary only as far as some of their biophors are concerned, and similarly for their determinates, as when a group of scales on a butterfly's wing that had previously been black turn out a brilliant blue. It can probably also happen that such variations within the determinants are transmitted to neighbouring determinants because the nutritive conditions which caused the first to vary have extended to those about them. The increase of brightly coloured spots in birds and butterflies gives us ground for concluding that there are processes of this kind within the germ-plasm.

I will refrain from following this idea into greater detail, and translating the observable relations and variations of the fully-formed parts of the body into the language of the germ-plasm; but so much may be taken as certain, that multitudinous inter-relations and influences exist between the elements of the germ-plasm, and that one variation brings another in its train, so that—usually at a very slow rate, that is, in the course of generations and of species-forming, definite variations occur from purely intra-germinal reasons—variations which as far as they remain outside the limits of good or bad may of themselves change the character of a species, but which when they are seized upon by personal selection may, by sifting and combination of the ids, be led on to still higher development.

If we consider further that the variation of a part must depend not only on the quality of the external stimulus but also upon the constitution, the reacting power of the part, we shall understand that similar nutritive variations may cause two different determinants to vary in different ways, and when we reflect that every nutritive change must extend from the point from which it started with diminishing strength in a particular direction, we have a further factor in the variation of determinants and one which influences even similar determinants differently.

Finally, if we remember that determinants of different constitution will also extract different ingredients from the nutritive stream and thus set up in it different kinds of chemical change, thus causing an altered supply of nutritive substances to flow to the neighbour determinants, we get some insight into a very complex and delicate but perfectly definite set of processes, into a mechanism which we can certainly only guess at, but whose results lie plainly before us in the spontaneous variations of the organism. We understand in principle the possibility of saltatory variation, as a more or less widespread, more or less marked disturbance of the species-type in this or that group of characters, and we may acknowledge that those 'kaleidoscopic variations' which Eimer supposed to be the sole basis of the transformation of species, and which have been brought to the foreground again quite recently by De Vries [1], are probably factors in transmutation operative within a limited sphere.

But we must think of all these struggles and mutual influencings as taking place on the smallest possible scale, so that it is only by long summation that they can produce any visible effect, and we must never forget the essential significance of the plurality of ids, for these 'spontaneous' variations may take place in a different and quite independent manner in each individual id. If this were not so no intervention of personal selection would be possible, natural selection would not exist, and the adaptation of the organism from the single

[1] See end of chap. xxxiii.

cell up to the whole would remain wholly unexplained. The whole crop of spontaneous germ-variations, whenever it ceases to be 'indifferent,' and becomes either 'good' or 'bad,' comes under the shears of personal selection and under its almost sovereign sway.

On the other hand, the sudden first appearance of a saltatory variation takes place quite independently of personal selection, depending on similar variations in a number of ids, which remain latent until they have by the process of reducing division which precedes amphimixis, chanced to attain a majority. In sudden bud-variations we may perhaps suppose that reducing division occurring in some still unverified abnormal manner is the reason why the germinal variation suddenly makes itself visible—a supposition previously suggested as the explanation of the reversion of these sports.

The rarity of bud-variation is thus explained, while the greater frequency of saltatory variations in plants propagated by seed may be accounted for by the regular occurrence of reducing division in sexual reproduction. But that the same or similar variations may occur in several, it may be in many, ids at the same time must depend upon similar general influences which affect the plant as a whole, as happens through cultivation, manuring, and so on. I shall return to this when discussing the influence of the environment.

In some quarters this whole conception of germinal selection has been characterized as the merest figment of imagination, condemned on this ground alone, that it is based on the differences in nutrition between such extremely minute quantities of substance as the chromosomes of nuclear substance within the germ-cell. The quantity of substance is certainly minute, but it needs nutriment none the less, and can we believe that the stream of nourishment for all the invisibly minute vital elements is exactly alike? It may be admitted that the nourishment outside the ids is usually abundant, although undoubtedly fluctuations occur in it also, but it certainly does not follow from this that every vital unit within the id is similarly disposed in relation to the nutritive supply, or has food in equal quantities at its command, or even that each has as much as it can ever need. To make an assertion like this seems to me much the same as if an inhabitant of the moon, looking at this earth through an excellent telescope and clearly descrying the city of Berlin with its thronging crowds and its railways bringing in the necessaries of life from every side, should conclude from this abundant provision that the greatest superfluity prevailed within the town, and that every one of its inhabitants had as much to live upon as he could possibly require.

We certainly ought not to conclude from the fact that we cannot see into the structure and requirements and methods of nutrition of a very minute mass of substance that its nutrition cannot be unequal, and that it cannot, by its inequalities, give rise to very material differences, especially when we are dealing with a substance to which we must attribute an extraordinarily complex organization built up of enormous numbers of extremely minute particles. That this complexity is undeniable is now admitted by many who formerly thought it possible to believe in the simple structure of the germ-substance. How complex not only the germ-substance but every cell of a higher organism is in its structure, and how far below the limits of visibility its differentiations and arrangements reach, is pressed upon our attention by the most recent histological researches, such as those we owe to Heidenhain, Boveri, and many others. The whole scientific world was amazed when it came to know the mysterious nuclear spindle in the seventies, and since then this has ,been quite thrown into the shade by the discovery of the centrosphere, the centrosome, and more recently even the centriole, and now we believe that these marvellous centres of force may, or must, possess their own dividing apparatus! In the face of discoveries like these no one is likely to be able to persist in recognizing as existing only what is disclosed or even hinted at by the most powerful lenses; no one can any longer doubt that far below the limit of visibility organization is still at the basis of life, and that it is dominated by orderly forces. To me, at least, it seems more cogent to argue from the phenomena of heredity and variation to an enormous mass of minute vital units crowded together in the narrow space of the id, than to argue from the calculated size of atoms and molecules to the number which we are justified in assuming to be present in an id. In my book on the germ-plasm I made a calculation of this kind, and I arrived at figures which seemed rather too small for the requirements of the germ-plasm theory. This has been regarded as a proof that I disregard the facts for the sake of my theory, but it should rather be asked whether the size of the atoms and molecules is a fact, and not rather the very questionable result of an uncertain method of calculation. Undoubtedly modern chemistry has established the *relative* weight-proportions of the atoms and molecules with admirable precision, but it can make only very uncertain statements in regard to the *absolute* size of the ultimate particles. It is therefore admissible to assume that these have a still greater degree of minuteness when the facts in another domain of science require this.

We *must* assume determinants, and consequently the germ-plasm must have room for these; the variations of species can only be explained through variations of the germ-plasm, for these alone give rise to hereditary variation. It is upon this foundation that my germinal selection is built up; whether I have in the main reached the truth the future will show: but that I have not exhausted this new domain, but only opened it up, I am very well aware.

LECTURE XXVII

THE BIOGENETIC LAW

Fritz Müller's ideas—Development of the Crustaceans—Of the Daphnidæ—Of Sacculina—Of parasitic Copepods—Larvæ of the higher Crustaceans—Change of phyletic stages in Ontogeny—Haeckel's *Fundamental Biogenetic Law*—Palingenesis and Cœnogenesis—Variation of phyletic forms by interpolation in a lengthened Ontogeny—Justification of deductions from Ontogeny to Phylogeny—Würtemberger's series of Ammonites—Phylogeny of the markings in the caterpillars of the Sphingidæ—Condensation of Phylogeny in Ontogeny—Example from the Crustaceans—Disappearance of useless parts—The variation of homologous parts, according to Emery—Germ-plasmic correlations—Harmony with the theory of determinants—Multiplication of the determinants in the course of the phylogeny.

WHAT I propose to discuss in this lecture should have been considered at an earlier stage, if we had pledged ourselves to adhere strictly to the historical sequence of scientific discovery, for the phenomena which we are about to deal with attained recognition shortly after the revival of the evolution idea, and indeed they formed the first important discovery which was made on the basis of the Darwinian Doctrine of Descent. I have introduced them at this stage because they have to do with phenomena of inheritance and modifications of these, the understanding of which—in as far as we can as yet speak of understanding at all—is only possible on the basis of a theory of inheritance. Therefore, in order to examine these phenomena and their causes, it was necessary first to submit a theory of heredity, as I have done in the germ-plasm theory. We have to treat of the connexion between the *development* of many-celled individuals and the *evolution* of the species, between germinal history and racial history, or, as we say with Haeckel, between ontogeny and phylogeny.

Long before Darwin's day individual naturalists had observed that certain stages in the development of the higher vertebrates, such as birds and mammals, showed a likeness to fishes, and they had spoken of a fish-like stage of the bird-embryo. The 'Natural Philosophers' of the beginning of the nineteenth century, Oken, Treviranus, Meckel, and others, had, on the basis of the transmutation theory of the time, gone much further, and had professed to recognize in the embryonic history of Man, for example, a repetition of the different animal stages, from polyp and worm up to insect and mollusc. But von Baer afterwards showed that such resemblances are never between different types, but only between representatives of the same general type, e. g. that of Vertebrata; and Johannes Müller maintained, from the standpoint of the old Creation theory, that an 'expression of the most general and simple plan of the Vertebrates' recurred in the development of higher Vertebrates, giving as an instance that, at a certain stage of embryogenesis, even in Man, gill-arches were laid down and were subsequently absorbed. But why this 'plan' should have been carried out where it was afterwards to be departed from remained quite unintelligible.

An answer to this question only became possible with the revival of the Theory of Descent, and the first to throw light in this direction was Fritz Müller, who, in his work *Für Darwin*, published in 1864, interpreted the developmental history of the individual, 'the ontogeny,' as a shortened and simplified repetition, a recapitulation, so to speak, of the racial history of the species, the 'phylogeny.' But at the same time he recognized quite clearly—what indeed was plain to all eyes—that the 'racial history' cannot be simply read out of the 'germinal history,' but that the phylogeny is often 'blurred,' on the one hand by the fusing and shortening of its stages, since development is always 'striking out' a more direct course from the egg to the perfect animal, while, on the other hand, it is frequently 'falsified' by the struggle for existence which the free-living larvæ have to maintain.

For the establishment of these views Fritz Müller relied chiefly upon larvæ, and in particular upon those of Crustaceans, and the facts, which were in part new and in part interpreted in a new manner, were so striking that it was impossible to deny their importance. In particular, he drew attention to the fact that in several of the lower orders of Crustaceans the most diverse species have a similar form when they leave the egg, all of them being small, unsegmented larvæ, with a frontal eye and a helmet-like upper lip, and with three pairs of appendages, the two posterior pairs being two-branched swimming-legs beset with bristles. In the size and form of the body, and especially of the chitinous carapace, these larvæ differ in the various systematic groups; thus, for instance, the larvæ of the Copepods are simply oval, while those of the Cirrhipedes are produced anteriorly into two horn-like processes, and so on, but in essentials they are all alike, and for a long time these larval forms had been distinguished by the special name of 'Nauplius' (Fig. 109).

The development of the perfect animal begins with the longitudinal growth of the Nauplius; the posterior end lengthens and becomes segmented, between the anterior portion and the tail more segments are interpolated, and on these new pairs of limbs may grow. The number of these segments and limbs varies according to the group to which the animal belongs. Thus the body of the perfect animal in the little Cyprids always consists of eight segments, seven of which bear a pair of limbs apiece; in the Branchiopods, on the other hand, the number of segments varies from twenty to sixty, with ten to over forty pairs of legs; in the Daphnids or water-fleas there are about ten segments, with seven to ten pairs of limbs, and in the Copepods about seventeen segments with eleven pairs of limbs. The difference between the orders depends not only upon the differences in the number of segments and limbs, but quite as much upon the form and development of the segments, and above all of the limbs, and in this

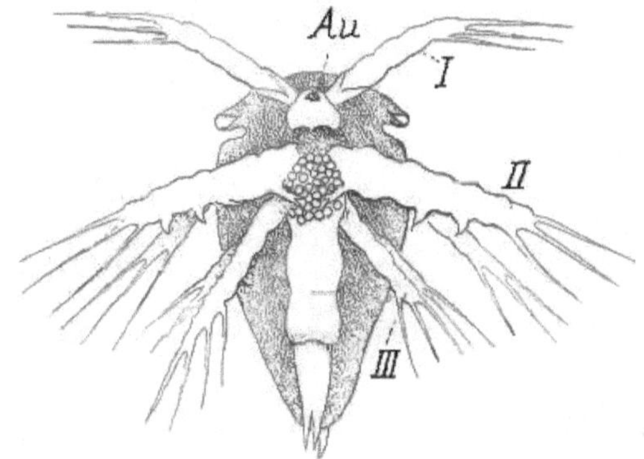

FIG. 108. Nauplius larva of one of the lower Crustaceans. After Fritz Müller. *Au*, the frontal eye; *I*, first pair of limbs, corresponding to the future antennæ; *II* and *III*, two biramose swimming appendages.

connexion it is worthy of note that the additional limbs which grow out usually appear at first as biramose swimming-legs, and are subsequently modified in form. Thus the pairs of jaws, three in number, which appear in the Copepods are developed from such swimming-legs, and so also is the second pair of antennæ in the Copepods and the jaws of the Branchiopods, Cirrhipedes, &c.

If then we have before us in the 'germinal history' (ontogeny) a fairly precise repetition of the 'racial history' (phylogeny), we may deduce from this that the primitive forms of the Crustacean race were animals which consisted of few segments, and that from these, in the course of the earth's history, the very diverse modern groups of Crustaceans have arisen, by the addition of new segments, and the adaptation of the limbs upon them, which were at first biramose

II. M

swimming-legs, to different kinds of functions, one becoming an antenna, another a jaw or a swimming-arm, a third, fourth, fifth, and so on, a jumping-leg, a copulatory organ, an egg-bearer, a gill-bearer, or a tail-fin.

That the development has in general followed those lines is made clear chiefly by the fact that the members of all these different orders of Crustaceans still arise from nauplius larvæ, even in those cases in which the perfect animal possesses a structure differing widely from the usual Crustacean form. *All* Crustaceans arise from the *nauplius*

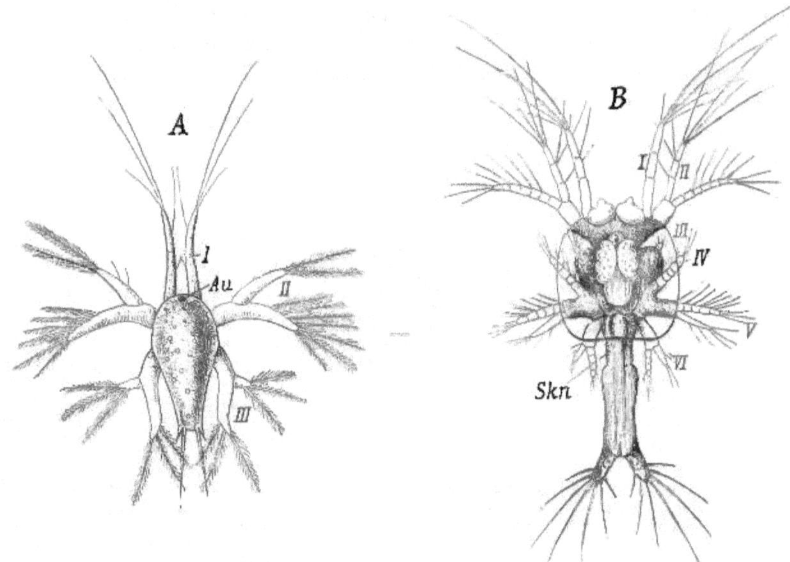

FIG. 109. Metamorphosis of one of the higher Crustacea, a Shrimp (*Peneus potimirim*), after Fritz Müller. *A*, the nauplius larva with the three pairs of appendages: *I*, the antennæ; *II* and *III*, the biramose swimming-feet. *Au*, the single eye. *B*, first Zoæa stage, with six pairs of appendages (*I-VI*). *Skn*, area where new segments are being formed.

form, even those of the higher orders, though they may not arise from a nauplius *larva*. But this very circumstance, that in most of the higher and many of the lower Crustaceans, the young animal, when it emerges from the egg, already possesses more numerous segments and limbs than a nauplius larva, again points to the connexion between phylogeny and ontogeny, for in these cases the nauplius stage *is gone through within the ovum*. The whole difference between this and the forms we considered first lies in the fact that, in the latter, the development is greatly shortened, condensed, as we might say, so that the nauplius stage forms a part of the *embryonic* development, and that new segments and limbs develop in the embryo nauplius within the egg, so that the young animal leaves the egg in a more advanced state, nearer to that of the perfect animal, to which it can, therefore, attain in a shorter time.

We should expect that this shortening of the larval period would be associated with a prolongation of embryogenesis, especially in those Crustaceans which possess a large number of segments and limbs, that is—in the higher forms—and in the main this is the case. But there are exceptions in two directions; in the first place there are some, even among the lower Crustaceans, which leave the egg not as a nauplius but in the perfect form of the adult, and secondly, there are, among the higher Crustaceans, certain species which emerge from the egg not in the more mature form but still in the primitive nauplius form. Fritz Müller was the first to furnish an example of this last case, a Brazilian shrimp, *Peneus potimirim.* Like the lowest Copepods or Branchiopods, this species, which belongs to the highest order of Crustaceans, goes through the whole long development, from the nauplius through a series of higher larval forms up to the perfect animal, and all *outside of the egg*, as an independent free-swimming larva (Fig. 109, *A–E*). This is in sharp contrast to its near relative, the freshwater craytish, which goes

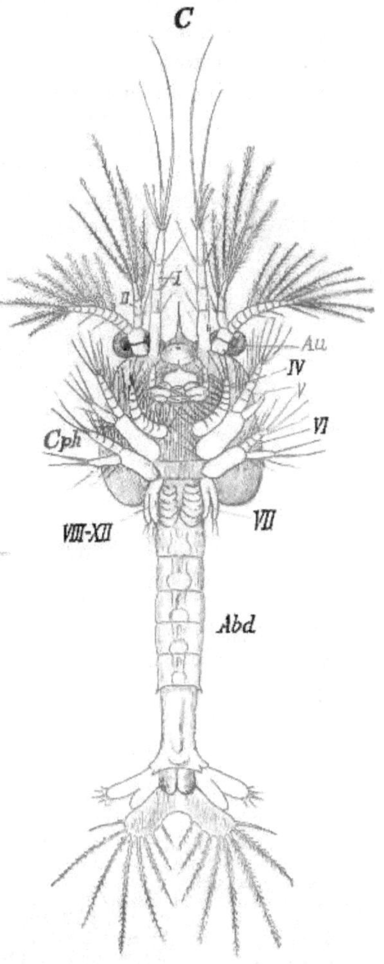

Fig. 109. *C*, second Zoœa stage. The thorax is now divided into cephalothorax (*Cph*) and abdomen (*Abd*); seven pairs of appendages are developed, and five more (*VIII–XII*) are beginning to appear. *Au*, paired eyes.

through this whole development within the egg, and emerges perfectly formed.

We see from this example that it is not some inward necessity which thus, in the higher and more complicated organism, contracts the ontogeny into the embryonic state, but that this depends upon external adaptive factors. Here again we have adaptation, mainly to

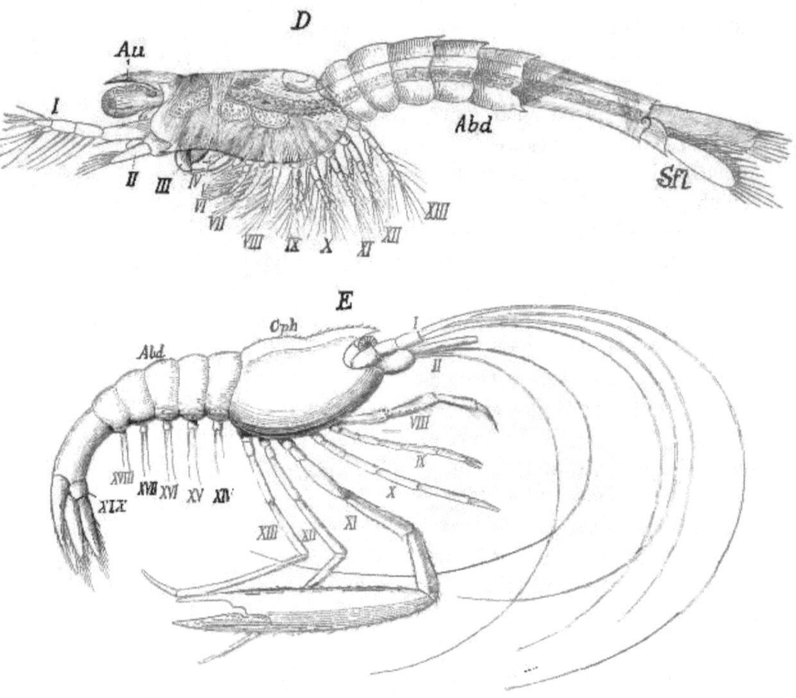

FIG. 109. *D*, Mysis-stage. Thirteen pairs of appendages are now formed: *I* and *II*, antennæ; *III*, mandibles; *IV* and *V*, maxillæ; *VI–XIII*, swimming appendages with one branch or with two. *Abd*, abdomen. *Sfl*, tail-fin. *E*, the fully-formed Shrimp, with thirteen pairs of appendages on the cephalothorax (*Oph*); *I* and *II*, the two pairs of antennæ; then follow the maxillæ and maxillipedes (*III–VIII*), the last of which is visible in the figure, and the five pairs of walking-legs (*IX–XIII*) of which the third bears a long chela. On the abdomen there are now six pairs of appendages (*XIV–XIX*).

the conditions of larval life. The elimination of the larvæ by enemies, for instance, will, other things being equal, be so much the more incisive the longer the larval development is protracted, but in that case the general ratio of elimination of the species, and the degree of fertility the species must possess in order to hold its own in the struggle for existence, will also play a part in determining the mode of development. For the higher the ratio of elimination the more eggs the female must produce, and the more eggs that have to be produced the smaller will be the quantity of nutritive material for the building up of the young embryo which each egg can be furnished with. I know of no records in regard to the eggs of that Brazilian shrimp in which embryonic development ends with the nauplius stage, but we shall certainly not be wrong in predicting that the eggs in this case will be very small and very numerous, in contrast to those of the freshwater crayfish, which are large and, as compared with others known to us, not very numerous.

It is a point of undeniable theoretical significance which the life-histories of these Crustaceans disclose, that embryogenesis is not condensed according to hidden internal laws when the structure increases in complexity, but that the condensation of the ontogenetic stages depends upon adaptation, and may be quite different in nearly related species. It shows us anew that all biological occurrences are dominated by the process of selection.

I have already mentioned that exceptions to the usual mode of development occur even among the lower Crustaceans, and I was thinking at the time of the Daphnids, which leave the egg as fully formed little animals, already equipped with all their segments and limbs. The nauplius stage is passed through in the egg, and it is an interesting indication that the ancestors of the modern species were in the way of moulting, that this embryo nauplius moults within the egg by forming a fine cuticle which is shed after a time. If it be asked why there should be direct development in the case of these small and not very complex water-fleas, while related species, the Branchiopods, which are much richer in segments and in limbs, should emerge from the egg in the form of a nauplius, and then pass through a longer larval period, we may answer that the reason probably lies in the fact that, in the former case, very few eggs are produced, sometimes only one, often two, seldom more than a dozen, that these eggs can thus be relatively well equipped with yolk, and that the formation of the little body which bears only from seven to nine pairs of limbs can be easily completed within this egg. Other things being equal, the direct development would always be an advantage, because reproduction can begin sooner in the young generation and the number of individuals will thus increase more rapidly. And this is of particular importance in the case of the water-fleas.

But if it be asked, further, why so few eggs are produced in this case, and whether these animals have no enemies, we must answer that, on the contrary, they are preyed upon and eaten in thousands by fishes and other freshwater animals, but that the drawback of the scanty production of eggs is counteracted on the one hand by their habit of reproducing parthenogenetically for the greater part of the year, and on the other hand by their habit of concealing the eggs in a special brood-chamber. This is the case not only in the summer eggs, to which nourishment is conveyed in the brood-chamber from the blood of the mother (Fig. 70), but also in the winter or 'lasting' eggs, which receive within the chamber a protecting covering (the shell or ephippium).

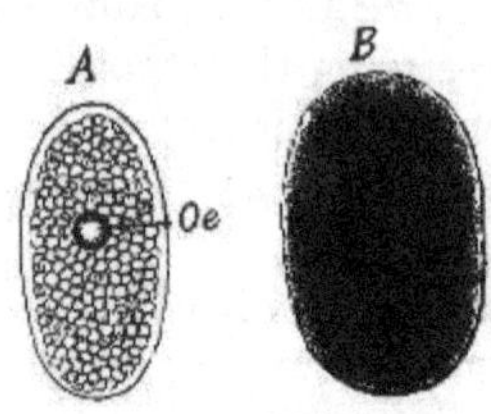

FIG. 70 (repeated). Daphnella. *A*, summer ovum, with an oil-globule (*Oe*). *B*, winter ovum.

In almost all the Daphnids the winter egg develops into a perfect animal just like that to which the summer egg gives rise, although it no longer receives any nourishment after it passes into the brood-chamber. But it receives a larger supply of yolk on this account, so that the nutritive provision within the egg is sufficient to develop the perfect animal. There is only one exception to this, and it is of special theoretical interest, because it shows more plainly than any other fact that the greater or less degree of condensation in the ontogeny depends upon the combined effect of the external conditions of life.

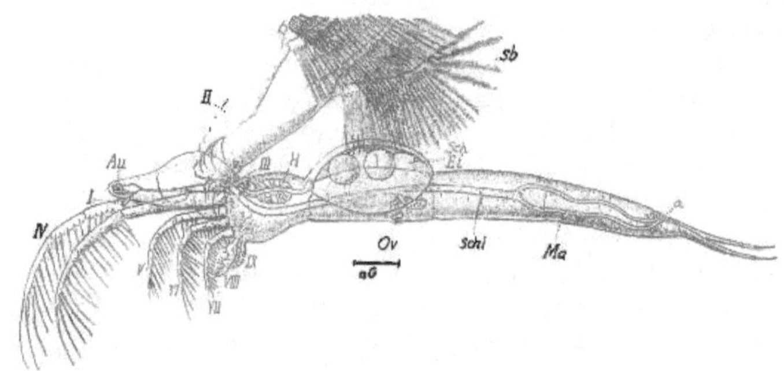

FIG. 110. The largest of the Daphnids (*Leptodora hyalina*), with summer ova (*Ei*) beneath the shell (*Sch*). *I–IX*, the appendages. *II*, the oars (second antennæ) which always remain biramose in Daphnids. *sb*, setæ. *ov*, ovaries. *Schl*, œsophagus. *Ma*, stomach. *a*, anus. *H*, heart. *Au*, eye. *nG*, natural size.

The largest of the Daphnidæ, *Leptodora hyalina*, a beautifully transparent inhabitant of our lakes, which measures about a centimetre in length (Fig. 110), also emerges from the summer egg as a perfect animal, but from the winter egg, which floats freely in the water and has only a small provision of yolk, it emerges as a nauplius, which then undergoes larval metamorphosis before it becomes a perfect animal (Fig. 111).

Fritz Müller concluded from the repetition of the nauplius form in all orders of Crustaceans that the primitive form of the Crustacean must have been a nauplius, and that from it all the modern Crustaceans must have evolved phyletically by the addition of segments varying in number and differentiation. Now, however, it is doubted whether there ever were nauplioid types capable of reproduction. But even if the nauplii only *represent what have been the larval* forms from very early times, they are equally important in illustrating the relations between ontogeny and phylogeny; they at any rate represent the primitive pre-cambrian larval form from which all modern Crustaceans are derived. This is borne out not only by the facts to which we have already referred, but also by those Crustacean-groups which have diverged far from the usual Crustacean habit and type.

Thus the sessile Cirrhipedes, with their mollusc-like shells, their soft, unsegmented bodies, degenerate heads, and their twelve vibratile food-wafting limbs, emerge from the egg as nauplius larvæ. But the remarkable parasites on the shore-crabs and the hermit-crab deviate much further from the type of the rest of the Crustaceans, for they hang like a sac or formless sausage-like soft mass to the abdomen of their host, growing into it by fine, pale, root-like threads, through which they suck up the blood of their hosts (Fig. 112, *C. Sacc.*). They possess neither head, nor thorax, nor abdomen, not even an indication of segmentation, no limbs of any kind, neither antennæ, nor mouth parts, nor swimming-legs. Nevertheless they are Crustaceans; indeed, we can say with certainty that they belong to the order of Cirrhipedes, for they leave the egg in the form of a nauplius larva (*A*), with 'horns' on their carapace which no other forms except themselves and the Cirrhipedes possess. That they are of the same stock as these is also proved by their further development, for the nauplius grows first, just as in the case of the Cirrhipedes proper, into a 'Cypris-like larva' (*B*), so called because it bears a certain resemblance to the Ostracods of the genus Cypris, and only from this point do their paths of development diverge. The Cypris-like larva of the true Cirrhipedes settles down somewhere, attached by its antennæ; it grows, and its body becomes that of the perfect Cirrhipede; but the Cypris-like

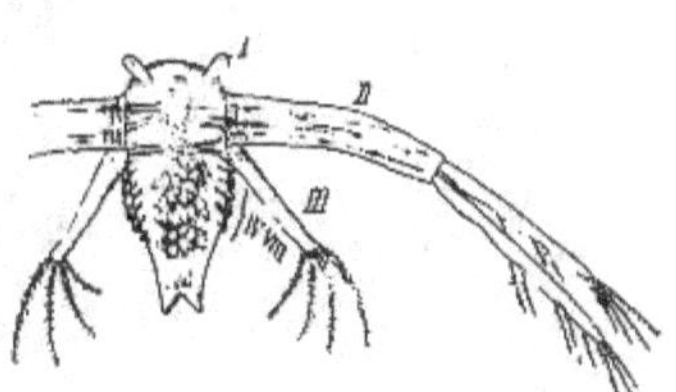

FIG. 111. Nauplius larva from the winter egg of *Leptodora hyalina*; after Sars.

larva of the Sacculinæ bores its way into the inside of a crab or hermit-crab, at the same time losing its limbs, segmentation, and its chitinous covering; and within the body of its host it is transformed into the sac-like organism we have already described. After a time it emerges again on the surface, and remains attached to the abdomen of its host (Fig. 112, *C. Sacc.*), drawing its nourishment from the blood which it sucks up by means of its numerous delicate roots (*W*, *W*).

From all this we may conclude that certain Cirrhipedes in times long past adopted a parasitic habit in the Cypris-larva stage, and that they gradually underwent adaptations to this mode of life, and that these went further and further, until the animal was transformed

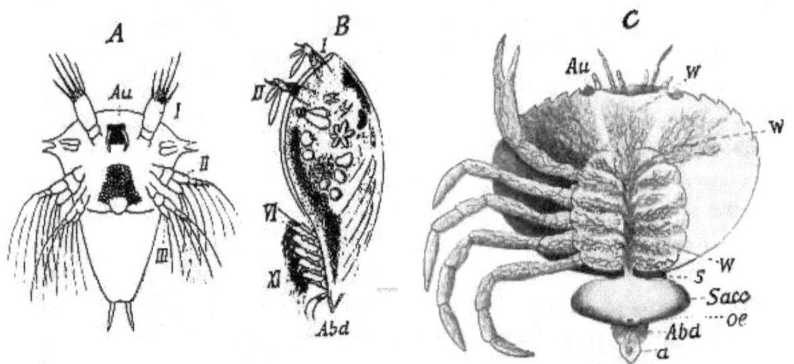

FIG. 112. Development of the parasitic Crustacean *Sacculina carcini*, after Delage. *A*, Nauplius stage. *Au*, eye. *I*, *II*, *III*, the three pairs of appendages. *B*, Cypris-stage. *VI–XI*, the swimming appendages. *C*, mature animal (*Sacc*), attached to its host, the shore-crab (*Carcinus mænas*), with a feltwork of fine root-processes enveloping the crab's viscera. *s*, stalk. *Sacc*, body of the parasite. *oe*, aperture of the brood-cavity. *Abd*, abdomen of the crab with the anus (*a*)

into the singular creature which we now see in the sexually mature form

The same is the case with the numerous fish-parasites of the order Copepoda. They all leave the egg as nauplius larvæ, however greatly they may be modified later on by adaptation to a parasitic habit, and in them we can still observe, in the fully developed animals, a whole series of grades of transformation. Thus many genera, like *Ergasilus*, are distinguished from the free-swimming Copepods only by the modification of their jaws into piercing and sucking organs, and of a single pair of antennæ into hooks, by means of which they attach themselves to the fish on which they feed. In other genera the degeneration and modification go further; the antennæ, the eye, and the appendages degenerate more or less, and very remarkable attaching organs are sometimes developed, in the form of hooks or of knobbed pincers, or of actual suckers. In several types the degeneration and modification go so far that the segmentation of the body disappears, and the animal looks more like an intestinal worm than like a Crustacean (*Lernæocera* and others). In all these forms adapted to a parasitic mode of life it is always only the mature animal which has been transformed in this manner, for previously it has gone through a series of stages which are quite similar to those of the free-swimming Copepods, beginning with the nauplius, and ending with the so-called Cyclops stage, that is, a larval form which possesses antennæ, eyes, and swimming-legs similar to our freshwater Copepods of the genus *Cyclops*.

Here again we see in the ontogeny the repetition of a series of phyletic stages before the mature form is assumed. Why these stages should have persisted it is easy enough to understand, for how could an animal which emerged from the egg as a worm-shaped *Lernæocera* find a fresh fish which would serve it as host? Yet these parasites could not possibly go on preying upon the same fish generation after generation. To secure the existence of the species it was therefore indispensable that the faculty of swimming should be retained at least in the young stages; in other words, that the free-swimming ancestral stages should be preserved in the ontogeny. In all these cases it is therefore beyond doubt that the germinal history recapitulates a series of stages comparable to those of the racial history, although not quite unchanged but adapted to the modern conditions of life, for instance in having shorter antennæ, smaller eyes, and with four instead of the usual five swimming-legs. The search for a host does not seem to last long, for fishes are usually found in large numbers together, and thus the young parasitic Crustacean does not require to make a long journey before it finds a refuge.

It is noteworthy that the males of parasitic Crustaceans are not only much smaller than the females (Fig. 113), but that they are also much less modified, and resemble the ancestral free-swimming Copepods to a much greater degree. They usually possess small but well-developed swimming-legs, and by means of these they seek out the female, dying after fertilization is accomplished. They are thus not sessile parasites at all, and have therefore to go through the stages of the free-swimming Copepods much more completely than the females, whose task is to accumulate within themselves from the blood of the fish as much material as possible for the forming of the eggs, and to produce the largest possible number of these. These therefore greatly surpass the free-swimming Copepods in fertility, as is evidenced by the enormous egg-sacs they bear at the posterior end of the body (Fig. 113, *ei*).

Even among the higher Crustaceans, the so-called Malacostraca, the germinal history not infrequently exhibits more or less of the racial history in distinct recapitulation.

It is true however, as we have already shown, that there are only a few of the higher Crustaceans which emerge from the egg in the form of a nauplius; in most of them this stage has been shunted backwards in the ontogeny, and most of the crabs and hermit-crabs leave the egg in a higher larval form, that of the so-called Zoæa (Fig. 114). This term is applied to a larva which already exhibits two main divisions of the body, a head and thorax portion (cephalothorax, *Cph*) and an abdomen (*abd*). The cephalothorax is frequently equipped with remarkable long spines (*st*), and it always bears from five to eight pairs of limbs, anteriorly the antennæ (*I* and *II*), then the mandibles (*III*), further back swimming-legs (*IV*, *V*), and behind these can be recognized the primordia of the other legs (*VI-XIII*), which will grow freely out later on. Large facetted and stalked eyes (*Au*) are borne on the head. This Zoæa form is not now found as a mature Crustacean form, so we cannot maintain with any confidence that it lived as a mature animal at an earlier period of the earth's history, but a second still more complex larval form of the higher Crustaceans is preserved for us in a group of marine Crustaceans, the Schizopods. These are Crustaceans which, though small, approach in external appearance our freshwater crayfish, only they have, instead of the ten walking-legs, biramose swimming-legs, by means of which they move freely in the water. The number of these branched legs is even greater than ten, there are sixteen of them (Fig. 109 *D*, p. 164, *VI-XIII*). In the aquaria of the Zoological Station at Naples one may often see these dainty little creatures swimming about in large companies. Here they are of interest to us chiefly because their structure occurs in the ontogeny of the highest Crustaceans, the Decapods; that is,

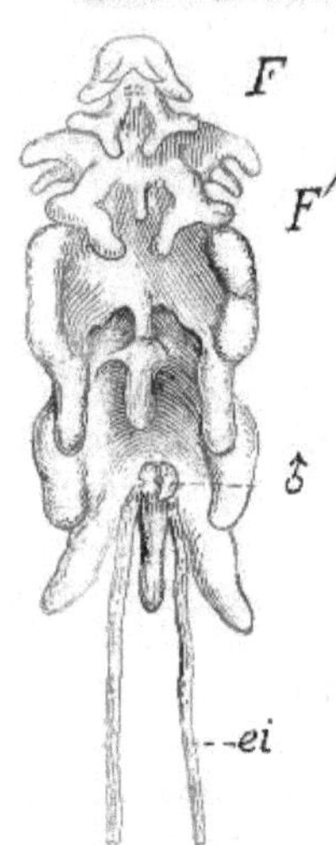

FIG. 113. The two sexes of the parasitic Crustacean *Chondracanthus gibbosus*, enlarged about six times; after Claus. The main figure is that of the female, whose body bears quaint blunt processes. At its genital aperture (♂) a dwarf male is situated. *F* and *F′*, the two pairs of appendages. *ei*, the long egg-sacs, portions of which have been cut off in the figure.

the phyletic stage represented by the Schizopods appears as an ontogenetic stage, just before the final metamorphosis of the larva to the perfect animal. This is the case in most of the marine Decapods, in those forms which do not go through the whole course of their development within the egg, but emerge as Zoea larvæ, or even, as in *Peneus potimirim*, as nauplii. In the last-named species (Fig. 109) the ontogeny contains at least three stages which must have lived, perhaps not as mature forms, but as primitive larval forms, for unthinkable ages—the stage of the nauplus (Fig. 109 *A*), that of the Zoea (Fig. 109 *B* and *C*), and that of the Schizopod (Fig. 109, *D*); from this last the fully developed Decapod Crustacean arises (Fig. 109, *E*).

We are, therefore, justified in saying that here the racial evolution is recapitulated in the individual development, although condensed and shortened in proportion as more numerous stages of the phyletic development are gone through within the egg, for there the different stages can succeed each other more rapidly and directly than in a metamorphosis of the free-swimming larvæ, since these must procure their own material for their further growth and their metamorphosis, while the yolk of the egg supplies a store of material which is sufficient for the production of a whole series of successive stages.

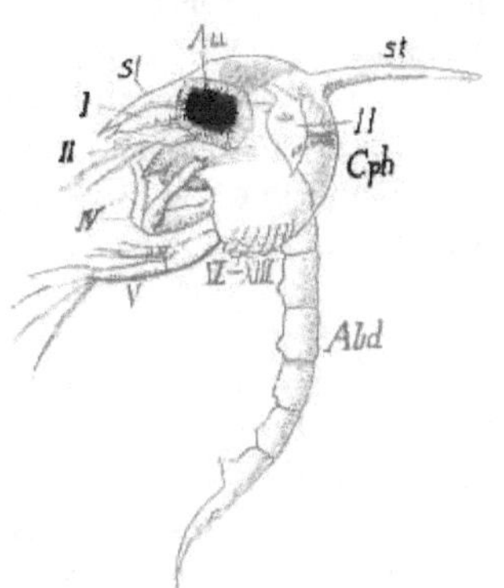

FIG. 114. Zoea-larva of a Crab, after R. Hertwig. *I–V*, the already functional anterior appendages—antennæ, mandibles, and swimming-legs. *VI–XIII*, rudiments of the posterior appendages of the cephalothorax (*Cph*). *Abd*, the abdomen. *st*, spine of the carapace. *Au*, eye. *H*, heart.

For this reason it inevitably resulted that the sharply defined characters of the phyletic stages were more and more lost as soon as they were transferred from larval stages to stages in embryogenesis. For, in the first place, these sharply defined characters, such as the spines of the Zoea larva, or the swimming bristles of the 'oars,' or the shape of thorax or abdomen characteristic of certain species, are adapted to a free life, and would be valueless in an embryonic stage; and secondly, in the transference of the free larval stages to embryonic development the greatest possible condensation and abbreviation of the stages must have been striven for, which could only come about by a continual mutual adaptation of the embryonic parts to one another, involving the suppression of everything superfluous. Otherwise the transference of the free stages to the embryogenesis would have brought no advantage, but rather a most prejudicial protracting of the development.

We must not, therefore, expect to find the stages of the phylogeny occurring unaltered in every ontogeny in the way we have found the nauplius, Zoœa, or Mysis stages in the larval development of the Decapods. I have noticed already that in the water-fleas (Daphnidæ) and other Crustaceans without metamorphosis the nauplius stage is still passed through, but within the egg, and as an embryonic stage, and this is quite true, but nevertheless it would hardly do to liberate a nauplius like this from its shell and place it in the water, for the influence of the water upon the delicate embryonic cells of its body would soon cause it to swell, and would destroy it utterly. And, even apart from this, it has no hard and resistant chitinous covering, no fully-developed appendages, but only the stump-like blunt beginnings of these without swimming-bristles and without muscles capable of function, so that it could not even move. Nevertheless it is a nauplius with all its typical distinctive characters, only it is not a perfect nauplius capable of life, but rather a 'schema' of one, which must be retained in the embryogenesis that it may give rise to the later stages.

Shall we therefore say that the statement that phylogeny repeats itself in ontogeny is false, that the nauplius stage within the embryo is not a true nauplius at all? That would be pushing precision beyond reasonable limits, and would obscure our insight into the causal connexion between phylogeny and ontogeny, which, as we have seen, undoubtedly exists.

A few years after the appearance of Fritz Müller's work *Für Darwin*, Haeckel elaborated Müller's idea, and applied it in a much more comprehensive manner. He formulated it under the name of 'the fundamental biogenetic law,' and then he used this 'law' to deduce from the ontogeny of animals, and more particularly of Man, the paths of evolution along which our modern species have passed in the course of the earth's history. In doing so the greatest caution was necessary, since ontogeny is not an actual unaltered recapitulation of the phylogeny, but an 'abridged' and in most cases—in my own belief, in all cases—*a greatly modified recapitulation*. Therefore we cannot simply accept each ontogenetic stage as an ancestral stage, but must take into consideration all the facts supplied to us by other departments of biological inquiry which afford help in the decision of such questions, especially those brought to light by comparative morphology and by the whole range of comparative embryology.

Haeckel was quite well aware of this difficulty, and repeatedly emphasized it by laying stress on the fact that a 'blurring' of the phyletic stages of development had arisen through the abridgement of the phylogeny in the ontogeny, and a 'falsification' of it through the secondary adaptation of individual ontogenetic stages to new conditions of life. He therefore distinguished between 'Palingenesis, that is, simple though abridged repetition of the ancestral history, and 'Cœnogenesis,' that is, modification of the racial history by later adaptation of a few or many stages to new conditions of life. As an example of cœnogenetic modification, I may cite the pupæ of butterflies. Since these can neither feed nor move from one spot, they can at no time have been mature forms, and cannot, therefore, represent independent ancestors of our modern Lepidoptera; they have originated through the constantly increasing difference between the structure of the caterpillar and that of the moth or butterfly. Originally, that is, among the oldest flying insects, the mature animal could be gradually prepared within the larva as it grew, so that finally nothing was necessary but a single moult to set free the wings, which had in the meantime been growing underneath the skin, and to allow the perfect insect to emerge, complete in all its parts. This is the case even now with the grasshoppers and crickets. In these forms the larval mode of life differs very little, if at all, from that of the perfect insect, and the main difference between the two is the absence of wings in the larva. But when the perfect insect adapted itself to conditions of life quite different from the larval conditions, as was the case with the nectar-sucking bees and butterflies adapted entirely for flight, while the larvæ were still adapted exclusively to an abundant diet of leaves and other parts of plants, and to a very inactive life upon plants, the two stages of development ultimately diverged so widely in structure that the transition from one to the other could no longer be made at a single moulting, and a period of rest had to be interpolated, in order that the transformation of the body could take place. In this way arose the stage of the resting and fasting pupa, a 'cœnogenetic' modification of the last larval stage, *not a recapitulation of an ancestral form*, but a stage which has been interpolated, or better, has 'interpolated itself' into the ontogeny on account of the widely different adaptations of the early and the final stages.

This is a perfectly clear idea, and Haeckel's distinction between palingenesis and cœnogenesis is undoubtedly justified.

But it is quite a different matter to be able to decide whether a particular stage or organ has arisen palingenetically or cœnogenetically with the same certainty as in the case of the insect-pupa, or even with any degree of probability, and we must admit that in very many cases, perhaps even in most cases, it is impossible. This is so chiefly because pure palingenesis is hardly likely to occur now; the ancestral stages were bound to be modified in any case if they were to be compressed into the ever-shortening ontogeny of later descendants, and particularly so if they were to be shunted back into embryogenesis. In the latter case they would not only be materially shortened, and, as I have already shown, modified by the mutual adaptations of the different developing parts, but time-displacements of embryonic parts and organs would be necessary, as has been very clearly proved by the excellent recent investigations, which we owe in particular to Oppel, Mehnert, and Keibel. A shunting forward or backward of the individual organs takes place—conditioned apparently by the decreasing or increasing importance of the organ in the finished state; for in the course of the phylogeny everything may vary, and not only may a new, somewhat modified, and often more complex stage be added on at the end of the ontogeny, but each one of the preceding stages may vary independently, whenever this is required by a change in its relations to the other stages or organs. Adaptation is effected at every stage and for every part by the process of selection, for all parts of the same rank are ceaselessly struggling with one another, from the lowest vital units, the biophors, up to the highest, the persons. If we reflect that, in the course of the phylogeny of every series of species, a number of organs always become superfluous and begin to disappear in consequence, we can understand what great changes must take place gradually as such a series of phyletic stages is compressed into the ontogeny, for all organs which are no longer used are gradually shifted further and further back in the ontogeny till ultimately they disappear from it altogether. But, while the primary constituents of these 'vestiges' play their part in ontogeny for a shorter and shorter time, new acquisitions are being more and more highly developed, and thus, in the course of the phylogeny, numerous time-displacements of the parts and organs in ontogeny must result, so that ultimately it is impossible to compare a particular stage in the embryogenesis of a species with a particular ancestral form. *Only the stages of individual organs can be thus compared and parallelized.*

But we must not on that account 'empty out the child with the bath,' and conclude that there is no such thing as a 'biogenetic law' or recapitulation of the phylogeny in the ontogeny. Not only is there such a recapitulation, but—as F. Müller and Haeckel have already said—ontogeny is nothing but a recapitulation of the phylogeny, only with innumerable subtractions and interpolations, additions and displacements of the organ-stages both in time and place. It would be a great mistake to conclude from the fact of these manifold alterations that the whole proposition of the recapitulation of the phylogeny in the ontogeny is erroneous, or at least valueless. If its only use were to enable us to read the racial history of a species out of its germinal history, it is intelligible enough that we might be led to give it up in despair, but I think that the main thing is to get some insight into the history of the ontogeny, and there can be no doubt that this can have been built up on no other foundation than upon the racial history. What is new could only have arisen from what was already in existence, and everything in ontogeny, not only the palingenetic stages which still represent in some measure the facies of fully-formed ancestral stages, but also the cœnogenetic stages, like the pupa-stage we have already discussed, have arisen historically, nothing *de novo*, but all in connexion with what was already present. But what was first present was in all cases the stages of the ancestral forms.

It is undoubtedly of the greatest value to be able to penetrate more and more deeply into embryonic development, and to discover more precisely the changes that have taken place throughout its course in the originally existing material of ancestral forms. But it must not be forgotten that, all transformations notwithstanding, so much of the racial history is still very plainly indicated in the germinal history, that this must always remain for us a most important source from which to draw conclusions in regard to the phyletic development of any animal group. I admit that these conclusions have sometimes been drawn with too great confidence, but even if we cannot regard as well founded Haeckel's view that in the ontogeny of Man there are fourteen different ancestral stages recognizable, a protist stage, a gastræa stage, a prochordate, an acranial, a cyclostome, a fish-stage, and so on, we must recognize that the unicellular stage of ontogeny, with which even now the development of every human being begins, undoubtedly repeats the facies of an ancestor, although greatly altered; for we must be descended from unicellular organisms. The essential part of this ancestral stage is thus preserved in the ontogeny, and only what is special and in some measure due to chance, that is, to adaptation to special conditions of existence, has been modified.

It has been supposed that the proposition that phylogeny is recapitulated in the ontogeny is disproved, because the ontogenetic stage must always contain within it the primordia of the later stages which have been added since the corresponding phylogenetic stage. It is certain that the egg-cell or the sperm-cell of Man contains, though in a form not recognizable by us, all the determinants of the perfect human body, but this neither affects its nature as a cell nor its particular form as ovum or spermatozoon. It is essentials that are important in this comparison, not accessories. Neither can I agree with Hensen's argument when he says that the 'recapitulation-idea' is erroneous, because the actual course of ontogeny is the 'best and only possible one,' which, apart from previous history altogether, must of necessity be followed. Certainly the actual course is the best, and under the given circumstances the only possible one, but that does not exclude recapitulation, on the contrary it implies it, for ontogeny could at no time have arisen from a *tabula rasa*, but only from what was historically existent.

I do not propose to examine each of Haeckel's ancestral stages in Man's pedigree, or to estimate the degree of probability with which they may be deduced from the ontogeny; but that Man's ancestry does, in a general way, include such a series of phyletic stages may be admitted, even if we grant that many of these stages are now no longer represented in the ontogeny as stages of the developing organism as a whole, but only by stages of individual organs or group of organs. Thus it may be disputed whether there is still a fish-stage in human development, but it cannot be disputed that the rudiments of 'gill-arches' and 'gill-clefts,' which are peculiar to one stage of human ontogeny, give us every ground for concluding that we possessed fish-like ancestors.

As we now know that the history of a given mode of embryogenesis has involved numerous time-displacements of the organ-rudiments, we must attach all the more weight to the developmental history of the individual parts and characters, in which the phylogeny can often be read more clearly than in the stages of the organism as a whole, and we can probably find out important laws in this way.

As far back as 1873 Würtemberger investigated the fossil ammonites with special reference to this point. He was concerned even more at that time with finding proofs of the theory of descent in general, and this was the first case in which any one succeeded in demonstrating phyletic transformation-series of species, deposited one above the other in a corresponding series of geological strata, and connected by transition forms lying between these. In studying this interesting material, of which many examples were at his disposal, Würtemberger proved that the variations which had taken place in the spirally coiled shell in the course of ages appeared first on the last whorl, and then subsequently extended to the one before this, and thence to the still younger whorls of the shell. Meanwhile the last whorl not infrequently exhibited another new character. Thus, for instance, protuberances on the shell were shifted in the course of the phylogeny from the last convolution to the second last, and later to the third last, and so on, while at the same time the last convolution showed the protuberance changed into spines. In other words, the new phyletic acquirements first appeared in the mature animal (in the last-formed whorl or chamber of the shell), but were subsequently shifted back in the ontogeny to younger stages in proportion as new transformations of the mature animal appeared. Thus there was, so to speak, a retraction of the phyletic acquisitions of the mature animal deeper and deeper into the germinal history of the species.

About the same time—in the seventies—I obtained similar results from living species when I was attempting to work out the ontogeny of the markings on the external skin of the caterpillars of certain butterflies, and I should like to submit a short account of these.

In one of the early lectures we discussed the protective and defensive colours of caterpillars in general, and those of caterpillars of the Sphingidæ in particular. I showed that those naked caterpillars which live on plants among the grass, or on the grass itself, are often not only green, like fresh grass-stalks, or yellowish-grey, like dry ones, but all the larger forms also exhibit light, usually white, longitudinal lines, which, by mimicking the sharp light reflections on the grass-stems, heighten the protective resemblance.

We also spoke of the light transverse stripes, often marked with pink or lilac-blue, of many of the large green caterpillars which live on trees and bushes, and whose likeness to the leaves is heightened by this imitation of the lateral veining of a leaf; and finally we mentioned the warning coloration indicative of unpleasant or nauseous taste, among which must be classed not only vivid contrasts of colour, but also specially conspicuous elements of colour such as light ring-spots upon a dark ground. These different colour schemes which protect the caterpillars from their enemies are usually only to be found in the adolescent caterpillar, not in the very small one which has just emerged from the egg, and the development of the markings in the individual life clearly shows that the phylogeny of the markings is more or less obviously contained in the ontogeny.

There are three different schemes of marking which occur in the caterpillars of hawk-moths or Sphingidæ—longitudinal striping, obliquely transverse striping, and spots. Longitudinal striping pure and unmixed is now found only in a few species, for instance in the caterpillar of the *Macroglossa stellatarum* (Fig. 115), in which a white longitudinal line, beginning at the tip of the tail, runs up each side of the body to the head as a 'subdorsal stripe' (*sbd*). These, with other two similar stripes, effectively secure the fairly large caterpillar from discovery when it is among grass and herbs.

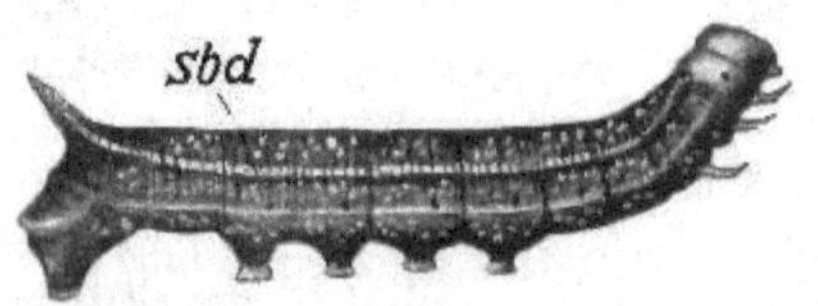

FIG. 115. Caterpillar of the Humming bird Hawk-moth, *Macroglossa stellatarum*. *sbd*, the subdorsal line.

Transverse striping occurs as the sole mode of marking in species which live on bushes and trees whose leaves have strong lateral veins, such as willows, poplars, oaks, privet, syringa, and so on, and these markings associated with the leaf-green of their colouring protect them most effectively from discovery.

The third scheme of marking, namely by spots, occurs in various forms in species of the genera *Deilephila* and *Chærocampa*, and it varies in its biological significance; in many species the spots serve as a warning colour, by making the caterpillar conspicuous and easily seen from a distance (*Deilephila galii*, Fig. 117); in others they imitate the eyes of a larger animal, and have a 'terrifying' effect, as we have already said (Fig. 4); in still other and rarer cases they heighten the resemblance of the caterpillar to its food-plant by mimicking parts of it, as, for instance, the red berries of the buckthorn (*Deilephila hippophaës*, Fig. 8, *r*).

FIG. 3 (repeated). Full-grown caterpillar of the Eyed Hawk-moth, *Smerinthus ocellatus*. *sb*, the subdorsal stripe.

Thus all three modes of marking possess a biological value, and protect the soft and easily wounded animal in some way, and, in the case of at least two of them, it is clear that they must have arisen at the very end of the caterpillar's development, since they can only be effective as the animal is approaching full size, and would be valueless in the very young caterpillar. The transverse striping only makes the caterpillar like a leaf when the stripes bear about the same relation to each other as those on the leaf, and eye-spots can only scare away lizards and birds when they are of a certain size. Only longitudinal striping is effective as a protection in the case of young caterpillars, supposing, that is, that they live in or on the grass (Fig. 116).

Let us consider the ontogeny of these different forms of markings, beginning with the eye-spots. It appears that these develop from a sub-dorsal stripe, which appears in the young caterpillar in the second stage of its life, and from it, in the course of the further development, two pairs of large eye-spots are formed. Even in the

Fig. 4 (repeated). Full-grown caterpillar of the Elephant Hawk-moth, *Chærocampa elpenor*, in its 'terrifying attitude.'

young caterpillar, scarcely one centimetre in length (Fig. 116), it can be observed that the fine, white sub-dorsal line takes a slight curve upwards on the fourth and fifth segments (*C*), and on the lower edge of these curves a black line is laid down (*D*). This is then continued to the upper side (*E*), and encloses the piece of the sub-dorsal stripe (*F* and *G*), and thus there arises a white-centred, black-framed spot which only requires to grow and to differentiate a blackish shadow-

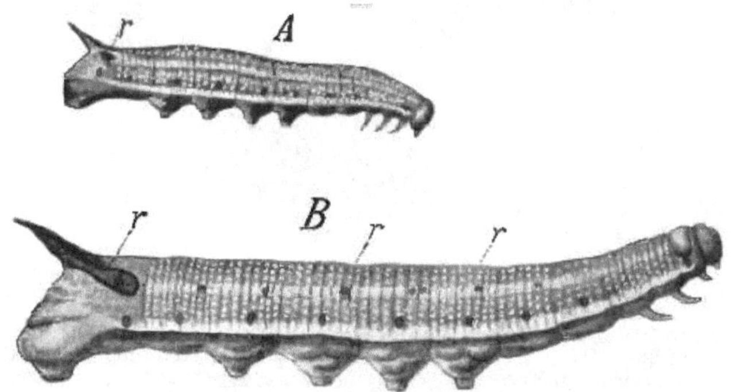

Fig. 8 (repeated). Caterpillars of the Buckthorn Hawk-moth, *Deilephila hippophaës*. *A*, Stage III. *B*, Stage V. *r*, annular spots.

centre, the pupil (*G*), to give the impression of a large eye. This occurs as the caterpillar goes on growing, and after the fourth moult or ecdysis the eyes have already some effect, as the animal is six centimetres in length, but they become even more perfect in the fifth and last stage. During this development of the eye-spot the sub-dorsal stripe disappears completely from the greater part of the caterpillar, persisting only on the first three segments (Fig. 116, *B-F*).

N 2

When we consider that this stripe in the little caterpillar a centimetre long, which lives on the large leaves of the vine, or on the obliquely ribbed willow-herb (*Epilobium hirsutum*), is quite without protective value, its occurrence at that stage can only be regarded as a phyletic reminiscence due to the fact that the ancestors of these species of *Chærocampa* possessed longitudinal stripes in the adult state, probably because at that time they lived on plants among the grass, and that, later, when the species changed their

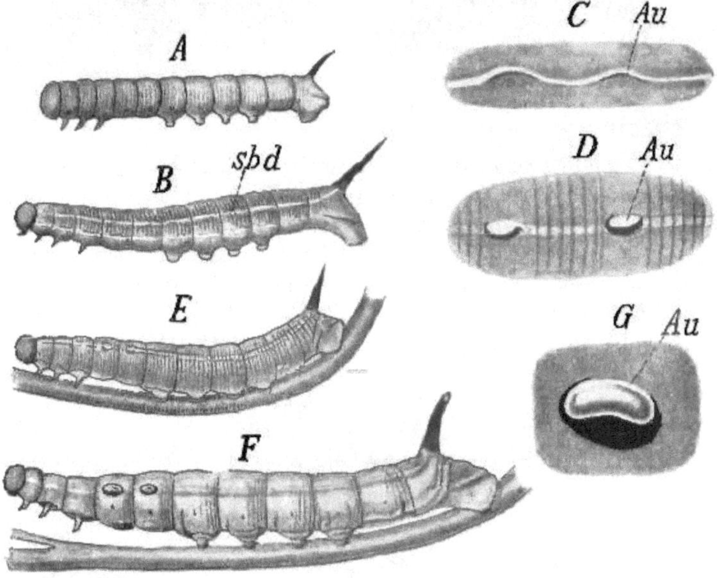

FIG. 116. Development of the eye-spots in the caterpillar of the Elephant Hawk-moth (*Chærocampa elpenor*). *A*, Stage I, still without marking, simply green. *B*, Stage II, with sub-dorsal stripe (*sbd*). *C*, sub-dorsal line somewhat later, with the first hint of the eye-spot (*Au*) on segments 4 and 5. *D*, eye-spots in Stage III of the caterpillar, somewhat further developed than in *E*, the third stage. *F*, Stage IV. *G*, the anterior eye-spot at the same stage.

habitat to plants with broad leaves which had arisen in the meantime, eye-spots were developed in addition to the green or brown protective colouring which they retained. Thus the modern development of these spots mirrors their phyletic evolution very faithfully; on the two segments there were formed, from pieces of the sub-dorsal line, first white spots ringed round with black, then unmistakeable eyes with pupils (*C*, *D*, *G*). This transformation can only have begun in the fairly well-grown caterpillar, because it was only of any use to it; but later on it was shunted further back in the ontogeny, from the sixth and fifth to the fourth and third caterpillar stage, not in its complete development, but in more and more incipient form; and nowadays the first traces of eyes, as we have already seen, are visible in the course of the second stage. The marking of the more remote ancestors, the longitudinal striping, is now lost in proportion as the eye-spots develop, perhaps because the former would take away from the full effect of the latter. The longitudinal stripes are still quite plainly visible on the first three segments, but these segments are drawn in and are scarcely noticeable when the caterpillar assumes a defiant attitude (Fig. 4).

In the case of marking with ring-spots, which is found especially in species of the genus *Deilephila*, the ontogeny discloses that it has developed phyletically from the sub-dorsal stripe; in the young stage of this caterpillar also, the sole marking is longitudinal striping; in *Deilephila zygophylli*, from the steppes of Southern Russia, this persists apparently through all the stages, but in the others it disappears almost completely in the later stages, but only on the segments on which the spot-marking has developed from it. This happens in a manner similar to that in which the eye-spot in *Chærocampa* arises, a piece of the white sub-dorsal stripe is enclosed above and below by a semicircle of black, and later these semicircles unite, and cut off the portion of the sub-dorsal line, and form a black spot with a light centre within which a red spot frequently appears (Fig. 117, *A*).

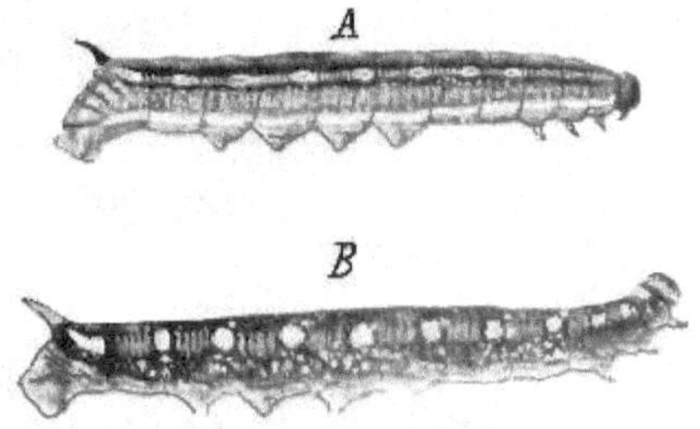

FIG. 117. Caterpillar of the Bed-straw Hawk-moth (*Deilephila galii*). *A*, Stage IV, sub-dorsal stripe still distinct, the annular spots are still incompletely enclosed in it. *B*, fully-formed caterpillar without trace of a sub-dorsal stripe, but with ten annular spots.

In most species these ring-spots occur on many segments (10–12) (Fig. 117, *B*), and in cases where they are of importance in making the caterpillar conspicuous and easily seen they sometimes form a double row. But we know one species, *Deilephila hippophaës*, in which only a single ring-spot exists, and it is a large brick-red spot on the second last segment, mimicking the red berry of the buckthorn (Fig. 8, *A* and *B*, *r*). But individuals also occur in which there are, on the five or six segments in front, smaller ring-spots which become less distinct the further forward they are, and in most caterpillars it is possible, on careful examination, to recognize little red dots on the faded sub-dorsal stripes of these segments (Fig. 8, *B*). We might be disposed to think, on this account, that the ancestors of *D. hippophaës* bore rings on all the segments, and that these had gradually become vestigial on the majority of them, because they had lost their earlier biological importance, and now, by adaptation to the buckthorn, could only be of use on the second last. But when we take the ontogeny also into account we find in the young caterpillar only a simple sub-dorsal line, upon which, in the third stage, the red spot of the tail-horn segment appears (Fig. 8, *A*).

No spots ever occur on the other segments at this stage; they only appear in the last stage, but as they may be entirely wanting, they must have arisen as the result of internal laws of correlation, that is, they must be recapitulations of the hindmost spots which arose in the phylogeny through natural selection. We may conclude

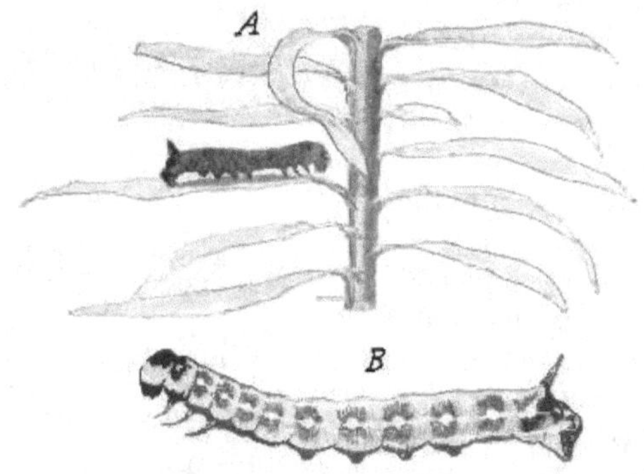

FIG. 118. Two stages in the life-history of the Spurge Hawk-moth (*Deilephila euphorbiæ*). *A*, first stage, the caterpillar dark blackish-green, without marking. *B*, second stage, the row of spots is distinctly connected by a light streak, the vestige of the sub-dorsal stripe.

this, at least, if we believe in the truth of the fundamental proposition of the biogenetic law, and admit that there is in the ontogeny some more or less distinct recapitulation of the phylogeny.

This proposition may be recognized as true in the case of *Deilephila* also, if we compare the different species with one another as regards their ontogeny. We find here too that not only the sub-dorsal, that is, the phyletically oldest marking of the Sphingid caterpillars, occurs everywhere in the young stages, but also that it is being shunted back to younger and younger stages, in proportion to the degree of the development of the spot-marking reached in the full-grown caterpillar. Thus, for instance, in the caterpillar of *Deilephila euphorbiæ* the highest form of spot-marking is reached, and in this species the sub-dorsal line is no longer the sole marking element at any stage. Leaving out of the question the absolutely unmarked little caterpillar which emerges from the egg (Fig. 118, *A*), there appears at once in the second stage a series of ring-spots connected by a fine white sub-dorsal line (Fig. 118, *B*). In the following stage, the third, this sub-dorsal line disappears without leaving a trace, and there remains only the spot-marking, which is subsequently duplicated.

Let us compare with this the ontogeny of the bed-straw hawk-moth, *Deilephila galii* (Fig. 117). The full-grown caterpillar possesses only a single row of ring-spots (*B*), and accordingly the young stages of the caterpillar up to the fourth show a distinct sub-dorsal line (*A*), although spots are seen upon it. A still earlier phyletic stage of development is illustrated by *Deilephila livornica*, in which the ring-spots are all connected by the sub-dorsal line.

It can thus hardly be doubted that the biogenetic law is guiding us aright when we conclude from a comparison of the ontogeny of the different species of *Deilephila*, that the oldest ancestors of the genus possessed only the longitudinal stripes, and that from these small pieces were cut off as ring-spots, and that these were gradually perfected and ultimately duplicated, while at the same time the original marking, the longitudinal stripe, was shunted back further and further in the young stages, until it finally disappeared altogether.

Let us now refer for a moment to the third form of marking in the caterpillars of the Sphingidæ—transverse striping. This has not arisen out of the sub-dorsal line, but quite independently and at a later date. This is proved with great certainty by the ontogeny of species of the genus *Smerinthus*. The full-grown, and usually also the young caterpillars, of these species have quite regularly the seven broad oblique stripes which run in the direction of the tail-horn at equal intervals on the lateral surfaces of the body (Fig. 3). They are absent only from the three anterior segments, and upon these a part of the older marking, the sub-dorsal stripe, has persisted. But we find this fully developed in the youngest stages of other species. In *Smerinthus populi*, the little caterpillar, which has no markings at all when it leaves the egg, very soon shows the white sub-dorsal line, and simultaneously with it the seven transverse stripes, which cut obliquely through it; in the older caterpillars the sub-dorsal then disappears (Fig. 119).

When I was investigating these matters at the beginning of the seventies I did not succeed in procuring eggs of the species of the genus *Sphinx*, which likewise almost all exhibit the oblique striping in their full-grown stages. But from what I knew of the ontogeny of *Smerinthus* species I was able to predict that, among the young stages of *Sphinx*, there must be some with sub-dorsal lines. This was confirmed later, for Poulton found in *Sphinx convolvuli* that in the first stage there are no oblique stripes, but only the sub-dorsal stripe, while in *Sphinx ligustri* both kinds of marking were present at the same time.

From all these facts, which I have summarized as briefly as possible, we see that the older phyletic characters are gradually crowded by the newer into ever-younger stages in the ontogeny, until ultimately they disappear altogether. We have now to ask to what this phenomenon is due; is it a simple crowding out of the old and less advantageous by the new and better characters as a result of natural selection, or is there some other factor at work? It is clear in regard to these forms of marking that they can have been developed at first only in the almost full-grown larva by natural selection, because they

Fig. 119. Caterpillar of *Smerinthus populi*, the Poplar Hawk-moth, at the end of the first stage, showing both the complete sub-dorsal stripe and the oblique stripes.

are of use only there, and that, at the same time, the old marking must have been set aside through the influence of the same factor, in as far as it prejudiced the effect of the new adaptation. This seems to be indicated by the persistence of the sub-dorsal line on those segments which are drawn in when *Chærocampa* assumes a terrifying attitude, or which do not bear oblique stripes in the leaf-like caterpillars, e. g. the three anterior segments in the species of *Sphinx* and *Smerinthus*. When newly acquired schemes of marking like the eye-spots of *Chærocampa* are transmitted from the last stage to the stage before, this can be explained by following the same train of thought, for the caterpillar is already of sufficient size to be able to inspire terror with its eyes; but in still younger stages the spots would not be likely to have that effect, and yet they occur in quite small animals (20 mm.). More obvious still is the uselessness of the oblique striping in the young stages of the *Sphinx* and *Smerinthus* caterpillars, for in the earliest stages of life the caterpillars are much too small to look like a leaf, and the oblique stripes stand much closer together than the lateral ribs of any leaf. Moreover, the little green caterpillars require no further protection when they sit on the under side of a leaf; they might then very easily be mistaken *in toto* for a leaf-rib. *Thus it is certainly not natural selection which effects the shunting back of the new characters.* Nor can this be caused by the fact that the new character can only be developed gradually and in several stages, for the oblique striping at any rate arises in the ontogeny all at once. There must therefore be some mechanical factor in development to which is due the fact that characters acquired in the later stages are gradually transferred to the younger stages. But this shifting backwards can be checked by the agency of natural selection as soon as it becomes disadvantageous for the stage concerned.

It is in this way that I explain the fact that the majority of the caterpillars of the Sphingidæ are absolutely without markings when they emerge from the egg. Thus, for instance, the caterpillars of *Chærocampa* (Fig. 116, *A*), of *Macroglossa* (Fig. 115), and of *Deilephila* (Fig. 118, *A*), as well as those of the *Smerinthus* species, are at first without stripe or mark of any kind; they are of a pale green colour, almost transparent, and very difficult to recognize when they sit upon a leaf. How very greatly the different stages *can be* independently adapted to the different conditions of their life, when that is necessary for the preservation of the species, is shown in the most striking manner by many species. Thus the little green caterpillar of *Aglia tau*, when it leaves the egg, bears five remarkable reddish rod-like thorns, which in form and colour resemble the bud-scales of the young beech-buds among which they live, and which disappear later on; the full-grown caterpillar shows nothing of these, but is leaf-green, marked with oblique stripes. Even if the use of these reddish thorns be other than I have indicated, we have in any case to deal with a special adaptation of *one*, and that the first caterpillar-stage, and what can happen at this stage is possible also at every other. Nor is it only animals which undergo metamorphosis that can exhibit independent phyletic variation at every stage, but those also with direct development, and indeed, in the case of these, we may assume adaptation of this kind at almost every stage in the history of the organs, as we have already seen, because the great abridgement of the phylogeny into the ontogeny necessitates a very precise mutual adaptation of the organ-rudiments and of the diverse rates of development.

We have thus been led by the facts discussed—and numerous others from other groups in the animal kingdom might be ranked along with them—to two main propositions, which express the relation of phylogeny to ontogeny. The first and fundamental proposition is the one already formulated. The ontogeny arises from the phylogeny by a condensation of its stages, which may be varied, shortened, thrown out, or compressed by the interpolation of new stages. The second proposition refers to individual parts, and may run as follows: As each stage can undergo new adaptations by itself, so can every part, every organ; such new adaptations very often show a tendency to be transferred to the immediately antecedent stage in ontogeny.

It is not my intention to formulate the laws of ontogeny just now, otherwise many others might be added to these, such as that of the regular transference of characters acquired at one end of a segmented animal to the other segments: I must confine myself here to bringing the two main propositions into harmony with the principles of our theory of heredity.

How phylogeny is condensed in ontogeny can be understood readily enough in a general way, although we cannot profess to have any insight into the detailed processes. The continuity of the germ-plasm brings about inheritance, in that it is continually handing over to the germ-plasm of the next generation the determinant-complex of the preceding one. Every new adaptation at any stage whatever depends on the variation of particular determinants within the germ-plasm, and this in its turn depends on germinal selection, that is, on the struggle of the different determinant-variants among themselves, and on the variation in a definite direction which arises from this, as we have already shown. A new kind of determinant can never arise of itself, but always only from already existing determinants, and through variation of these. But as spontaneous variation never causes all the homologous determinants of a germ-plasm to vary in quite the same way, but only a majority of them, there always remains a minority of the old determinants, which may, under certain circumstances, predominate again, as is proved by the aberrations in *Vanessa* species due to cold, and by many other kinds of reversion.

But it is not this variation which leads to the prolongation of ontogeny, and the repetition of the phyletic stages within it. In this case it is rather that a new character takes the place of an old one, not that it is added to it. A black spot may arise instead of a red one, but not first a black spot and then a red one. Of course we still know far too little in regard to the intimate succession of events in the stages of ontogeny to be able to say definitely that, in such apparently simple transformations, the older stage does not, in every ontogeny, precede the more recent one as a preparation for it, though it may be only for a brief and transient period.

It is certain, however, that variations such as the addition of a new stage in ontogeny are undergone, and that this implies the occurrence of something really quite new. Therefore such a new stage can arise only from the germ-plasm, by the duplication, and in part variation, of the determinants of the preceding stage. If, for instance, the body of a Crustacean be lengthened by a segment, this must be due to a process of this kind, and in such a case it is intelligible enough that the new segment can be formed in the ontogeny only after the development of the older preceding one, for its determinants come from that, and are from the beginning so arranged that they are only liberated to activity by the formation of the preceding segment.

Now, if in the course of the phylogeny numerous new segments were added to the body of the Crustacean, the ontogeny would be materially prolonged, and condensation would become necessary in the interests of species-preservation. To bring this condensation about, whole series of segments which were added successively in the phylogeny succeeded each other with gradually increasing rapidity in the ontogeny, until finally they appeared *simultaneously*: the determinants of the segments $n, n+1, n+2 \ldots n+x$ varied in regard to their liberating stimuli, and were roused to activity no longer successively, but simultaneously, in the cell complexes controlled by them. We have thus recapitulation, but with abridgement and compression, of the phyletic stages in the ontogeny. Thus in the nauplius of *Leptodora* we see the rudiments of five of the pairs of legs of the subsequent thorax (Fig. 111, *IV–VIII*), and in the Zoæa larva the rudiments of six thoracic legs may be seen behind the already developed swimming-leg (Fig. 114, *VI–XIII*).

But in the course of the phylogeny a segment may also become superfluous, and we know that it then degenerates and is ultimately eliminated altogether. Thus in a parasitic Isopod, which lives within other Crustaceans, a segment of the thorax is wanting in the relatively well-developed larva, and in the Caprellidæ among the Amphipod Crustaceans the whole abdomen of from six to seven segments has degenerated to a narrow, rudimentary structure. In such cases the gradual degeneration of the relative determinants has preceded step for step the degeneration of the part itself, and when this is complete the ontogeny shows nothing of what was previously present, and so we may speak of a 'falsification' of the phylogeny.

But that the complete disappearance of the determinants only comes about with extreme slowness, so that whole geological periods are sometimes not enough for its accomplishment, we have already learnt from our study of rudimentary organs, instances of which can be demonstrated in every higher animal, bearing witness to the presence of the relevant organs or structures in the ancestors of the species.

We can infer with certainty, from the observational data at our disposal, that the disappearance of useless parts is regulated by definite laws; but it is too soon to attempt to formulate these laws, or even to trace them back to their mechanical causes. As we have already said, a much more comprehensive collection of facts, and above all one which has been made on a definite plan, is a necessary preliminary condition to this. But so much at least we may gather from the facts before us, that the degeneration of an organ begins at the final stage, and is transferred gradually backwards into the embryogenesis. Thus the two fingers of birds which have disappeared since Cretaceous times are still indicated in every bird-embryo, though they subsequently degenerate. In various mammals 'pre-lacteal tooth-germs' have been demonstrated in the jaws of embryos, which show us that not only did ancestors exist whose dentition was the modern 'milk-teeth,' but that still more remote ancestors possessed another set of teeth, which was crowded out by the 'milk-teeth': thus the teeth of the ancestors of the modern right whale (*Balæna mysticetus*) are only represented in the embryo of to-day in the form of dental pits. And, as we saw already, the Os centrale so characteristic of the wrist of lower vertebrates only appears in Man at a very early embryonic stage, and disappears again as such in the further course of the embryogenesis.

We may perhaps give a preliminary statement of this law as follows: It is impossible that any part or organ should be removed suddenly from the ontogeny without bringing the whole into disorder, and the least serious disturbance of the course of development will undoubtedly be caused if the final stage of the part in question become rudimentary first. Only after this has happened, and the neighbouring parts have adapted themselves to the disappearance, can this extend to the stages immediately preceding it, so that these too degenerate, and allow the surrounding parts to adapt themselves. The further back into the ontogeny the disappearance extends the greater will be the number of other structures affected in some way or other by the degeneration, and these must not all be brought suddenly into new conditions, else the whole course of development would suffer. Thus at first only those determinants may disappear—and *can* disappear according to the laws of germinal selection—which control the final form of the useless organ, then those just preceding them, which controlled, let us say, its size, and thus more and more of the previously active determinants disappear, and hand in hand with this disappearance there is variation of all the parts correlated with the dwindling condition of the organ, so that their own development and that of the animal as a whole suffers no injury. If it were otherwise, if when a part became useless its collective determinants were all to disappear at the same time, the whole ontogeny would totter, in fact it would be much as if a man who wished to remove the breadth of a window from a house standing on pillars were to begin by taking away the foundation pillar.

It is, of course, to be understood that these processes go on so exceedingly slowly that personal selection takes a share in them, at least at the beginning. Later on, the further degeneration of a useless organ or rudiment has no effect on the individual's power of life, and therefore depends solely upon the struggle of the parts within the germ-plasm (germinal selection).

If we could see the determinants, and recognize directly their arrangement in the germ-plasm and their importance in ontogeny, we should doubtless understand many of the phenomena of ontogeny and their relation to phylogeny which must otherwise remain a riddle, or demand accessory hypotheses for their interpretation. Several years ago Emery rightly pointed out that the phenomena of the variation of homologous parts might be inferred by reasoning from the germ-plasm theory. If one hand has six fingers instead of five, it not infrequently happens that the other also exhibits a superfluity of fingers, and sometimes the foot does so too. The phyletic modification of the limbs in the Ungulates has taken place with striking uniformity in the fore and hind extremities; no animal has ever been one-hoofed in front and two-hoofed behind. Although I might suggest that this primarily depends on adaptation to different conditions of the ground, and that the Artiodactyls were evolved in relation to the soft marshy soil of the forest, and the Perissodactyls for the steppes, it cannot be denied that germinal conditions may have co-operated in bringing about this uniformity of the direction of variation, especially as the whole structure of the fore- and hind-limbs exhibits such marked similarity. Emery is inclined to refer this to 'germ-plasmic correlations,' and we have assumed from the very first that the different determinants and groups of determinants do indeed stand in definite and close relations to one another. But it seems to me premature to say anything more precise and definite than that in the meantime. I should like, however, to say that determinants or groups of determinants which had in old ancestral germ-plasms to give rise to a series of quite similar structures by multiplication during the ontogeny, and therefore only needed to be present *singly* in the germ-plasm, would, in later descendants, have to shift their multiplication back into the germ-plasm itself, if necessity required that the homologous parts which they controlled should become *different* from each other. Then the previously single group of determinants in the germ-plasm would have to become multiple. But as new determinants can only arise from those which already exist, these new ones must have had their place beside the old, and would therefore probably be exposed to any intra-germinal causes of variation in common with them—that is to say, they will tend to vary even later in a similar manner. For instance, we might think of the segments of primitive Annelids, which in form and contents are for the most part alike, as arising from one germ-rudiment, from which, when, in the higher Annelids, the various regions of the body had to take a different form, several primary constituents of the germ-plasm separated themselves off; and in a similar way the much higher and more complex differentiation of the somatic segments in the Crustaceans must have been brought about. Thus we understand how the determinant groups of the germ-plasm multiplied according to the need for increasing differentiation, but remained in intimate relation, which exposed them in some measure to a common fate, that is, to common modifying influences, and in many cases determined them to similar variation.

But we cannot see directly into the germ-plasm, and are therefore thrown back on the inductions we can make from the facts presented to us by the phenomena of visible living organisms. As yet the material for such inductions is scanty, because it has been got together haphazard, and not collected on a definite plan. I therefore refrain for the present from attempting any further elaboration of my germ-plasm theory. It is only when an abundance of observation material, collected according to a definite plan, lies at our disposal that anything more in regard to the intimate structure of the germ-plasm, or the mutual influences and relations of its determinants and its modification in the course of phylogeny can be deduced with any certainty. Meanwhile, we must content ourselves with having, through the hypothesis of determinants, made intelligible at least the one fundamental fact, how it is possible that in the course of the phylogeny single parts and single stages can be thrown out or interpolated, or even only caused to vary, without giving rise to variation in all the rest of the parts and stages of the animal. A theory of epigenesis cannot do this, for, if no representative particles were contained in the germ-plasm, then every variation of it would affect the whole course of development and every part of the organism, and variations of individual parts arising from the germ would be impossible.

LECTURE XXVIII

THE GENERAL SIGNIFICANCE OF AMPHIMIXIS

Twofold import of amphimixis—It conditions the continual changing of individuality—Analogy from game of cards—The germ-plasm is at once variable and persistent—The two roots of individual variation: germinal selection and new combinations of the ids—'Harmonious' adaptation conditions amphimixis—Difference between adaptation and mere variation—Is a 'direct' use of amphimixis to be insisted upon?—Ceaseless intervention of personal selection in the lineage of the germ-plasm—Far-reaching effects of personal selection—Fixing of the arrangements for amphimixis in the course of generations of species—Increase of the constancy of a character with its duration—Characters in the same species variable in different degrees—The upper and under surfaces of Kallima—Wild plants brought under cultivation do not at first vary—Amphimixis very ancient, therefore very firmly established—Does amphimixis bring about equalization (Hatschek, Haycraft, Quetelet)?—Galton's frequency curves—Ammon's free scope for variations—De Vries' assymetrical curves of frequency.

We have already made ourselves familiar with the process which in unicellular organisms is called conjugation and in multicellular organisms fertilization, and we have seen that its most obvious significance lay in the fact that through it the germ-plasms of two individuals are united. Since, according to our view, this germ-plasm or idioplasm is the bearer of the hereditary tendencies of the organism concerned, the mingling or amphimixis of two germ-plasms brings together the hereditary tendencies of two individuals, and the organism whose development is derived from this mingled germ-plasm must therefore exhibit traits of both parents, and must to a certain extent be made up of the traits of both. This is *one* result attained by amphimixis.

But we went further than this, and saw that there is a second result implied in amphimixis, namely, that the individual character of the germ-plasm is being continually altered by new combinations of the ids contained in it. We inferred from what I believe to be the demonstrated hypothesis that the germ-plasm is composed of ids, that its reduction to half the original mass must mean a reduction of the ids to half the number, and as the ids contain primary constituents which are individually different, this must effect a new arrangement, a new mingling of these individual peculiarities. The reduction of the germ-plasm to half, that is, the diminution of the number of its ids to half, is a phenomenon generally associated with amphimixis, and has been established in the case of all animals which have hitherto been investigated, and of all the most carefully studied plants, and finally, it has been shown to be very probable in unicellular organisms, for the processes of conjugation in Infusorians and many other Protozoa include phenomena very similar to those of reducing division in the higher animals. The prediction made on theoretical grounds has here been verified by observation, and it is obvious that the assumption of ids, that is, of units in the germ-plasm which are handed on from one generation to the succeeding one, involves a reduction of their number in each amphimixis. Without this the number of ids would be doubled at each amphimixis, and would therefore gradually amount to something enormous. We see therefore why this normally recurrent reduction of ids before each amphimixis was established in the course of evolution, and we see that it inevitably involves that a new combination of ids should be associated with each amphimixis.

If nothing persists unless it be purposeful, that is, necessary, what is the meaning of the fact that arrangements for amphimixis occur over almost the whole known domain of life, from the very simple organisms up to the highest, in unicellular and multicellular organisms, in plants and animals alike? Why is it that this arrangement has been departed from only in a few small groups of forms, while it occurs everywhere else, in almost every generation, so indissolubly associated with reproduction that it has even been regarded—with a lack of clearness—as itself a form of reproduction, and is even now generally called 'sexual reproduction'? And why is it that in many organisms, especially lowly ones, it is not associated with every reproduction, though it recurs at regular or irregular intervals? Such a universal arrangement must undoubtedly be of fundamental importance, and we have to ask wherein this importance lies. That is the problem to the solution of which we must now apply ourselves.

So much we may say at once: The significance of amphimixis cannot be that of making multiplication possible, for multiplication may be effected without amphimixis in the most diverse ways—by division of the organism into two or more, by budding, and even by the production of unicellular germs. Even though these last are usually in various ways so organized that they must undergo amphimixis before they can develop into new organisms, yet there are numerous germ-cells which are not subject to this condition (e.g. spores), and there are—as we have seen—many germ-cells, adapted for amphimixis, which always, or in certain generations, or even only occasionally, emancipate themselves from this condition under certain external influences: I refer to egg-cells which develop parthenogenetically.

If amphimixis is not a universal preliminary condition of reproduction, wherein lies the necessity for its general occurrence among living organisms?

We have already learned that there are two results produced without exception by amphimixis; one of these is the antecedent reduction of the original number of ids by one half, and the consequent new combination of ids which results from this; the other is the union of two such halved germ-plasms from two different individuals. The first we may, with Hartog, compare to the removal of half of a pack of cards previously mixed, the second to the combination of two such halves from different packs. The first process brings nothing new into the complex of primary constituents, but rather removes a part—larger or smaller—of its characters: not necessarily exactly half of these, since each individual kind of id may be represented by doubles or multiples. But the reduction simplifies the composition of the germ-plasm, and might by itself, through the struggle of the ids in ontogeny, lead to a resultant different from the parent, that is, to a new individuality. Through the second process, however, new individual traits are of necessity added, and make the resultants still more markedly diverse, that is, if the ids of both parents attain to expression in the struggle of ontogeny, and this, as we have already seen, is usually the case, though not always and certainly not always in all parts. Thus amphimixis, together with the preparatory reduction of the ids, secures the constant recurrence of individual peculiarities through the ceaseless new combinations of individual characters already existing in the species.

When sixteen years ago I first inquired into the actual and ultimate significance of sexual reproduction, I thought I had found it in this ceaseless production of new individualities. This seemed to me a sufficient reason for the introduction of amphimixis into nature, since the difference between individuals is the basis of the process of selection, and thus the basis of all the transformations of organisms, which we may refer to natural or sexual selection. Now these differences of selection-value are—as I believed then, and do still—not only by far the most frequent organic changes, but also the most important, since they not only initiate, but control new lines of evolution. Therefore I still regard amphimixis as the means by which a continual new combination of variations is effected a process without which the evolution of this world of organisms so endlessly diverse in form and so inconceivably complex, could not have taken place.

But I do not regard this amphimixis as the real root of variation itself, for that must depend not on a mere exchange of ids, but rather upon a variation of the ids. The ids of a worm of the primitive world could not without variation now make up the germ-plasm of an elephant, even if it be true that mammals are descended from worms. The ids must have been meanwhile transformed times without number by the modification, degeneration, and new formation of determinants. Amphimixis, that is, the union of two germ-plasms, does not of itself cause variation of the determinants, it only arranges the ids (the ancestral plasms) in ever-new combinations. If the origin of variation were limited to that alone, a transmutation of species and genera would only be possible on a very limited scale; there could at most be a narrow circle of variations, just as in the example already given of the packs of cards: even if the taking away and mixing up of the halves were repeated a thousand times, a definite though undoubtedly large number of card-combinations would in the long run recur again and again. But the case is different with the germ-plasm and amphimixis, where there is an infinitely more varied series of results, because the individual cards—the ids—are variable, even between one time of sifting and shuffling and another, and therefore infinitely productive of variety in the course of numerous repetitions of the shuffling.

I have been frequently and persistently credited with maintaining that the germ-plasm is invariable—a misunderstanding of my position, due perhaps to a somewhat too brief and terse statement which I made at an earlier period (1886). I had described the germ-plasm as 'a substance of great power of persistence,' and as varying with difficulty and slowly, basing this statement upon the age-long persistence of many species in which the specific constitution of the germ-plasm must have remained unchanged. The idea of 'germinal selection,' of a ceaseless struggle between the 'primary constituents' of the germ, and of the resulting continual slight and invisible rising and falling of individual characters, had not yet dawned upon me, nor had I at that time formulated the conception of 'determinants.' I was even doubtful at that time whether development, heredity, and variation were not interpretable on the assumption of an undifferentiated substance without primary constituents. But at no time was I unaware that the whole phyletic evolution of the organic world is only conceivable on the assumption of continual variation of the germ-plasm, that it actually depends upon this, even

O 2

if these variations come about with exceeding slowness, and are thus in a certain sense 'difficult.'

Now that I understand these processes more clearly, my opinion is that the roots of all heritable variation lie in the germ-plasm, and furthermore, that the determinants are continually oscillating hither and thither in response to very minute nutritive changes, and are readily compelled to *variation in a definite direction*, which may ultimately lead to considerable variations in the structure of the species, if they are favoured by personal selection, or at least if they are not suppressed by it as prejudicial. But selection is continually keeping watch over both kinds of variation, and if the conditions of life do not further the variation or do not even allow it to persist, selection eliminates everything that lessens the purity of the specific type, everything that transgresses the limits of utility, or that might endanger the existence of the species. Thus we understand how the germ-plasm may be variable, and yet at the same time remain unvaried for thousands of years, how it is ready and able to furnish any variation that is possible in a species if that is required by external circumstances, and yet is able to preserve the characters of the species in almost absolute constancy through whole geological ages; in short, how it can be at once readily variable and yet slow to vary.

The importance which amphimixis thus has in connexion with the adaptation of organisms lies, if I mistake not, in the necessity for co-adaptation, that is, in the fact that in almost all adaptations it is not merely a question of the variation of a single determinant, but of the correlated variations of many—often very numerous—determinants, of 'harmonious adaptation,' as we have already said. Many-sided adaptation of this kind seems to me impossible without a continually recurrent sifting and recombining of the germ-plasms, and this can only be effected by amphimixis.

It may be objected that, apart from amphimixis, variation can be brought about in many parts of an organism, as in purely asexual reproduction. A plant, for instance, may vary when it is transferred to a strange soil or climate; and even in that case the variations seem to be harmonious, at least the harmony of the parts is so far maintained that the plant continues to flourish, at any rate under cultivation. A plant species may be incited by abundant nourishment to gigantic growth, and caused to vary in many of its parts, and the abundant food may even directly affect the germ-plasm so that all or some of these variations may become hereditary; and yet this is far from being a case of adaptation, it is merely a case of simultaneous variations, and it is questionable whether they will make the continued existence of the plant under the new conditions possible or not. It might easily happen, for instance, that the plant, though it became larger and bore more abundant blossoms, would be sterile, and therefore unfitted for continued existence in a natural state. Variations are not necessarily adaptations; the latter can never come about solely through direct influence upon the germ-plasm. What direct influence upon the germ-plasm could, for instance, make the hind-legs of a mammal long and strong and the fore-legs short and weak? Obviously neither an increase nor decrease in the food-supply, nor a higher or lower temperature—in short, no direct influence, because all these affect the germ-plasm as a whole, and therefore cannot possibly influence two homologous groups of determinants in opposite directions.

This, it seems to me, is only possible when amphimixis brings about in one individual a favourable coincidence of the chance germinal variations of the determinants of the fore- and hind-limbs; and just as it is with the two variations in this simple hypothetical case, so it will be in the actual processes of adaptation where there are involved numerous—we know not how numerous—variations essential to a 'harmonious adaptation.'

It need not be objected that the very number of variations necessary to a 'harmonious adaptation' makes its occurrence impracticable; for it is *the complete* harmony of the parts that makes the adaptation, and without this the individual was only imperfectly adapted, and therefore incapable of survival. It is certainly not mathematically demonstrable that this is the case, but as the whole process of transformation which makes an old adaptation into a new one begins with minimal fluctuations of the determinants, which must first be brought by germinal selection to the level of selection-value, and must then be subject to personal selection,so the whole process goes on so gradually and by such small steps that the harmony of the parts is maintained by functional adaptation during the individual life in a great number of individuals. But these are just the individuals which survive in the struggle for existence, and at the same time possess at every stage of the process *the best combination of favourably varying determinants.* As these favourable variations are, in consequence of germinal selection, not mere isolated variations of fluctuating importance, but variations in a *definite direction,* the whole process of variation must persist in every single part in the direction imposed upon it by personal selection. But since at every reducing division the ids of the germ-cells are brought down to half their number, a possibility is offered for gradually removing the unfavourable ids from the germ-plasm of the species, since the descendants resulting from the most unfavourable id-combinations always perish, and so from generation to generation the germ-plasm gets rid of its unfavourably varying ids, and the most propitious combinations afforded by amphimixis are preserved, till ultimately there remain only those combinations which are varying appropriately, or at least only those in which the appropriately varying determinants are in the majority, and so have controlling influence.

Logically this deduction is undoubtedly indisputable, from the standpoint of the germ-plasm theory: but whether it may be regarded as a sufficient reason for the introduction of amphimixis, and for its extremely tenacious persistence throughout the course of the long and intricate phylogeny, cannot be maintained without special investigation.

Against my position the objection has often been urged that an arrangement cannot arise or be maintained through natural selection unless it is *of direct use* to the individual in which it occurs. Sexual reproduction cannot therefore have been established simply because it advances, or even because it makes possible the adaptations of species, for these adaptations only came about occasionally, perhaps once in a thousand generations or even less frequently; thus the intervening generations could derive no advantage of any kind from the arrangement in question, and therefore, according to the law of the degeneration of unused characters, it must have long since been lost. I mentioned this objection before, but was obliged to postpone a detailed consideration of it until we had discussed germinal selection.

We admit, of course, that characters are only preserved intact as long as they are of advantage sufficient to turn the scale in favour of their possessors, and that they begin to fall from their height of perfection when that is no longer the case; we admit also that new adaptations are not continually necessary, but are so only at intervals of long series of generations, and yet the objection cited seems to me baseless.

Leaving out of account, for the moment, the first introduction of amphimixis, let us deal with it as an existing occurrence, for the tenacious persistence of which we wish to find reasons.

Is it really the case that amphimixis is only of importance in connexion with the new adaptation of a species, and that it has nothing to do with the persistence of the species in the state of adaptation already attained? According to the conception of the processes within the germ-plasm which we have already stated, it is impossible that this should be the case, for continual slight fluctuations are occurring in the determinants in consequence of the fluctuations of the nutritive stream, and these slight variations, plus or minus, do not in many cases equalize one another or counteract one another by turning again in a contrary direction; they go on increasing in the direction in which they have begun. It is only when personal selection opposes them that they come to a standstill, and this can only happen when they attain to selection-value, that is to say, when they reach a level at which they become disadvantageous in the struggle of persons. But as germinal variations of this kind are continually occurring, personal selection must keep continual watch over them, and eradicate them as soon as they have attained selection-value.

Therefore, when a species is most perfectly adapted to its conditions, it would of necessity begin to degenerate if personal selection were not continually guarding it, and setting aside everything that is in excess or deficient as soon as it begins to be prejudicial. But the adaptation of a species does not depend upon *one* character persisting at its normal level, but on the persistence of very many, and many of these vary simultaneously upwards or downwards, and reach the limit of selection-value at one time or another. If there were no amphimixis, then either all individuals with any excessive variant would be at once eliminated, or the species would go on deteriorating until this excessive variant was so numerously and strongly represented in all its individuals that it would perish through degeneration. But even in the first of these cases the species would drift towards the fate of extinction, because excessive variations do occur even in every asexual generation, and would appear in an increasingly large number of determinants if there were no possibility of rejecting them and eliminating them from the lineage of the species.

This is made possible through the periodic intervention of amphimixis; it is actually effected thereby; and in this way alone the species is kept at its high-water mark of adaptation. It is not necessary to assume that every single determinant which is varying in an unfavourable direction is at once eliminated as soon as it becomes prejudicial, that is, reaches negative selection-value, or—to make use of an expression introduced by Ammon—as soon as it oversteps the boundaries of the 'playground of variations,' the limits within which variations are neither favourable nor unfavourable. But *in the course of generations* they are unfailingly eliminated, especially when a large number of unfavourably varying determinants are coincident in the germ-plasm. Then the individuals which arise from a germ-plasm thus composed must perish in the struggle for existence, and thus the id-combinations with excessive determinants are eliminated from the germinal constitution of the species. As this is repeated as often as excesses of the ids occur, the species is kept pure.

It might be objected that, through such a continual weeding-out of rebellious determinants, the germ-plasm would become so constant in its constitution that it would ultimately be secure from all such aberrations of it on the part of its determinants, and therefore would in time become quite incapable of diverging from its proper path at all, and would thus no longer require this continual correction through amphimixis.

I do not wish to contradict this conclusion; indeed, I believe that the constitution of the species becomes more and more constant in the way I have indicated, and that an ever more perfect and stable equilibrium of the whole determinant system is thus brought about. It follows that in the course of generations the diverse determinants of the germ-plasm will vary within a progressively shortened radius, and will thus more and more rarely overstep the limits of the 'variation-playground'—and yet I still believe that this justifiable conclusion tells in favour of my interpretation of the utility of the persistence of amphigony once introduced.

Let it be remarked, in the first place, that it is by no means essential to the preservation of a useful institution that it should practically justify its utility in *every* generation. Although, for instance, the warm winter coat of a species of mammal may be necessary to its survival, it does not disappear at once when a winter happens to occur which is so warm that even individuals with poor pellage can survive. Indeed, several such mild winters might occur in succession, in which there was no weeding-out of the individuals with poor fur, and yet the thickness of the winter fur of the species would not become less fixed, just because this character no longer varies perceptibly in an old-established species which has long been perfectly adapted, and it could only be brought into a state of marked fluctuation very slowly through direct influence on the germ-plasm, or through panmixia. But exactly the same thing is true in regard to the determinants of the reproductive cells, in respect of their adaptation to amphimixis, only very much more emphatically.

Before going further, I should like to show that the conclusion we have just deduced from the theory, namely, that the equilibrium of the determinant system of a species increases in stability with the duration of its persistence, holds good not only for the whole system, but for its individual parts, that is, for the individual characters and adaptations. Experience teaches that characters are the more exactly and constantly transmitted the older they are; generic characters are more constant than species-characters, order-characters more persistent than family-characters—this is implied even in their name. But we are able to show even in relation to the characters of a species that those which have been fixed for a long time are most precisely and purely transmitted; that is, that their determinants are least inclined to overstep the limits of the 'variation-playground' either in an upward or downward direction.

Two groups of facts prove this: first the observed fact that the very different degree of variability which the different species exhibit is by no means common to all the characters of the species in the same measure; for individual characters may be variable or constant in very different degrees.

Many years ago[1] I drew attention to the fact that the different stages in the life-history of insects, especially of Lepidoptera, might be variable in quite different degrees. Thus, for instance, the caterpillar might be very variable, and yet the butterfly which arises from it might be extremely constant. I concluded from this—what probably no one now will dispute—that the various stages may vary phyletically independently of one another, that, for instance, the caterpillar may adapt itself to a new manner of life, a new food-plant, a new means of defence, while the butterfly, unaffected by this, goes on quietly as it was before. Every new adaptation necessarily implies variability, and so the stage which is in process of transformation must have its period of variability, which gradually returns again to greater constancy, and this the more completely the longer the series of generations through which the weeding out of the less well-adapted has endured.

But it is not only the individual stages of development that may be unequally variable; the same is true of the characters of a species which occur simultaneously. The most striking example of this known to me is the leaf-butterfly, which I have already mentioned many times in the course of these lectures—the Indian *Kallima paralecta*. In this species the brown and red upper surface is almost alike in colour and marking in all individuals, but the under surface, the colour and marking of which is so deceptively mimetic of a leaf,

[1] *Studien zur Descendenztheorie*, Leipzig, 1876.

is variable to such a degree that it is difficult, among a large number of specimens, to find even a few which are as like one another as are the members of species in which the under side is constant. It need not be urged that this is due to the complexity of the marking on the under side. In many of our indigenous butterflies the under side is just as complex in coloration and marking, and nevertheless it is very constant, being almost identical in all individuals, as for instance in *Vanessa cardui*. In *Kallima* the great variability of the under surface certainly depends not merely on the fact that the mimetic character has been only recently acquired (phyletically speaking), but chiefly on the fact that the dead leaves to which they approximate are themselves very diverse in appearance, for many are dry, others moist and covered with mould, and that the adaptations have therefore gone in different directions, and as yet, at least, have neither combined to form a single constant type, nor diverged to form two or three distinct types. The various 'leaf-pictures' seem equally effective in concealing the insects from their enemies, and thus there is still a continual crossing and mingling of the different essays at leaf-picturing.

A second group of facts, which indicates that old-established characters have less tendency to overstep the limits of the neutral 'variation-playground,' is to be found in the experience of breeders, and especially that of gardeners who have brought wild plants under cultivation in order to procure varieties.

It has been proved that the wild plants often exhibit no hereditary variations for a long series of generations, notwithstanding the greatly altered conditions of life, but that then a moment comes in which isolated variations crop up, which may then be intensified by the manipulations of the breeder to form sport-species with large conspicuously coloured flowers, or with some other distinctive character. Darwin called this a shattering of the constitution of the plant; but the stable and slowly varying 'constitution' simply means that in old-established and well-adapted species the determinants possess only a very restricted 'variation-playground,' and because of their firmly based harmonious correlation are not easily and never very quickly induced to overstep its limits in any marked degree.

Let us now apply all this to the institution of amphimixis and amphigony, and it is immediately obvious that these determinants of the germ-plasm which control the characters relating to sexual reproduction must be *more stable and less variable than all others which a species possesses, for they are infinitely older.* They are older than all species-characters, older than the characters of the genus, of the family, of the class, and indeed of the whole series or phylum to which a higher animal, a vertebrate, for instance, belongs. We cannot wonder, therefore, that amphigony has persisted through hundreds and thousands of generations, even if it had not been reinforced in the germ-plasm during this period by selection. We should rather wonder that an institution so primaeval, and so firmly engrained in the germ-plasm, can ever be departed from, even when its abandonment is to the advantage of the species, as has happened in parthenogenesis.

I have entered upon this long discussion because I believe that we require to appreciate this power of persistence on the part of the sexual determinants before we can explain the general occurrence of amphigony. The occurrence of pure parthenogenesis, unaccompanied by any degeneration of the species, can hardly be understood except on the assumption that the constancy of the species, when it has once been attained, may be preserved without the continual intervention of amphimixis. How long it can be preserved is another question, which it is difficult or impossible to answer, since species exhibiting *pure* parthenogenesis are rare, and since we cannot tell with certainty how long it is since amphimixis ceased to occur in them. Generally speaking, the answer in regard to the few species which have to be taken into account in this connexion would be 'not long,' but whether this 'not long' signifies hundreds of generations or thousands of generations we must leave undecided. So much only we can say, that in all species of animals in which the male sex has quite died out or has dwindled to a minimal remnant, there are as yet no traces of degeneration to be found, and that even organs which have fallen into disuse and become functionless because amphigony has disappeared, are nevertheless in several cases retained in perfect completeness. I shall return to this subject later on, but in the meantime I wish to work out our conception of the actual efficacy of amphigony or ordinary sexual reproduction, and thereby increase our understanding of its significance and power of persistence.

We have seen that amphigony not only renders possible the novel 'harmonious adaptations' which are continually required, but that it also leads, by a continual crossing of individuals, simultaneously with the elimination of the less fit, to a gradually increasing constancy of the species. This has been regarded by some writers as its sole effect: thus recently by Hatschek, whose view has already been refuted.

Haycraft also finds the significance of amphigony simply in the equalizing or neutralizing of individual differences which it effects.

Quetelet and Galton have attempted to show that intercrossing leads to a mean which then remains constant. Haycraft supposes that a species can only remain constant if its individuals are being continually intercrossed, and that otherwise they would diverge and take different forms, because the 'protoplasm' has within itself the tendency to continual variation. The transformation of species is effected by means of this variation tendency, and the persistency and constancy of species which are already adapted to the conditions of their life are secured by the constant intercrossing of the individuals, and the consequent neutralization of individual peculiarities.

Although the cases already mentioned in which great constancy of species is associated with purely parthenogenetic reproduction do not tell in favour of the accuracy of the view just stated, yet the fundamental idea, that amphigony is an essential factor in the maintenance and even in the evolution of species, is undoubtedly sound. We should certainly find neither genera nor species in Nature if amphigony did not exist; but we cannot simply suppose that amphigony and variation are, so to speak, antipodal forces, the former of which secures the constancy of the species, the latter its transformation. In my opinion, at all events, there is no such thing as a 'tendency' of the protoplasm to vary, although there is a constant fluctuation of the characters—dependent on the imperfect equality of the external influences, especially of nutrition. This certainly results, as far as it takes place within the germ-plasm, in a continual upward and downward variation of the hereditary tendencies, and it would lead to increasing dissimilarity of the individuals were it not that amphigony is continually equalizing the differences by a constantly repeated mingling of individuals. Quetelet and Galton have shown that the tendency of this mingling is towards the establishment of a mean; the characters of Man, such as bodily size, fluctuate about a mean, which at the same time shows the maximum of frequency; and the frequency curve of the various bodily sizes assumes a perfectly symmetrical form, so that the average size is the most frequent, and deviations from it upwards or downwards occur more rarely in proportion to the amount of deviation, the largest and the smallest sizes occurring least frequently.

Thus an equalizing of variations by means of amphimixis really exists, and the question we have to ask is, How does it come about? The case is assuredly not the same as that in which equal quantities of red and white wine are mixed to make a so-called 'Schiller.' This is proved even by the fact that the mixture may turn out quite different even when the wines—the two parents—are alike: for the children of a pair are often dissimilar. And while the 'Schiller' cannot be separated again into red wine and white, this happens often in sexual reproduction, and sometimes to such an extent that the grandchild exactly resembles one or other of the grand-parents, as is most clearly proved in the case of plant-hybrids.

There is thus a deep-seated difference, depending on the fact that what is mingled in amphigony is not simple but composite, not a simple uniform developmental tendency associated with a simple and definite substance, but a combination of several or many developmental tendencies, associated with several equivalent but different material units. These units are the ids or ancestral plasms, and we have seen how they are not only halved by reducing division, but are also arranged in new combinations in amphimixis.

These ids differ very little within the same germ-plasm; in species which have long been established the majority probably only differ in correspondence to the individual differences of the fully-formed organisms, but they are only absolutely alike in the case of two ids which have been formed by the division of a mother-id. Let us disregard this for the moment, and assume that all the ids of a germ-plasm are different: the germ-plasm of a father, *A*, will be composed of ids *A* 1–100, that of the mother, *B*, of the ids *B* 1–100. But in each mature germ-cell of these two parents only fifty ids are contained, and if we assume that the mingling of the ids is controlled solely by chance, then in the various germ-cells *A* × *B* the most diverse combinations of ids may be contained; for instance, *A* 1, 3, 5, 7, 9, 11, ... to 99, or *A* 1–10 and 20–30, and 40–50, and so on, and similarly in the germ-cells *B*. If all germ-cells produced by *A* and by *B* attained to development, or even if all the ova succeeded, the thousand or hundred thousand children of this pair would necessarily exhibit every possible mingling of their characters, and each in the same number according to the rules of probability calculations. But it is well known *that this does not happen*; of the thousands of human ova, for instance, which come to maturity in the course of the life of a female individual more than ten rarely develop, and more than thirty never, and these are determined solely by chance and quite independently of the mixture of ids which they contain. It is thus purely a matter of chance which of the complexes of primary constituents contained in the germ-plasm of an individual are transmitted to descendants, and it is also purely a matter of chance which combination of ids comes to be developed. Therefore we may say that no regular neutralizing of contrasts, either in the primary constituents of the parents or as regards the differences in their characters, can occur. In one case there is a blended inheritance; in another the child takes after the father or after the mother; in a third, and this probably occurs most frequently, the child resembles the father in some characters and the mother in others.

But how then does Galton's curve of frequency of variations come about? Why does the mean of any character occur by far the most frequently, and why does the frequency of a variation diminish regularly in proportion to its approximation to either extreme? To this it is answered: Because the process of mingling through amphigony goes on through numerous generations, and thus an elimination of chance, and the establishment of an average, must be brought about.

But this does not quite suffice to explain matters, for experience shows that asymmetrical frequency-curves of variations also occur, even in species with sexual reproduction. As De Vries has recently shown, there are also 'half-Galton curves,' that is, curves which suddenly break off at their highest point. We must conclude from this that the frequency of the different variations depends not only on their degree, but also on the greater or less facility with which they arise from the constitution of the species.

This consideration can be readily elucidated with the help of Ammon's exposition, and especially of his graphic representation of the 'playground of variations.' If we think of the indifferent variations occurring in any character of a species as arranged in a series ascending from the smallest to the largest, this line may be regarded as the abscissal-axis, and from it ordinates may be drawn which express the frequency of the variation in question by the differences in their length. If the tips of these ordinates be united, we have the curve of frequency (Fig. 120, *A*), which according to Galton ought to be symmetrical, and in most cases really is so. Ammon calls the space between the smallest and the largest variations the 'variation-playground,' that is, the playground within which all variations are equally advantageous to the species. This is not co-extensive with the variation-area, for there may be more marked deviations below the beginning or above the upper end of the variation-playground, but these, being disadvantageous, fall under the shears of personal selection. The variation-playground may also be called the area of indulgence of variation, because the variations falling within it are spared from the eliminating activity of selection, or the variation-area of survivors, because on an average only those survive whose variations do not overstep the limits of this area.

This implies that variations below *U* (the lower limit of the area of exemption) and above O (the upper limit) can occur, but do not survive and leave descendants, and we can therefore easily understand why characters, of which different degrees arise with equal ease from the constitution of the species, must gradually develop a symmetrical curve of frequency because of the constant crossing. Obviously those individuals which stand just upon the borders of admissible variation will, other conditions being equal, leave behind them fewer descendants than those which approximate to the middle of the area of exemption; for as the characters concerned can vary in the offspring in both directions, there will always be at the lower end some of the descendants of a pair which will fall below the limits of exemption, and at the upper end some which will

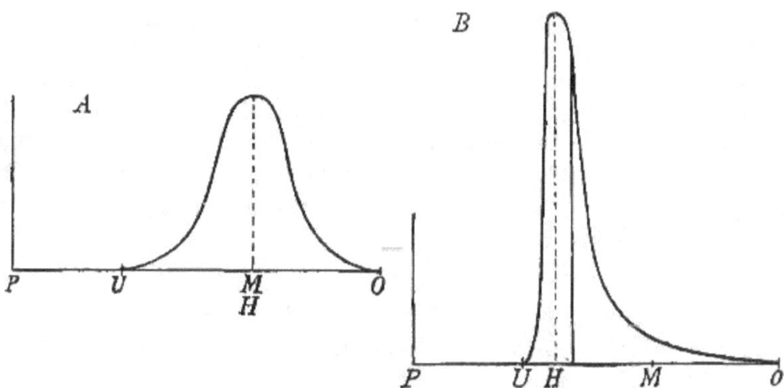

FIG. 120. *A*, symmetrical, and *B*, asymmetrical curve of frequency; after Ammon. *U*, minimal, *O*, maximal limit of individual variation. *U–O*, the 'variation-playground.' *M*, the mean of variation. *H*, the greatest frequency or mode of variation.

rise above it. This will happen even when pairing takes place between parents at the middle or at the other end of the abscissa, for there are always cases of the preponderance of one parent in heredity. A higher percentage of the descendants of individuals on the borderline will therefore be eliminated, and their frequency *must therefore be less.* Even if at the beginning of the series of observations a condition obtained in which all the ordinates of the area of exemption were equally high, those nearest the boundaries would of necessity very soon become lower, and this in proportion to their distance from the boundary, and the frequency-curve, which at first would be a straight line (according to our assumption, which of course does not tally with natural conditions), would become a symmetrical curve, highest in the middle and falling equally at either side.

Ammon has worked out the hypotheses on which the curve of frequency would become asymmetrical. Firstly, when the fertility is greater towards the upper or lower limit of the area of exemption: secondly, when germinal selection forces the variation in a particular direction, upwards or downwards; and thirdly, 'when natural selection intervenes diversely at the upper or lower limit.' Of these three possibilities the first two must be acknowledged as quite probable, but the third, it seems to me, could only cause a temporary asymmetry of the curve, lasting, that is, only until a state of equilibrium has again been reached: but that may in certain conditions take a long time.

Asymmetrical curves of frequency (Fig. 120, *B*) therefore arise, for instance, when the intra-germinal conditions (the 'constitution of the species') more easily and therefore more frequently produce extreme variations. In this case the area of exemption can only extend on one side, and must remain in this state. In *Caltha palustris*, the marsh marigold, we may find, according to De Vries, among a hundred flowers, those with five, six, seven, and eight petals, in the following proportions:—

Petals	5	6	7	8
Number of flowers	72	21	6	1

and thus there is an asymmetrical curve of frequency. But if we take the whole area of variation as the area of exemption, that is, if we assume that it is indifferent for the species whether the flowers have five, six, seven, or eight petals, the preponderance of the five-petalled flowers may have its reason in the fact that it is much easier for five than six or more petals to be produced because of the internal structure of the whole plant.

In this case the maximum of frequency lies at the lower limit of variation, but it may also lie at the upper. Thus. according to De Vries, the blossoms of *Weigelia* vary, in regard to the number of their petal-tips, in the following manner. Six-tipped corollas were not found, and among 1,145 flowers there were the following proportions:—

Tips of the corolla .	3	4	5
Number of flowers .	61	196	888

It is thus clear that amphimixis is an essential factor in the fixing of forms, but that it certainly does not of itself determine these, and that it is not always the average of the variations that is the most frequent, but that the form of the curve of frequency is determined by other factors also, namely, by germinal and personal selection and by the directive control which these exert on variations.

The equalizing effect of amphigony may perhaps be expressed thus: In the case of every new adaptation there is at first a large area of variation, but this gradually decreases owing to a continual restriction on the part of natural selection, until ultimately—when the highest degree of constancy of the character or species has been attained—it only extends very little beyond the 'adaptation-playground' or the 'area of exemption.'

One of the effects of amphimixis is thus to bring about an increasing restriction of the area of variation, or, as we usually say, a constancy of the facies of a given form, a condensation into a species. How far this result is necessary or useful, and therefore how far it may be regarded as accounting for the persistence of amphimixis, we shall discuss in the chapter on the formation of species. My own view is that even the fact that new adaptations are rendered possible through amphimixis and amphigony, the mode of reproduction associated with it, affords in itself a sufficient reason why amphimixis should have been retained when once it had been introduced.

LECTURE XXIX

THE GENERAL SIGNIFICANCE OF AMPHIMIXIS (*continued*)

Association of amphimixis with reproduction—Origin of amphimixis—Its lowest forms—Amphimixis in Coccidia—Chromosomes in unicellular organisms—*Coccidium proprium*—'Amœba-nests' as a preliminary stage to amphimixis—Plastogamy of the Myxomycetes—Result: a strengthening of the power of adaptation—Strengthening of the power of assimilation—Use of complete amphimixis—Proof of its constant efficacy to be found in the rudimentary organs of Man—Allogamy—Means taken to prevent the mingling of nearly related forms—Amphimixis is not a 'formative' stimulus—Attraction of the germ-cells—Effects of inbreeding compared with those of parthenogenesis—Nathusius's case of injurious inbreeding—Hindrances to fertilization in the crossing of species—Probable reason for the injurious effect of inbreeding.

We have endeavoured to understand why amphimixis should have been established among the processes of life, and we have now to turn to the question when and how, that is, in what form, it was first introduced. But first I should like to refer for a little to the association of amphimixis with reproduction, which we find in all multicellular organisms, and among the higher types so unexceptionally that, until not very long ago, amphimixis and reproduction were looked on as one and the same thing, and all multiplication was believed to be associated with 'fertilization.' We have seen that this is not the case, that on the other hand the two processes are quite distinct, and may be called contrasts rather than equivalents, for reproduction always means an increase in the number of individuals, while amphimixis implies—originally at least—their diminution by a half.

Accordingly we found that, in unicellular organisms, amphimixis is not associated with reproduction, but interpolated between the divisions, and not even in such a manner that amphimixis precedes every multiplication by division, but so that the conjugation of two animals occurs only from time to time, after numerous divisions, sometimes hundreds, have occurred. It is obvious that this must be so, since, if amphimixis occurred regularly between every two divisions, no increase in the number of individuals would be brought about, at least if the fusion of the two conjugating individuals were complete.

Why, then, is there such an intimate, and in the case of the higher types, such an indissoluble, association between reproduction and amphimixis that 'fertilization' appears to be a *sine qua non* of reproduction, and not very long ago seemed to us to be the 'quickening of the ovum,' the 'burning spark' which causes the powder-barrel to explode?

The reason of this is not difficult to discover; it lies in the structure of multicellular animals, and in their differentiation according to the principle of division of labour, for since only particular cells are capable of reproduction, that is, of giving rise to the whole, it is in these necessarily that the process of amphimixis has to occur if its significance lies in its effects on the succeeding generations. It is true that in the lowest multicellular organisms, such as the species of *Volvox,* there are, in addition to the sex-cells, other reproductive cells quite similar to the ova, whose development into a new colony takes place without amphimixis, but the higher we ascend in the animal and plant series the rarer are these 'asexual' germ-cells or 'spores,' and in the highest animal types they are entirely absent and reproduction occurs only by means of the 'sex-cells.'

I am inclined to look for the cause of this striking phenomenon mainly in the fact that, if amphimixis had to be retained, this was effected with increasingly great difficulty the more highly and complexly differentiated the organisms became, and that more complicated adaptations were therefore necessary in order that the union of the two germ-cells might be rendered possible at all. There is first of all the separation into two kinds of sex-cells, whose far-reaching differentiations and precise adaptations to the most minute conditions we have already discussed; then follow the innumerable adaptations to bring about the meeting of the sex-cells, the arrangements for copulation, and, finally, the instincts which draw the two sexes together, the means of attraction which are employed, whether decorative colours or attractive shapes, stimulating odours or musical notes, in short, all the diverse and intricate arrangements, which seem to be more subtly elaborated the higher the organism stands upon the ladder of life. When we call to mind that sexual differentiations finally go so far that they dominate the whole organism, alike in its external appearance and in its internal nature, its feelings, inclinations, instincts, its will and ability, as well as its structure down to the finest nerve-elements, we can understand that a mode of reproduction which demands such a composite disposition of details, involving a moulding of the whole organism, so to speak, from birth till death, must of necessity remain the only one, and that there was no room for the persistence of any essentially different mode of reproduction with quite different adaptations. Or, to speak metaphorically, the power of adaptation which is innate in the organism so exhausted itself in the establishment of this marvellous amphimixis adjustment that the possibility of any other was totally excluded.

It is true that it is only among the Vertebrates that we find 'the reproductive apparatus' so highly developed, but even among Molluscs and Arthropods 'sexual' reproduction, that is, reproduction associated with amphimixis, is the prevailing mode. In these, indeed, parthenogenesis does occasionally occur, that is to say, sexually differentiated female germ-cells are, by means of some slight variations in the maturation of the egg, rendered capable of developing without previous amphimixis, but this happens only in quite special cases as an adaptation to quite special circumstances, and can only be regarded as a temporary cessation of the association between reproduction and amphimixis. In some cases it is a moiety of the ova adapted for amphimixis which develop parthenogenetically, as it is the same sexually differentiated animals, true females, which produce both sorts, and this is often true to some extent when the differentiation in the direction of parthenogenesis has advanced further, and the ova have been separated into those requiring fertilization and those which are parthenogenetic (e.g. the winter and the summer eggs of the Daphnidæ). Parthenogenesis is not asexual but unisexual reproduction, a mode of multiplication which shows us that even in highly differentiated animals the apparently indissoluble association between reproduction and amphimixis can be dissolved if circumstances require it.

But if amphimixis had to be retained in the higher animal forms —and we have seen reasons why this must be—it could only be effected by means of unicellular germs, for amphimixis is in essence a fusion of nuclei, and this is the reason why 'vegetative' reproduction, so-called, becomes less and less prominent in animals at least, and above the level of the Arthropods disappears almost entirely.

Let us now return to the question we asked at the beginning— When and in what form was amphimixis first introduced into the world of organisms? The best way to answer this is by observation. We must turn to the lowest forms which now exhibit it, and see whether it occurs in them in a simpler form, so that we may draw conclusions as to its origin and its primitive significance, for it would be possible, *a priori*, that this was something different from what it is now in the relatively higher organisms, and that a change of function has gradually come about.

Assuredly the whole intricate complex of adaptations which is now exhibited on the conjugation of the two sex-cells in animals and plants, the differentiation of two kinds of 'sexually' antagonistic cells, with all their special adaptations, the reduction of the chromosomes, the institution of the karyo-kinetic apparatus, together with the centrospheres and so on, cannot possibly have arisen all at once by fortuitous variation, but can only have arisen gradually, step by step, and as the result of 'innumerable external and internal influences.' But why should not these arrangements, nowadays so complex, have had a simple beginning? Why might not this beginning have been the simple union of the protoplasmic bodies of two non-nucleated Monera; followed, after the origin of nuclear substances, by the union of these, and, finally, after the differentiation of a nucleus with a definite number of chromosomes, with a dividing apparatus, with a membrane, and so on, by complete amphimixis as we now know it? And how many transition stages may not be added to fill up the gaps between these three main stages?

But how much we can actually prove in regard to these conceivable preliminary stages of amphimixis is another matter. If we take a survey of the observations that have been made up till now, we are confronted at first by the undoubtedly striking fact that very little is known about it as yet, for in fact the whole process is gone through even in quite lowly forms of life in a manner very similar to that in the higher forms. Amphimixis has been shown to be widespread even among unicellular organisms, yet not in an *essentially* simpler mode than among multicellulars. We have seen that even in ciliated Infusorians reducing division obtains, and that of the four nuclei which arise from twofold division of the original nucleus three break up again, and only the fourth, by a further division, separates into a male and a female pronucleus, 'which then complete the amphimixis with the corresponding pro-nuclei of another animal' (compare Fig. 85, 4–7, vol. i. p. 321). This, and the existence of a dividing apparatus and of chromosomes, make the process appear very little less complicated than the fertilization of higher animals. The case is similar even in much lower unicellular organisms, such as *Noctiluca* (Fig. 83, vol. i. p. 317). In this form and in Rhizopods it is true that reducing divisions have not yet been made out, but their occurrence in the lower Algæ (*Basidiobolus*), and above all in those simple unicellular organisms which give rise to malaria, and their allies, which live as 'Coccidia' in the blood-cells and intestinal cells of animals, leads us to expect that they may prove to be of general occurrence among unicellulars.

In the Coccidia, which are extremely simple unicellular organisms, equipped, however, with a nucleus, the adaptations relating to amphimixis are more extensive and more complex than in the Rhizopods. For while in the latter the two conjugating cells are absolutely alike in external appearance, in the former the male cell is distinct from the female, and indeed the differences are as marked as those that usually occur in multicellular animals.

We owe our present knowledge of these processes especially to

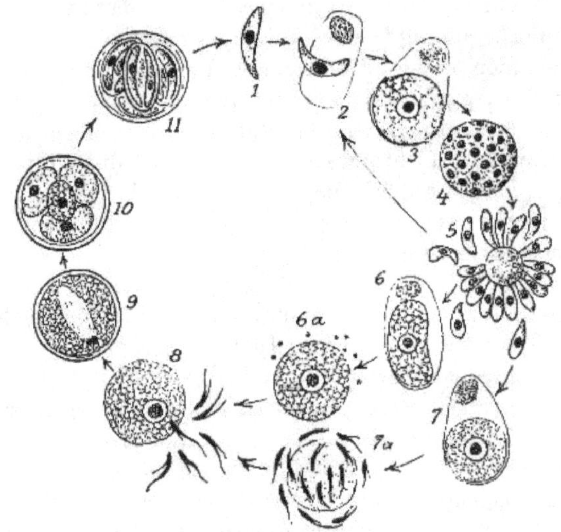

Fig. 121. Life-cycle of *Coccidium lithobii*, a cell-parasite of the centipede *Lithobius*; after Schaudinn. 1, a 'sporozoite'; 2, the same penetrating into an intestinal epithelial cell; 3, the same growing into a 'schizont' capable of division; 4, the same dividing, and 5, breaking up into numerous pieces which separate from the 'residual body' in the centre, and either, as in 1, migrate into epithelial cells and repeat the history, or pass on to the phase of sexual reproduction. In the latter case, after eliminating a portion of the nucleus (reduction) in 6 and 6 *a*, they form the 'macrogamete' (the ovum); or within the mother-cell they produce microgametes (or sperm-cells), 7 and 7 *a*. The penetration of a sperm-cell into an egg-cell (amphimixis) is shown in 8, the fertilized egg-cell (9) becomes the so-called oocyst or permanent spore, from which by repeated division (10 and 11), new sporozoites, as in 1, arise, and begin the cycle afresh.

Schuberg, Schaudinn, and Siedlecki, and, because of their theoretical importance, I should like to summarize the essential points.

One of these Coccidia lives in the intestinal cells of a small centipede, *Lithobius*; in Fig. 121 the parasite is shown as a so-called 'Sporozoite,' that is, as a minute sickle-shaped cell, which at first moves freely about the intestine of the host (1), but then soon penetrates into an epithelial cell (2). There it grows to a spherical shape (3), and then, after having devoured the cell, it gives rise, by a peculiar process of division (Schizogony), to a number of very minute nucleated pieces, again sickle-shaped, the Schizonts, each of which bores its way into an epithelial cell as in 2, and follows the same path of development, so that a large number of cells in the intestine of the same host are attacked in this manner. But there is still another mode of reproduction, with which amphimixis is associated, which leads directly to the formation of 'lasting' germs which are enclosed in a capsule or cyst, reach the exterior with the excrement of the host, and thus spread the infection to other centipedes. The Schizonts which take this course develop into so-called macrogametes and microgametes, the former being the female, the latter th male germ-cells. Then follows the penetration of a male gamete, actively motile because of its two flagella, into the female gamete (8). Amphimixis is accomplished, and the product of the fusion of the two sex-cells (9) surrounds itself with a thinner cyst, within which it multiplies by twofold division into four cells (10). These are the 'lasting' spores, which may dry up within the voided excrement of the centipede (11), and if they be eaten by another animal of the species, they infect it, for the sporozoites which have been formed by the previous divisions creep out, and in form 1 begin the life-history anew.

We have thus an alternation of four generations which are all unicellular, and of which one series (1–5) shows multiplication by fission, while the other (6–11) includes, besides multiplication by fission and as a condition of this, the process of amphimixis. Amphimixis *must* occur in order that the formation of 'lasting' spores and new sporozoites may result. We have thus a regular alternation of 'asexual' and 'sexual' reproduction, and the latter shows great resemblance to that of multicellular organisms. The macrogamete corresponds to the ovum, the microgametes to the spermatozoa, and they resemble these also in their greater numbers and in their structure.

But the resemblance goes even further. The ovum is much larger than the sperm-cell, and undergoes a kind of reduction of its nuclear substance; shortly before fertilization the ovum-nucleus ('the germinal vesicle') comes to the surface—just as in the case of animal ova—bursts, and extrudes a part of its substance in the form of a sphere (Fig. 121, 6 and 7). A reduction of the nuclear substance in the male cell has not been demonstrated in all cases, but in one of the *Lithobius*-Coccidia, *Adelea ovata*, the relatively large microgamete (the sperm-cell, Fig. 122, *Mi*) places itself close to one pole of the female macrogamete (the egg-cell) and then divides twice in succession, so that four small cells arise (Fig. 122, *A–C*): of these only one penetrates into the egg-cell (*D*, ♂*K*) and unites with it, the other three come to nought (*D*, *Mi*). What a surprising resemblance this bears to the twofold division of the mother sperm-cell in multicellular animals, through which the number of chromosomes is reduced to half! In the conjugation itself the thread-like chromosomes of the female nucleus are plainly recognizable, while those of the male remain coiled up (Fig. 118, *D*).

That the nuclear substance can be separated into chromosomes (ids) even in lowly unicellular organisms was probably first demonstrated by R. Hertwig for *Actinosphaerium*, a Heliozoon or freshwater sun-animalcule, then by Lauterborn in regard to Diatoms, by Blochmann for an indigenous Rhizopod, *Euglypha*, and by Ishikawa for

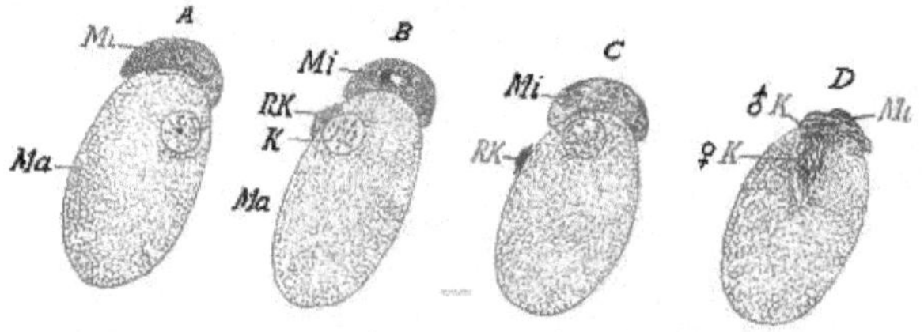

FIG. 122. Conjugation of a Coccidium (*Adelea ovata*), after Schaudinn and Siedlecki. *A*, the microgamete (sperm-cell) (*Mi*) has become closely apposed to the macrogamete (*Ma*). *B*, the reduction division of the nucleus of the macrogamete has been effected; *Rk*, directive corpuscles. In the microgamete the first division of the nucleus has begun. *C*, four nuclei in the microgamete, of which three come to nought. *D*, the fourth microgamete-nucleus (♂*K*) has become apposed to the nucleus of the ovum, in which distinct chromosomes are seen.

the marine *Noctiluca*. Fresh cases have been added in the last decade, so that we can now say that a considerable number of unicellulars, from the ciliated Infusorians and lower Algæ down to the Coccidia and Diatoms, exhibit a germ-plasm composed of ids. These structures behave in the same way as those in higher organisms, and Berger was able to demonstrate, in 1900, in the case of a Radiolarian, their multiplication by spontaneous splitting.

From our point of view all this cannot surprise us, since all these organisms, though only single cells, possess great complexity of structure; we need only call to mind the extremely fine differentiation of structure in numerous ciliated Infusorians, such as *Stentor*, which has already been mentioned, or the bell-animalcule (*Vorticella*) with its long and peculiarly ciliated gullet, its retractile ciliated disk, its muscular or myophane layer, its spirally retractile stalk with the ribbon-like, rapidly acting muscular axis; or the regular geometrically constructed flinty skeleton of the Radiolarians, with their radially disposed sword-like or rod-like needles and their complex interlacing lattice-work shells. In the latter case the complexity of the living substance becomes visible only through its product, the shell, for the protoplasm itself does not show any visible intricacy, and the same is true of the Coccidium whose life-history we have just been tracing, for in each of its stages it seems to be of very simple organization, though the succession of numerous different forms shows that its germ-substance must be composed of numerous determinants.

We cannot doubt, however, that, in all unicellular organisms, the protoplasm can be hardly less complicated as regards its minute invisible structure, since otherwise it would be impossible that the delicate vital processes which we observe in them should run their course. In this I agree, at least in principle, with the beautiful picture drawn by Ludwig Zehnder in his recent book [1] already mentioned, though he reached it in quite a different way, namely, by a purely synthetic method. He made the daring attempt to build up the organic world from below, starting from atoms and molecules, and ascending from these to the lowest vital units, our biophors, to which he attributes a tubular shape and therefore calls fistellæ. He imagines the cell to be made up of a large number, perhaps millions, of different kinds of fistellæ, of which one presides over the power of turgidity, another over endosmosis, a third over contraction, a fourth over the conduction of stimuli, &c., so that there results a high degree of cellular complexity, a composition out of numerous kinds of biophors arranged on a definite architectural plan. All this corresponds perfectly with the views I have so long championed, and which alone make the existence of a nucleus intelligible, if it is composed—as I assume—essentially of an accumulation of determinants, that is, of hereditary substances. And that such a high degree of complexity of structure is not a mere fanciful picture we see occasionally even in the case of unicellular organisms. Thus, for instance, in *Coccidium proprium*, parasitic in the newt (*Triton*), the macrogamete or egg-cell (Fig. 123, *Ma*) before fertilization by the sperm-cell or microgamete (Fig. 123, *Mi*) surrounds itself with a capsule, at one pole of which a minute opening, the micropyle, remains for the entrance of the male cell. This proves, it seems to me, that this particular spot of the capsule is hereditarily determined, just as much and just as definitely as the ray of the flint-skeleton of a Radiolarian. But if any spot of the capsule can vary by itself alone, may

[1] Zehnder, *Die Entstehung des Lebens*, Freiburg-i.-Br., 1899.

not numerous other points in the animal also be hereditarily determinable? With such complexity of the invisible structure it would not greatly surprise us if we should find amphimixis occurring in all unicellular organisms, and in many of them at a high level of elaboration. These apparently lowly and simple organisms are obviously very far from being the lowliest and simplest, as we shall discover later in a different connexion. But that amphimixis is found as a periodically recurring process even among these, must depend upon the fact that here too the preservation of the best-adapted structure, as well as adaptability to new conditions, requires that the best variants of many different parts of the cell should be brought together, and since the hereditary substance lies in the ids of the nucleus, the union

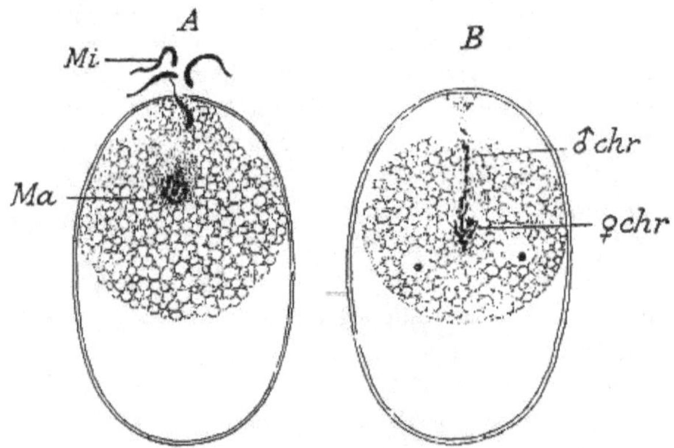

FIG. 123. Conjugation of *Coccidium proprium*, a cellular parasite of the newt (*Triton*), after Siedlecki. *A*, a microgamete (*Mi*) in the act of penetrating the shell of a macrogamete (*Ma*) through the micropyle. *B*, the male and the female nuclear constituents are uniting ♂ *chr* and ♀ *chr*.

of the ids of two unicellulars will make harmonious and many-sided adaptation materially easier. It will thus give an advantage in the struggle for existence, and we may therefore expect to find that the nuclear substance in all unicellular organism is made up of ids.

The observations hitherto made do not, however, appear to bear this out, for in the lower Flagellata and Algæ the nuclear substance does indeed consist of chromatin, but—as far as it can be made out—of a compact unarranged mass of it. But even though deeper investigations should succeed in demonstrating chromosomes in many of these, the nucleus *must have arisen at some time,* and we must assume that it did so through a more intimate union of previously loose aggregates of determinants, which were gradually arranged and bound together by the combining forces (affinities) we have assumed to obtain among them, thus giving rise to the first chromosomes or ids which were complete in themselves. Then came the multiplication of these ids by the process of division, and only then was the state arrived at from which amphimixis, as we now know it, could have arisen, namely, the existence of a considerable number of identical ids, half of which could be exchanged for the identical ids of another individual in conjugation.

But as to our question, In what organisms did amphimixis first arise, and how? there seems, from what we have already learned with regard to the Coccidia, little prospect of our being able to give a definite answer, for if amphimixis occurs even in these lowly organisms, and occurs, too, in the same manner as in the higher unicellular organisms, and not very much more simply than among the highest multicellular organisms, we may conclude that the preliminary stages will now be very difficult or impossible to detect, either because they are extinct, or because they occur only in ultra-microscopic organisms.

Nevertheless there do appear to be preliminary stages, and they are exactly those which we should have assumed if we had been obliged to construct them theoretically.

The first phenomenon of this kind is the mere juxtaposition of two or more unicellular organisms, without the occurrence of fusion. This was probably first observed by Gruber in Amœbæ, and it was theoretically interpreted at a later date by Rhumbler. As many as fifty Amœbæ gather together to form a 'nest,' and remain closely apposed to each other for a fortnight. Although no fusion took place, and there were no visible results of this juxtaposition, it may be concluded that the animals had some sort of attractive effect upon each other, and it may be supposed that some sort of advantage must have been associated with this state of quiet, close apposition against one another. Cytotropism, the mutual attraction of similar cells, which Wilhelm Roux first observed in the segmentation-cells of the frog's egg, seems to occur also in unicellular organisms, and this may help us to understand how a fusion of cell-bodies may have come about.

Fusion of this kind was demonstrated in the Myxomycetes almost forty years ago by De Bary, and it has been observed more recently in various unicellular organisms, especially in Rhizopods and in Heliozoa. These last often place themselves close together in pairs, threes, or even more at a time, and then the delicate cell-bodies coalesce, though no fusion of the nuclei takes place. With Hartog, we call this process 'Plastogamy,' but we cannot agree with that observer when he regards the importance of the process as consisting in the fact that the nuclei thus come into contact with fresh cell-substance, after having been surrounded for a very long time with the same cytoplasm. If this were the import of amphimixis, then an *exchange of nuclei* would take place, and this we find nowhere even among the lowest forms of life, for everywhere there is a union of the nuclear substance of two individuals. But this is by the way! Further cases of plastogamy have been observed in many of the limy-shelled Rhizopods. A union of this kind does not usually lead to any visible consequences, but in some Foraminifera a group of young animals is developed within the cell-bodies by the division of the nuclei and the cell-body; thus multiplication follows the fusion just as in perfect amphimixis, and we may therefore assume that there is a causal connexion between the two. In the slime-fungi, too, the union of several amœba-like cells into a multi-nucleated plasmodium is followed later by the development of numerous encapsuled spores, but only after the plasmodium, which to begin with is microscopically small, has grown to a macroscopically visible, reticulated mass (*Æthalium*) sometimes a foot in extent. In this case the fungus, creeping slowly over its foundation of decaying substance, takes up nourishment from it, and it is not possible to tell whether the union of the amœbæ yields any further advantage than that of facilitating the spreading over large uneven surfaces, and through this, later, the development of large fruit-bodies. But in the case of the Foraminifera the plastogamy has obviously another effect, unknown and mysterious, which as yet no one has ever been able to define precisely. Words like 'stimulus to growth,' 'stimulating of the metabolism,' and even 'rejuvenation,' give no insight into what happens, but that something happens, that through the fusion of two or more unicellulars a stimulus is exerted, which reveals itself later in increased rapidity of growth, we may, and indeed must assume, because this process has become a permanent arrangement in so many unicellular organisms. Only what is useful survives, and the uniting individuals must derive some advantage from the process of fusion, and it remains to be seen whether we can find out with any clearness what this advantage may be.

Till within a few decades ago it was believed that in this process one individual devoured the other, but this can now no longer be maintained. If any one still seriously considers this possible, Schaudinn's observations would convince him of his error, for in *Trichosphærium*, a marine, many-nucleated Rhizopod, he observed, on the one hand, the union of two or more animals, i. e. plastogamy, and on the other hand, the swallowing and digesting of a smaller member of the species by a larger one—two processes which are absolutely different, for in the first case the cell-bodies of the two animals remain intact, while an animal that is eaten becomes surrounded by a food-vacuole, and is dissolved and digested within it. In the former case the vital units (biophors) of each animal obviously remain intact and capable of function; in the second, those of the over-mastered animal are at once dissolved and chemically broken up; as biophors, therefore, they cease to exist. Whether one or the other process takes place may perhaps depend on whether the two animals differ greatly in size, so that the smaller can be quite surrounded by the larger.

In a former lecture I have emphatically expressed my dissent from the view which interprets amphimixis as a process of rejuvenation, meaning thereby a necessary renewal of life, and I need not go into this again in detail: for that the metabolism can continue through uncounted generations without being artificially stimulated—that is, in any other way than by nutrition—is proved by all those lowly organisms which exhibit neither plastogamy nor complete amphimixis, and also by the occurrence of purely parthenogenetic reproduction, &c. In what, then, can the advantage lie which the conjugating unicellular organisms derive from conjugation? Obviously not in that they impart to each other what each already possessed, but only in the communication of something special and individual, something that was peculiar to each, and becomes common to both.

Haberlandt believed that the development of auxo-spores in Diatoms pointed towards the processes which form the deepest roots of amphimixis. As is well known, the hard and unyielding flinty shell of these lowly Algæ involves a diminution of the organism at every division, so that the Diatoms become smaller and smaller as they go on multiplying, and if that went on without limit they would come rapidly to extinction. But a corrective is supplied in the periodical occurrence of conjugation of two organisms which have already materially diminished in size, and this is followed by the growth of the two fused individuals to the original normal size of the species.

It is, of course, obvious that in this case the union of two organisms which have become too small may be of advantage in bringing them back to the requisite normal size; but this is an isolated special case, which certainly does not justify our regarding conjugation as a means whereby diminished bodily size may be brought back to its normal proportions. By far the greater number of unicellular organisms are not permanently diminished in size by division, and even in the Diatoms the mass of the two fused individuals does not amount to the normal size of the species, so that even in this case there must be growth subsequent to the conjugation before the normal is re-attained. It may be doubted, therefore, whether the increase in mass is, even in the case cited, the essential event in conjugation, and whether there are not other effects which we cannot clearly recognize. Here, too, there must be differences between the two conjugating individuals, as we have just seen, for if they only communicated something similar to each other, the result would be an increase only in their mass, not in their qualities.

Although we cannot demonstrate differences of this kind in the case of the lowly organisms with which we are now dealing, we may assume their existence from analogy with the higher organisms. We know, especially through G. Jäger, that in Man every individual has a specific exhalation, his particular odour, and that in the secretions of his glands there are incalculably minute differences in chemical composition, which justify the conclusion that the living substance of the secreting cells themselves exhibits such differences, and that all the various kinds of cells in an individual are not absolutely identical with the corresponding cells of another individual, but that they are distinguished from them by minute yet constant chemical differences. The assumption that differences of this kind exist even in unicellulars, and in all lowly organisms generally, is not a merely fanciful one, but has much probability.

How far the combination of these individual differences of chemical, and at the same time vital, organization is able to quicken, to strengthen the metabolism, to bring about 'physiological regeneration,' or whatever we may choose to call it, we do not yet understand. It has been said that in plastogamy an exchange of 'substances' takes place; that each gives to the other the substances which it possesses and the other lacks, and that this causes an increase of vital energy. But it is unlikely that we have here to do merely with chemical substances, although these, of course, as the material basis of all vital processes, are indispensable; it seems to me more probable that the vital units (biophors) themselves in their specific individuality must play the chief part. But even this is saying very little, for we have not yet reached an understanding of these processes, and if we were not forced by the fact of plastogamy to the conclusion that this union must have some use, no one would have been likely to postulate it as useful, still less as necessary. It has, of course, been frequently suggested that multiplication by fission, if long-continued, results in 'exhaustion,' and that this is corrected by amphimixis, but who can tell why this 'exhaustion' might not be remedied, and even more effectually remedied, by a fresh supply of fuel, that is, of food? One might have thought that the vital processes would be thus more readily recuperated than by the co-operative combination of two already 'exhausted' cells. Two exhausted horses may perhaps be able to pull the load that one of them was no longer equal to, but in the case we are considering it is the combined burdens of two units that have to be borne, although each was no longer equal to its own share! That is more than we can understand.

Zehnder has recently defined the effect of amphimixis as a 'strengthening of the power of adaptation,' and he infers that the 'digestive fistellæ' (Biophors) of two individuals, which have somewhat different powers of digestion, are, when they combine, able to assimilate more kinds of food than either was able to assimilate by itself. But I confess that I do not see how an advantage for the whole would be gained through this alone, since half of the digestive biophors would have to work for the nutrition of the mass of the individual *A*, the other half of the differently constituted biophors for that of the individual *B*, and the nutritive capacity would thus remain exactly what it was before conjugation. Nevertheless I believe that Zehnder was right in his supposition that conjugation is concerned with strengthening the power of adaptation, and I have long maintained and defended this interpretation with regard to true amphimixis in nucleated organisms. In these cases it is quite obvious that the communication of fresh ids to the germ-plasm implies an augmentation of the variational tendencies, and thus an increase of the power of adaptation. Under certain circumstances this may be of *direct* advantage to the individual which results from the amphimixis, but in most cases the advantage will be only an indirect one, which may not necessarily be apparent in the lifetime of this one individual, but may become so only in the course of generations and with the aid of selection. For amphimixis must bring together favourable as well as unfavourable variations, and the advantage it has for the species lies simply in the fact that the latter are weeded out in the struggle for existence, and that by repetition of the process the unfavourable variational tendencies are gradually eliminated more and more completely from the germ-plasm of the species.

But this cannot have been the efficient cause in the introduction of amphimixis into the series of vital phenomena; the reason for this must be found in some *direct* advantage, such as that it improved and increased the assimilating power, the growth, and the multiplication of the particular individual, so that it gained an advantage over individuals which had not entered into conjugation. This advantage *must exist*, at least in the lower forms of conjugation, in pure plastogamy, i.e. in the mere coalescence of the protoplasmic bodies. But, as it seems to me, we have not yet clearly recognized what the advantage precisely is; we do not yet see how such a mingling or combination of two plasms should every time be of advantage for the combined conjugate. If we assume with Zehnder that two kinds of 'nutritive' biophors are brought together which differ slightly from each other in digestive capacity, three cases may occur. Either the food *a*, adequate for the animal *A*, is just as abundant as the food *b*, suitable for the animal *B*, and then half the conjugated animal will be nourished by means of the biophors *a*, the other half by means of the biophors *b*, and the state of matters is the same as it was before conjugation; or the food *b* is more abundant than the food *a*, or conversely, and then the biophors *b* will have to take the larger share in the nourishment of the conjugate $A + B$, and they will therefore multiply more rapidly and the biophors *a* will decrease relatively in number. Nutrition and growth will then go on more slowly for a time, but will soon attain to their former intensity. The combined individual $A + B$ has then certainly gained an advantage over the isolated animal *A*, and the living substance of *A* which, if left to itself would probably have perished, can continue to live in combination with *B*. But in that case it is not obvious where the advantage in the union can lie, as far as *B* is concerned. An advantage to *B* only results if there be a combination not of *one* kind of biophor only, but of several or many kinds of biophors. If for instance *A*, whose digestive biophors were weak, brought with it into the partnership 'secretory' or nervous biophors stronger than those of *B*, then there would be an advantage for both in the combination, and it is thus that, in the meantime, I interpret the direct benefit which results from pure plastogamy. This benefit must be the more important and far-reaching the longer multiplication by fission continues without the occurrence of conjugation.

We thus reach what is perhaps a not wholly unsatisfactory conception of amphimixis, in so far at least that we do not require to assume that there has been a fundamental change in its significance between its expression in the lowest organisms and in the higher and even highest forms. Everywhere it is the same advantage: an increase in the power of adaptation; but it sometimes finds expression directly in the product of conjugation, sometimes only indirectly, sooner or later, among the descendants of the product.

How far below the Myxomycetes pure plastogamy reaches we do not know; whether it also occurs among non-nucleated organisms (Haeckel's Monera) we cannot tell from experience, since these assumed organisms have not yet been observed with certainty. Perhaps they all lie below the limits of visibility, and then we could never do more than *suppose* that plastogamic processes occur among them. Logically and purely theoretically we may *suppose* that amphimixis occurred first between the plasmic bodies of non-nucleated Monera, then between the cell-bodies of true cells, and finally between the nuclei of cells.

Let us hold fast to what we have found to be probable, namely, that the fusion of individually different simple organisms must or may bring about a direct advantage—a stimulation of the metabolism, and at the same time an improvement of the constitution in different directions, and let us go on to the consideration of cell-fusion combined with nuclear fusion, or complete amphimixis. In this something is added which we can recognize as an important advantage, namely, the combination of two hereditary substances, and thus the union of two variation-complexes which, according to our view, is necessary if transformation of species is to take place. In mere plastogamy such a union of two hereditary masses could only take place in Monera, not in nucleated organisms. If then there are really unicellular organisms which exhibit plastogamy without karyogamy (certain Foraminifera), we have a further proof that these processes of plasmic fusion imply direct advantage, which is distinct from the indirect advantage lying in the mingling of two different hereditary contributions, since in these cases of plastogamy there is no demonstrable mingling of hereditary bodies, no karyogamy.

But as soon as karyogamy or nuclear fusion was associated with mere plastogamy, complete amphimixis could never be lost again, because it alone made it possible that there should be harmonious transformation and adaptation in organisms which were becoming ever more complex; the primary effect of the mingling would be more and more transcended, since, without amphimixis, transmutation with harmonious adaptation in all directions would be less and less possible as organisms became more complex in structure. I have already referred to the manifold details in the structure and development of the lowest organisms which make this conclusion appear luminous to us, but we can also infer the necessity for an unceasingly active selection, from a quite different set of facts, namely, from what we know of rudimentary organs in Man.

We may regard Mankind as a species which has its local races and sub-races, but which is fixed in its essential characters, and only fluctuates hither and thither in individual variation in each sub-race, just like any other modern mammal, such as the marmot or the hare.

Nevertheless we know that Man, as regards certain fairly numerous parts, is continually and persistently varying in a definite direction. Wiedersheim, in his book *On the Structure of Man*[1], enumerates a long series of parts and organs of the human body, which are in process of gradual degeneration, and of which it may be predicted that they will disappear from the human structure since they have lost functional significance. Among these dwindling structures are the two last ribs, the eleventh and twelfth, while the thirteenth has already disappeared, and only occurs exceptionally as a small vestige in the adult human being of to-day. The series includes also the seventh cervical rib, the *os centrale* of the wrist, the wisdom teeth, and the vermiform appendix of the intestine. The last is much larger in many mammals, and represents an important part of the digestive apparatus, but in Man it has dwindled to an unimportant appendage, which is a source of danger when foreign bodies (cherry stones and such like) lodge in it and set up inflammation. The variations in its length warrant us in concluding that it is still in process of degeneration: its average length is about 8½ cm., but it varies from 2 cm. to 23 cm. in length, and in about 25 per cent. of cases a partial or entire closing up of its opening into the intestine may be observed.

Wiedersheim enumerates nearly a hundred parts thus in process of degeneration: this means that nearly a hundred structures in Man are at the present time in process of variation, and this could not be so unless amphimixis were continually mingling the hereditary contributions anew from generation to generation, so that the minus-variations of the parts in question, starting from the germ-plasm in which they arose at one time as chance variations, and confirmed in their direction by means of germinal selection, are gradually being transmitted to all the germ-plasms of the species. We thus see that even in a period of species-life, which we may fairly call a period of constancy, variations of a phyletic kind are continually in process, which could not become general without the co-operation of amphimixis.

Now, we have already seen that personal selection plays no part, or, at least, no important part in such degenerations, because the variations which are here concerned do not usually attain to selection value, but it is just such variations proceeding with infinite slowness that occur in functionally important organs likewise, and in the progressive advance of which personal selection and mutual adaptation probably play a part, so that in this way we can understand why the preservation of amphigony by natural selection must be effected. It is impossible—for obvious reasons—to name particular instances with

[1] *Ueber den Bau des Menschen*, 2nd ed., Freiburg-i.-Br., 1893. Trans. London, 1896.

certainty, as we can do in the case of the rudimentary organs, but even on general considerations we might expect that among the incipient variations of the determinants of the germ-plasm there would be some which were in an ascending direction, and that among these there would be some which, advanced by germinal selection, would go on ascending until they attained selection value. Wiedersheim reckons, for instance, the gradually increasing differentiation of the cortical zone of the human brain among the parts which are still in process of ascending variation, and he is probably right in doing so.

But if variations, so slow as to be unnoticeable, are still of abundant occurrence in Man, we have no reason to doubt that similar processes are going on in other animals; among the higher Vertebrates at least there is hardly a species which does not exhibit regressive variations even now, and in many cases progressive variations also are occurring, although we cannot give definite proofs of this.

The appearance of fixity which most species have is, therefore, illusory; in reality they exhibit a slow flux, gradually setting aside the superfluities they received from their ancestors, perfecting the important parts to more precise adaptation and greater functional capacity, and at the same time endeavouring to maintain all the parts in constant harmony. We can understand that as long as this process of gradual perfecting goes on, amphimixis will not readily be given up. Those that retain it must always, in the long run, have the preference. Moreover, as we have seen, *it cannot be given up*, when it has existed through æons, because of the power of persistence which the germ-plasm has gradually acquired in the course of such a long hereditary succession. It could only be given up if an advantage decisive as to survival were associated with its abandonment, such as can be actually recognized in most cases of parthenogenesis, among animals at least.

In my opinion this indirect effect of amphimixis, that is, the increasing of the possibilities of adaptation by new combinations of individual variational tendencies, is the main one, while the direct nutritive effect of the two germ-cells upon one another is quite subsidiary. In this opinion I find myself in opposition to the views of many if not most naturalists, who assume that amphimixis has a direct, sometimes, indeed, only a direct effect, and believe that they can prove it by facts.

In support of this position it has been pointed out that allogamy, that is, the mingling of individuals of different ancestry, occurs even among lowly unicellulars, and then higher up among most organisms; but the question has not been asked whether this mutual attraction of the unlike really expresses a primary characteristic of organisms, and may not possibly be a secondary acquisition adapted to ensure the occurrence of amphimixis. If we examine the facts we find that even in the lowly Algæ, such as *Pandorina* and *Ulothrix*, only the migratory cells or swarm-spores of different cell-colonies conjugate with one another, but not those of the same lineage, and this phenomenon may be observed in many unicellular plants and animals. We are justified in concluding from this that a fairly large degree of difference between the conjugating gametes secures the best results, whether this result is to be looked for in a 'rejuvenation' or in an increased adaptive capacity; but it is erroneous to regard the stronger attraction between individuals of different descent as a direct outcome of this. To me, at least, it seems to be an adaptive arrangement. The whole of the long and complex phylogenetic history of the sex-cells, the gametes, shows clearly that we have here to deal with a succession of adaptations, and that the degree of attraction which obtains between gametes has gradually been increased and specialized in the course of the phylogeny. I need only briefly recall what we have discussed in a former lecture, that at first the copulating cells were exactly alike in appearance and size, that then one kind of cell became rather larger than the other, and that only gametes which were thus different in size were mutually attractive—the micro-gametes and the macro-gametes, or male and female germ-cells; we have seen that these differences between the two became more and more accentuated, that the female cell continued to grow larger than the male, and to accumulate more and more nutritive material for the building up of the young organism which arises from its union with the male cell, and that the male cells became smaller, but more numerous, as was essential if their chances of finding the often remote female cell were not to disappear altogether. And besides, there are all the innumerable adaptations of the egg-cell to the countless special circumstances which obtain in the different groups, and the innumerable varieties in the form of the sperm-cell, with all its delicate and complicated adaptations to the special conditions under which the egg-cell can be reached and fertilized in this or that group of organisms. Of a truth, he is past helping who does not regard with wonder and admiration the adaptations which have been worked out in this connexion in the course of evolution! But if all these details are adaptations, so is the beginning of the whole process of differentiation; allogamy, the attraction of conjugating cells of different lineage, is not a primary outcome of individual diversity; gametes of different descent did not strongly attract each other of themselves, but they were equipped with a strong power of mutual attraction, because the union of very different individualities was the more advantageous.

This is an important distinction, for the adaptation to allogamy is widely distributed, and its latest manifestations have frequently been misunderstood in the same way as its beginnings. The widespread occurrence of allogamy has been interpreted as evidence in favour of the rejuvenation theory, and the endeavour on Nature's part to secure the union of the unlike has been associated with the hypothetical 'rejuvenating' power of amphimixis, and regarded as a direct and inevitable outcome of this. That this view is erroneous we shall see even more clearly from what follows.

As among unicellular Algæ it is frequently only gametes of different lineage which conjugate, so among animals and plants there are numerous cases in which the union of nearly related gametes is more or less strictly excluded, both by the prevention of self-fertilization (autogamy) in hermaphrodites, or by the prevention of inbreeding, that is, the continued pairing of near relatives. Now all the preventive measures which effect this are of a secondary nature; they are adaptations which result from the advantage involved in the mingling of unrelated germ-plasms, even though it sometimes seems as if they were an outcome of the primary nature of the germ-cells.

The primary result of the mutual chemical influence of the two germ-cells upon one another is—apart from the impulse to development which the centrosphere of the sperm-cell supplies—as far as I see, only the more favourable or the more unfavourable mingling of the biophor- or determinant-variants, and the resulting increase or decrease in adaptive capacity, which leads to the better thriving of the offspring, or conversely to its degeneration. Everything else is secondary and depends upon adaptation, effected in very diverse ways, to secure the most favourable mingling of the germ-plasms for the particular species concerned. Undoubtedly the parental ids united through amphimixis have an effect upon each other, since throughout the building up of the organism of the child the homologous determinants struggle with one another for food, but they do not affect each other in the way that many prominent physiological and medical writers suppose, namely, that the union of the parental germ-plasms sets up a 'formative stimulus' which 'advances' or even 'greatly advances' the process of development in the egg.

Parthenogenetic development goes on just as rapidly, sometimes even more rapidly than that of the fertilized ova of the same species!

How can the supposed 'formative stimulus' be so entirely dispensed with in this case?

Of course I am well aware that the two kinds of germ-cells have a strong attraction for each other, and that the protoplasm of the ovum actually exhibits tremulous movement when the spermatozoon penetrates through the micropyle. I myself observed this in the case of the lamprey (*Petromyzon*) when Calberla instituted his investigations on the fertilization of that animal, but has that anything to do with a formative stimulus? Is it anything more than the result of the chemotactic stimulus exerted by the substance of the ovum upon that of the spermatozoon and conversely? And have we any ground for seeing anything more in this than an adaptation of the sex-cells to the necessity of mutually finding each other out and thereafter combining? Two quite different things are often confused with one another in this connexion: the mutual attraction of the two kinds of sex-cells which tends to secure their union, and the results of this union. A more exact distinction is necessary between the effects and the advantages which allogamy brings in its train and the means by which it is secured in the different species.

If amphimixis really set up a 'formative' stimulus, and if the amount of this was regulated by the differences between the two parental germ-plasms, then parthenogenesis, which implies the entire absence of the mingling of two parental cells, would necessarily be even less advantageous than amphimixis between near relatives; but this is not the case. Continued inbreeding leads in many cases to the degeneration of the descendants, and particularly to lessened fertility and even to complete sterility. Thus in my prolonged breeding experiments with white mice, which were later carried on by G. von Guaita, strict inbreeding, effected throughout twenty-nine generations, resulted in a gradually diminishing fertility, and similar observations have been made by Ritzema Bos and others. But why does not the same thing happen in pure parthenogenesis? My experiments in breeding parthenogenetic Ostracods (*Cypris reptans*) shows that these crustaceans, in the course of the eighty generations which I have observed till now[1], have lost nothing of their prolific fertility and vital power; and the same is true in free nature of the rose-gall wasp (*Rhodites rosæ*), which enjoys the greatest fertility notwithstanding its purely parthenogenetic reproduction, the females not infrequently

[1] The cultures were begun in 1884 and are still continued (March 6, 1902), still multiplying as abundantly as at the outset. I reckon that there are on an average five generations in a year, which means about eighty generations in sixteen years

laying a hundred eggs in a single bud. How does it happen that 'the mutual influence of two different hereditary substances which so powerfully promotes individual development' can be here altogether dispensed with? Only because it does not really exist, except in the imagination of my opponents, still influenced by the old dynamic theory of fertilization.

But it may be asked, whence come the injurious results of inbreeding, if not from the union of two nearly related germ-plasms? They certainly do arise from that cause, but it is not through a 'formative stimulus,' *too slight* in this case, exercising a direct formative chemical effect upon the two hereditary substances, but through the indirect influences exerted by these *too similar* hereditary contributions during the development of the new individual. Lest it be imagined that I am tilting against windmills, I will refer to one of the numerous examples of the evil effects of inbreeding which have been submitted to me as specially corroborative of the conception of amphimixis as a 'formative stimulus' whose strength depends upon the difference between the germ-substances. The renowned breeder, Nathusius, allowed the progeny of a sow of the large Yorkshire breed, imported from England when with young, to reproduce by inbreeding for three generations. The result was unfavourable, for the young were weakly in constitution and were not prolific. One of the last female animals, for instance, when paired with its own uncle—known to be fertile with sows of a different breed—produced a litter of six, and a second litter of five weakly piglings. But when Nathusius paired the same sow with a boar of a small black breed, which boar had begotten seven to nine young when paired with sows of his own breed, the sow of the large Yorkshire breed produced in the first litter twenty-one and in the second eighteen piglings.

How could this really remarkable difference in the fertility of the sow in question be the result of a formative stimulus, exercised by the sperm-cells of the unrelated boar upon the ova of the female animal? If the progeny of the sow had been more fertile than herself, then we should have been at least logically justified in concluding that this was the case, but it is not intelligible that the egg-cells of this mother sow should be increased twice or three times because they were fertilized by a new kind of sperm as they glided from the ovary. The number of ova which are liberated from the ovary depends in the first instance upon the number of mature ova contained in it; and unless we are to make the highly improbable assumption that the crossing with the strange boar had as an immediate result the maturing of a large number of ova, we must look elsewhere than in the ovary of the animal for the cause of this sudden fertility, possibly in chance circumstances which we are unaware of and which make the ovary occasionally more productive, possibly however in the fact that inbreeding may have brought about various slight structural variations in the animal, and among these some which made the fertilization of the abundantly produced ova by the sperm of the related boar less easy, and caused it to fail more frequently. As will be readily understood, I cannot say anything definite on this point, but we know that very slight variations in the sperm-cell or the ovum may make fertilization difficult, or may even prevent it. I need only remind you of the interesting experiments in hybridization which Pflüger and Born made with Batrachians nearly thirty years ago, which showed that in two nearly related species of frog the ova of the species A were frequently fertilized by the sperms of the species B, but not conversely, the ova of the species B by the sperms of A. This is the case, for instance, with the green edible frog (*Rana esculenta*), and the brown grass-frog (*Rana fusca*), and the reason of this dissimilarity in the effectiveness of the sperm lies simply in 'rough mechanical conditions,' in the width of the micropyle of the ovum, and the thickness of the head of the spermatozoon. If each species possesses a micropyle which is exactly wide enough to admit of the passage of the spermatozoon of its own species, another species will only be able to fertilize these eggs if the head of its spermatozoon be not larger than that of the first species. Thus, as experiment has proved, the spermatozoa of *Rana fusca* fertilize the ova of almost all other related species, for they have the thinnest head and it is at the same time very pointed. In this case, therefore, it depends upon the microscopic structure of the ovum whether fertilization can take place or not, and we can imagine that similar or perhaps other minute variations had taken place in the ova in the case of Nathusius's sow, and that these made it difficult for the sperms of boars of the same family to effect fertilization. These variations may have arisen as a result of the continued inbreeding, because the same ids were constantly being brought together in the fertilized ova, and thus any unfavourable directions of variations which existed were strengthened.

It seems to me that in this way alone can the injurious effect of inbreeding be made intelligible. From both parents identical ids meet in the fertilized ovum, in greater numbers the longer inbreeding continues, for at the maturation of every germ-cell the number of different ids is diminished by a few, and their number must therefore gradually decrease, and it is conceivable that ultimately it may sink to one kind of id, that is, that the germ-plasm may then consist entirely of identical ids. If chance variations of certain determinants in unfavourable directions occur in some of the ids composing the germ-plasm, these are brought together in the offspring from both the maternal and the paternal side, and will occur in an increasing number of ids the longer the inbreeding has gone on, that is, the smaller the number of different ids has become. The unfavourable variation-tendency is therefore persisted in, and its influence upon the development of a new descendant will be the greater the larger the number of identical ids with these unfavourable variations. It is obvious that the crossing of an animal, which is thus, so to speak, degenerating slightly, with a member of an unrelated family must immediately have a good effect upon the descendants, for in this way quite different ids with other variations of their determinants are introduced into the inbred germ-plasm which had become too monotonous.

From this theoretical interpretation of the injurious consequences of inbreeding we may at once infer that not every inbreeding necessarily implies degeneration, for the occurrence of unfavourable variational tendencies in the germ-plasm is presupposed as the starting-point of degeneration, and if these do not exist there can be no degeneration. This harmonizes with the fact that the evil effects of inbreeding are observed *to vary greatly in amount, and may not occur at all.* But they are greatest in breeds artificially selected by man, which have long been under unnatural, directly influential conditions, and are also removed from the purifying influence of natural selection. In such cases, therefore, there is every probability that diverse unfavourable variational tendencies in the determinants will occur.

But how are we to understand the fact that pure parthenogenesis may last through innumerable generations, and yet no degeneration sets in? I believe very simply. In this case too, the same ids which were peculiar to the mother of the race are contained in the descendants, but they do not diminish in number, for in pure and normal parthenogenesis, such as that of *Cypris reptans*, the second maturation-division of the ovum does not take place, and this is precisely the nuclear division which effects reduction. In addition, the introduction of identical ids, which must take place in the case of inbreeding at every amphimixis, does not occur, and, what is certainly of great importance, all these cases are old species, living under natural conditions—the same conditions under which they lived as amphigonous species, and not newly formed breeds under artificial conditions, as has probably always been the case in the experiments in inbreeding.

It is true that even in old species, living in a state of nature, unfavourable variations may arise in the germ-plasm, and may go on increasing during purely parthenogenetic multiplication, for the ids with unfavourably varying determinants will no longer be set aside by means of reducing division. But those individuals in which the unfavourable variational tendency increases until it has attained selection-value will be subject to selection and will be gradually eliminated; indeed, the weeding out of the inferior individuals will be more drastic here than where amphigony obtains, because in this case all the offspring of one mother are nearly alike, so that the whole progeny is exterminated if the mother varies unfavourably.

On the other hand, a transformation in a favourable direction, an adaptation to new conditions of life, as far at least as that implies the simultaneous variation and harmonious co-adaptation of many parts, cannot, as far as I can see, be effected in the course of purely parthenogenetic reproduction, nor can a degeneration of complicated parts which have become superfluous. For both these changes, in my opinion, require that the ids of the germ-plasm should be frequently mingled afresh, since apart from this there cannot be a harmonious readjustment of complicated structures, nor can a uniform degeneration affecting all parts set in. As an example of this last case we may take that organ which became functionless in the purely parthenogenetic species of Ostracods when amphigonous reproduction was given up—the sperm-pocket or receptaculum of the female. All these species still possess an unaltered receptaculum seminis, a large pear-shaped bladder with a long, narrow, spirally coiled entrance-duct, very well adapted for allowing the enormous spermatozoa of the males to make their way in singly, and to arrange themselves within the receptacle side by side in the most beautiful order, like a long ribbon, and finally to migrate out again singly to fertilize the liberated ova. In *Cypris reptans* and several other species, however, no males have been found in any of the places which have been carefully searched, and the receptaculum of the female is always found to be empty. Nevertheless it shows no hint of degeneration. It is possible enough that, as in *Apus cancriformis*, which is of similar habit, the males have become extinct in most colonies of these species, but that nevertheless they do occur here and there from time to time in the area inhabited by the species, and if this should prove to be the case, it would confirm the conclusion, which is very probable on other grounds, that the pure parthenogenesis of these species has not existed in most of their habitats for a long time, speaking phylogenetically. For this reason we must not over-estimate the significance of the complete persistence of the receptaculum even with exclusively parthenogenetic reproduction. It proves, however, that degeneration of a superfluous organ does not necessarily set in even after hundreds of generations, and in this fact there is certainly a corroboration of the view that it is 'chance' germinal variations which give the impulse to degeneration. These first induce a down-grade variation through germinal selection, and this, if it concerns an organ of no importance to the survival of the species, is not hindered in its progress by personal selection. Whether degeneration of the receptaculum would have occurred in these parthenogenetic species if they had retained even a periodic sexual reproduction, as is actually the case in the generations of the alternately parthenogenetic and sexually reproducing Aphides, we cannot decide, since we know nothing in either case as to the length of time that parthenogenesis has prevailed among them, nor have we any method of computing the number of generations that must elapse before a superfluous organ begins to vacillate. We only know that the parthenogenetic generations of Aphides no longer possess a receptaculum, while other forms with alternating bi-sexual and parthenogenetic modes of reproduction, which are in this respect possibly more modern, e. g. some of the gall-wasps, possess one similar to that of the Ostracods.

I must refer to one other case of parthenogenesis, since it has been hitherto regarded as a formidable puzzle for the germ-plasm theory, and has only recently found its solution, I mean the facultative parthenogenesis of the queen-bee. As the 'male' eggs of the bee remain unfertilized, and yet undergo two reducing divisions, which must diminish the number of ids in the ovum-nucleus by a half, the number of ids in the germ-plasm of the bee must be steadily decreasing, and this state of things has therefore been regarded by some English biologists as convincing evidence of the untenability of the conception of ids and of the whole germ-plasm theory. Apparently, indeed, it is contradictory to the theory, and we must inquire whether the contradiction is merely an *apparent* one, disappearing when the facts are more precisely known. It was mainly on this ground that I instituted the researches carried out by Dr. Petrunkewitsch, the results of which I have already in part communicated in a former lecture. These results confirmed the previous conclusions that the 'male' eggs of the queen-bee remain unfertilized, that two reducing divisions occur, and that in consequence the ovum-nucleus only contains half the normal number of chromosomes. That these increase again by division to the normal number does not save the theory, for only *identical* ids can arise in this way, while the significance of the multiplicity of the ids lies mainly in their difference. The halving of the number of ids in each 'male' ovum would necessarily lead, if not to a permanent diminution in the number of ids, at least to a monotony of the germ-plasm, since the number of *different* ids would be steadily decreasing and the number of *identical* ids as steadily increasing. This too would be a contradiction of the theory. But Dr. Petrunkewitsch's investigations have shown that, of the four nuclei which are formed by the two reducing divisions, the two middle ones (Fig. 79, *K* 2 and *K* 3) recombine with one another, and fuse into a single nucleus, and that

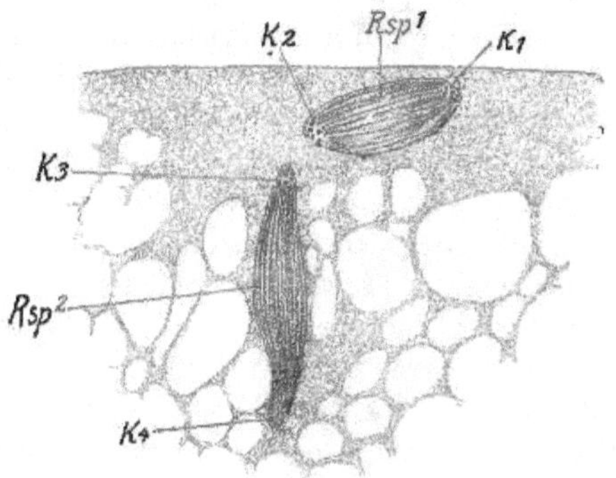

FIG. 79 (repeated). The two maturation divisions of the 'drone eggs' (unfertilized eggs) of the bee, after Petrunkewitsch. *Rsp* 1, the first directive spindle. *K* 1 and *K* 2, the two daughter-nuclei of the same. *Rsp* 2, the second directive spindle. *K* 3 and *K* 4, the two daughter-nuclei. In the next stage *K* 2 and *K* 3 unite to form the primitive sex-nucleus. Highly magnified.

from this copulation-nucleus in the course of development the primitive germ-cells of the embryo arise. Now all the ids which were originally present in the nucleus of the immature ovum may be reunited in this 'polar copulation-nucleus' if the two nuclei *K* 2 and *K* 3 turned towards each other in Fig. 79 contain different ids. That this is the case cannot of course be seen from the ids themselves, but it seems to me extremely probable, since it is dissimilar poles of the two nuclear spindles which here unite, namely, the lower pole (daughter-nucleus) of the upper spindle and the upper pole of the lower spindle. In the first directive or polar spindle there lay thirty-two chromosomes, which had increased by duplication from sixteen, and of these sixteen passed over into the first polar nucleus, while sixteen formed the basis of the second directive spindle. These two sets of sixteen chromosomes must have been quite similar, since the two sets arose by division of the sixteen mother-chromosomes. Let us call the chromosomes *a*, *b*, *c*, *d–q*, then similar sets of chromosomes must have been contained in the two nuclear spindle figures depicted in Fig. 79 at the beginning of the division, and eight of these went to each daughter-nucleus. Now, if *a–k* migrated to the upper pole of the spindle and *l–q* to the lower pole, then the union of *K* 2 with *K* 3 would bring together again all the ids that had before been present. In consideration of this I predicted to Dr. Petrunkewitsch that this copulation-product might be the basis of the formation of the germ-cells in the drone-bee, and his painstaking and difficult researches have confirmed this prediction, strange though it may seem, that the male germ-cells have a different origin from the female germ-cells. But this discovery gives a strong support to the germ-plasm theory. It may, of course, be objected that the assumed regular distribution of the ids in the two daughter-nuclei cannot be proved, but we know already that this dividing apparatus does *very exact* work, and we are at liberty to assume it in an even higher degree. Moreover, what other interpretation of the unexpected development of the germ-cells discovered by Petrunkewitsch could be given if this had to be rejected? A clearer proof of the individual differences of ids and of their essential importance could not be desired, than lies in the fact that in the 'male' eggs of the queen-bee a different and novel mode of germ-cell formation is instituted, after half the ids have been irrecoverably withdrawn from the ovum-nucleus. We see from this that for individual development a duplication of individual ids may suffice, but that for the further development of the species a retention of the diversity of the ids is important.

LECTURE XXX

INBREEDING, PARTHENOGENESIS, ASEXUAL REPRODUCTION, AND THEIR CONSEQUENCES

The separation of the sexes exists even among the Protozoa—Conditions determining the occurrence of Hermaphroditism—Tape-worms, Cirrhipeds—Primordial males—Advantages of parthenogenesis—Alternation with bi-sexual generations—In Gall-wasps—In Aphides—Cross-fertilization secured in plants—Self-fertilization is avoided whenever possible—The mechanism of fertilization and the mingling of germ-plasms must be clearly distinguished from one another—Cases of persistent self-fertilization—The effects of inbreeding compared with those of parthenogenesis—The effect of purely asexual reproduction—In sea-wracks—In lichens and fungi—In cultivated plants—Degeneration of the sex-organs—Summary.

We have seen that continued inbreeding must make the germ-plasm monotonous, and therefore unplastic as regards the requirements of adaptation. Accordingly, we found that the gametes of many unicellulars are so constituted that they only possess a power of attraction for gametes of a different lineage, not for those of their own stock. Among multicellular organisms the most intense mode of inbreeding is to be found in the uninterrupted self-fertilization of hermaphrodites: in such cases the monotony of the germ-plasm must reach extreme expression more readily than in the case of ordinary inbreeding. We can thus understand why, in the scale of organisms, there is such an early occurrence of gonochorism, the separation of the species into male and female individuals. Even among unicellular plants or Protophytes this occurs occasionally, as it does in the Vorticellids among Infusorians.

In the Metazoa and Metaphyta the separation of the sexes finds emphatic expression; it is absent from no important group, and in many, such as, for instance, among the Vertebrates, it has become the absolutely normal condition, with hardly any exception. But in many divisions of the animal and plant kingdoms hermaphroditism also plays an important part, as, for instance, in terrestrial snails and in flowering plants.

Obviously the sexual adaptations of a species are definitely related to the conditions of its life, and, though Nature's endeavour to prevent inbreeding and to secure cross-fertilization is evidenced by the occurrence of separate sexes in such a multitude of forms yet in many cases gonochorism has been relinquished, and always where this was necessitated by the conditions of life to which the group concerned was subject. In such a case inbreeding is regulated as far as possible, for instance, by an arrangement which ensures that individuals shall be crossed at least from time to time. But cases of exclusive and constant self-fertilization do also seem to occur, and even these may be brought into harmony with our conception, according to which cross-fertilization is an advantage, but only an advantage which must be weighed against others, and which may eventually be given up in favour of greater advantages. This occurrence of persistent autogamy can no more be reconciled with the rejuvenation theory than can continuous parthenogenesis, because, according to this theory, the mingling of different individuals is a *sine qua non* for the continued life of the species.

It is impossible for me here to discuss in detail all the deviations from pure gonochorism or bi-sexuality which occur in nature, but I must at least attempt to take a general survey, and to arrange the chief phenomena of these various modes of 'sexual reproduction' in an orderly scheme. I must take a survey of both plants and animals, but I shall give the precedence to animals, as being to me more familiar ground.

Where do we find, in the animal kingdom, that Nature has departed from gonochorism, from the separation of the sexes, and for what reasons was this departure necessary? And further, what means does Nature take to compensate for this renunciation of the simplest method of securing the continual cross-fertilization of individuals?

Let us glance over the animal kingdom with special reference to these questions: we find that hermaphroditism prevails chiefly among species which at maturity have lost their power of free locomotion, and have become sedentary, such as oysters, barnacles among Crustaceans, the Bryozoa, and the sea-squirts (Ascidians) which are fixed to the rocks at the bottom of the sea. For forms such as these it must often have been advantageous that each individual could function both as male and as female, especially when it was capable of self-fertilization, since individuals which settled down singly, or in very small numbers together, would not be lost as regards the persistence of the species. The continuance of the species is thus better secured than it would be by separation of the sexes, because in the latter case it might frequently have happened that the animals which had settled beside each other by chance were of the same sex, and would therefore remain unfertile.

But many of these species do not fertilize themselves, but fertilize each other mutually; and this, too, carries a great advantage with it, because in sedentary animals the sperms will fertilize twice as many individuals, if each contains eggs, than if half were exclusively male. It is thus to some extent an economy of sperms, but at the same time also of ova, which is effected by hermaphroditism: the result is that these valuable products are wasted as little as possible. On this account we find that not only sedentary, but also sluggish, slow-moving animals are equipped with male and female organs of reproduction, as, for instance, all our terrestrial snails. They fertilize each other mutually: when two meet it is always as males and females, and notwithstanding the sluggishness of movement, it is not likely to happen that a snail does not attain to reproduction because it has not found a mate. The same is true of the earthworms, which are likewise not adapted for making long journeys in search of the opposite sex; they, and the leeches also, function as male and female simultaneously, while their nearest relatives, the marine Chætopods, are of separate sexes, which may be associated with their much greater power of free movement in the water.

In these cases self-fertilization is often absolutely excluded; it may be physically impossible, and hermaphroditism therefore secures cross-fertilization in such cases just as effectively as if the sexes were separate. Similarly, in many hermaphrodite flowers, as we have already seen, the pollen is so constituted and so placed within the flower that it cannot of itself make its way to the stigma. In oysters, for instance, the young animal is male, and liberates into the water an enormous quantity of minute spermatozoa, and therewith fertilizes the older individuals, functioning only as females, which have grown upon the same bank. At a later stage of its development the oyster which was male becomes female, and produces only ova. This state of affairs, of which I shall shortly mention another case, has been called *temporary* hermaphroditism. In this case not only is self-fertilization excluded, but close inbreeding also, since it is always a young generation functioning simultaneously as males that mingles with an older generation which has become female.

It is quite otherwise with parasites which live singly within the body of a host: for these it was indispensably necessary that they should not only produce both kinds of germ-cells, but that they should unite the two kinds in fertilization, and they therefore possess the power of self-fertilization. Thus, in the urinary bladder of the frog, there occurs a flat-worm (*Polystomum integerrimum*) which possesses special organs for pairing with another individual, but which is also capable of self-fertilization when, as frequently occurs, it has no companion in its place of abode. But this self-fertilization is always liable to be interrupted by cross-fertilization, for not infrequently there are two, three, or even four such parasites within the bladder of a single frog.

In the tape-worms, too, cross-fertilization is not excluded, for there are often two or more of these animals together in the intestine of a host at the same time. But even where there is only one, self-fertilization on the part of the joints, that is, the sexual individuals, is prevented, and by the same device, metaphorically speaking, as in the case of the oyster, for in each joint the male elements mature first and the female elements afterwards. In certain parasitic Isopods of the genus *Anilocra* and related forms close inbreeding is prevented in the same way—by a difference in the period at which the two sets of gonads in the hermaphrodite individual become mature (dichogamy).

This is secured in a different way in Crustaceans which have grown to maturity in a sedentary state, like the Cirrhipeds. These animals, known as 'acorn-shells' and 'barnacles,' are sedentary, sometimes on rocks and stones, sometimes on a movable object, the keel of a ship, floating pieces of wood, cork, or cane, or sometimes attached to turtles or whales, and although they generally occur in great numbers together, they are probably only able to fertilize each other occasionally, and are therefore essentially dependent upon self-fertilization. But Charles Darwin discovered long ago that many of them, notwithstanding their hermaphroditism, have males which are small, dwarf-like, and very mobile organisms, destined only for a very brief life. These seemed quite superfluous in association with hermaphrodite animals, and they have therefore long been regarded as vestigial males, as the last remnant, so to speak, of a past stage of the modern Cirrhipeds, in which the sexes were separate. It is obvious, however, that we must now attribute to them a deeper significance, for these so-called 'primordial males,' although extremely transitory creatures without mouth or intestine, represent a means of securing the cross-fertilization of the species. What importance nature attaches to their preservation is shown especially by the parasitic Cirrhipeds which have been so carefully studied by Fritz Müller and Yves Delage—those sac-like Rhizocephalidæ or root-crustaceans which are altogether disfigured by parasitism. The fully developed animals are hermaphrodite and live partly in, partly upon crabs and hermit-crabs (Fig. 112, *C*, *Sacc*). These hermaphrodites indeed fertilize themselves, but in their youth they are of distinct sexes, and the females are so constituted that they lay eggs for the first time just when the males of the current year are appearing. Thus the first batch of eggs liberated by the females are fertilized by the minute free-swimming 'primordial males,' but after that the females themselves develop testes, and then fertilize themselves; the males die very soon after copulation, and only appear the following year in a new generation. They are therefore far from being mere historic reminiscences, vestiges of the early history of the modern species, for they are the instruments of a regular cross-fertilization of the species, and therefore of a constant mingling of new ids in the germ-plasm. This is not the place to discuss the marvellous life-history of these parasites in detail; I can only say

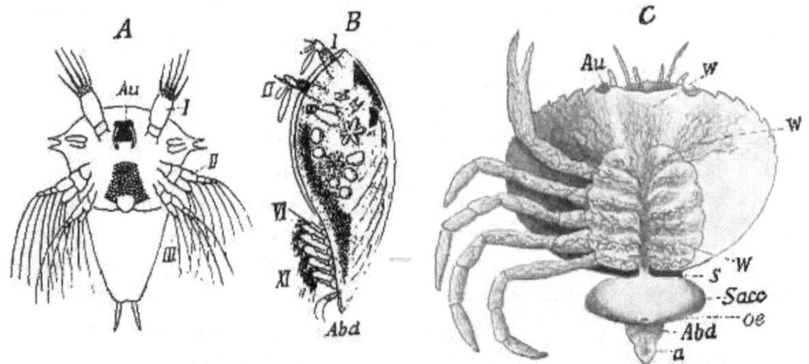

FIG. 112 (repeated). Development of the parasitic Crustacean *Sacculina carcini*, after Delage. *A*, Nauplius stage. *Au*, eye. *I*, *II*, *III*, the three pairs of appendages. *B*, Cypris stage. *VI–XI*, the swimming appendages. *C*, mature animal (*Sacc*), attached to its host, the shore-crab (*Carcinus mænas*), with a feltwork of fine root-processes enveloping the crab's viscera. *S*, stalk. *Sacc*, body of the parasite. *oe*, aperture of the brood-cavity. *Abd*, abdomen of the crab with the anus (*a*).

that when we inquire into the whole story, and appreciate the difficulties associated with the persistence of these 'primordial males,' we can no longer doubt that crossing is an indispensable feature of amphimixis—a feature which must at least occasionally occur if amphimixis is to retain its significance. This is shown, it seems to me, especially by these numerous instances of what we may call compulsory retention of ephemeral males in hermaphrodite, self-fertilizing animals; it follows also from the theory, for with continued self-fertilization all the ids in the germ-plasm of an individual would tend to become identical, and the mingling of two germ-plasms which contained *identical* ids would, at least according to the germ-plasm theory, have no meaning at all.

Thus we see that in the animal kingdom hermaphroditism is always associated with cross-fertilization in some way or other, even though the latter may occur rarely, being usually periodically interpolated, and thus bringing new ids into the germ-plasm which is rapidly becoming monotonous or uniform. Adaptations quite analogous to these are found in relation to parthenogenesis, and it will repay us to give a brief summary of these.

Parthenogenesis effects a very considerable increase in the fertility of a species, and in this increase the reason for its introduction among natural phenomena obviously lies. By the occurrence of parthenogenesis, the number of ova produced by a particular colony of animals may be doubled, because each individual is a female, and as the multiplication increases in geometrical ratio a few parthenogenetic generations result in a number of descendants enormously in excess of those produced by bi-sexual reproduction. We can therefore understand why parthenogenesis should obtain among animals whose conditions of life are favourable only for a short time, and are then uncertain and dangerous for a long period. This is the case with the water-fleas, the Daphnids (see Figs. 57 and 58), whose habitats —pools, ponds, and marshes—often dry up altogether in summer, or freeze in winter, so that it becomes almost if not quite impossible for the colonies to go on living, and the preservation of the species can only be secured by the production of hard-shelled 'lasting' eggs, which sink to the bottom, dry up in the mud, or become frozen, or at least remain latent in a sort of slumber. As soon as the favourable conditions reappear, young animals which emerge from the eggs are all females and reproduce parthenogenetically, so that after a few days there is a numerous progeny swimming freely about, which in their turn are all females, and reproduce after the same manner. In many Daphnids this goes on for a series of generations, and there thus arises an enormous number of animals, which may fill a marsh so densely that, by drawing a fine net a few times through the water, one can draw out a veritable animal soup. In our ponds and lakes these little Crustaceans form the fundamental food of numerous fishes. But notwithstanding the enormous havoc wrought among them by enemies, large numbers remain at the end of a favourable season, and these produce the lasting eggs, *after fertilization*. For shortly before the end of the season males appear among the progeny of the hitherto purely parthenogenetic females. Although each female will only produce a few of these 'lasting' eggs, which require fertilization and are richly supplied with yolk, the whole number in each colony is a very large one, because the number of individuals is very large;

and it must be so, since the eggs, though secure against cold and desiccation, are very imperfectly protected against the numerous enemies which may do them injury.

Of course the number of individuals which form a colony may vary greatly in the different species, and the same is true of the number of parthenogenetic generations which precede the bi-sexual generation. I have already shown in detail that this depends precisely on the average duration of the favourable conditions, so that, for instance, a species which lives in large lake-basins will produce many purely parthenogenetic generations before the bi-sexual one, which only appears towards autumn, while species which live in quickly-drying pools have only a few parthenogenetic generations, and the true puddle-dwellers give rise to males and sexual females along with the parthenogenetic females as early as the second generation.

We thus find in the Daphnids an alternation, regulated and made normal by natural selection, of purely parthenogenetic with bi-sexual generations, and the result is that the uniformity of the germ-plasm, which is the necessary consequence of pure parthenogenesis, is interrupted after a longer or shorter series of generations by the occurrence of amphimixis. That the number of parthenogenetic generations may be so varied, though with a definite norm for each species, indicates again that amphimixis is not an absolute condition of the maintenance of life, not an indispensable rejuvenation, designed to counteract the exhaustion of vital force—whether this be meant in a transcendental sense or otherwise—but that it is an important advantage calculated to keep the species at its highest level, and that its influence appears whether it occurs in the species regularly, or frequently, or only rarely.

This kind of alternation of generations, that is, the alternation between unisexual (female) and bi-sexual generations, has been called heterogony. In the Daphnids, certainly, a difference in form between the parthenogenetic and the bi-sexual generation does not exist, for the same females which produce eggs requiring fertilization can also produce parthenogenetic ova, although these are very different from each other, as we have already seen. The difference between generations, therefore, does not lie in their structure, but in their tendency to parthenogenetic or to amphigonous reproduction, and in the absence or presence of male individuals. There are, however, other cases of alternation of generations in which the different generations diverge from each other in structure. One of the most remarkable of these is that of the gall-wasps (Cynipidæ). In many of these little Hymenoptera, which form galls on leaves, blossoms, buds, and roots, especially of the oak, two generations occur annually, one in summer, the other in early spring, or even in the middle of winter. The latter consists of females only and reproduces parthenogenetically. We can readily understand this from the point of view of adaptation to particular conditions, since the young wasps which emerge from their galls in winter, or in the middle of a raw spring, are exposed to many dangers and are terribly decimated before they can succeed in laying their eggs in the proper place on the plant. Moreover, much precious time would be lost by the mutual search of the sexes for each other, —a search which would often be entirely without result. Thus the wingless female of *Biorhiza renum* (Fig. 124, *A*), which is not unlike a plump ant, attempts, without taking food, and often interrupted by a spell of cold or a snowstorm, to reach a neighbouring oak-shrub,

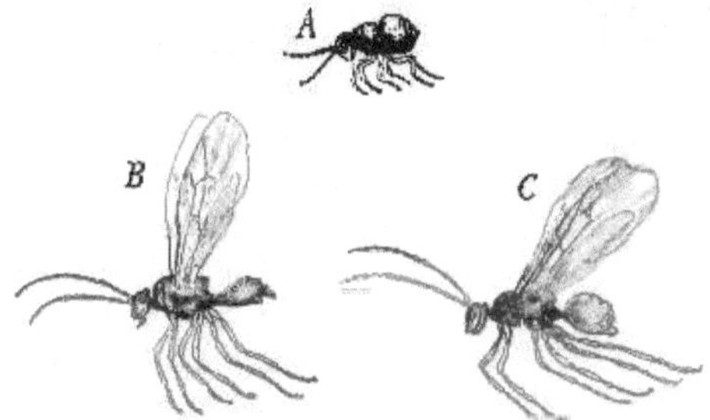

Fig. 124. Alternation of generations in a Gall-wasp. *A*, winter generation (*Biorhiza renum*). *B* and *C*, summer generations (*Trigonaspis crustalis*). *B*, male. *C*, female. After Adler.

creeps up on it, and lays its eggs in the heart of a winter bud, whose hard protecting scales it laboriously perforates by means of its short, thick, sharp ovipositor.

After it has succeeded in sinking its ovipositor into the heart of the bud, it goes on working for hours, piercing the delicate tissue with a multitude of fine canals, one close beside the other, and then deposits an egg in each of these. The whole detailed piece of work requires, according to Adler, uninterrupted active exertion for about three days, even though in the end only two buds may be filled with eggs. If at every egg-laying the arrival of a male had to be waited for, an even larger number of females would fall victims to the unfavourable weather and other dangers, while at the same time the number of emerging females could be only half as large as it is. It is obvious that in this case parthenogenesis is of very great advantage.

In summer the climatic conditions are incomparably more favourable for the gall-wasps, and accordingly we find that the summer generation is bi-sexual, but, strangely enough, is so different from the winter generation that the relationship of the two forms was for a long time overlooked. The antennæ, the legs, and particularly the ovipositor, the whole shape of the animal, its size, the length of the abdomen, the structure of the thorax, and many other points are so different that as long as the structural features afforded the only criterion of relationship, the systematists quite naturally placed the winter and summer forms in different genera. It was only when Dr. H. Adler succeeded in breeding the one form from the other that people were convinced that such marked differences in structure could be found within the same life-cycle.

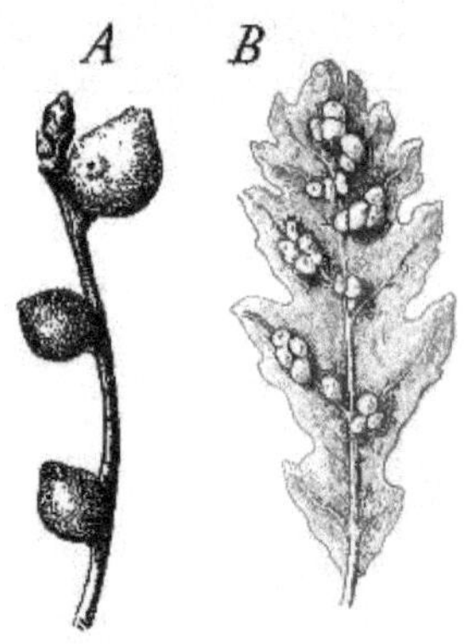

FIG. 125. The two kinds of Galls formed by the species. *A*, the many-chambered galls produced by the parthenogenetic winter form, *Biorhiza renum*. *B*, those produced on oak-leaves by *Trigonaspis crustalis*, the bi-sexual form. After Adler.

But we see here quite clearly why the two generations had to become so different; simply because the winter generation had to adapt itself to different conditions from the summer generation, above all as to the laying of its eggs within the tissues of a plant of a different constitution. In our example, the winter form *Biorhiza renum* pierces the terminal buds of the oak, and lays in each of them a large number of eggs, sometimes as many as 300, so that a very large gall is formed, in which a great many larvæ can find food, and grow on to the pupa-stage. From this spongy gall, something like an inverted onion in shape, and about the size of a walnut (Fig. 125, *A*), there emerge in July the slender, delicately formed male and female gall-wasps which were long known as *Trigonaspis crustalis*. Both males and females are winged, and fly rapidly about in the air (Fig. 125, *B* and *C*). The sexes pair, and the females lay their eggs in the cell-layers on the under side of an oak-leaf, on which arise small, wart-like, kidney-shaped galls (Fig. 125, *B*) which fall to the ground in autumn, and from which there emerge, in the middle of winter, the plump, wingless females, to which, as we have already seen, the name *Biorhiza renum* was given.

One generation, therefore, lays its eggs in the parenchyma of tender leaves, and has only to pierce through a thin layer of plant-tissue, while the other must penetrate deep down into the hard winter bud, to be able to deposit its eggs in the proper place, and we therefore find that in the two kinds of female the ovipositor differs in length, thickness, and general structure, and so also does the whole complex apparatus by which the ovipositor is moved. But these differences are associated with the form of the abdomen, in which the ovipositor lies, and with the strength and shape of the legs, which must be shorter and stronger when the boring has to be performed through a hard plant-tissue or to a considerable depth. We can readily understand how numerous must be the secondary variations which a transformation of the ovipositor brings in its train when we compare the ovipositor apparatus in the two generations of one of these species (Fig. 126).

Figure 126 shows the ovipositor of another gall-wasp, of which the winter form, *Neuroterus laeviusculus*, also perforates the hard winter buds of the oak, while the summer form, *Spathegaster albipes*, lays its eggs in the tender young leaves of the same tree. The ovipositor of the former is thin and long, that of the latter short and strong (Fig. 126, *A* and *B*), and corresponding also to the depth at which the egg must be sunk, or, so to speak, sown in the tissue of the plant, the egg of the summer generation differs from that of the winter generation by having a much shorter stalk (Fig. 126, *ei*). These little wasps thus afford a beautiful example of the way in which even marked changes in the conditions of life of a generation may be associated with transformations in bodily structure, and we understand how it was possible that by means of processes of selection the generations which alternate periodically in the year should come to diverge very considerably in structure. The example may also serve to illustrate how diverse are the harmonious co-adaptations which such transformations require,

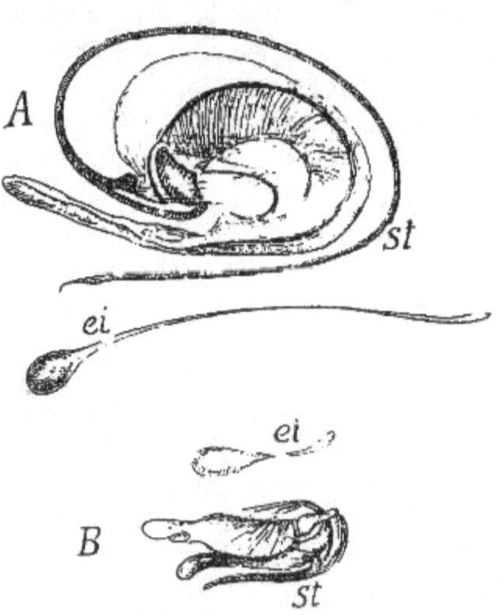

FIG. 126. Ovipositor and ovum of the two generations of the same species of Gall-wasp. *A*, those of the winter form, *Neuroterus laeviusculus*. *B*, those of the summer-form, *Spathegaster albipes*. *st*, ovipositor. *ei*, ovum. Similarly magnified. After Adler.

and how necessary, therefore, the continual re-combination of the ids of the germ-plasm by means of amphimixis must be. We understand why bi-sexual reproduction was only abandoned in one generation, and that the one in which parthenogenesis was of considerable advantage. But such transformations must have come about with extreme slowness, since they were the result of climatic changes which only come about very gradually. We thus come again to the same conclusion to which we were led by our study of vestigial organs in Man, that numerous species which appear to be at a standstill are continually working towards their own improvement. But for this amphimixis is essential; consequently the descendants which have arisen through amphimixis, and whose ancestors have arisen in the same way, have an advantage over those of parthenogenetic origin. On the whole, at least, this must be so; in special cases it may be otherwise, namely, when the advantage offered by parthenogenesis in respect to the maintenance of the species preponderates over the advantage which amphimixis implies as regards possibilities of transformation.

As far as we have seen from the case of the gall-wasps, the absence of amphimixis in every second generation implies no disadvantage in regard to the capability for transformation which the species exhibits. As to whether any disadvantage would ensue if the number of parthenogenetic generations in the life-cycle were greater we can only guess, since no case is known which enables us to decide this point, *pro* or *con*, with any certainty. The heterogony of the plant-lice, the Aphides, and their relatives might be cited as against the probability, for in this case a long series of parthenogenetic generations often alternates with a single bi-sexual one, but the difference in structure is not so great in this case, although it does exist, and moreover we can quite well assume that the adaptation to parthenogenesis was effected at the beginning of heterogony, when it still consisted of a cycle of only two generations, and that further virgin generations were interpolated subsequently.

This assumption is supported by the fact that in some species of our indigenous Ostracods, in *Cypris vidua* and *Candona candens*, in contrast to the Daphnids, several bi-sexual generations alternate with one parthenogenetic generation. But in this case again there is no difference whatever in the structure of the two generations, the parthenogenetic generation being distinguished from the bi-sexual generation simply by the absence of males.

The alternation of generations in the plant-lice is particularly instructive, because it emphatically indicates how much Nature is concerned with the retention of amphimixis, and how little mere multiplication has to do with this. This is especially striking in the case of the bark-lice; for instance, in their notorious representative, the vine-pest, *Phylloxera vastatrix*.

As in all plant-lice, the advantage for the sake of which sexual reproduction was given up depends upon the fact that a practically unlimited food supply is at the disposal of these parasites of the vine, which can be made full use of during the proper season, and which, since every animal is female and produces eggs, results in an

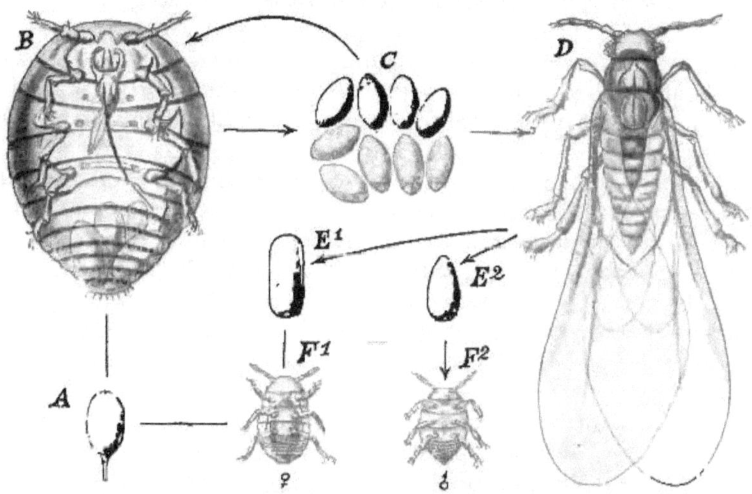

FIG. 127. Life-cycle of the Vine-pest (*Phylloxera vastatrix*), after Leuckart and Nitsche, and Ritter and Rübsamen. *A*, the fertilized ovum. *B*, the resulting apterous and parthenogenetic Phylloxera. *C*, its eggs, from which, as the uppermost arrow indicates, there may arise similar apterous, parthenogenetic forms, or, as the horizontal arrow indicates, winged forms (*D*), which produce 'female' and 'male' ova (E^1 and E^2); from these the sexual generation arises, the female (F^1) and the male (F^2); the former lays the fertilized ovum (*A*).

enormous increase in the number of individuals, and thus secures the continuance of the species. These insects emerge in spring from small fertilized eggs, which have lain dormant throughout the winter (Fig. 127, *A*), and they develop rapidly into wingless females (*B*), which, sucking the juice of the vine, multiply by producing large numbers of little white eggs (*C*). These develop without fertilization into similar wingless females. Several generations of females succeed each other, but then, usually from August onwards, differently formed winged females (*D*) make their appearance, and these, flying from plant to plant, effect the distribution of the species. But these, too, lay parthenogenetic eggs (E^1 and E^2), and from these there emerge, late in autumn, the members of the single bi-sexual generation, males and females (F^1 and F^2), both very minute and wingless, without a piercing proboscis, and thus incapable of taking food. These pair, and the female lays a single egg (*A*) under the bark of the vine, from which the leaves are now falling; this egg survives the winter, and from it in the following April or May there emerges once more a parthenogenetic female.

It could hardly be more plainly shown than it is by this case that the importance of amphimixis is something quite apart from reproduction and multiplication, for here the number of individuals is not only not increased by amphimixis, but is materially diminished, being indeed lessened by a half. By the retention of amphimixis, the species gains in this case no advantage *except* the mingling of two germ-plasms.

Something similar occurs in plants which exhibit alternation of generations, for instance the ferns, in which the sexual generation, the so-called prothallium or prothallus, contributes nothing to the *multiplication* of the plant, since only a single egg-cell is developed; and the same is true of the mosses. In both cases *multiplication* depends solely on the asexual generation, which, as the so-called 'moss-fruit' or 'fern-plant proper,' produces an enormous number of spores, in addition to multiplying by runners.

To sum up: we have seen that self-fertilization does occur in hermaphrodite animals, where otherwise the species would be in danger of extinction, but this is never the *sole* and exclusive mode of fertilization[1], for hermaphrodite species have always the possibility of securing inter-crossing of individuals, and that in various ways, whether by the intervention of 'primordial males' or by an occasional or a periodic alternation of self-fertilization and mutual fertilization. Pure parthenogenesis enduring through innumerable generations does appear to occur, but in most cases unisexual generations alternate with bi-sexual, so that a stereotyping of the germ-plasm with complete uniformity of ids is obviated.

We must now briefly consider the higher plants with reference to the maintenance of diversity in the germ-plasm through crossing.

We saw in an earlier lecture that most flowers are hermaphrodite, but that they do not fertilize themselves, and are adapted for crossing,

[1] As to the cases Maupas has brought into notice, of permanent and apparently exclusive self-fertilization in Rhabditidæ (round worms), it seems fair to say that they have not been as yet sufficiently investigated to admit of a secure appreciation of their value in their theoretical bearings. Cf. *Arch. Zool. Exper.*, 3rd ser., vol. viii, 1900.

since the pollen of one flower is carried by insects to the pistil of another, which cannot be reached by its own pollen, either because it ripens too early or too late, or because the stigma, notwithstanding its proximity, is so placed as to be out of reach of the pollen from the adjacent stamens. I showed, following the fundamental investigations of Sprengel, Charles Darwin, Hermann Müller, and other successors of Darwin, that the flowers may in a sense be regarded as the resultants of the insect-visits, since all their accessory adaptations—large coloured petals, fragrance, nectar, and even little minutiæ of colour and markings (honey-guides)—as well as their detailed shape, as seen in 'landing stages,' corolla tubes, and so on, are only intelligible when we refer their existence to natural selection. We assume that each of these adaptations secured some advantage for the species concerned, and that therefore their first beginnings as slight germinal varieties were accepted, and were brought gradually to their full expression by the united operation of germinal and personal selection. This at least is how we should express ourselves now that we have become acquainted with the factor of germinal selection. The advantage secured by every such improvement in a flower's means of attracting insects is obvious, as soon as it is established that cross-fertilization is more advantageous for the species than self-fertilization.

We have discussed this already; we saw that experiments instituted by Darwin proved that seedlings which had arisen through cross-fertilization were superior to those arising through self-fertilization, and that in many cases the mother-plant itself produced fewer seeds when self-fertilized than when cross-fertilized. This discovery afforded an explanation of the cross-fertilization of flowers by insects which Sprengel had previously observed. We understand how the flowers must have become so adapted through processes of selection that they were unable to fertilize themselves, but attracted insects, and, so to speak, compelled these to dust them with pollen from another plant of the same species. We also understand how self-fertilization remained possible for many flowers in the event of cross-fertilization through insects not being effected, since after a certain period of waiting, a curvature of the stamens or the pistil may take place and lead to the stigma being dusted with the pollen of the same flower. Obviously the development of *fewer* seeds is preferable to complete sterility. It is a well-known fact that peculiar inconspicuous and closed flowers, designed solely for self-fertilization, may occur along with the open flowers, as in the case of the so-called cleistogamous flowers of the violet (*Viola*) and the little dead-nettle (*Lamium amplexicaule*), and the phyletic origin of these becomes intelligible as soon as it is established that cross-fertilization is more advantageous than self-fertilization.

Now, however, it seems as if the fundamental proposition of this theory of flowers will have to be rejected. Not only do the cleistogamous flowers just mentioned exhibit a great fertility, not at all less than that of the open flowers of the same species which are adapted for cross-fertilization, but there is a small number of plants which produce seeds by *self-fertilization alone*. Thus in *Myrmecodia* cross-fertilization is absolutely prevented by the fact that the flowers never open, and according to Charles Darwin *Ophrys apifera* also reproduces by self-fertilization alone, and is nevertheless a thoroughly vigorous plant. There are several other cases of this sort, and particularly among the orchids, though the whole of the structure of their flowers is specially adapted for pollination by insects. Many of them are only rarely visited by insects, some not at all, we know not why, but it is readily intelligible that in such cases they should have adapted themselves to self-fertilization wherever that was possible. For this *no great* variation was necessary; it was enough that the pollinia, which formerly only became detached from their attachment at a touch or a push from an insect, should free themselves spontaneously. And this, according to Darwin, is what happens, for instance, in *Ophrys scolopax*, which at Cannes is frequently self-fertilizing. For the development of seed, however, it is not enough that the pollen should reach the stigma; the pollen-grain has to send out its tube and penetrate into the ovary, and in many orchids this does not happen; they are infertile with their own pollen. Various other plants are also non-fertile with their own pollen, for instance the common corydalis, *Corydalis cava*, or the meadow cuckoo-flower, *Cardamine pratensis* (Hildebrand).

How are we to reconcile these apparently absolutely contradictory facts? On the one hand, the innumerable devices for securing crossing lead us to conclude that it is necessary, or at least advantageous, and on the other we find a small number of plants which reproduce continually by self-fertilization and yet remain strong and vigorous. And again there are many plants which yield seed when fertilized with their own pollen, and others which remain absolutely sterile in the same circumstances, yielding no seed or very little, and there is indeed one on which its own pollen has the effect of a poison, for if it reaches the stigma the flower dies. If there is anything injurious in self-fertilization (Darwin), we can understand that it will be avoided, but how can it be continued so long in many cases, and even become in others the exclusive method of fertilization without visible evil results?

It seems to me that in these facts, established by observation, the results of two quite different processes have been confused, and that we can only gain clearness by studying them apart from one another; I mean the processes involved in the mechanism of fertilization and those involved in the mingling of the germ-plasms.

In many cases self-fertilization is said to yield less seed and weaker seedlings. Let us for the present take this statement as the basis of our consideration; it does not seem to me conceivable, though here I am not in agreement with views that have been expressed by others, that both effects should depend upon the same causes, for the smaller number of seeds cannot possibly depend upon the mingling of the two parental germ-plasms, and thus not upon the process of amphimixis itself, since the effect of the mingling does not make itself felt until the organism of the offspring is being built up. Of course the plant seed is the embryo of the young plant, but it will hardly be thought probable that its development could be absolutely prevented by the too close relationship of the two germ-cells, and thus the number of the developing seeds cannot depend on the quality of the ids co-operating in the segmentation-nucleus, but presumably on the number of ova awaiting fertilization in the ovary, which are reached by a pollen-tube and then by a paternal sex-nucleus. This again will depend upon the impelling and attracting forces of the pollen-grain on the one hand, and of the stigma and 'embryo-sac' of the flower on the other. In other words, the fertility of a flower with its own pollen will depend upon whether the two products of the flower are adapted for mutual co-operation, and in what degree they are so. We are here dealing not with the *primary* reactions of the germ-plasms, which are as they are and cannot be varied, but with secondary relations, which may be thus or thus—in short, with *adaptations*.

By what adaptations the pollen of a flower can be made ineffective for that flower is a question which we must leave the botanists to answer; in any case it must have been possible, and we see clearly that it depends upon adaptation when we consider the numerous stages which occur—from the rare case of the actually poisonous influence of self-pollination already noticed, to complete sterility, and from lessened fertility to greater or even perfect fertility. It is possible that chemical products, secretions of the stigma or the pollen-grain, or the so-called synergid-cells, have to do with this, or that the size and therewith the penetrating power of the pollen-cell in self-fertilization stand in inverse ratio to the length of the pistil, as has been proved in regard to heterostylism by Strasburger; but in any case it was possible for Nature, by means of slight variations in the characters of the male and female parts of the flower, to diminish the certainty of the meeting of the two germ-cells, even to the total exclusion of the possibility of any union of these.

If, then, self-fertilization had to be guarded against or at least rendered difficult because its consequences were injurious, all variations pointing in the direction of safeguarding would necessarily be preserved and increased. In many cases variations in the structure of the flower were sufficient; but when, as in *Corydalis cava*, the pollen could not readily be prevented from falling upon the stigma, the pollen might be made sterile as far as its own flower was concerned by a process of selection, in which on an average those plants would

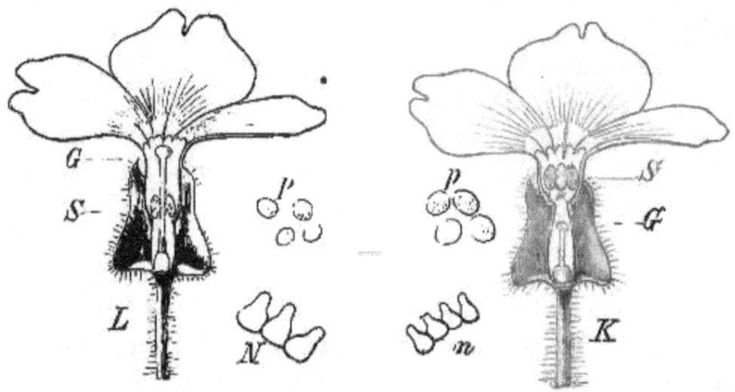

FIG. 128. Heterostylism (*Primula sinensis*), after Noll. Two heterostylic flowers from different plants. *L*, the long-styled form. *K*, the short-styled form. *G*, style. *S*, anthers. *P*, *p*, pollen-grains. *N*, *n*, stigmatic papillæ of the long-styled and short-styled forms respectively. *P*, *p*, *N*, *n*, magnified 110 times.

remain successful which produced the largest number of cross-fertilized seeds, and in this case those which did so were those whose pollen reacted most feebly to the stimulus of their own stigma.

That self-sterility in all these different degrees is not a primary character of the species, but an adaptation to the advantages of cross-fertilization, is apparent—if indeed it seems doubtful to any one—especially from cases of heterostylism. I refer to the dimorphism and trimorphism which Darwin discovered in many flowers, and which shows itself in the fact that flowers otherwise almost exactly alike, as, for instance, primroses, may exhibit a long style in some individuals, and in others a short one (Fig. 128). At the same time, there is a difference in the position of the stamens, which are placed higher up in flowers with short styles, and much lower down in those with long styles. Experiments have proved that the dusting of the stigma has the best results if pollen from the short-styled reaches the stigma of the long-styled form, or if pollen from the long-styled form reaches the stigma of the short-styled. Thus we have again to deal with an arrangement for crossing, an adaptation to the advantages of cross-fertilization, and we can in this case see the reason why the pollen has a different effect upon the two stigmas; the pollen-grains of the flowers with short style are larger than those of the flowers with long style, and as the length of the pollen-tube that can be sent out must depend upon the mass of protoplasm within the pollen-grain, it follows that the smaller pollen-grains will send out too short a tube to reach through the long style to the embryo-sac. In addition to this there is a difference in the papillæ of the stigmas, and it is possible that these may form an obstacle to the penetrating of pollen from a similar type. The process of selection which gives rise to such arrangements as we find in Primulas may easily be imagined, as soon as we are able to assume that cross-fertilization is more advantageous than self-fertilization as regards progeny, that is, as regards the continuance of the species.

We have already seen that uninterrupted self-fertilization is unknown among animals, but that it is not even very rare among plants, and this emphatically corroborates our previous conclusion, that the reason for which amphimixis was introduced as a normal event in nature is not to be sought for in the necessity for a renewing of life, or 'rejuvenation.' It cannot be a necessity, but only an advantage, which can in certain circumstances be dispensed with.

Although it is obvious enough that continued inbreeding in its most extreme form, self-fertilization, does not imply an absolute abandonment of amphimixis, the adherents of the rejuvenescence theory have regarded the unfavourable consequences of pure inbreeding as a confirmation of their assumption, according to which amphimixis is indispensable to the continuance of the life of the species, and it is therefore an important fact, if it can be proved, that continued self-fertilization can occur persistently, among plants at least, and yet not cause any injurious results to the species.

But how can this fact be understood from our point of view? How does it happen that crossing is striven after in so many different ways and yet so often given up again, and continued self-fertilization resorted to?

To this it may be answered, in the first place, that it is not, as far as we can see, for *internal* reasons that persistent self-fertilization becomes the rule; there is no peculiar condition of the germ-plasm which makes it disadvantageous or superfluous that the diversity of the id-combinations should be maintained; self-fertilization is due to *external* influences which bring it about that the plant has only the alternative of producing no seeds at all or of producing them by self-fertilization. In this connexion Darwin's experiments with orchids are particularly noteworthy.

In this very diversified order of plants there are numerous species whose flowers are infertile with their own pollen, although it does not reach the stigma in natural conditions, and therefore there was no necessity—as far as we can see—for guarding against self-fertilization by 'self-sterility.' These flowers are thus doubly adapted, so to speak, for crossing by means of insects. But as regards many of these, as well as many other modern orchids, insect-visits are very rare, and in some cases do not occur at all, and therefore these species cannot produce seed or can do so only exceptionally.

This is true of most of the Epidendra of South America, and of *Coryanthus triloba* of New Zealand, two hundred blossoms of which only yielded five seed-capsules, and also of our *Ophrys muscifera* and *O. aranifera,* the latter of which yielded only a single seed-capsule from 3,000 flowers gathered in Liguria. We might expect that the species in question must have become very rare, but this is not always the case, since each of these capsules contains an enormous number of seeds, sometimes many thousands. As soon as the visits of insects cease altogether, the species must die out in the particular locality concerned, unless it can revert to self-pollination and self-fertility. There is a whole series of species in which the stigma of the flower is sensitive to its own pollen, and in many of these an adaptation to self-fertilization has actually been effected, for the pollinia detach themselves from their anthers at maturity and fall upon the stigma. I have already mentioned *Ophrys apifera*, which, according to Charles Darwin, is no longer visited by insects, although its flowers still possess the structure required for insect-fertilization. This species has saved itself from extinction by the normal occurrence of self-fertilization.

This seems to me noteworthy in two respects. In the first place, it shows that pure self-fertilization need not necessarily result in a weakening of the species, and secondly, it affords a clear instance of a species being transformed in one minute character only, all the other characters remaining unaltered. In this case it was only the pollinia that required to vary a little in their mode of attachment and maturation, in order to effect the transformation of the flower for self-fertilization, and in point of fact that is all that has varied. The case is not relevant to our investigation at this moment, but cases of the kind can so rarely be clearly demonstrated that I cannot lose the opportunity of calling attention to it. The germ-plasm of this *Ophrys* must have varied at an earlier stage, for otherwise the detachment of the pollinia would not have become normal and hereditary, but it can only have varied to the extent that the structure of this one small part of the flower was affected by the variation; something must have varied in the germ-plasm that had no influence upon the other parts of the flower, that is, solely the *determinants* of the pollinia.

Let us return after this digression to our previous train of thought: we have to inquire how we can interpret the fact of continued self-fertilization without any visible injurious results to the species. If cross-fertilization be a material advantage as regards the continuance of the species, how can it be transformed into its opposite without evil effects? And there are no visible evil effects in *Ophrys apifera*. It is indeed not so abundant as *Ophrys muscifera*, or other allied species, but it certainly does not follow from that that it is on the way to extinction: certainly no decrease either of vigour of growth or of fertility can be observed.

If we inquire from the standpoint of our theory, how the composition of the germ-plasm must have altered through continual inbreeding, we have already found the answer—that through the reduction of the number of ids at the maturation of every germ-cell the diversity of the germ-plasm would gradually be lessened, that the number of different ids would thereby be lessened possibly even to the identity of the whole of the ids.

The consequences of such extreme uniformity of the germ-plasm would not, according to our theory, necessarily be that the species would be incapable of continued existence, but it would be that the species would become incapable of adaptations in many directions. Adaptations in one direction, such, for instance, as the variation in the mode of attachment and detachment of the pollinia of an Orchid, would still be possible. Thus a species which has long been perfectly adapted will be able to make the transition to inbreeding without injury to its chances of continued existence, if it be compelled by circumstances to do so. Species, on the other hand, which are still undergoing considerable transformations in many directions must be exposed by these to the danger of degeneration, just as happens in the artificial experiments with domesticated animals, whose secret weaknesses are greatly exaggerated by inbreeding.

We might be inclined to regard the effects of inbreeding as similar to those of parthenogenesis; they are certainly analogous, for both modes of reproduction must lead to a certain degree of uniformity in the germ-plasm. But there seems to me to be a difference and one which is not without importance.

In parthenogenesis no amphimixis occurs, but neither does any reduction of the number of the ids to one-half; all the ids present at the beginning of parthenogenesis are retained; they are only no longer mingled with strange ids. In inbreeding both amphimixis and reduction take place, but the former soon *ceases* to convey any really strange ids to the germ-plasm, but only the same as those which it already contains, so that a rapidly increasing monotony of the germ-plasm must result. To this must be added the possibility that among the few ids which now—many times repeated—form the germ-plasm, some must occur which exhibit unfavourable variational tendencies in one or many determinants, and then the same thing will occur which usually occurs in experimental inbreeding of domesticated animals, namely, *degeneration of the progeny*. In parthenogenesis the case is otherwise; unfavourable variational tendencies, as soon as they attain selection-value, are, so to speak, eliminated root and branch, because the individuals which exhibit them, and their whole lineage, are exterminated, without their having any effect upon the other collateral lines of descent. A purely parthenogenctic species will, therefore, not degenerate as long as individuals of normal constitution are present, for these reproduce with perfect purity. But if in later generations unfavourable variational tendencies crop up in the germ-plasm through germinal selection, the process of personal selection will be reinforced on these or on their descendants, and it is conceivable, and even probable, that in perfectly adapted species parthenogenesis may last for a very long time without doing any injury to the constitution of the species.

The same is true of purely asexual reproduction, to the investigation of which we shall now turn.

Let us leave out of account the simplest animals (Monera) without amphimixis, which we have already discussed. In simple animals reproduction by budding or by fission is frequent, or it occurs in alternation with sexual reproduction; in higher animals, Arthropods, Mollusca, and Vertebrates, asexual reproduction is wholly absent. In plants it plays an enormously greater part, and what is called 'vegetative reproduction,' which is purely asexual without any amphimixis, is to be found in all groups of plants, especially in the form of budding and spore-formation, besides which there is multiplication by runners, rhizomes, tubers, bulbs, and bulbils. In most cases there is, in addition to the purely asexual reproduction, so-called sexual reproduction associated with amphimixis, and often the sexual and asexual generations alternate with each other, so that 'alternation of generations' occurs, as is common in lower animals, especially polyps, medusæ, and worms.

But it sometimes happens among plants that the sexual reproduction is absent, and that a species reproduces by the asexual mode only, and this is the case which we must now consider more closely.

Let us first of all seek to gain clearness as to the composition of the germ-plasm in the case of purely asexual multiplication, and what conclusions may be drawn from this, and then let us compare these with the known observational data, and it will be apparent that in individuals which have arisen by budding the complete germ-plasm of the species must be contained; the number of ids will not only remain the same in the bud as it was in the mother plant, but the number of *different ids* will not be diminished. The case is analogous to that of pure parthenogenesis, in which the absence of the second maturation-division of the ovum allows the germ-plasm to retain the full complement of ids. Charles Darwin held that purely asexual multiplication was 'closely analogous to long-continued self-fertilization,' yet, as we have seen, according to our theory there must be a not inconsiderable difference between the two processes, depending on the fact that in exclusive self-fertilization the number of different ids is continually decreasing, while in purely asexual reproduction the germ-plasm loses nothing of the diversity of its ids. If, therefore, the germ-plasm in purely asexual reproduction no longer receives fresh ids through amphimixis, it at least loses none of those it formerly possessed. Although we cannot consider it adapted for entering upon new adaptations in many directions, yet we may expect that the species will continue to reproduce unchanged for longer than in the case of exclusive self-fertilization, the more so since all unfavourable variational tendencies which crop up are eliminated as soon as they attain to selection-value, and, as in the case of parthenogenesis, they are eliminated without being mingled with other lines of descent.

Let us take, for instance, the purely asexual reproduction which obtains in Algæ of the genus *Laminaria*, in regard to which it is stated that it multiplies only through asexual swarm-spores. There are quite a number of species of this large tangle, and if it should be established that in all these the spore-cells really do not conjugate, then the case would prove that the species of a genus can maintain a well-defined existence for a long time after amphimixis has been given up. But this would not be a proof of the possibility of *species-formation*, for that the ancestral forms of the Laminarians must have possessed amphigony may be assumed, since their nearest relatives

S 2

exhibit it still. It cannot be proved, but there seems nothing against the assumption that these tangles have existed for a long time under uniform conditions, and have become adapted to these with a high degree of constancy.

The conditions are similar in the marine Algæ of the genus *Caulerpa*, the nearest relatives of which reproduce sexually, though they themselves, as far as is known, reproduce only by spores.

In the Lichens, which represent, as we have already seen, a life-partnership between Fungi and Algæ, amphimixis appears not to occur at all: the unicellular Alga reproduces by cell-division, the Fungus by producing a great number of swarm-spores, which do not conjugate with one another. As far as the Alga is concerned we might perhaps suppose that the simplicity of its structure makes it possible for it to dispense with a constant recombination of its few characters to bring about the most favourable composition in its idioplasm: in support of this we may note that even the life-long combination with the Fungus has caused no visible variation in the Alga, as we must conclude from the fact that these Algæ can also live independently, and that the same species of Alga may combine with several different Fungi to form different species of lichen, just as the same Fungus may also form part of several species of lichen. We might also imagine that we have here no more than a direct influence of the Alga and Fungus upon one another, and that there is no adaptation to the new conditions of life at all, yet that can hardly be seriously maintained in regard to species which live under such definite and diverse conditions. It now seems to be established —contrary to the older statements—that the lichen-fungus only reproduces asexually, and in face of this it seems to me that nothing remains except to make the assumption that lichens formerly possessed sexual reproduction, but that they have lost it, though whether all have done so is, perhaps, not yet quite certain.

The same assumption must be made in regard to the Basidiomycetes among the Fungi, and for most of the Ascomycetes, for in these groups of Fungi sexual reproduction has only been demonstrated 'with certainty in a few genera.' That in these cases also there has been a degeneration of amphigony, until it has completely disappeared, seems probable from the two other groups of Fungi, the Zygomycetes and Oomycetes, since in these 'a reduction of sexuality amounting in some cases to complete disappearance' can be demonstrated even in existing forms. But whether it may be assumed that the Fungi which are now asexual are no longer capable of new adaptations, and whether their parasitic habit may be regarded as making up in some way for the lack of the remingling of the germ-plasm, as the botanist Möbius supposes, I am not able to decide. It is obvious that data in regard to amphimixis among the Fungi are still incomplete, and recent investigations lead us to suspect that sexual mingling may not be absent, but only disguised. Dangeard, Harold Wager, and others have observed that a fusion of nuclei precedes the formation of spores, and this may be regarded as amphimixis, although the conjugating nuclei belong to cells of the same plant and sometimes even to the same cell. But although we are here dealing with a set of facts which cannot yet be satisfactorily formulated in terms of our theory, it is nevertheless not contradictory to it that amphimixis should be wholly absent in the higher Fungi. But the fact would be contradictory to the unadulterated rejuve-

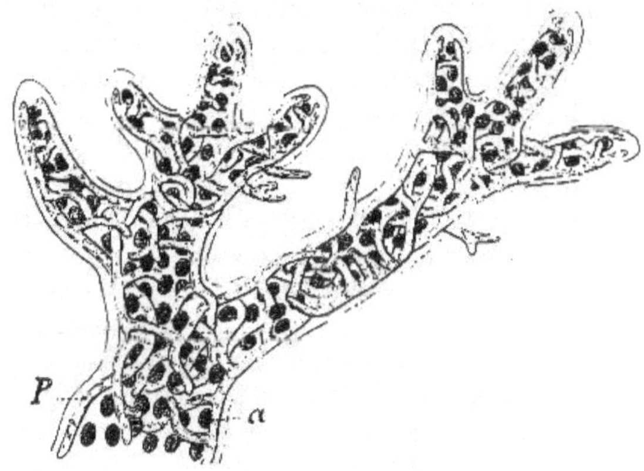

FIG. 38 (repeated). A fragment of a Lichen (*Ephebe kerneri*), magnified 450 times. *a*, the green alga-cells. *P*, the fungoid filaments. After Kerner.

nescence-theory, for if amphimixis were really a condition of the continuance of life, no species—as we have already said—could continue to exist without it for countless generations.

The same argument holds true for the higher plants, which have become purely asexual under the influence of cultivation. I refer to many of the well-marked varieties of our cultivated plants which multiply exclusively, or almost exclusively, by means of tubers and slips, as is the case with the potato, the manioc, the sugar-cane, the arrowroot-plant (*Maranta arundinacea*), and others. All these facts can easily be reconciled with our interpretation of the meaning of amphimixis, although the attempt to range them as evidence against our theory has more than once been made. We have thus arrived at the conclusion that while many-sided adaptations, that is, variations which transform the plant in accordance with the indirect influences of new conditions of life, cannot be brought about without a persistent mingling of germ-plasms, simple modifications may readily appear although amphimixis is altogether absent. If a wild plant be permanently transferred to a well-manured culture-bed, it is probable that certain changes will occur in it, either gradually or at once. But these are not adaptations: they are, so to speak, direct reactions of the organism which do not even require selection to make them increase, but depend upon the influencing of certain determinants of the germ-plasm, and which, like all germinal variations, will follow their course steadily until a halt is called either by germinal or by personal selection. When a given plant is exposed to these new and artificial conditions, the changes in question make their appearance sooner or later, and follow their course, and go on increasing as long as that is compatible with the harmony of the structure and functioning of the plant, this depending, as in all individual development, on the struggle between the parts, that is to say, on histonal selection. Only in this respect is the utility or injuriousness of the change of importance, for personal selection, the struggle between individuals, does not affect plants which are under cultivation.

That such modifications may increase and may persist through many generations, even with asexual multiplication, depends upon the fact that the budding cells contain germ-plasm, as well as the germ-cells, and if particular determinants of the germ-plasm in general are caused to vary by these new influences, the variation may be transmitted from bud to bud, from shoot to shoot, and so go on increasing as long as the new conditions persist, as well as in amphigonic (bi-sexual) reproduction, where they are transmitted from germ-cell to germ-cell. It is not inconceivable that an individual adaptation, that is to say a useful adjustment, might be effected in the course of asexual reproduction, although it is improbable that direct influences would give rise to just those changes which would be useful under the new conditions. But there are a number of cases which have been interpreted in this way. In several of the cultivated plants named, the reproductive organs have themselves degenerated, either only the male, or only the female, or both at the same time; and some observers, accepting the hypothesis of an inheritance of functional modifications, have regarded this as the direct result of disuse during the long period of asexual reproduction.

Leaving out of account this erroneous presupposition, we may ask how asexual reproduction, such as that of the potato by tubers instead of by seed, which has gone on exclusively for several centuries, could exercise any influence upon the flowers and seed-forming of this species? In point of fact it has exercised none in most potatoes, for the flowers and seeds are just as fertile now as they were when the potato was first discovered.

Whether the pollen of a flower is utilized in one or other of its thousands of pollen-grains by reaching the stigma of another plant of the same species, or whether all the pollen-grains are uselessly scattered abroad, cannot possibly affect the flower so as to cause degeneration; the theory of disuse cannot be applied in this case. What is true of the potato holds good also of the manioc (*Manihot utilissima*), but, on the other hand, many of the best varieties of common fruits—pears, figs, grapes, pine-apples, and bananas—are seedless. In *Maranta arundinacea* 'the whole wonderful structure of the flower has persisted, but the pollen-grains, that is the germ-cells, are wanting.' Whether this implies a permanent degeneration of the sexual organs, that is to say, one that is embodied in the primary constituents of the species, or whether it is only the result of over-abundant nourishment, or of other causes in the circumstances affecting the particular plant, can only be decided by experiment. Probably both occur. The common ivy, for instance, does not now blossom in the northern parts of Sweden and Russia, but it does so still in the southern provinces. If plants were brought to us from the most northerly zone of distribution, they would in all probability flower and bear fruit with us, and in that case the absence of bloom in these plants must have been a direct effect of the cold climate. But it is quite conceivable that cultivated plants have in many cases become hereditarily infertile, when they are constantly propagated only by means of buds, layering, and so on, not however because of any direct effect of this mode of propagation, but through chance germinal variations. For in regard to many of them man has lost all interest in the flowers and fruit, as, for instance, in the case of the potato; in other cases he is even interested in procuring seedless fruits.

In the first case he will quite readily make use of plants with imperfect flowers for propagating, if they are otherwise fit and exhibit what he wants in other respects; in the second case, he will give a preference to individuals with seedless fruits, and thus increase and strengthen the tendency to degeneration of the seeds in the race concerned.

All these cases are quite in harmony with our conception of amphimixis, which, now that we have investigated the facts throughout the animate kingdom, we may sum up in the following propositions. In the whole organic world, from unicellular organisms up to the highest plants and animals, amphimixis now means an augmentation of the organism's power of adaptation to the conditions of its life, since it is only through amphimixis that simultaneous harmonious adaptation of many parts becomes possible. It effects this by the mingling and constant recombination of the germ-plasm ids of different individuals, and thus gives the selection-processes the chance of favouring advantageous variational tendencies and eliminating those which are unfavourable, as well as of collecting and combining all the variations which are necessary for the further evolution of the species. This indirect influence of amphimixis on the capacity of organisms for surviving and being transformed is the fundamental reason for its general introduction and for its persistence through the whole known realm of organisms from unicellulars upwards.

The reason for its *first* introduction among the lower forms of life must have been a direct effect which had a favourable influence on the metabolism, and this is so far coincident with the subsequent import of amphimixis, inasmuch as it may be regarded not only as a heightening of the power of adaptation, but as an immediate and direct increase and extension of the power of assimilation. In any case, amphimixis is not necessary to the actual preservation of life itself, but it does bring about a wealth and diversity of organic architecture which without it would have been unattainable.

If amphimixis has been abandoned in the course of phylogeny by isolated groups of organisms, this has happened because other advantages accrued to them in consequence, which gave them greater security in the struggle for existence; but it must be admitted that they thereby lost their perfect power of adaptation, and that they have thus bartered their future for the temporary securing of their existence.

In addition to this variational influence, amphimixis has also played a part in the evolution of sharply defined organic types, especially of specific types; but of this we shall have more to say later on.

LECTURE XXXI

THE INFLUENCES OF ENVIRONMENT

Different modes and grades of selection—Changes due to the influences of environment—Superfluity and lack of food—The horses and cattle of the Falkland Islands—Angora animals—Protection against cold in Arctic and marine mammals—Plant-galls—Nägeli's *Hieracium* experiments—Experiments with *Polyommatus phlæas*—Artificially produced *Vanessa*-aberrations—Vöchting's experiments on the influence of light in the production of flower-forms—Heliotropism and other tropisms—Primary and secondary reactions of organisms—Herbst's 'lithium larvæ'—Schmankewitsch's experiments with *Artemia*—Poulton's caterpillars with facultative colour adaptation—Colour-change in fishes, chamæleon, &c.—Actual scope of those influences which directly produce organic changes.

THROUGH a long series of lectures we have devoted our attention to those phenomena which bear some relation to the processes of selection: we have attempted to gain clearness in regard to the modes and stages of these, and we reached the result that all variations which have taken place in organisms since the first appearance of living matter are directed by processes of selection, that is, their direction and duration are determined by these processes, although they may have their roots in external influences. But it is not to be supposed that this guidance is due solely to that one kind of selection which, with Darwin and Wallace, we designate 'natural selection': on the contrary, we must regard this as only one of the different modes of the processes of selection, necessarily occurring between all living units which are equivalent to one another, and which, therefore, must maintain a continual struggle with one another for space and food. If the expression 'natural selection' were not already so firmly fixed in its meaning, I should propose that it should be employed in the most general sense for all the processes of selection collectively, but we must keep to its original meaning and use it only for personal selection.

We have seen that processes of selection take place even between the elements of the germ-plasm in all organisms which possess a germ-plasm as distinguished from the mass of the body, and that through these processes there arise those hereditary individual variations which, under some circumstances, form the basis of transformations in the species.

Obviously this may come about in a twofold manner: firstly,

a variation movement originating in the germ-plasm may go on increasing till it attains to selection-value, and then 'personal selection' steps in, and seeks to make it the common property of the species. But it is obviously also conceivable that variational tendencies arising in the germ-plasm may never attain to selection-value at all, and then in most cases they will only continue to exist through a longer or shorter series of generations as individual distinguishing characters, without being transmitted to a larger number of individuals or becoming a constant character of the species. Their persistence will depend essentially on the chance of mingling with other individuals, and on the halving of the germ-plasm which precedes sexual reproduction. Sooner or later these individual peculiarities disappear again, as may often be observed in the case of abnormalities or morbid tendencies in man, in as far as these do not weaken vitality. In the latter case they attain selection-value, though only negatively.

But even quite indifferent germinal variations, which neither raise nor lower the individual's power of survival, may, under some circumstances, increase and lead to permanent variations of all the individuals of a species, and this happens when they are conditioned by external influences which affect all the individuals of a species, or of the particular colony concerned, and it is this kind of organismal change which we shall now study for a little in detail.

The ordinary never-ceasing, always active germinal selection depends, we must assume, upon intra-germinal fluctuations of nutrition, or inequalities in the nutritive stream which circulates within the germ-plasm. The variations which it produces may, therefore, be different in each individual, since these fluctuations are a matter of chance and may affect the determinants *A* in one individual and the determinants *B*, *C*, or *X* in another, or alternating groups of these. Or it may be that the homologous determinants *A* may vary in a plus direction in one individual, and in a minus direction in another, while in a third they may remain unchanged, and although the same direction of variation of a determinant *N* may occur in many individuals, it will certainly not do so in all, and still less will it occur in all along with the same combination of fluctuations in the rest of the determinants. It is only if this occurs that the variation can become a specific character.

We might expect on *a priori* grounds that not only the chance fluctuations of nutrition within the germ-plasm would cause its elements to vary in this or that direction, but that there would also be influences of a more general kind, especially those of nutrition and climate, which would in the first place affect the body as a whole, but with it also the germ-plasm, and which would therefore bring about variations, either in all or only in certain determinants. In this case all the individuals would vary in the same way, because all would be similarly affected by the same causes of change.

This is actually the case; it is indubitable that external influences, such as those emanating from the environment or media in which species live, are able to cause direct variation of the germ-plasm, that is, permanent, because hereditary variations. We have already referred to this process and called it 'induced germinal selection.'

That such influences of environment may bring about changes in *individual* organisms is obvious enough: that, for instance, good nutrition makes the body strong and vigorous, that too abundant food makes it fat and causes degeneration, that insufficient food lessens its stamina and vigour, are well-known facts. We have to inquire, on the one hand, to what extent such influences are able to cause changes in the individual body in the course of a lifetime, and, on the other hand, more particularly, how far such changes or modifications of the soma can call forth corresponding variations in the determinant system of the germ-cells, and whether and under what circumstances they may be transmitted; for where this is not the case there can be no permanent hereditary variation of the whole species, and the variation will only persist as long as the conditions which gave rise to it endure, and will disappear again with these.

The influence of nutrition as a cause of variation has often been over-estimated. The old statement which has gone the round of the textbooks since the time of John Hunter, that the stomach of carnivores may be transformed by vegetable diet into a herbivore stomach, is absolutely unproved. Brandes at least, who not only subjected all the statements in the literature on this point to a critical investigation, but also instituted experiments of his own, regards the statement as altogether unfounded. All the 'cases' cited, in which the stomach of a gull or of an owl fed on grain became transformed into an organ with stronger muscles and covered with horny plates, depend, according to Brandes, upon inexact observation. There can therefore be no question of any inheritance of this fictitious stomach-transformation, and the idea that such a fundamental histological adaptation as the alleged transformation of the stomach of the grain-eating bird should arise as a direct effect of the food is wholly without foundation.

But it is quite otherwise with purely quantitative differences in nutrition. That meagre diet influences individuals unfavourably is indubitable, and we are certainly justified in considering whether this may not have an effect on the germ-cells, and one which will correspond to the changes induced on the body, so that if the poor nutrition should last through many generations an hereditary degeneration of the species would occur, which would not at once disappear though the animals were transferred to more favourable conditions.

We certainly know nothing of how far the minuteness of the determinants of the germ-plasm, the whole quantity of the germ-plasm, or the reduced size of the germ-cell, may bear an internal relation to the smallness of the animal which develops therefrom, but it surely cannot be regarded as absurd to suppose that there is some such relation. There are no experiments known to me which prove that meagre diet brings about a progressive decrease in the size of the body. Carl von Voit has observed that dogs of the same litter grew to very different sizes of body according as they received abundant or scanty food, but it would be difficult to make animals small through scantiness of food and at the same time to keep them capable of reproduction, and thus proofs of the inheritance of the dwarfing are lacking. Moreover, the experiments which Nature herself has made are never quite convincing, because we never can definitely exclude the indirect effect of altered circumstances. The case of the feral horses of the Falkland Islands, so often cited since the time of Darwin, which have become small 'through the damp climate and scanty food,' seems to me, of all known cases of the kind, the one we should most readily attribute to the direct effect of continued scanty diet; but even here we cannot altogether exclude the possibility of the co-operation of adaptations of some kind to the very peculiar conditions of life in these islands, as far as the feral horses are concerned. I have not been able to find any record of more modern exact investigations either regarding these feral horses, or in regard to the others which are reared in the Falklands under conditions of domestication. Darwin himself, however, in the Journal of his famous voyage tells us much that is interesting in regard to the mammals of the Falkland Islands. Cattle and horses were brought there in 1764 by the French, and have increased greatly in numbers since that time; they roam about wild in large herds, and the cattle are strikingly large and strong, while the horses both wild and tame are rather small, and have lost so much of their original strength that they cannot be used for catching wild cattle with the lasso, and horses have to be imported from La Plata for this purpose. From this contrast between the horses and the cattle we may at least conclude that it cannot be 'scanty food' alone which causes the horses to become smaller, but that the climatic conditions as a whole are concerned in the matter. Whether the total amount of variation which has taken place in the horses which have lived wild there for a hundred years would take place in the course of a single life, or whether it is a cumulative phenomenon, has still to be decided.

Similar statements, for the most part still more uncertain, are made in regard to changes in the hair of goats, sheep, cattle, cats, and sheep-dogs, which are referred to climatic influence. The raw climate of many highlands, like Tibet and Angora, is said to have directly produced the long and fine-haired breeds. But there is a lack of proof that adaptation or artificial selection did not also play a part, and the fact that similar long-haired breeds have arisen among rabbits and guinea-pigs in quite different places and under quite different climatic conditions, but under the directing care of man, speaks in favour of our supposition. But, on the other hand, it does not seem impossible that the climate may have a variational influence upon certain determinants of the germ-plasm, for we have already seen that the influence of cultivation may incite plants and animals to hereditary variations, and that slowly increasing disturbances in the equilibrium of the determinant system may thereby be produced, which may suddenly find marked expression as 'mutations.' But there is little probability that *adaptations*, that is, transformations corresponding to the altered climate, can arise in this way. The thick fur of the Arctic mammals is assuredly not a direct effect of the cold, although it has developed in all Arctic animals, not only in the modern polar bears, foxes, and hares of the polar regions, but also in the shaggy-haired mammoth of diluvial Siberia, whose tropical relatives of to-day, the elephants, have an almost naked skin. Another interesting case, recently brought to light, shows that a group of animals which, in correspondence with their otherwise exclusively tropical distribution, have only a moderately developed coat of hair, may, on migrating to a cold country, grow as good a fur as the members of other families. I refer to one of the higher apes, *Rhinopithecus roxellanae*, which live in companies in the forest on the high mountains of Tibet, notwithstanding that the snow lies there for six months [1].

But we should assuredly make a mistake if we were to regard the thick fur of these apes as a direct reaction of the organism to the cold. We see at once that this cannot be the case if we compare them with marine mammals, which differ just as much from one

[1] See Milne-Edwards, *Recherches pour servir à l'histoire nat. d. mammifères*, Paris. 1868–74.

another in this respect and yet are exposed to the same low temperature. The whale and the dolphin are quite naked, absolutely hairless, but the seals possess a thick hairy coat. This striking difference is obviously connected with the mode of life; the whales remain always in the water, the seals leave it often and therefore require the hairy coat, especially in colder climates, since otherwise they would be too rapidly cooled by the evaporation of the water from their bodies. For the whales, on the other hand, even a very thick hairy coat would not have sufficed as a protection against cold, since water is a much better conductor of heat than air, and so it was necessary for them to become enveloped with the well-known thick layer of blubber, a deposit of fat lying under the skin, and this—after it was once developed—made the hairy coat superfluous, so that it disappeared. The seals certainly also possess a layer of fat under the skin, but it is only in the largest of them that it affords sufficient protection against the cooling effect of evaporation when they go upon land or on the ice, and it is therefore only in these larger ones that the hairy coat has markedly degenerated, as, for instance, in the walrus and the sea-lion; in all the smaller seals, in which the mass of the body is much less, the hairy coat is necessarily very thick and protected from soaking by being very oily, because the layer of fat under the skin would not be sufficient to prevent excessive cooling when on land. But the thick coat of hair is no more *produced* by the cold than is the layer of fat. As Kükenthal has shown, all these characters are adaptations, and may depend here as elsewhere upon natural selection and upon the 'fluctuating' variations of the germ-plasm upon which that process is based. They are directed by personal selection because there is the need for them, and they are produced and augmented by germinal selection.

In all these cases the *direct* effect of external influences has nothing to do with the matter, but in other cases that alone brings about the whole change, which is then limited to the individual and does not affect the species as a whole at all.

Plant-galls afford striking illustration of the extraordinary changes that may be brought about in an organism or in its parts by external influence in the course of the individual life. All possibility of adaptation on the part of the plant is excluded in this case. The gall can only depend upon the direct influence of a stimulus, which is exercised by the young animal, the larva, upon the cells which surround it; and yet these cells vary to a considerable extent, become filled with starch or form a woody layer, secrete special substances, such as tannic acid, in large quantities, or develop hairs, moss-like growths, pigments, and so on, which do not otherwise occur in that particular part of the plant. Since Adler and Beyerinck have proved that it is not a poison conveyed by the mother animal into the leaf or bud when laying the eggs, which gives rise to the gall-formation, the matter has become rather clearer. We can now understand that different stimuli in succession affect the cells which enclose the larva, and that the ordered succession of these and the exactly graded stimulation incite the cells to activity in various ways, whether to mere growth and multiplication in a given direction, or to the secretion of tannic acid, or to the formation of wood, or to the deposition of reserve material, and so on. Even the feeble movements of the young larva may form a stimulus that increases with its growth; then the movements made by the larva in feeding, and not least the different secretions emanating from the salivary glands of the animal, which must contain some substances capable of acting as stimuli and probably changing in character as time goes on. All these factors must act as specific stimuli to the plant-cells, influencing and modifying their processes of growth and metabolism in one direction or another. In principle at least, if not in detail, we understand the possibility that through the ordered succession and exact balancing of these different cell-stimuli the really marvellous structure of the gall may be brought about as the product of the direct influence, exercised only once, of the gall-insect upon the plant's parts. But the animal's power of exercising such a succession of finely graded stimuli upon the plant must be referred to long-continued processes of selection, and the structure of the gall, which is adapted to its purpose down to the minutest details, can thus be understood. The assumption of substances which can act even in minute quantities as specific cell-stimuli, which we require to make in this attempt to explain galls, is no longer without corroboration since we find analogies in the Iodothyrin of Baumann, the specific secretions of the thymus and the supra-renal bodies in the higher animals, not to speak of the 'anti-toxins' of the pathogenic bacteria, which are only known by their effects.

The case of plant-galls is thus of great theoretical interest because we can exclude all preparation of the plant-cells for the stimuli exercised by the animal, since the gall is quite useless for the plant, though many have endeavoured to discover some utility. We have therefore here a clear case of modification due to the effect, exercised once only, of external influences, an adaptation of the animal to the mode of reaction of particular plant-tissues.

It might be supposed that if any inheritance of somatogenic

modifications, any transmission of the acquirements of the personal part to the germinal part, were possible at all, it would occur in this case, for many species of gall-insects attack plants, particularly oaks, in great numbers every year. It has actually been maintained that galls may arise spontaneously, that is without the presence of a gall-insect. But no proof of this has ever been found, and the fact that no one has paid any attention to the assertion probably implies an unconscious condemnation of the hypothesis of the transmissibility of acquired characters.

It has been proved by Nägeli's often discussed experiments on hawkweeds (*Hieracium*) that much less specialized external influences can give rise to changes which are not hereditary. The Alpine species of hawkweed varied considerably in their whole habit in the rich soil of the Botanic Gardens at Munich, but their descendants, when transferred to a poor flinty soil, returned to the habit of the Alpine species. The changes which occurred in garden soil were therefore somatic and, as I have called them, 'transient,' and they did not depend upon variations of the germ-plasm. It may be objected in regard to these experiments that they were not continued long enough to prove that hereditary variations would not also have cropped up in consequence of the altered conditions. But in any case they prove that marked changes in the whole body of the plant may occur without any obvious variation of the germ-plasm. This does not mean, however, that the possibility of variations of the germ-plasm through such direct external influences is disputed. We must assume the occurrence of these on *a priori* grounds, if we refer—as we have done—individual hereditary variation to fluctuations in the nutrition of the individual determinants of the germ-plasm. It is probable that many general nutritive variations or climatic factors affect the germ-plasm as well as the soma, and it is by no means inconceivable that it is not all, but only certain definite determinants that are caused to vary.

A proof of this may be found in the results of experiments made upon the little red-gold fire-butterfly (*Polyommatus phlæas*), to which I have briefly referred in a former lecture. This little diurnal butterfly of the family Lycænidæ has a wide distribution and occurs in two climatic varieties. In the far north and also in the whole of Germany the upper surface is red-gold with a narrow black outer margin, but in the south of Europe the red-gold has been almost crowded out by the black. I reared caterpillars in Germany from eggs of *P. phlæas* found at Naples and exposed them directly after they had entered on the pupa-stage to a relatively low temperature

(10° C.). Butterflies emerged which were not quite so black as those of Naples, but considerably darker than the German form. Conversely, German pupæ were exposed to greater warmth (38° C.), and these gave rise to butterflies which were rather less fiery gold and considerably blacker than the ordinary German form. If I had to repeat these experiments I should use a much lower temperature in the case of the cold experiments, because we now know from the experiments of Standfuss, E. Fischer, and Bachmetjeff, that most of the pupæ of diurnal butterflies can stand a temperature below zero for a considerable time; probably the results would be even more marked then.

But even from the results of my former experiments we are justified in concluding that the blackening of the upper surface of the wing is really the direct result of the increased temperature during pupahood, and that the pure red-gold results from the lowered temperature. Similar experiments made by Merrifield with English *Phlæas* pupæ agree exactly with mine. But we may conclude further from these experiments that both warmth and cold only give rise to slight variations in the individual pupæ, and that the pure red-gold of the northern form and the black of the southern are the result of a long process of inheritance and accumulation, in which the germ-plasm has been caused to vary in as far as the relevant determinants are concerned, so that these yield the respective northern and southern forms even in less extreme temperatures.

As it is to be assumed that these determinants are present not only in the primordium of the wing in the pupa, but also in the germ-cells, both must be affected by the varying temperature, and, in accordance with the continuity of the germ-plasm, each variation of these determinants, however slight, would be continued in the next generation. It is thus intelligible that somatic variations like the blackening of the wings through warmth appear to be directly inherited and accumulate in the course of generations; in reality, however, it is not the somatic change itself which is transmitted, but the corresponding variation evoked by the same external influence in the relevant determinants of the germ-plasm within the germ-cells, in other words, in the determinants of the following generation.

This interpretation of these experiments, which I offered some years ago, has been confirmed in several ways in regard to various other diurnal Lepidoptera. By employing a temperature as low as 8° C. in the case of fresh pupæ of various species of *Vanessa* Standfuss and Merrifield, and especially E. Fischer, succeeded in getting great deviations in the marking and colour of the full-grown insects,—so-called aberrations, such as had previously been found only very rarely and singly under natural conditions. The deviations from the normal must undoubtedly be ascribed to the effect of cold, but it does not follow that they are new forms which have suddenly sprung into existence, as many have assumed without further experiment. Dixey, on the other hand, has attempted to establish, by a comparison of the different species of *Vanessa*, the phyletic development of their markings, and has found that these aberrations due to cold are more or less complete reversions to earlier phyletic stages. As regards the common small painted lady (*Vanessa cardui*), the small tortoise-shell butterfly (*Vanessa urticæ*), the 'Admiral' (*Vanessa atalanta*), the peacock (*Vanessa io*), and the large tortoise-shell (*Vanessa polychloros*), I can agree with this interpretation, and I do so the more readily because some years ago I suggested that the alternation of differently coloured generations of seasonally dimorphic Lepidoptera might be considered as a reversion. But this by no means excludes the possibility that other than atavistic aberrations may be produced by cold or heat. There is nothing against this theoretically. Yet we must not, without due consideration, compare these abruptly occurring variations to the sport-varieties of plants which we have already discussed; there is an important difference between the two sets of cases. In the Lepidoptera a single interference, lasting only for a short time, modifies the wing-marking, but in the plant varieties the visible appearance of the variation is preceded by a long period of preparatory change within the germ-plasm. This period required for the external influences to take effect was already recognized by Darwin, and it has recently been named by De Vries the 'premutation period.'

We may explain these remarkable aberrations theoretically in the following way: The determinants of the wing-scales in the wing-primordium of the young pupa are influenced by the cold in different ways, some kinds of determinants being strengthened by it, others markedly weakened, even crippled so to speak, and in this way one colour-area spreads itself out more than is normal on the surface of the wing, and another less, while a third is suppressed altogether. That this disturbance of the equilibrium between the determinants leads usually to the development of a phyletically older marking pattern leads us to the conclusion that in the germ-plasm of the modern species of *Vanessa* a certain number of determinants of the ancestors must be contained in addition to the modern ones. We might even inquire whether these were not better able to endure cold than their modern descendants, since their original possessors, the old species of the Ice age, were accustomed to greater cold, but this idea is contradicted by the experiments of E. Fischer, which go to show that the same aberrations are evoked by abnormally high temperature. That the old ancestral determinants are present in *different* numbers in the germ-plasm of the modern species, I am inclined to infer from the fact that among a large number of experiments made by me in the course of several years the aberrations have always occurred in very different numbers in the different broods, although the greatest care was taken to have the conditions as nearly alike as possible: absolutely alike, of course, they never can be.

But it would lead me too far if I were to enter on a detailed discussion of these cases, which have not yet been fully worked up: only one thing more need be mentioned, that is, that the aberrations induced by cold are to a certain extent transmissible. Standfuss first succeeded in making some aberrant specimens of *Vanessa urticæ* reproduce, and from their eggs he procured butterflies which showed a much slighter deviation from the normal, which however was still so decided that it could not be regarded as due to chance. I myself succeeded in doing the same, but the deviation in this case was much slighter. But that these observed cases are rightly referred to the cold to which their parents had been subjected is proved by other observations recently published by E. Fischer. These refer to one of the Bombycidæ (*Arctia caja*), which flies by day, and accordingly has a gay and very definite marking and coloration. A large number of pupæ were exposed to cold at 8° C., and some of these resulted in striking and very dark aberrant forms (Fig. 129, *A*). A pair of these yielded fertilized eggs; in the progeny, which were reared at a normal temperature, there were among the much more numerous normal forms a few (17) which exhibited the aberration of the parents, though to a considerably less degree (Fig. 129, *B*).

This shows that the cold had affected not only the wing-primordia of the parental pupæ, but the germ-plasm as well, and at the same time that this latter variation was less marked than that of the determinants of the wing-rudiments. This gives rise *to an appearance* of the transmission of acquired characters.

In the case of many of these cold-aberrations in Lepidoptera the cold gives rise to variations, but does so not by creating anything new, but by giving the predominance to primary constituents which have long been present, but are usually suppressed, and so it is also among the plants. I have in mind, for instance, the interesting experiments of Vöchting on the influence of light in the production of flowers in phanerogams. These showed that the common balsam (*Impatiens noli me tangere*) produces its familiar open flowers in a strong light, but in weak light only bears small, closed, so-called 'cleistogamous' flowers. But it would be utterly erroneous to suppose that the strong or weak light is the real cause, the *causa materialis*, of these two forms of flowers; the degree of illumination is merely the stimulus which provokes one or other of the primary constituents to development, both kinds being present in the constitution of the plant. As has long been known, the balsam normally possesses two kinds of flowers, and the slumbering primary constituents of these are so arranged that the open flowers develop where there is a prospect

FIG. 129. *A*, an aberration of *Arctia caja*, produced by low temperature. *B*, the most divergent member of its progeny. After E. Fischer.

of insect visits and cross-fertilization, that is, in sunny weather or in a strong light, while closed and inconspicuous flowers adapted for self-fertilization develop in weak light, that is, in shady places and in concealed parts of the plant, where insect visits are not to be expected.

Among plants we find thousands of instances of such reactions of the organism to external stimulus—reactions which are not of a primary nature, that is, are not the inevitable consequences of the plant's constitution, but which depend upon adaptations of the special constitution of a species or group of species to the specific conditions of its life. To this category belong all the phenomena of heliotropism, geotropism, and chemotropism, which have been discovered by the numerous and excellent observations of the plant physiologists. That all these are adaptations and secondary reactions to stimuli is proved by the fact that the same stimuli affect the homologous parts of different species in very different, and often in opposite ways. For instance, while the green shoots of most plants turn towards the light, being positively heliotropic, the climbing shoots of the ivy and the gourd are negatively heliotropic, which is an adaptation to climbing. In this case the reason of the difference in the mode of reaction must lie in the difference of constitution of the cellular substance of the shoot, and since this may differentiate so very diversely in its relation to light, the power of reaction which plant substance in general has to light must not be regarded as a primary character, like the specific gravity of a metal or the chemical affinities of oxygen and hydrogen, but as adaptations of the living and varying substance to the special conditions of life. And the origin of these adaptations must depend upon processes of selection, and on these alone. This is just the difference between living and non-living matter,—that the former is variable to a high degree, the latter is not; it is the fundamental difference upon which the whole possibility of the origin of an animate world depends.

Among animals also we must distinguish between the direct effects of external influence to which the organism is not already adapted, and those reactions which imply a previously established adjustment to the stimulus. That is, we must distinguish between primary and secondary reactions.

For instance, Herbst made artificial sea-water in which the sodium was partially replaced by lithium, and the eggs of sea-urchins developed in this artificial sea-water into very divergent larvæ of peculiar structure. We have here a primary reaction of the organism to changed conditions of life—not an adaptation, not a prepared reaction. Accordingly these 'lithium larvæ' eventually perished.

The increasing blackness of *Polyommatus phlœas*, which we have already discussed, must also be regarded as a primary reaction, but not so the variations—often misinterpreted—of those species of *Artemia* which live in the brine-pools of the Crimea, in regard to which Schmankewitsch showed that, when the amount of salt in the water is diminished, they undergo certain changes which bring them nearer to the fresh-water form *Branchipus*, while when the salt is increased in amount they vary in the contrary direction. Probably these are adaptations to the periodically changing salinity of their habitat.

There can be no doubt of this in the case of the caterpillars of different families, in regard to which Poulton showed that in their early youth they possess the power of adapting themselves exactly to the colour of their chance surroundings. It is obvious that the protection which the caterpillar would gain from being coloured *approximately* like its surroundings would be insufficient, for instance because the surroundings may be very diverse, since the species lives upon different, variously coloured plants and plant-parts. Thus a facultative adaptation arose. Selection gave rise to an extraordinarily specialized susceptibility on the part of the different cell elements of the skin to differences of light, and the result of this is that the skin of the caterpillar invariably takes on the colouring which is reflected upon it in the first few days of its life from the plants and plant-parts by which it is surrounded. Thus the caterpillars of one of the Geometridæ, *Amphidasis betularia*, take on the colours of the twig between and upon which they sit, and they can be made black, brown, white, or light green quite independently of their food, according to the colour of the twigs (or paper) among which they are reared.

Colour-change in fishes, Amphibians, Reptiles, and Cephalopods, depends upon much more complex adaptations. In their case a reflex-mechanism is present which conducts the light-stimulus affecting the eye to the brain, and there excites certain nerves of the skin: these in their turn cause the movable cells of the skin which condition the colouring to change and rearrange themselves in the manner necessary to bring about the harmonization of colour. On this depends the colour-change of the famous chamæleon, and also the scarcely less striking case of the tree-frog, which is light green when it sits on trees, but dark brown when it is kept in the dark. All these are secondary reactions of the organism in which the external stimulus is, so to speak, made use of to liberate adaptive variations, either permanently or transitorily. In the caterpillars colour-changes are permanent, that is, it is only the young caterpillar which takes on the colour of its surroundings; later it does not change, even when it is exposed to different light, or intentionally placed upon a food-plant of a different colour. In fishes, frogs, and cuttlefishes, on the contrary, the reaction of the colour-cells to light only lasts a little longer than the light-stimulus, and it changes with it. The purposiveness of this difference of reaction is obvious.

We cannot say to what degree the direct influence of external conditions is effectively operative on the germ-plasm, or how far, by persistently repeated slight changes, the determinants and the parts of the body determined by them may be made to vary in the course of generations; that is to say, how large a part this direct influence of climate and food may play in the transmutation of species. We can give no answer from experience, because there is an entire lack of perfectly satisfactory and clear experiments; we only know in a few cases how great the variations are which can be brought about in the body during the individual life by means of any of these factors. In most cases it is uncertain whether actually hereditary effects play any part, that is, whether the germ-plasm itself is affected. But if we wish to be theoretically clear as to how far direct climatic effects may go, we may say this, that they may operate as long as they cause no disturbance in the life of the species concerned, for at the moment that such a direct effect begins to be prejudicial to the species personal selection will step in, and, by preferring the individuals which react least strongly to the climatic stimulus, will inhibit the variation. If in any case this should be physically impossible, the species would die out in the climate in question. That a species of plant or animal has climatic limits indicates that individuals which go beyond these are exposed to influences which make life impossible and which natural selection is unable to neutralize. We are here brought face to face with one of the limits to the scope of natural selection. There is no doubt that the influences of the environment must always have a powerful effect upon the soma of the individual, but we have seen, in the case of Alpine plants and of galls, how very far this effect may go without leaving any trace in the germ-plasm.

LECTURE XXXII

INFLUENCE OF ISOLATION ON THE FORMATION OF SPECIES

Introduction—Isolated regions are rich in endemic species—Is isolation a condition in the origin of species?—Moriz Wagner, Romanes—'Amiktic' local forms, the butterflies of Sardinia, of the Alps, and of the Arctic zone—Periods of constancy and periods of variation in species—Amixia furthered by germinal selection—The thrushes of the Galapagos Islands—The intervention of sexual selection—Humming-birds—Central American thrushes—Weaver-birds of South Africa—Papilionidæ of the Malay Archipelago—Natural selection and isolation—Snails of the Sandwich Islands—Influences of variational periods—Comparison with the edible snail and with the snail fauna of Ireland and England—Changed conditions do not always give rise to variation—Summary.

In an earlier lecture I endeavoured to show, by means of Darwinian arguments and examples, how important for every species, in relation to its transmutation, is the companionship of the other species which live with it in the same area. We saw that the 'conditions of life' operated as a determining factor in the composition of an animal and plant association quite as momentously as any climatic conditions whatsoever, and, indeed, Darwin rated the influences of vital association even more highly, and attributed to them an even greater power of evoking adaptation than he granted to the physical conditions of life.

We are, therefore, prepared to recognize that even the transference of a species to a different fauna or flora may cause it to vary, and this occurs when the species gradually extends the area of its distribution, so that it penetrates into regions which contain a materially different association of forms of life. But these migrations are not necessarily only gradual, that is, due to the slow extension of the original area of distribution in the course of generations as the species increases in numbers; they may also occur suddenly, when isolated individuals or small companies of a species transcend in some unusual manner the natural boundaries of the old area, and reach some distant new region in which they are able to thrive.

Species-colonies of this kind may be due to the agency of man, who has spread many of his domesticated animals and plants widely over the earth, but who has also intentionally or unintentionally forced many wild animals and plants from their original area to distant parts of the earth, as, for instance, when the English humble-bees were imported into New Zealand with a view to securing the fertilization of the clover; but such colonies also occur in thousands of cases independently of man's agency, and the means by which they are brought about are very diverse. Little singing-birds are sometimes driven astray by storms, and carried far away across the sea, to find, if fortune favours them, a new home on some remote oceanic island; fresh-water snails, which have just emerged from the egg, creep on to the broad, webbed feet or among the plumage of a wild duck or some other migratory bird, and are carried by it far over land and sea, and finally deposited in a distant marsh or lake. This must happen not infrequently, as is evidenced by the wide distribution of our Central European fresh-water snails towards the north and south. But terrestrial snails can also, though more rarely, be borne in passive migration far beyond limits which are apparently impassable, as is evidenced by the presence of land-snails on remote oceanic islands.

The Sandwich Islands are more than 4,000 kilometres from the continent of America; they originated as volcanoes in the midst of the Pacific Ocean; and yet they possess a rich fauna of terrestrial snails, the beginnings of which can only have reached them by the chance importation of individual snails carried by strayed land-birds. Charles Darwin was the first who attempted to investigate the problem of the colonization of oceanic islands by animal inhabitants, and the chapter in *The Origin of Species* which deals with the geographical distribution of animals and plants still forms the basis of all the investigations directed towards this point. We learn from these that many land-animals, of which one would not expect it on *a priori* grounds, may be carried away by chance over the ocean, either, as in the case of butterflies and other flying insects, and of birds and bats, by being driven out of their course by the wind, or by being concealed—either as eggs or as fully-formed animals—in the clefts of driftwood, where they can resist for a considerable time the usually destructive influence of salt water. Thus eggs of some of the lowest Crustacea (Daphnidæ), which are contained in large numbers in the mud of fresh water, may be transported with some of the mud on the feet of birds, and this may happen also to encysted infusorians and other unicellulars, and to the much more highly organized Rotifers as well. In all these cases, and in many others, it may happen occasionally that single individuals, or a few at a time, may be carried far afield, and may reach regions from which their fellows of the same species are entirely excluded. If they thrive there they may establish colonies which will gradually spread all over the isolated area as far as it affords favourable conditions of life.

But oceanic islands are not the only cases of isolated regions: mountains and mountain-ranges which rise in the midst of a plain also form isolation-areas for mountain-dwelling plants or animals which have not much power of migrating. In the same way marine animals may be completely isolated from each other by land-barriers, as the inhabitants of the Red Sea, for instance, are from those of the Mediterranean, as has been clearly expounded by Darwin. The idea of an isolated region is always a relative one, and the region which seems absolutely insular for a terrestrial snail is not so at all for a strong-flying sea-bird. There is no such thing as *absolute* isolation of any existing colony, for otherwise the colony could never have reached the region; but the degree of isolation may be *absolute* as far as the time of our observation is concerned, if the transportation of the species concerned occurs so rarely that we cannot observe it in centuries, or perhaps in thousands of years, or if the extension of its range could only take place through climatic or geological changes, such as a subsidence of land-barriers between previously separated portions of the sea, or, in the case of land animals such as snails, the elevation of the sea-floor and the filling up of arms of the sea which had separated two land-areas. But even the transportation of a species by the accidental means already indicated will occur so rarely, if the isolated insular region is very distant, that the isolation of a colony by such a chance may be regarded as almost absolute as far as the members of the same species in the original habitat are concerned.

If we examine one of these insular regions with reference to the animal inhabitants which live upon it in isolation, we are confronted with the surprising fact that it harbours numerous so-called *endemic* species, that is to say, species which occur nowhere else upon the earth, and that these species are the more numerous the further the island is removed from the nearest area of related species. It looks at first sight quite as if isolation alone were a direct cause of the transformation of species.

The facts which seem to point in this direction are so numerous that I can only select a few of them. The Sandwich Islands, to which we have already referred, possess eighteen endemic land-birds, and no fewer than 400 endemic terrestrial snails, all belonging to the family group of Achatinellinæ, which occurs there alone.

The Galapagos Islands lie 1,000 kilometres distant from the coast of South America, and they too harbour twenty-one endemic species of land-birds, among them a duck, a buzzard, and about a dozen different but nearly related mocking-birds, each of which is found in only one or two of the fifteen islands. The group of islands also possesses peculiar reptiles, and they take their name from the gigantic land-tortoises, sometimes 400 kilogrammes in weight, which in Tertiary times inhabited also the continent of South America, but are now found in the Galapagos Islands only. The islands also possess endemic lizards of the genus *Tropidurus*, and although the lizards can no more have been transported across the ocean than the tortoises, but corroborate the conclusion drawn from geological data, that the islands were still connected with the mainland in Tertiary times, the occurrence of a particular species of *Tropidurus* upon almost every one of the fifteen islands testifies anew to the mysterious influence of isolation, for most of these islands are quite isolated regions for the different species of lizard, even more than for the mocking-birds, which have also split up into a series of species.

We are thus led to the hypothesis, which was first introduced into the Evolution Theory by Darwin, that the prevention of constant crossing of an isolated colony with the others of the same species from the original habitat favours the origin of new endemic species, and his conclusion is confirmed when we learn that islands like the Galapagos group possess twenty-one endemic land-birds, but only two endemic sea-birds out of eleven, for the latter traverse great stretches of sea, and crossings with others of the same species on the neighbouring continental coasts will often take place. The Bermuda Islands also afford a proof that the development of endemic species is prevented by regular crossing with other members of the species from the original habitat, for although they are 1,200 kilometres distant from the continent of North America—that is, further than the Galapagos Islands from South America—they possess no endemic species of bird, and we may undoubtedly associate this with the fact that the migratory birds from the continent visit the Bermudas every year.

Madeira also confirms our conclusion, for only one of the ninety-nine species of bird occurring there can be regarded as endemic, and it has often been observed that birds from the neighbouring African mainland (only 240 kilometres distant) are driven across to Madeira. Terrestrial snails, on the other hand, will seldom be carried to Madeira by birds, and accordingly we find there an extraordinary number of endemic terrestrial snails, namely, 109 species.

Although these and similar facts indicate strongly that isolation favours the evolution of new species, it would be erroneous to imagine that every isolation of a species-colony conditions its transmutation to a new species, or, as has been maintained, first by Moritz Wagner, and later by Gulick and by Dixon, that isolation is a necessary preliminary to the variation of species—that not selection but isolation alone renders the transmutation of a species possible, and thus admits of its segregation into several different groups of forms. Romanes went so far as to regard the natural selection of Darwin and Wallace as a sub-species of isolation, and isolation in its diverse forms he regarded as the sole factor in the formation of species. He assumed that it was only by the segregation of individuals which did not vary that the constant reversion to the ancestral species could be prevented, and he regarded the process of selection as essentially resulting in the 'isolation' of the fittest through the elimination of the less fit. The idea is correct in so far, that selection undoubtedly aids the favourable variation to conquest over the old forms, precisely because the latter, being less favourably placed in the struggle for existence, are gradually more completely overcome and weeded out, so that a constant mingling of the new forms with the old is prevented, just as it is by isolation of locality. Obviously the new and fitter forms could not become dominant, could not even become permanent, if they were always being mingled again with the old. But whether it serves any useful purpose to bring this under the category of 'isolation,' and to say that mingling with the ancestral form during transmutation is prevented by natural selection, in that favourably varying individuals *are isolated* by their superiority from the inferior ones, that is, the non-varying individuals which are doomed to elimination, is somewhat doubtful. For my part, I should prefer to retain the original meaning of the word, and to call 'isolation' the separation of a species-colony by spatial barriers.

Whether this factor by itself prevents the mingling with the ancestral form as effectually as selection does, and whether isolation alone and by itself can lead to the evolution of new forms, or perhaps *must* lead to them, must now be investigated.

I look at this question from exactly the same point of view as I did nearly thirty years ago, when in a short paper[1] I endeavoured to show that, under favourable circumstances, an individual variation of a species may become the origin of a local variety if it finds itself in an isolated region. Suppose an island had no diurnal butterflies, until one day a fertilized female of a species from the continent was driven thither, found suitable conditions of life, laid its eggs, and became the founder of a colony; the prevention of constant crossing

[1] *Ueber den Einfluss der Isolirung auf die Artbildung*, Leipzig. 1872.

between this colony and the ancestral continental species would not in itself be any reason why the colony should develop into a variety. But suppose that the foundress of the colony diverged in some unimportant detail of colouring, such as may at any time arise through germinal selection, from the ancestral species; then this variation would be transmitted to a portion of her progeny, and there would thus be a possibility that a variety should establish itself upon the island which would be the mean of the characters of the surviving progeny. The greater the divergence was in the first progeny of the mother-colonist, and the stronger this variational tendency was, the greater also would be the chance that it would be transmitted further and become a characteristic aberration from the marking of the original species. I then designated this effect of isolation as due to *amixia*, that is, to the mere prevention of crossing with the members of the same species in the original habitat.

We have examples of this from the Mediterranean islands, Sardinia and Corsica, which possess in common nine endemic varieties of butterflies, most of which diverge from the species of the continent in a quite inconsiderable degree, though quite definitely and constantly. Thus there flies in these islands a variety (*Vanessa ichnusa*) of our common little *Vanessa urticæ* in which the two black spots on the anterior wing exhibited by the original species are wanting. The large tortoise-shell (*Vanessa polychloros*) also occurs there, but it has not varied and still exhibits the black spots. Our little indigenous butterfly (*Pararga megæra*), which is abundant on warm, stony slopes, quarries, and roads, flies about in Sardinia, but as a variety (*tigelius*), which is distinguished from the original species by the absence of a black curved line on the posterior wings.

That of two nearly related and similarly marked species, like the large and small tortoise-shell, one should remain unvaried, while the other has become a variety, shows us that amixia alone does not necessarily lead to the evolution of varieties in every case. It might of course be objected that one species may have migrated to the islands at a much earlier period than the other, and that it might be a direct effect of the climate which found expression in this way. But we have other similar cases in which one of two species has varied in an isolated region, while the other has not, and in regard to which we can prove definitely that both were isolated at the same time.

An instance of this kind is to be found in Arctic and Alpine Lepidoptera, which inhabited the plains of Europe during the Glacial period, and subsequently, when the climate became milder again, migrated some to the north into countries within the Arctic zone, and some to the south to the Alps to escape in their heights from the increasing warmth. There are many diurnal Lepidoptera which now belong to both regions, and of these some have remained exactly alike, so that the Arctic form cannot be distinguished from the Alpine form: others show slight differences, so that we can distinguish an Arctic and an Alpine variety. To the former category belong, for instance, *Lycæna donzelii* and *Lycæna pheretes*, *Argynnis pales*, *Erebia manto*, and others; to the second category belong, for instance, *Lycæna orbitulus*, Prun., *Lycæna optilete*, *Argynnis thore*, and some species of the genus *Erebia*.

This cannot be an instance of the direct effect of general climatic influences, for in that case all the nearly related species of a genus would have varied or not varied; nor have we to do with adaptations, for the differences in marking are seen on the upper surfaces of the wing, which do not exhibit protective colouring, at least in these Lepidoptera. It can only have been the prevention of crossing that has fixed the existing variational tendencies in the isolated colonies—variations which would have been swamped and obliterated if there had been constant crossing with all the rest of the members of the species.

But there is another factor to be considered. Those Alpine Lepidoptera, for instance, which have not remained exactly the same in the far north, have formed local varieties in the rest of the area of their distribution also, while species which have remained quite alike in isolated regions, such as the Alps and the north, exhibit no aberrations in other isolated regions, such as the Pyrenees, in Labrador, or in the Altai. Thus one species must have had a tendency in the Glacial period to form local varieties, and the other had not; and I have already attempted to explain this on the hypothesis that the former at the time of their migration and segregation into different colonies were at a period of dominant variability, the latter at a period of relatively great constancy. Leaving aside the question of the causes of this phenomenon, we may take it as certain that there are very variable and very constant species, and it is obvious that colonies which are founded by a very variable species can hardly ever remain exactly identical with the ancestral species; and that several of them will turn out differently, even granting that the conditions of life be exactly the same, for no colony will contain all the variants of the species in the same proportion, but at most only a few of them, and the result of mingling these must ultimately result in the development of a somewhat different constant form in each colonial area.

If we were to try to imitate this 'amixia' artificially we should only require to take at random from the streets of a large town a number of pregnant bitches, and place each of them upon an island not previously inhabited by dogs, and then a different breed of dog would arise upon each of these islands, even if the conditions of life were exactly similar. But if, instead of these variable bitches, the females of a Russian wolf were placed on the islands, the developing wolf-colonies would differ as little from the ancestral species as the various Russian wolves do from one another—similar climate and similar conditions of life being presupposed.

There is thus an evolution of varieties due to amixia alone, and we shall not depreciate the significance of this if we consider that individual variations are the outcome of the fluctuations in the equilibrium of the determinant system of the germ-plasm, to which it is always more or less subject, and that variations of the germ-plasm, whether towards plus or minus, bear within themselves the tendency to go on increasing in the direction in which they have begun, and to become definite variational tendencies. In isolated regions such variational tendencies must continue undisturbed for a long period, because they run less risk of being suppressed by mingling with markedly divergent germ-plasms.

The probability that variational tendencies set up in some ids of the germ-plasm by germinal selection will persist and increase is obviously greater the more the germ-plasms combining in amphimixis resemble each other. For instance, let us call the varying determinants *Dv*, and assume as a favourable case that these are represented in three-fourths of all the ids in the fertilized eggs of a butterfly-female which has been driven astray on to an island, that is, that they are present in twelve out of sixteen ids; then of 100 offspring of the first generation it is possible that seventy-five or more will contain the determinants *Dv*, some of them in a smaller number of ids, some in a great number than the mother, according as the reducing division has turned out. If the pairing of the second generation be favourable —and this again is purely a matter of chance—a third generation must arise which would contain the variants *Dv* throughout, and thus the fixation of this particular variation on this particular island would be begun. In other words, the possibility would arise, that, if individuals with a majority of *Dv* ids predominated, they would gradually come to be the only ones, since by continual crossing with the minority which possessed only the determinants *D*, they would mingle the varied ids with those of the descendants of these last, till ultimately germ-plasm with only the old ids would no longer occur.

In following out this process it is not necessary to assume that the first immigrant possessed the variation *visibly*; if determinants varying in a particular direction occurred in the majority of its ids, these would, as a consequence of persistent germinal selection, go on varying gradually until the externally visible variation appeared. This would not have appeared at all if the animal concerned had remained in the original habitat of its species, for there it would have been surrounded by normal germ-plasms, and its direct descendants, even if they had been as favourably situated for the origin of variations as we have assumed, would not have reproduced only among themselves, and therefore even in the next generation the number of *Dv* ids would have diminished.

Obviously it is to a certain extent a matter of chance whether in the isolated descendants the variation or the normal form remains the victor, for it depends on the number of *Dv* ids originally present in the fertilized eggs, then on the chances of reducing divisions, and finally on the chance which brings together for pairing individuals in which the similarly varied ids preponderate. The probability of the conquest of the variation will depend in the main on the strength of the majority of the varied ids in the fertilized eggs of the parents; if this be an overwhelming majority, then the chances of favourable reducing divisions and pairings will also be great. The origin of a pure amixia variety will thus depend upon the fact that *the same* variational tendency *Dv* was present in a large number of the ids of the ancestral germ-plasm. We need not wonder therefore that of the numerous diurnal butterflies of Corsica and Sardinia only eight have developed into endemic, probably 'amiktic,' varieties.

But since we know that so many species in oceanic islands and other isolated regions are endemic or autochthonous, i.e. of local origin, there must obviously be some other factor in their evolution in addition to the mere prevention of crossing with unvaried individuals of the same species. The variational tendencies which have arisen in the germ-plasm through germinal selection may—as we have already seen—gain the ascendancy in various ways: first, by being favoured by the climatic influences, then by being taken under the protection of personal selection, whether in the form of natural or of sexual selection.

As the inhabitants of insular areas are not infrequently subject to special climatic conditions, we may assume at the outset that many of the 'endemic' species are climatic varieties, but in many cases this explanation is insufficient. For instance, special local forms of mocking-bird live on several of the Galapagos Islands, but this cannot depend upon differences of climate, for the islands are only a few kilometres apart, and resemble one another as regards the conditions of life which they present. But as the differences between these local forms show themselves especially in the male sex, as colour variations of certain parts of the plumage, we must take account of sexual selection, which, though with its basis in germinal selection, has in many islands followed a path of its own. Sexual selection operates especially in the case of sporadically occurring characters which are in any way conspicuous. But it is just such variations as these that are called into existence by germinal selection, whenever it is allowed to continue its course undisturbed through a long series of generations. Characters of this kind, such, for instance, as feathers of abnormal structure or colour in a bird, or new colour spots in a butterfly, make their appearance when a group of determinants has been able to go on varying in the same direction for a long time unimpeded, that is, without being eliminated as injurious by natural selection or obliterated by crossing. This is very likely to happen in the case of an isolated area, and as soon as the conspicuous character thus brought about makes its appearance, sexual selection takes control of it, and ensures that all the individuals, that is, all the germ-plasms which possess it, have the preference in reproduction.

I believe, therefore, that a large number of the endemic species of birds and butterflies in isolated regions result from amixia based upon germinal selection, whose results have been emphasized by sexual selection. Experience corroborates this, as far as I can see, for many of the endemic species of birds in the Galapagos and other islands differ from one another solely or mainly in their colouring, and in many it is especially the males which differ greatly.

As to the humming-birds we may say, without going into details regarding their sexual characters and their distribution, that the many endemic species which inhabit the Alpine regions of isolated South American volcanic mountains differ from one another chiefly in the males and in the secondary sexual characters of these. The family of humming-birds is characteristically Neotropical, that is, it has its centre in the Tropics of the New World, and by far the greater number of humming-bird species—there are about a hundred and fifty —occur there only, while a few occur as migrants north of the Tropical zone, and visit the United States as far north as Washington and New York. We know that many of the most beautiful species have quite a small area of distribution, that many are restricted to a single volcanic mountain, living in the forests which clothe its sides. These species are isolated there, for they do not migrate; apparently they cannot endure the climate of the plains, but remain always in their mountain forests. Without doubt they originated there, chiefly, I am inclined to think, through the variation of the males due to sexual selection. Any one who has seen Gould's magnificent collection of humming-birds in the British Museum in London knows what a surprising diversity of red, green, and blue metallic brilliance these birds display, what contrasts are to be found in the diverse colour-schemes, and what differences they exhibit in the length and form of the feathers of the head, of the neck, of the breast, and especially of the tail. There are wedge-shaped, evenly truncate and deeply forked tails, some with single long, barbless feathers, and so on. All these characters are confined to the males, and are at most only hinted at in the female; in no species does the female even remotely approach the male in brilliance or decorativeness of plumage.

I do not believe that so many species with very divergent plumage in the males could have developed if they had all lived together on a large connected area. But here, distributed over a large number of isolated mountain forests, the decorative colouring or the distinctive shape which chances to arise through germinal selection on any of these terrestrial islands can go on increasing, undisturbed by crossing with individuals of the ancestral species, and furthered, moreover, by sexual selection.

In this way, if I mistake not, numerous new species have arisen as a result of isolation, and it is quite intelligible that several new species may have arisen from one and the same ancestral species, as we may see from the nearly related yet constantly different species of mocking-bird on the different islands of the Galapagos group.

A number of similar examples might be given from among birds. Thus Dixon calls attention to the species of the thrush genus *Catharus*, twelve of which live in the mountain forests of Mexico and of South America as far as Bolivia, all differing only slightly from one another and all locally separated. They came from the plains, migrated to the highlands, were isolated there, and then no longer varied together all in the same direction, but each isolated group evolved in a different direction according to the occurrence of chance germinal variations: one developed a chestnut-brown head, another a slate-grey mantle, a third a brown-red mantle, and so on. From what we have already seen in regard to the importance of sexual selection in evolving the plumage of birds, it is probable that this factor has been operative in this case also.

Another example is afforded by the weaver-birds (*Ploceus*) of South Africa, those ingenious singing-birds resembling blackbirds in size and form, whose pouch-shaped nests, hanging freely from a branch, usually over the water, and with their little openings on the under side, are excellently protected from almost every form of persecution. These birds have in South Africa split up into twenty or more species, but the areas of each are not sharply isolated, and the division into species cannot, therefore, be due to isolation. But it is not difficult to guess upon what it depends, when we know that the males alone are of a beautiful yellow and black colour, while the females are of a greenish protective colouring all over.

Thus, in my opinion, sexual selection plays a part more or less important in the origin of the numerous endemic species of diurnal Lepidoptera which are characteristic especially of the islands of the Malay Archipelago, and which make the Lepidopteran fauna there so rich in individuality. A large number, indeed the majority of the types of Papilionidæ, have a peculiar species, a local form, on most of the larger islands, which is sharply and definitely distinguished from those of the other islands, usually in both sexes, but most markedly in the much more brilliantly coloured males.

Thus each of these types forms a group of species, each of which is restricted to a particular locality, and has usually originated where we now find it, although of course the diffusion of one of these large strong-flying insects from one island to the other is in no way excluded. As an example we may take the *Priamus* group, the blackish yellow *Helena* group, the blue *Ulysses* group, and the predominantly green *Peranthus* group.

If we inquire into the causes of this divergence of forms and their condensation into numerous species, we shall find that their roots lie in this case, as in that of all transformations, in germinal selection and the variational tendencies resulting therefrom, but we must *regard their fixation as the result of isolation*, which prevented the variational tendencies which happened to develop on any one island from being neutralized and swamped by mingling with the variations of other islands. But that sexual selection took control of these striking colour-variations and increased them still further is obvious from the rarely absent dimorphism of the sexes. Even if the females do not consciously select mates from among the males, they will more readily accept as a mate the one among several suitors which excites them most strongly. And that will be the one which exhibits the most brilliant colours or exhales the most agreeable perfume, for we know from their behaviour in regard to flowers how sensitive butterflies are to both these influences.

Although isolation has an important rôle in the formation of all these species, it seems to me an exaggeration to maintain, as many naturalists do, that the splitting up of a species is impossible without isolation. Certainly the splitting up of species is, in numerous cases, facilitated by isolation, and indeed could only have been brought about in its present precision by that means, but it is underestimating the power of natural selection not to credit it with being able to adapt a species on one and the same area to *different* conditions of life, and we shall return to this point later on in a different connexion. But in the meantime it must suffice to point out that the polymorphism of the social insects affords a proof that a species may break up into several forms in the same area through the operation of natural selection alone.

I am therefore of opinion, with Darwin and Wallace, that adaptation to new conditions of life has, along with isolation, had a material share in the evolution of the large number of endemic species of snail on the oceanic islands. This brings us to the co-operation of natural selection and isolation. If, thousands of years ago, by one of the rarest chances, an *Achatina*-like snail was carried by birds to the Sandwich Islands, it would spread slowly, at first unvaried, from the spot where it arrived over the whole of the snailless island. But during this process of diffusion it would frequently come in contact with conditions of life which would not prevent it from penetrating further, but to which it was imperfectly adapted, and in such places a process of transformation would begin, which would consist in the fostering of favourably varying individuals, and which would run its course quietly by means of personal selection, based upon the never-ceasing germinal selection, and unhindered by any occasional intrusion of still unvaried members of the species from the original settlement on the island. But these new conditions were not merely different from those of the ancestral country; the island region itself presented very diverse conditions, to which the snail immigrant had to adapt itself in the course of time, as far as its constitution allowed. Terrestrial snails are almost all limited to quite definite localities with quite definite combinations of conditions; none of our indigenous species occurs everywhere, but one species frequents the woods, another the fields; one lives on the mountains, another in the valleys; one on gneiss soil, another on limy soil, a third on rich humus, a fourth on poor river-sand; one in clefts and hollows among damp moss, and another in hot, dry banks of loess, and so on. Although we cannot see in the least from the structure of the animal why this or that spot should be the only suitable one for this or that species, we may say with certainty that each species remains permanently in a particular place because its body is most exactly adapted to the conditions of life there, and therefore it remains victorious in the competition with other species in that particular spot.

In this way the immigrants to the Sandwich Islands must have adapted themselves in the course of time to their increasingly specialized habitats, and in doing so have divided up into increasingly numerous forms, varieties, and species, and indeed into several genera.

But this alone is not sufficient to explain the facts. According to Gulick's valuable researches there live on one little island of the Sandwich group no fewer than 200 species of Achatinellidæ, with 600–700 varieties! This remarkable splitting up of an immigrant species is regarded by him as a result of the isolation of each individual species and variety, and I do not doubt that this is correct as far as a portion of these forms is concerned, and that isolation plays a certain part in regard to them all. Gulick, who lived a long time upon the island, attempts to prove that the habitats of all these nearly related varieties and species are really isolated as far as terrestrial snails are concerned; that intermingling of the snails of one valley with those of a neighbouring one is excluded, and that the varieties of the species diverge more markedly from one another in proportion as their habitats are distant. On the other hand, species of different genera of Achatinellidæ often live together on the same area; but they do not intermingle.

Although Gulick's statements are worthy of all confidence, and though his conclusions have great value as contributions to the theory of evolution, I do not think that he has exhausted the problem of the causes of this remarkable wealth of forms among the terrestrial snails of oceanic islands. It is not that I doubt the relative and temporary isolation of the snail-colonies at numerous localities in the island of Oahu. But why have we not the same phenomenon in Germany, in England or Ireland? Gulick anticipates this objection by pointing out the peculiar habits of the Oahu snails. Many of the species there are purely arboreal animals, living upon trees and never leaving them, even during the breeding season, or in order to deposit eggs, for they bring forth their young alive. Active migration from forest to forest seems excluded by the fact that on the crests of the mountains there is a less dense forest of different kinds of trees, and dry sunny air, which could not be endured by the species of *Achatinella* and *Bulimella*, which love the moist shades of the tropical forests. Active migration over the open grass-land at the mouths of the valleys is also excluded.

It must be admitted that the isolation of these forest snails in their valleys is for the time being very complete, and that intermingling of two colonies which live in neighbouring valleys *does not occur by active migration, within the span of one or several human generations.* It will also be admitted that our terrestrial snails in Central Europe are much less isolated in their different areas, that, for instance, they could get from one side of a mountain to the other by active migration; but we must nevertheless repeat the question: how does it happen that in Oahu every forest, every mountain-crest, and so on, has its own variety or species, while our snails are distributed over wide stretches of country, frequently without even developing sharply defined local varieties? The large vineyard or edible snail (*Helix pomatia*) occurs from England to Turkey, that is, over a distance of about 3,000 kilometres, and within this region it is found in many places which might quite as well be considered isolated as adjacent forest valleys in Oahu. It occurs also on the islands of the Channel and of the Irish Sea, and lives there without intermingling with the members of the species on the mainland. But even on the Continent itself it would be possible to name hundreds of places in which they are just as well protected from intermingling with those of other areas as they are in Oahu. There too the snails must *somehow* have reached their present habitat some time or other, perhaps rather in an indirect way, by means of other animals; but this is true also of the snails of a continent, as we shall show more precisely later on. In the meantime let us assume that this is so, and that the vineyard snail (*Helix pomatia*), or some other widely distributed snail, is relatively isolated. *Why then have not hundreds of well-marked varieties evolved—a special one for each of the isolated areas?*

Obviously there must have been something in operation in the Sandwich Islands which is absent from the continental habitats of *Helix pomatia*, for this species shows fluctuations only in size, but is otherwise the same everywhere, and the few local varieties of it which occur are unimportant. I am inclined to believe that this 'something' depends on two factors, and especially on the fact that the immigrant snail enters upon a period of variability. This will be brought about in the first place by the fact that the climate and other changes in the conditions of life will call forth a gradually cumulative disturbance in the equilibrium of the determinant system, and thus a variability in various directions and in various combinations of characters. To this must be added the operation of natural selection, which attempts to adapt the immigrant to many new spheres of life, and thus increases in diverse ways the variational tendencies afforded by germinal selection. These two co-operating factors bring the species into a state of flux or lability, just as a species becomes more variable under domestication, likewise as a direct effect of change of food and other conditions, such as the consciously or unconsciously exercised processes of selection. It follows from this that, in the gradual diffusion of snails all over the island, similar localities would almost never be colonized by exactly similar immigrants, but by individuals containing a different combination of the existing variations, so that in the course of time different *constant forms* would be evolved through amixia in relatively isolated localities.

But everything would be different in the diffusion of a new species of snail in a region which was already fully or at least abundantly occupied by snail-species. Let us leave out of account altogether the first factor in variation, the changed climate, and we see that a species in such circumstances would have no cause for variation, because it would find no area unoccupied outside of the sphere to which it was best adapted; it would therefore not be impelled to adapt itself to any other, and in most cases could not do so, because in each it would have to compete with another species superior to it because already adapted.

The case would be the same if an island were suddenly peopled with the whole snail-fauna of a neighbouring continent, with which a land connexion had arisen. If the island had previously been free from snails, all the species of the mainland would be able to exist there in so far as they were able to find suitable conditions of life, but each species would speedily take complete possession of the area peculiarly suited to it, so that none of their fellow migrants would be impelled, or would even find it possible, to adapt themselves to new conditions and thus to become variable and split up into varieties. If Ireland were at present free from snails, and if a land connexion between it and England came about, then the snail-fauna of England would probably migrate quite unvaried to Ireland, and in point of fact the snail-fauna of the two islands, which were formerly connected, is almost the same. For the same reason the fauna of England, as far as terrestrial snails are concerned, is almost the same as that of Germany.

On the other hand, it may be almost regarded as a law that an individual migrant to virgin territory must become variable. This could not be better illustrated than by the geographical distribution of terrestrial snails, which emphasizes the fact that a striking wealth of endemic species is to be found on all oceanic islands. Moreover, the fact that the number of these endemic species is greater in proportion to the distance of the island from the continent, indicates that the variability sets in more intensively and lasts longer in proportion to the small number of species which become immigrants in the island,

and in proportion to the number of unoccupied areas which are open to the descendants of the immigrant species. This is undoubtedly the reason why the Sandwich Islands do not possess *a single species* which occurs elsewhere, and the segregation of the unknown ancestral form into many species and several (four) sub-genera is also to be interpreted in the same way. There was probably in this case only one immigrant species, which found a free field, and adapted itself in its descendants to all the conditions of snail-life which obtained there, and in doing so split up into numerous and somewhat markedly divergent forms. But the number of different forms is much greater than the number of distinctive habitats, as Gulick indicates and substantiates in detail, for similar areas, if they are relatively isolated from one another, are inhabited not by the same forms, but by different though nearly related varieties, and this depends on the fact that from the species which was in process of varying a different combination of variations would be sent out at different periods, and the temporary isolation would result in the evolution of special local varieties.

But I do not believe that this would continue for all time. I rather think that these—let us say—representative varieties would diminish in numbers in the course of a long period. For the isolation of single valley-slopes or of particular woods is not permanent, individuals are liable to be carried from one to another in the course of centuries as they were at the beginning of the colonization of the isolated woods; forests are cleared or displaced by geological changes, connexions are formed between places which were formerly separated, and in the course of another geological period the number of representative varieties, and probably even of species, will have diminished considerably,—the former will have been fused together, the latter in part eliminated. Even now Gulick speaks regretfully of the decimation of rare local forms by their chief enemies, the mice.

But even if the number of endemic forms in insular regions diminishes from the time when they were first fully taken possession of, it nevertheless remains a very high one, for even now Madeira possesses 104 endemic terrestrial snails, the Philippines have more than the whole of India, and the Antilles as many as the whole American continent.

Many naturalists believe that each isolated variety must diverge further and further from its nearest relatives as time goes on. Although I entirely admit that this is possible, for I have endeavoured to show that variational tendencies which have once arisen in the germ-plasm go on in the same direction until they are brought to a full stop in some way or other, yet I cannot admit that this must always be so. The species which has been carried to a strange area need not always contain particular variational tendencies in its germ-plasm, and need not in every case be impelled to such variations by the influence of new conditions. We know species which have made their way into new regions, and, without varying at all, have held their own with, or even proved superior to, the species which were already settled there. Many cases of this kind are known, both among plants and animals; these have been brought by man, intentionally or by chance, from one continent to another, and have established themselves and spread over the new area. I need only recall the evening primrose (*Œnothera biennis*[1]), whose fatherland is Virginia, but whose beautiful big yellow blossoms now display themselves beside nearly every river in Germany, having migrated stream-upwards along the gravelly soil; or the troublesome weed (*Erigeron canadense*), which is now scarcely less common in our gardens than in those of Canada; or the sparrow (*Passer domesticus*), which was introduced into the United States to destroy the caterpillars, but which preferred instead to plunder the rich stores of corn, and in consequence of these favourable conditions increased to such an extent that it has now become a veritable pest, all imaginable means for its extirpation having been tried—as yet, however, with no great results.

In all these cases the migration is certainly of recent date, and it is quite possible that, when a longer time has elapsed, some variations will take place in the new home, but in any case these instances prove that an immigrant species can spread over its new area without immediately varying.

Similarly, it must be admitted that species which have belonged to two continents ever since Tertiary times need not have diverged since that time, and we know, for instance, thirty-two species of nocturnal Lepidoptera which are common to North America and to Europe and yet exhibit no differences, while twenty-seven other nocturnal Lepidoptera are, according to Grote, represented in America by 'vicarious' species, that is, by species which have varied slightly in one or other of the two areas, perhaps in both.

To sum up: we must undoubtedly admit that isolation has a considerable influence in the evolution of species, though only in association with selection in its various grades and modes, especially

[1] This was written before the appearance of the researches which De Vries has made on the variations of *Œnothera* in Europe. Thus the illustration may not be quite apposite, for it seems to remain undetermined whether the 'mutations' which occur in Holland do not also occasionally appear in America. See end of lecture xxxiii.

germinal selection, natural selection, and sexual selection. We can say generally that each grade and mode of selection will more readily lead to the transformation if it be combined with isolation. Thus germinal selection may call forth slight divergences in colour and marking, which will be permanent if the individuals concerned are in an isolated region. In isolation these variations will increase undisturbed, and in some circumstances will be intensified by sexual selection, so that the male sex will vary alone in the first place, though the female may follow, so that ultimately the whole species will be transformed. Finally, the most marked effect of isolation is seen when individual members of a species are transferred to virgin territory which offers unoccupied areas, suitable not to one particular species alone, but to many nearly related species, so that the immigrant colony can adapt itself to all the different possibilities of life, and develop into a whole circle of species. But we saw that such an aftergrowth of new forms, whether varieties, species, or even genera, may far exceed the number of different kinds of localities, if there be relative isolation between the different groups of immigrants within the insular region, as happens in the case of slow-moving animals like the terrestrial snails, or of small singing-birds, to which each island of a little archipelago is a relatively isolated region (Galapagos).

We may thus fully recognize the importance of local isolation without regarding the absence of crossing with the members of the species in the original habitat as the sole cause of species-formation, without setting 'isolation' in the place of the processes of selection. These last, taken in the wide sense, always remain the indispensable basis of all transformations, but they certainly do not operate only in the form of personal selection, but, wherever indifferent characters are concerned, in that of germinal selection. Here, too, we see the possibility of reconciliation with those naturalists who regard transformations as primarily dependent upon internal forces of development. The fact is that *all variations depend upon internal causes*, and their course must be guided by forces which work in an orderly way. But the actual co-operation of all these forces and variations is not predetermined, but depends to a certain extent upon chance, for of the possible modes of evolution the one which gains the upper hand in the play of forces at the moment is alone followed, the better are everywhere preferred, from the most minute vital units of the germ-plasm, up to the struggle between individuals and between species.

LECTURE XXXIII

ORIGIN OF THE SPECIFIC TYPE

Transition species of Celebes snails, according to Sarasin—Possible variations in the shell due to nutrition—Natural selection plays a part—Germinal selection—Temporary transitions between species—The fresh-water snails of Steinheim—How do sharply-defined species arise?—Nägeli's Developmental Force—The species a complex of adaptations—Adaptive differences between species—Adaptive nature of specific characters—The case of Cetaceans—Of birds—Additional note: the observations and theories of De Vries.

Our study of the influence which geographical isolation may have in transforming old and giving rise to new forms of life has led us naturally to a much more important problem, that of the origin of species as more or less sharply defined groups of forms, and I wish to make the transition to this problem by discussing another case of species-splitting effected in association with, or, as is usually said, *through* isolation. The naturalists Paul and Fritz Sarasin, well known through their excellent studies on many components of the tropical fauna, have published in their latest work interesting discoveries in regard to the terrestrial snails of Celebes. These observations show that on this island a great transformation of snails has taken place, even since the later Tertiary period. A large number of new species of snail have arisen on this island since that time, and this, as the authors show to be probable, in association with the receding of the sea, that is, with the elevation of the island further out of the water, and thus with the increase of its surface. The modern terrestrial snails show chains of forms connected in many ways so that a series of species is connected by transition forms, and therefore does not really consist of separate species at all, although the extremes would seem to be separate species if they were studied by themselves without taking the transition forms into account. The state of things is exactly as if a Tertiary snail had spread from any small area over the whole island, and had been transformed slowly and in a definite direction in accordance with its distance from its starting-point. It is thus that we must interpret this discovery; we have here, beside each other in space, and indeed often disposed along geographical lines, the individual stages of a phyletic process of transformation, which has reached different levels at different places. One of the longest of these chains of forms is that of *Nanina cincta*, which runs across the island from east to west, and, beginning with the smallest and most delicate forms, ascends through many intermediate stages to the giant form *N. limbifera*. Such chains of forms have been previously recognized; thus Kobelt described one in the case of the Sicilian land-snails of the genus *Iberus*, and other cases are recorded in literature, but in all instances they refer to areas which must be regarded as isolated for the snails, and which have been colonized from a single starting-point.

We have now to inquire whether and how we can explain the origin of these chains of forms. The cousins Sarasin tell us how they at first attempted to refer the differences between the individual links of such a chain to the diverse influence of the external conditions of life, but in vain; neither the height above sea-level nor the character of the soil was sufficient, and natural selection was no more so; 'for why should a high *Obba*-form twisted like a beehive be either better or worse equipped for the struggle for existence than a smaller and flatter one?' It is true that we do not understand why, but this does not seem to me any reason to doubt that natural selection should be regarded as one of the causes of the divergence of these species, for we could not answer the same question in regard to any of the other structural differences between two species of snail, for the simple reason that we have far too little knowledge of the biological value of the parts of a snail. Or could any one tell of what use it would be to a snail-species to have the horns slightly longer, the foot somewhat narrower, the radula beset with rather larger or more numerous teeth? We might indeed imagine many ways in which it might be of advantage, but we are not in a position to say definitely why, for instance, longer horns should be better for one species than for another, and yet we do not believe that the structure of snails is less well adapted to the life of each species than that of any other animals. The snail's structure is certainly built up of hundreds and thousands of adaptations, like that of every other animal species, but while in many others we can, at least in part, recognize the adaptations as such, we cannot do so at all in regard to the snail. Simroth has pointed out that the spiral asymmetrical shell bears a relation to the one-sided opening of the genital organs, but that only states the general reason for the coiling of the shell. In studying the differences in the shell one is apt to think of its external appearance alone, of the protection which it affords to the soft internal organs of the easily wounded animal; perhaps also of the distribution of weight, which must be different in a high tower-like structure and a low flat spiral; possibly, too, of the varied obstacles and resistance the snail has to encounter in creeping into clefts and holes, or among a tangle of plants, according to the form of its shell; but is it not also conceivable that the form of the shell has been determined by its contents? As Rudolph Leuckart taught, the snail may be regarded as composed of two parts, one of which is formed by the head and foot, the other by the so-called 'visceral sac': the former may be called the animal half, because it chiefly contains the dominant organs—the nerve-centres, almost the whole mass of muscle, and the sense-organs; the latter the vegetative half, since it contains the main mass of the nutritive and reproductive systems—the stomach and intestine, the large liver, the heart, the kidneys, the reproductive organs, and so on. The vegetative half of the animal is always concealed within the shell; would not therefore any great variation in the size of liver, stomach, intestine, and so on, bring with it a variation in the size and form of the shell, as well as in the expansion or contraction of its coils? And might not such variations become necessary because of some change in the food-supply? It is only a supposition, but it seems to me very probable that becoming accustomed to a new diet, less easily broken up and dissolved and of diminished nutritive value, would cause modification not only of the radula and jaw-plate, but also of the stomach and the liver, the intestine and the kidneys, whose activity is closely associated. The stomach must become more voluminous, the liver which yields the digestive fluid must become more massive, and so forth. I will not follow this hypothethical example further, for I merely wished to recall the fact that the snail shell, to the form of which no biological significance can be commonly attributed, is actually a sort of external cast of the visceral sac, and consequently dependent on the variations to which that is liable in accordance with the conditions of its life. To give precise proofs for such processes is certainly not yet possible, for we do not even know with certainty what the diet of the various species of snail is, much less the difference between the modes of nutrition in two varieties, or the nutritive value of the materials used, or the changes in secretion, absorption, assimilation, and excretion which must be brought about by these differences. But we can at least see that variations in nutrition must be enough in themselves to give rise to new adaptations in the size, constitution, and mutual adaptation of the internal vegetative organs, and we cannot overlook the possibility that the form and size of the vegetative half, and therefore the form and size of its secretion, the shell, may also be caused to vary[1]. The fact that we cannot recognize, for instance, the beehive shape of an *Obba* as an adaptation, is thus no proof that it is not one. But let us assume for the moment that it is not, and that it cannot be referred to natural selection any more than the other variations in the Celebes chain of forms, and we may further admit that they cannot be referred to sexual selection, still less to some 'inherent principle of perfecting,' not only because there is no question of perfecting in the matter, but because such a mystical principle is outside of the scope of natural history and its principles of interpretation.

But that transformations in a definite direction can and must arise from fresh disturbances in the equilibrium of the determinant system, that is from germinal selection, we have already shown.

Even if the changes of form with which we are here dealing had really no biological importance, they might quite well have been brought about by germinal selection, and only one thing remains obscure, that is, why the different stages on the path of distribution of a species are at a different level of evolution and not all at the same level. Why have not all been transformed? Why have some colonies remained near the ancestral form, while others have varied only a little, and others again a great deal? This cannot be explained by any assumption of an internal power of development, and the explanation can only be found in germinal selection associated with isolation, since the internal processes in the germ-plasm can quite well run a different course in different colonies. Nevertheless I am inclined to infer from these differences in the individual colonies of these chains of forms, that natural selection in the accepted sense has also played a part in the evolution of these snail varieties.

Such series of forms are especially interesting, because they show us the process of species-formation in its different stages beside each other in space, and thus simultaneously. They represent, so to speak, a horizontal branch of the genealogical tree of the species, as the Sarasins well express it, that is, a series of species arising from

[1] That this suggestion was not unjustified is evident from a recent contribution by Simroth ('Ueber die Raublungenschnecken,' *Naturwissenschaftliche Wochenschrift*, December 8 and 15, 1901). In this paper the author, who is an expert as regards the biology of Gastropods, shows that a change of diet may evoke many kinds of changes in the structure of the food-canal, which may indirectly compel changes in the shell. Thus in a small indigenous snail, *Daudebardia*, the pharynx has grown so enormously in thickness and length in adaptation to the predatory mode of life, that the head and the anterior part of the body can no longer be retracted within the shelter of the shell. For this reason, and also because of the snail's habit of following earthworms into their burrows, the shell has been shunted far back and obliquely downwards. It has at the same time markedly changed in its shape, as may still be verified by comparing the form of the shell in the young stages with that of the adult.

each other, which do not break off, but are all capable of life at the same time, and so exist simultaneously on different areas; they are species adapted to different localities, not to different times. The same is true of the snails of other isolated regions, except that the chains of forms are usually not simple, but split up into several chains of forms arising from one ancestral form, and under certain circumstances each of these may break up into two or more diverging series. The great number of related species in Madeira, or in the Sandwich Islands, compels us to this assumption, although the branching of the genealogical trees can no longer be demonstrated with certainty.

This splitting up of forms into several series on a varied insular region shows us once more that it is germinal selection alone which forms the basis of all transformations, and that there is not, as earlier naturalists, especially the botanists Nägeli and Askenasy, maintained, any peculiar impelling Force of Development innate in organisms. If there were such a force, a species would be obliged to go on continuously in the same direction, exactly like the Sarasins' chains of forms, but no breaking of the species into one or many forms could occur. But this breaking up into series is easy to understand when we take germinal selection into consideration, for the germ-plasm contains many ids and determinants, and each of these can enter upon new variations, so that one colony can vary in this direction, another in that, and a great diversity of forms living in isolation must, or at least may be the result, as we see in the case of the Sandwich Islands.

Let us delay a moment over the Sarasins' case of the Celebes snails. We are dealing here with series of forms in regard to which the ordinary conception of species fails us, for they contain varieties whose extremes are as far apart as distinct species usually are, which are not, however, distinct, since they are connected with one another by one and often by several transition forms. Thus we can only break them up into two or more 'species' by an arbitrary division at one place or other. The phenomenon itself is not new to us; we have seen that even Lamarck and Treviranus made use of similar series of forms, connected by transition stages, in their attack upon the old theory of creation, and sought to prove by means of these that the idea of species is an artificial one, read into nature by man, and not innate in nature, and that the forms of life were only apparently fixed and sharply defined, being in reality in process of slow transformation. Such beautiful and convincing examples as we now possess were not available at that time, but it might even then be said that it was the easier to make a new species the fewer examples one had to deal with, and the more difficult the more numerous these became, because with the number of individuals, especially if they come from a wide area, the number and diversity of the divergences increases also, so that in many cases, as in that of the Celebes snails, it becomes impossible to draw a line between the different species.

There are, however, many animal and plant forms which do not show such marked divergences, but rather exhibit a great harmony of individuals even in detail, and the conception of species is more readily applied to these. It would certainly be foolish to give it up, since we should then lose all possibility of arriving at any sort of orientation among the enormous wealth of forms in nature. But at the same time we must not forget that these 'typical' species only appear so to our short-sighted vision—short-sighted as far as time is concerned—and that they are connected from long-past times with 'species' which lived at an earlier date, by just such transition stages as connect the Celebes species of to-day, which are all living at the same time. The world of life on the earth only presents at any given time a 'cross-section of its genealogical tree,' and according as its branches grow out vertically or horizontally we receive an impression of typical, sharply defined species or of circles or chains of forms. In the first case the evolution of new species was associated with the dying out of the horizontal branches, and the end-twigs of the branch stand beside each other now apparently isolated and sharply defined; in the other case only a portion of the ancestral species has been transmuted, and the other part continues to live alongside of the species derived from it, and perhaps repeats the process of giving off a varied race of descendants.

The last thirty years have yielded much palæontological evidence of the successive stages of species-transformation. In quietly deposited horizontal strata of the earth's crust, lying one above another, the whole phyletic history of a group of snail-species has repeatedly been found in historic order, the oldest in the deepest layer, the youngest in the uppermost, and the numerous and often very divergent 'species' of a particular deposit are connected by transition forms in the intermediate strata. From the point of view of time, therefore, these are not 'typical' species, but circles of forms in a state of variability.

The most beautiful of such cases are the *Planorbis* species from the small lacustrine deposits of Steinheim in Swabia, the *Paludina* strata of Slavonia, and various groups of Ammonites.

These cases have been described and discussed so often that I need only refer to their most essential features.

The *Planorbis* strata of Steinheim were first investigated, from the point of view of the theory of descent, by Hilgendorf (1866). He described nineteen different varieties, which, as they are all connected in chronological succession with each other, he grouped together under the name of *Planorbis multiformis*. These little freshwater snails are found in millions in the strata of the former lake-basin of Steinheim, and they are arranged in so orderly and regular a manner that two observers, working independently and at different times, succeeded in building up the genealogical tree in almost the same way. According to Alpheus Hyatt, the later investigator, all the forms are derived from one ancestral form, *Planorbis lævis*, from which four different series have descended, one of them splitting up again into three subordinate series.

All the individual members of these series are connected by intermediate forms in such a manner that a long period of constancy of forms seems to be succeeded by a shorter period of transformation, from which again a relatively constant form arises.

We see, therefore, that the idea of species is fully justified in a certain sense; we find indeed at certain times a breaking up of the fixed specific type, the species becomes variable, but soon the medley of forms clears up again and a new constant form arises—*a new species*, which remains the same for a long series of generations, until ultimately it too begins to waver, and is transformed once more. But if we were to place side by side the cross-sections of this genealogical tree at different levels, we should only see several well-defined species between which no intermediate forms could be recognized; these would only be found in the intermediate strata.

The problem we have now to discuss is, how it comes about that relatively sharply defined species exist which are connected with ancestral forms further back, but which form among themselves an exclusive, more or less homogeneous, host of individuals. How does it happen that we everywhere find a specific type, and not an endless number of individual forms connected with one another in all directions?

This would require no further explanation if a phyletic evolutionary force impelled the forms of life to vary in a definite manner, and thus to become transmuted into new forms in the course of generations. In that case the whole genealogical tree of the organisms on the earth must have been potentially contained in the lowest moneron, so that, given time and the most indispensable general conditions of existence, the living world just as we know it must have resulted. Nägeli was the first to express this view, and he followed it out consistently, not even hesitating to deny the existence of all processes of selection, and to represent the whole of evolution as a process conditioned by this phyletic force, which would have given rise to the world of organisms which has actually arisen, even if the conditions of life at the different periods of the earth's history had been other than they were. I have always combated this idea, without however overlooking that it is based upon facts which—at that time at any rate—gave it a certain justification. We cannot pass it by without giving some other interpretation of the facts. Following Nägeli, the botanist Askenasy championed this view of 'variation in a different direction,' which gives rise to new forms; and in more recent times Romanes, Henslow, and Eimer expressed similar views, and—although they did not actually dispute the existence of processes of selection—they attributed a much less important rôle to them, and referred the phyletic genealogical tree of organisms in the main to other and internal causes.

Like Nägeli himself, his followers have laid stress upon the fact that natural selection cannot be the cause of the evolution and succession of particular species, because the differences which separate species from species are not of an adaptive nature, and therefore cannot depend upon selection; but if the step from one species to the next succeeding one does not depend upon adaptation, then the greater steps to genera, families, and orders cannot be referred to it either, since these can only be thought of as depending upon a long-continued splitting up of species. Genera, families, and all higher groups must be recognized as conventional categories, not as real divisions existing in nature itself. Even Treviranus and Lamarck maintained that the differences between genera depended just as much upon our estimate, our intellectual convenience, as do the differences between species. All forms were originally connected, though they may not be so now, and if the species are really not distinguished by adaptive characters, then neither are any other grades of our classificatory system, neither order nor classes, since they all depend originally on the transmutation of species. It was therefore quite consistent of Nägeli to seek the mainspring of organic evolution, not in adaptation, but in an unknown evolutionary force. Thus he refused to recognize adaptation as a consequence of selection, but regarded it, as Lamarck had done, as the direct effect of external conditions, and as an entirely subordinate factor in the transmutation of forms.

Nägeli and his modern successors conceive of phyletic evolution as depending upon definitely directed variation, resulting from internal causes and occurring at definite times, which of necessity causes the existing form to be transformed into a new one. To them the species appears, so to speak, as a vital crystallization, or to use Herbert Spencer's phraseology, as an equilibrium of living matter, which becomes displaced from time to time, and passes over into a new state of equilibrium, being transmuted into a new species, something like the pictures in a kaleidoscope. The species is thus something conditioned from within, which must be as it is and could not be otherwise, just like a crystal which crystallizes in one particular system and not in another; it must be just thus or it could not be at all. From the point of view of this theory it would be easy to understand that the thousands or millions of individuals composing a species all agree in essentials—that a specific type exists.

But this conception can hardly be entirely correct, although there is some truth at its foundation, namely, that germinal variations which arise independently are the basal roots of all transmutation. But the species is not simply the result of these internal processes, it is not even mainly so; it is not the result of an internal, definitely directed developmental force, even if we attempt to think out such a force in a purely scientific or mechanical, instead of a mystical, sense. It seems clear to me that the species is not a life-crystal in the sense that it must, like a rock-crystal, take form in a particular way and in no other for purely internal reasons and by virtue of its physical constitution; the species is essentially a complex of adaptations, of modern adaptations which have been recently acquired, and of inherited adaptations handed down from long ago—a complex which might quite well have been other than it is, and indeed must have been different if it had originated under the influence of other conditions of life.

But of course species are not exclusively complicated systems of adaptations, for they are at the same time 'variation-complexes,' the individual components of which are not all adaptive, since they do not all reach the limits of the useful or the injurious. All transformations arise from a basis of spontaneous chance variations, just as all forest plants grow from the soil of the forest, but do not all grow into trees, the adaptive forms which determine the essential character of the forest; for many species remain small and low, like the mosses, grasses, and herbs; and these too have a share, though a subordinate one, in determining the character of the forest, which depends definitely, though only partially, on the loftier growths.

According to my view all adaptation depends on an alteration in the equilibrium of the determinant system, such as must arise from intragerminal or even general fluctuations in the nutritive supply, affecting larger or smaller groups of determinants and causing variation in them to a greater or less degree. And these variations may be in a quite definite direction, persisted in for internal reasons, as we have already seen in the section dealing with germinal selection. These variations are the building-stones out of which, under the guidance of personal selection, a new specific type, that is, a new complex of adaptations, can be established. In this type many indifferent characters are involved, which are just as constant characters of the species as the adaptations.

The opponents of the selection theory have often urged against it this constancy of indifferent characters, but as soon as we cease to restrict the principle of selection to 'persons,' and extend it also to the lower categories of vital units, the occurrence of indifferent characters is easily understood. To illustrate characters of this kind, Henslow has recently called attention to the species of gentian, whose flowers have a corona split into five tips in some species and into six or seven in others, and we cannot possibly ascribe any biological significance to these specific characters. It is quite possible that they possess none; but did not even Darwin express his belief that many peculiarities of form 'are to be attributed to the laws of growth, and to the mutual influence of parts,' forces which he rightly refrained from including under 'natural selection' in his sense of the word, but which we now regard as an expression of intra-selection or of histonal selection? It is this, in our opinion, which brings about the coadaptation of the parts to form a harmonious whole, which admits of the primary adaptations to the conditions of life being followed or accompanied by correlative secondary variations, and which plays an important part in directing the course of every individual development, and is therefore uninterruptedly active within the organism. We cannot analyse the factors precisely enough to be able to demonstrate in an individual case why the corona should be divided into four in one species of gentian and into five in another, but we can understand in principle that all adaptations of a species which are not primary are determined by the compelling influence of intra-selection. And we need not now rest content even with that, for we know that this intra-selection—as we have already seen—is active within the germ-plasm, and it is only a logical consequence of the principle of germinal selection to suppose that variations of definite determinants due to personal selection may in the germ-plasm itself give rise to correlative variations in determinants next to them or related to them in any way, and that these may possess the same stability as the primary variation. This seems to me a sufficient reason why biologically unimportant characters may become constant characters of the species. Correlation is not effected only in the perfect organism; it exists at every period of its life, from the germ till death, and what it brings about is quite as inevitable as what is evoked through adaptation by means of personal selection.

We can thus also understand that indifferent characters may be contained not only in individual ids of the germ-plasm, but also coincidentally in a great majority of them, as soon as we think of them as dependent upon the characters established through personal selection, for these must be contained in a majority of the ids.

But there is still another reason why indifferent characters should become stable, and that is the effect of general variational influences on all the individuals of a species, as, for instance, in many climatic varieties, and probably also in many cultivated varieties.

But even when we have fully recognized that, from the arcana of the germ-plasm, new minimal variations are continually cropping up, which are biologically indifferent, and nevertheless become variational tendencies, and may increase even to the extent of causing *visible* differences, and that therefore varieties of snails or of butterflies, or of any animal or plant whatever, may originate through germinal selection alone, it cannot for a moment be supposed that the transmutation of species depends upon this process exclusively or even preponderantly. This was Nägeli's mistake, and that of his followers as well, that he ascribed to his 'principle of perfecting' the essential rôle in directing the whole movement of evolution, while the general structure of all species shows us that they are, so to speak, built up of adaptations. But adaptations could not be—or could only be fortuitously and exceptionally—the *direct* result of an internal power of development, since the very essence of adaptational changes is that they are variations which bring the organism into harmony with the conditions of its life. We are therefore forced either to underestimate greatly the part played by adaptation in every organism—and that is what Nägeli did—or to leave the standpoint of natural science altogether, and assume a transcendental force which varied and adapted the species of organisms *pari passu* with the changes in the conditions of life during the geological evolution of our earth. This would be a sort of pre-established harmony, through which the two clocks of evolution—that of the earth and that of organisms—kept exact time, although they had quite different and independent works!

But that the determining significance of adaptations in organic forms is underestimated even now is evidenced by the continually repeated statement that species differ, not in their adaptive characters, but in purely morphological characters, whereas it is obvious that we are far from being able to estimate the functions of a part with sufficient precision to be able to say definitely whether the differences between two nearly allied species are or are not adaptations to different conditions. The same is true with regard to the other side of the problem—the conditions of life. These are often to all appearances identical in two allied species, but even where they are visibly different it is often difficult to assert that the differences between the two species can be interpreted with certainty as adaptations to the specific conditions of life. At an earlier stage we discussed the protective coloration of butterflies, and we saw that the forest butterflies of the Tropics frequently mimicked a dry leaf on their under surfaces. In the various regions of the extensive forest districts of the Orinoco and the Amazon in South America there are fifty species of the genus *Anaea* alone, and in the resting pose all these bear a most deceptive resemblance to a leaf, yet each of them differs from the rest in the mingling of its colours, its brilliance, and usually in markings when these are present. If we wished to be able to decide whether these specific differences were of an adaptive nature or not, we should first of all require to know in what kind of forest two neighbouring species lived, and in what places, among what sort of leaves, they were in the habit of settling. Even then we should at best only know whether the species *A* was better protected, as far as our own eyes were concerned, among the leaves of the forest *A′* than the species *B*, and conversely; but we could not tell whether they *required* this protection, or whether the species *A*, if transferred to the forest *B′*, would be more frequently discovered and destroyed by its enemies than in its own forest-home, and that alone could prove the difference to be biologically important, that is, to have selection-value. The difficulty, indeed the impossibility, of arriving at such decisions can perhaps be better illustrated by an example from our indigenous fauna. No one doubts that the upper surface of the anterior wing in the so-called banner-moth (*Catocala*) possesses a very effective protective colouring; by day the moths rest with wings spread out flat upon tree trunks, wooden fences, walls, &c., and they are so excellently suited to their environment that they are usually overlooked both by man and animals. But each of the twelve German species of *Catocala* has a special protective colouring; in *Catocala fraxini* it is a light grey, in *Catocala nupta*, a dark ash-grey, in *Catocala elocata* rather a yellowish-brown grey, in *Catocala sponsa* an olive brown, in *Catocala promissa* a mingling of whitish-grey and olive brown, and so on. All these colourings are protective; but could any even of our most experienced and sharp-sighted entomologists prove that each of these different shades of colour depends upon adaptation to the usual resting-place of the particular species to which it belongs? And yet it is on *a priori* grounds highly probable that this is the case. But even this would by no means dispose of the whole problem, for each of these protective colour schemes is composed of several, often many, tints; it must be so if they are to fulfil their end at all, for a uniformly coloured wing would contrast with the bark of every tree and with every wooden fence. The wing-surface must therefore bear on a lighter background a number of lines and streaks varying from brown to black, and usually running zigzag across the wing; beside these are spots of lighter colour, which complete the deceptive picture. This 'marking' of the wing is similar in all twelve species, and yet in each it is different in detail. It is constant in each, and thus is a specific character. But who would venture to undertake the task of proving that each of these streaks, spots, zigzag lines, &c., is or is not adaptive—that the details are necessary adaptations to the resting-place which had become habitual to the species, or, on the other hand, simply expressions of the variational tendencies of the elements of marking, depending upon germinal selection? This would be an impossible task, and yet we are here dealing with a character which, *as a whole*, is undoubtedly adaptive; in many of the differences between other species even that is not certain.

It seems to me, therefore, hardly reasonable to talk of the 'insufficiency of natural selection' because we are not able to demonstrate that the minutiæ of specific characters are adaptational results. Personal selection intervenes whenever the variations produced by germinal selection attain to selection-value; and whether we can determine the exact point at which this takes place in individual cases is, as I have said before, theoretically quite indifferent.

Moreover, there are cases in which we *can* prove that specific differences are of an adaptive nature. When, of two nearly related species of frog, the spermatozoon of one possesses a thick head and that of the other a thin head, and when at the same time the micropyle through which alone the spermatozoon can make its way into the ovum is wide in the first species and narrow in the second, we have before us a specific character which is obviously adaptive.

In order to gain clearness as to the significance of natural selection in the restricted sense, that is of personal selection, it seems to me much more important to study the different groups of animals and plants with special reference to what they undoubtedly exhibit in the way of adaptation. For that reason I discussed different groups of adaptations in detail in some of the preceding lectures, although, or rather because, they all teach us that every part of every species, whether animal or plant, even every secretion, and indeed every habit, every inherited instinct, is subject to adaptation to the conditions of life. It seems difficult to refuse to admit that this is the natural impression which this study conveys, and it is strengthened as our knowledge increases; *that every essential part of a species is not merely regulated by natural selection, but is originally produced by it,* if not in the species under consideration at the time, then in some ancestral species: and, further, that every part can adjust itself in a high degree to the need for adaptation. It was not without a purpose that I discussed the phenomenon of mimicry so fully, for it, above all others, teaches us how great a power of adaptation the organism possesses, and what insignificant and small parts may be transformed, in a remarkable degree, in accordance with some actual need. We saw that a butterfly might assume a colouring which diverged entirely from that of its nearest relatives, but which caused it to resemble an immune species of a different family, and thereby protected it more effectively from persecution. Such a case can no more be due to a dominating phyletic force than to a chance and sudden displacement of the state of equilibrium of the determinant system; it can depend only on natural selection, that is, on a sifting out of the diverse variations offered by germinal selection, and the unhampered expression and augmentation of those favoured.

But it is not only these minute variations, insignificant in relation to the whole structure of the animal, which can be determined by natural selection. The same applies to the phyletic evolution as a whole; even that is not directed by the assumed internal principle of development.

Adaptations, from their very nature, can only depend upon selection, and not upon an internal principle of evolution, since that could take no account whatever of external circumstances, but would cause variations in the organism altogether independently of these. Thus, in considering the origin of any of the larger groups of animals, we may exclude a phyletic power as the guide of its evolution as soon as we can prove that all its essential structural relations, as far as they diverge from those of nearly related groups, are adaptations. We may not be able to do this for nearly all of the animal groups, and it will hardly be possible in regard to a single group of plants, because our insight into the *biological* significance of characters, which means more than the functional significance of the individual parts, and their correlation as parts of a whole, is seldom sufficiently intimate or thorough. But among animals we can do this in regard to some groups; one of these is the order of whales or Cetaceans.

Cetaceans, as is well known, belong to the Mammalia, that is to say, to a class whose structure was built for life on the land. The ancestors of Cetaceans were similar to the other mammals, and possessed a coat of hair and four legs, and a body the mass of which was so distributed that it could be borne by those four legs. But all the modern Cetaceans live in the sea, and they have therefore entirely changed their bodily form; they have become spindle-shaped like fishes, well adapted for cleaving the water, but incapable of moving upon land. At the same time, their hind-legs have completely disappeared, and can now be demonstrated only as rudiments within the mass of muscle (Fig. 130, *Br*, *Tr*, *Fr*), while the fore-legs have been transformed into flippers, in which, however, the whole inherited, but greatly shortened, skeleton of the mammalian arm is concealed (*OA*, *UA*, *H*). The skin has lost its covering of hair so completely that in some cases no traces of it are demonstrable except in the embryo. All these changes are adaptations to an aquatic life, and could not have been produced independently of the influence of external conditions. But there is much more than this. A thick layer of blubber under the skin gives this warm-blooded animal an effective protection against being cooled down by the surrounding water, and at the same time gives it the appropriate specific gravity for life in the sea; an enormous tail-fin similar to that of fishes, but placed horizontally, forms the chief organ of locomotion, and for this reason the hind-legs became superfluous and degenerated. Similarly, the muscles of

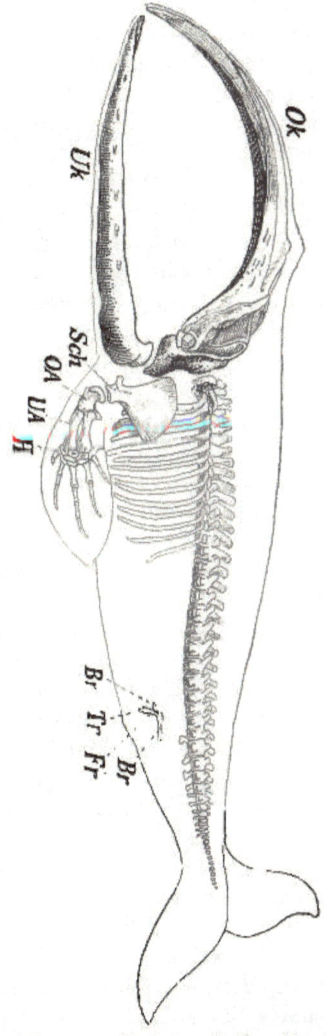

Fig. 130. Skeleton of a Greenland Whale with the contour of the body. *Ok*, upper jaw. *Uk*, lower jaw. *Sch*, shoulder-blade. *OA*, upper arm. *UA*, bones of fore-arm. *H*, hand. *Br*, vestige of the pelvis. *Fr*, vestige of the femur. *Tr*, vestige of the lower part of the leg. After Claus.

the ear have also disappeared, for the hearing organ of this aquatic type is no longer suited for receiving the sound-waves through an air-containing trumpet, but receives them by a shorter route from the surrounding water, directly through the bones of the skull. Remarkable changes in the respiratory and circulatory organs make prolonged submersion possible, and the displacement of the external nares from the snout to the forehead enables the animal to draw breath when it comes up from the depths to a frequently stormy surface. It would take a long time to enumerate all that can be recognized as adaptive in these remarkable aquatic mammals to a life in what to their ancestors would have been a strange and hostile element. Let us study particularly the case of the whalebone whales, for instance the Greenland whale, and we are at once struck by the enormous size of the head, which makes up about a third of the whole body (Fig. 130). Can this, which has such an important effect in determining the whole type of animal, be an outcome of some internal power of development? By no means! It is rather an adaptation to the mode of nutrition peculiar to this swimming mammal, for it does not, like dolphins and toothed whales, feed on large fishes and Cephalopods, but on minute delicate molluscs—Pteropods and pelagic Gastropods, on Salpæ, and the like, which often cover the surface of the Arctic Ocean in endless shoals, sometimes extending for many miles. To enable the whale to sustain life on such minute morsels it was necessary that it should be able to swallow enormous quantities; teeth were therefore useless, and they have become rudimentary, and can only be demonstrated in the embryo as rudiments (dental germs) in the jaw; but in place of these there hang from the roof of the mouth-cavity great plates of 'whalebone,' a quite peculiar product of the mucous membrane of the mouth, the ends of which are frayed into fibres, and form a sieve-net for catching the little animals which are engulfed with the sea-water. The mouth-cavity itself has become enormous, so that great quantities of water at a time can be strained through the net of whalebone-plates.

When I mention that peculiar changes have occurred also in the internal organs, that the lungs have elongated longitudinally and thus enable the animal more readily to lie in the water in a horizontal position, that peculiar arrangements exist within the nostrils and the larynx which enable the animal to breathe and swallow simultaneously, and that the diaphragm lies almost horizontally because of the length of the lung, I think I have said enough to indicate that not only does almost everything about the whale diverge from the usual mammalian type, but that all these deviations are adaptations to an aquatic life. If everything that is characteristic, that is, typical either of the order or of the family to which animals belong, depends upon adaptation, what room is left for the activity of an internal power of evolution? How much is left of the whale when the adaptations are subtracted? Nothing more than the general scheme of a mammal; but this was implicit in their ancestors before the whales originated at all. But if what makes whales what they are, that is, the whole 'scheme' of a whale, has originated through adaptation, then the hypothetical evolutionary power—wherever its seat may be—has had no share in the origin of this group of animals.

I said all this more than ten years ago, but the idea of an internal directive evolutionary force is firmly rooted in many minds, and new modifications of the idea are always cropping up, and of these the most dangerous seem to me to be those which are not clear in themselves, but suppose that the use of a shibboleth like 'organic growth' means anything. That organic growth is at the base of the phyletic evolution of organisms may be maintained from any scientific standpoint whatsoever, from ours as well as from Nägeli's, for no one is so extreme and one-sided as to regard the process of evolution as due *solely* to internal or *solely* to external factors. The process may thus always be compared to the growth of a plant, which likewise depends on both internal and external influences. But that is saying very little; we have still to show how much and how little is effected by these internal and external factors, what their nature precisely is, and what relation they bear to one another. There is thus a great difference between believing, with Nägeli, that 'the animal and plant kingdoms must have become very much what they actually are, even had there been on the earth no adaptation to new conditions and no competition in the struggle for existence,' and sharply emphasizing, in accordance with the facts just discussed, that, in any case, a whole order of mammals—the Cetaceans—could never have arisen at all if there had been no adaptation.

The same thing could be proved in regard to the class of Birds, for in them too we are able to recognize so many adaptive features, that we may say everything about them that makes them birds depends upon adaptation to aerial life, from the articulations of the backbone to the structure of the skull and the existence of a bill; from the transformation of the fore-limbs into wings, and of the hind-limbs to very original organs of locomotion on land or swimming organs in water, to the structure of the bones, the position, size, and number of the internal organs, down even to the microscopic structure of numerous tissues and parts. What could be more characteristic of a class of animals than feathers are of birds? They alone are enough to distinguish the class from all other living classes; an animal with feathers can now be nothing but a bird, and yet the feather is a skin-structure which has arisen through adaptation, a reptilian scale which has been so transformed that an organ of flight could develop from its anterior extremity. We find it thus even in the two impressions of the primitive bird *Archaeopteryx*, which have been preserved for us in the Solenhofen slate since the Jurassic period in the history of the earth. And into what detail does adaptation go in the case of the feathers! Is not the whole structure, with its quill, shaft, and vane, precisely adapted to its function, although that is purely passive? What I have just said of the whole class of Birds holds true for this individual structure, the feather; everything about it is adaptation, and indeed illustrates adaptation in two directions, for in the first place the feathers, by spreading a broad, light, and yet resistant surface with which to beat the air, act as organs of flight, while they are also the most effective warmth-retaining covering conceivable. In both these directions their achievements border on the marvellous. I need only recall the most recent discovery in this domain, the proof recently given by the Viennese physiologist, Sigmund Exner, that the feathers become positively electric in their superficial layer, and negatively electric in their deeper layer, whenever they rub against one another and strike the air. But they are rubbed whenever the bird flies or moves, and the consequence of the contrast in the electric charging of the two layers is that the covering feathers are closely apposed over the down-feathers, while, on the other hand, the similar charging of the down-feathers makes them mutually repel each other, with the result that a layer of air is retained between them, and thus there is between the skin and the covering feathers a loose thicket of feathers uniformly penetrated by air—the most effective warmth-preserver imaginable. The electric characters of the feathers—and the same is true of the hairs of animals—are thus not indifferent characters, but with an appreciable biological importance, and the same is true of the almost microscopical series of little hooklets which attach the barbs of the covering feathers to one another, and thus form a relatively firm but exceedingly light wing-surface which offers a strong resistance to the air. But as we must regard these hooklets as adaptations, so must we also regard the electrical characters of the feathers, and we must think of them as having arisen through natural selection, as Exner himself has insisted.

If we are able to recognize all the more prominent features

of the organization in Cetaceans and Birds as due to adaptation, we must conclude that, in the rest of the great groups of the animal kingdom, the main and essential parts of the structure are adaptations to the conditions of life, even although the relations between external circumstances and internal organization are not so readily recognizable. For if there were an internal evolutionary force at all, we should be able to recognize its operation in the origin of the races of Cetaceans and Birds; but if there be no such power, then even in cases where the conditions of life are not so conspicuously divergent as in Cetaceans and Birds, we must refer the typical structure of the group to adaptation. Thus everything about organisms depends upon adaptation, not only the main features of the organization, but the little details in as far as they possess selection-value: it is only what lies below this level that is determined by internal factors alone, by germinal selection; but this is not an imperative force in the sense in which the term is used by Nägeli and his successors, for it is capable of being guided; it does not necessarily lead to an invariable and predetermined goal, but it can be directed according to circumstances into many different paths. But it is precisely this that constitutes the main problem of the evolution theory—how development due to internal causes can, at the same time, bring about adaptation to external circumstances.

This lecture had been transcribed so far, and was ready for the press, when I received the first volume of a new work by De Vries, in which that distinguished botanist develops new views in regard to the transformation of species, based upon numerous experiments, carried on for many years on the variation of plants. As not only his views, but the interesting facts he sets forth, seem to contradict the conclusions as to the transmutation of organisms which I have been endeavouring to establish, I cannot refrain from saying something on the subject.

De Vries does not believe that the transformation of species can depend on the cumulative summation of minute 'individual' variations; he distinguishes between 'variations' and 'mutations,' and attributes only to the latter the power of changing the character of a species. He regards the former as mere fluctuating deviations which may be increased by artificial selection, and may even, with difficulty, if carefully and purely bred for a long period, be made use of to give character to a new breed, but which play no part at all in the natural course of phylogeny. As regards phylogeny, he maintains that only 'mutations' have any influence, that is, the larger or smaller saltatory variations which crop up suddenly and which have from the very first a tendency to be purely transmitted, that is, to breed true.

The facts upon which these views are mainly based are observations on and breeding experiments with a species of evening primrose (*Œnothera*) which was found in quantities on a fallow potato-field at Hilversum in Holland. It had been cultivated previously in a neighbouring garden, and had sown itself thence in the field. The numerous specimens of this *Œnothera lamarckiana* growing there were in a state of marked 'fluctuating' variability, but in addition there grew among them two strongly divergent forms which must have arisen from the others, and which led De Vries to bring the parent stock under cultivation, in the hope that it would yield new forms, in the Botanical Gardens at Amsterdam. This hope was fulfilled; in the second cultivated generation there were, among the 15,000 plants, ten which represented two divergent forms, and in the succeeding generations these forms were repeated several times and in many cases, and five other new forms cropped up, most of them in several specimens and in different generations of the original stock. All these new forms, which De Vries calls 'elementary species,' breed true, that is to say, when they are fertilized with their own pollen they yield seed which gives rise to the same 'elementary species.' The differences between the new forms are usually manifold, and of the same kind as those between the 'elementary' species of the wild Linnæan species. But, according to De Vries, what we have been accustomed since the time of Linné to call a 'species' is a collective category, whose components are these 'elementary' species which De Vries has observed in his experiments with *Œnothera*. In other species, such as *Viola tricolor* and *Draba verna*, true-breeding varieties have long been known to botanists, and these have been studied carefully and tested experimentally, especially by A. Jordan, and more recently by De Bary.

All 'species,' according to the Linnæan conception, consist, De Vries maintains, of a larger or smaller number (in *Draba* there are two hundred) of these 'elementary' species, and these arise, as is proved by the case of *Œnothera*, by saltatory or discontinuous 'variations' which occur periodically and suddenly break up a species into many new species, because the variations of the germ-plasm, which are for a time merely latent, suddenly find expression in the descendants of one individual or another. According to this view, species must be the outcome of purely internal causes of development, which reveal themselves as 'mutations,' that is as saltatory variations, which are stable and transmissible from the very first, and among which the struggle for existence decides which shall survive and which shall be eliminated. For the mutations themselves occur in no particular direction; they are sometimes advantageous, sometimes indifferent, sometimes even injurious (for instance, when one sex is left out), and so it is always only a fraction of the mutations, often only a few, which prove themselves capable of permanent existence. Thus 'species do not arise through the struggle for existence, but they are eliminated by it' (p. 150); natural selection does nothing more than weed out what is unfit for existence, it does not exercise any selective, in the sense of directive, influence on the survivors. A difference in the nature of variations was previously maintained by the American palæontologist Scott, though for different reasons and also with a different meaning. He believed that variations in a definite direction were necessary to explain the direct course of development which many animal groups, such as the horses and the ruminants, have actually followed, and which he thought could not be ascribed to cumulative adaptation to the conditions of life. The 'mutations' of De Vries are not distinguished from the 'fluctuating' variations by following a definite direction, but in that they are strictly heritable, that they 'breed true.' It is true that 'fluctuating' individual differences are also transmissible, and can be increased by artificial selection, but they lack one thing that would make them component parts of a natural species, namely, constancy; they do not breed true, and are therefore never independent of selection, but require to be continually selected out afresh in order that they may be kept pure. They form 'breeds,' not species, and if left to themselves they soon revert to the characters of the parent species, as is well known of the numerous 'ennobled races' among our cereals. De Vries therefore denies absolutely that a new species could be developed by natural selection from 'fluctuating' variations, and not alone because there is no constancy of character, but also because the capacity of the character for being increased is very limited. Usually nothing more can be achieved than doubling of the original character, and then progress becomes more difficult and finally ceases altogether.

These are incisive conclusions, based upon an imposing array of weighty facts. I readily admit that I have rarely read a scientific book with as much interest as De Vries's *Mutationstheorie*. Nevertheless I believe that one might be carried away too far by De Vries, for he obviously overestimates the value of his facts, interesting and important as these undoubtedly are, and under the influence of what is new he overlooks what lies before him—the other aspect of the transmutation of species, to which the attention of most observers since Darwin and Wallace has been almost exclusively devoted—I mean the origin of adaptations. Not that he does not mention these, he assumes in regard to his mutations 'a selection working in a constant direction,' and seeks to interpret them in terms of it, but as the mutations occur from purely internal reasons—I mean without any connexion with the necessity for a new adaptation—and occur only in a small percentage of individuals, and in no definite direction, they cannot possibly suffice to explain *adaptation*, which seems to dominate the whole organic world. But this is precisely the point at which many botanists cease to understand the zoologists, because among plants there are fewer adaptations than among animals; or, in any case, adaptations in plants are not so readily demonstrated as among animals, which not infrequently seem to us to be entirely built up of adaptations.

In this book, and in this chapter itself, I have discussed adaptations and their origin so much already that I need only refer to these pages for convincing evidence that we cannot think of them as being brought about by the accumulation and augmentation of individually occurring saltatory 'mutations.' Not even if we assume that the leaps of mutation can be increased in the course of generations; in short, even if we say that mutations are all those variations which breed true and lead to the development of species, while variations are those which do not. This would only be playing with words, so let us say that the fluctuating variations are really different in their nature, that is, in their causes, from mutations. De Vries lays great stress on the fact that these two kinds of variations must be sharply distinguished from one another, and this may have been useful or necessary for the first investigation of the facts before him, for we must first analyse and then recombine, but that variations and mutations are in reality different in nature can assuredly not be assumed, since innumerable adaptations can only have arisen through the augmentation of individual variations. These must therefore be able to become 'pure breeding,' even although they may not have done so in the cases of artificial selection which have hitherto been observed. How is it possible that chance mutations, in no particular direction, occurring only rarely and in a small percentage of individuals, can explain the origin of the leaf-marking of a *Kallima* or an *Anœa*—the shifting of the original wing-nervures to form leaf-veins, and the exact correlation of these veins across the surfaces of both pairs of wings? And even if we were to admit that a mutation might have occurred which caused the veins of the anterior and posterior wings to meet exactly by chance, that would still not be a leaf-adaptation, for there would still be wanting the instinct which compels the butterfly, when it settles down, to hold the wings in such a position that the two pictures on the anterior and posterior wings fit into each other. Correlated mutations of the nervous system suited to this end are required, but that is too much to attribute to happy chance! The same holds true in regard to the whole leaf-picture on the two wings, for it could not possibly have arisen as a whole by a sudden mutation. The whole litany of objections which have been urged throughout several decades against the Darwin-Wallace theory of natural selection, which were based on the improbability that chance variations not in a definite direction should yield suitable material for the necessary adaptations, may be urged much more strongly against mutations, which make their appearance in much smaller numbers and with less diversity.

But it is—as we have already seen—in regard to the necessity which exists almost everywhere for the co-adaptation of numerous variations of the most different parts, that the 'mutation theory' breaks down utterly. The kaleidoscopic picture, the mutation, is implicit from the first, and must be accepted or rejected just as it is in the struggle for existence; but harmonious adaptation requires a gradual, simultaneous, or successive purposive variation of all the parts concerned, and this can be secured only through the fluctuating variations which are always occurring, and are increased by germinal selection and guided by personal selection.

Many naturalists, and especially many botanists, regard adaptation as something secondary, something given to species by the way, to improve the conditions of their existence, but not affecting their nature—comparable perhaps to the clothing worn by man to protect himself from cold; but that is hardly the real state of the matter.

The deep-sea expedition conducted by Chun in 1898 and 1899 made many interesting discoveries in regard to animals living in the depths of the ocean, all of which exhibit peculiar adaptations to the special conditions of their life, and especially to the darkness of the great depths. One of the most striking of these discoveries was that of the luminous organs which are found not in all but in a great many animals living on the bottom of the abyssal area, and also among the animals occurring at various levels above the floor of the abyss. These are sometimes glands which secrete a luminous substance, but sometimes complex organs, 'lanterns' which are controlled by the will of the animal, and suddenly evolve a beam of light and project it in a particular direction, like an electric searchlight. These organs have a most complex structure, composed of nerves and lenses, which focus the light, and on the whole are not unlike eyes. That this sort of structure should have arisen all at once through a 'mutation' is inconceivable; it can have originated only from simple beginnings by a gradual increase of its structure along with continual strict selection among the variations which cropped up. They all depend upon complicated 'harmonious' adaptation, and cannot possibly have been derived from mutations, that is, from ready-made structural 'constellations,' unless we are to call in the aid of the miraculous. But lanterns of this kind are found in many different kinds of animals—in Schizopod Crustaceans, in shrimps, in fishes of different genera and families. Many fishes have long rows of luminous organs on the sides and on the belly, and these probably serve to light up the sea-floor and facilitate the finding of food; in others the luminous organs are placed upon the snout just above the wide voracious mouth, and in that position they have undoubtedly the significance attributed to them by Chun, namely, that they attract small animals, just as the electric lamps allure all sorts of nocturnal animals, and especially insects, in large numbers to their destruction. But not fishes only, but molluscs, e. g. the Cephalopods of the great depths, have developed luminous organs, and one species of Cephalopod has about twenty large luminous organs, like gleaming jewels, ultramarine, ruby-red, sky-blue and silvery, while in another the whole surface of the belly is dotted over with little pearl-like luminous organs. Even if we cannot be quite clear as to the special use of these lanterns of deep-sea animals, there can be no doubt that they are adaptations to the darkness of the great depths, and when we find the *same* adaptations (in a physiological sense) in many animals belonging to the most diverse groups, there is no possibility of referring them to sudden mutations which have arisen all at once in these groups with no relation to utility, and yet have not occurred in any animals living in the light. Only 'variations' progressing and combining in the direction of utility can give us the key to an explanation of the origin of such structures.

The same is true of the eyes of deep-sea animals. It was believed at one time that all the inhabitants of dark regions had lost their eyes. This is the case with many cave animals and the inhabitants of the lightless depths of our lakes, but in the abyssal zone of the sea it is only some fishes and Crustaceans whose eyes have degenerated to the vanishing point. Moreover, the disappearance apparently occurs in species which are restricted to the ocean-floor in their search for food, which therefore can make more use of their tactile organs than of their eyes, for while the ocean-floor undoubtedly contains over wide areas an abundance of food for these mud-eaters, it is only partly illuminated, that is, only in places where there are luminous animals such as polyp-colonies, &c. The fact that so many of the animals of the great depths are luminous obviously conditions, not that most of the immigrants into the abyssal zone should lose their eyes as useless, but that they should adapt them to the light which is very weak in comparison with that of the superficial layers. The eyes of deep-sea fishes, for instance, are either enormously large, and therefore suited for perceiving the faint light of the depths, or they have varied in another and very characteristic manner: they have become elongated into a cylinder, which projects far beyond the level of the head. It looks almost as if the animals were looking through an opera-glass, and Chun has called these eyes 'telescope-eyes.' A. Brauer has recently shown what far-reaching variations of the original eye of fishes were necessary in order to transform it into an organ for seeing in the dark. These variations, however, have occurred in the eyes of the most diverse animals in the deep sea, and not only do different families of deep-sea fishes possess 'telescope-eyes,' but Crustaceans and Cephalopods as well. Even our owls possess quite a similar structure, although it does not project beyond the head in the same way. Here again we have to deal with the phenomenon which Oscar Schmidt in his time called *convergence*, that is, corresponding adaptations to similar conditions in animal forms not genealogically connected with one another. These telescope-eyes are not all descended from one species which chanced in one of the 'mutation-periods' suddenly to produce this combination of harmonious adaptations, but they have risen independently through variation progressing step by step in the direction of the required end, that is to say, through natural selection based upon germinal selection. Only thus can their origin be understood.

But what is true of eyes adapted to darkness is true in some measure of all eyes, for the eyes of animals are not mere decorative points which might be present or absent; they cannot have arisen in any animal whatever through sudden mutation—they have been laboriously acquired with difficulty, by the slow increase of gradually perfecting adaptations; they are parts which bear the most precise internal correlation with the whole organization of the animal, and which can only cease to exist when they become superfluous. Thus the origin of eyes seems to me only conceivable on the basis of germinal selection controlled towards what is purposeful by natural selection, that is to say, on a basis of fluctuating variation, and not through chance.

This is the case with all adaptations. Just as the eyes of animals are adaptations which utilize the light-waves in the interest of the organism and its survival, the same is true of all the sense-organs, tactile organs, smelling and tracking organs, organs of hearing, and so on. The animal cannot do without these; first the lower sense-organs arose and then the higher; the increasingly high organization of the animal conditioned this, and a multicellular animal without sensory structures is inconceivable. The same may be said of the nervous system as a whole, whose function it is to translate into action the stimuli received through the sense-organs, whether directly or by means of intervening nerve-cells, which form central organs of ever-increasing complexity of composition. As telescope-eyes have evolved in some groups of deep-sea animals, independently of one another, and certainly not through the fortuitous occurrence of a mutation, but under the compulsion of necessity in competition, so all the organs we have just named, the whole nervous system with all its sense-organs, must have arisen through the same factors of evolution in numerous independent genealogical lines. And it must not be supposed that this is all; what is true of the sense-organs—that they are necessities—is undoubtedly true also of all parts and organs of the animal body, both as a whole and in every detail. It cannot be demonstrated in all cases, but it is nevertheless certain that this applies also to all the organs of movement, digestion, and reproduction, to all animal groups and also to the differences between them, even although these may not always be obvious adaptations to the conditions of life. What part is left for mutation to play if almost everything is an adaptation? Possibly the specific differences; and these in point of fact cannot in many cases be interpreted with certainty as adaptations, though this can hardly be taken as a proof that they are not. Possibly also the geometrical skeletons of many unicellulars, in which again we cannot recognize any definite relation to the mode of life. It is easy enough to conceive of the wondrously regular and often very complex siliceous skeleton of the Radiolarians or Diatoms as due to saltatory mutations, and 'leaps' of considerable magnitude must certainly have been necessary to produce some of the manifold transformations here as everywhere else. But whether these are or are not without importance for the life of the organisms, we are in the meantime quite unable to decide. Here too it is well to be cautious in concluding that these organic 'crystallizations' are without importance, and therefore to infer that they have arisen suddenly from purely internal causes. One of the experts on Diatoms, F. Schütt, has shown us that differences in length in the skeletal process of the Peridineæ have a definite relation to their power of floating in the sea-water, that the long skeletal arms or horns which these microscopic vegetable organisms extend into the surrounding water form a float-apparatus, for their friction against the particles of the water prevents sinking and enables them to float for a considerable time at approximately the same level. These skeletal forms are thus adaptations, and Chun has recently been able to corroborate the conclusion that this adaptation is exactly regulated, for the length of these horns varies with the specific gravity of the different ocean-currents, species with 'monstrously long' horns occurring, for instance, in the Gulf of Guinea, which is distinguished by its low salinity and high temperature (Fig. 131, *A*), while in the equatorial currents with higher salinity and cooler water, and thus a higher specific gravity, there is a predominance of species of Peridineæ with 'very short' processes and relatively undeveloped float-apparatus (Fig. 131, *B*). It could be seen clearly in the course of the voyage that the long-armed Peridineæ became more abundant as the ship passed from the North Equatorial current into the Gulf of Guinea, and that by and by they held the field altogether, but later, when the 'Valdivia' entered into the South Equatorial current, they disappeared 'all at once.' Thus in this case, in which the veil over the relations between form and function in unicellular organisms has been lifted a little, we recognize that the smallest parts of the cell-body obey the laws of adaptation, and consistent thinking must lead us to the conviction that even in the most lowly organisms the whole structure in all its essential features depends upon adaptation.

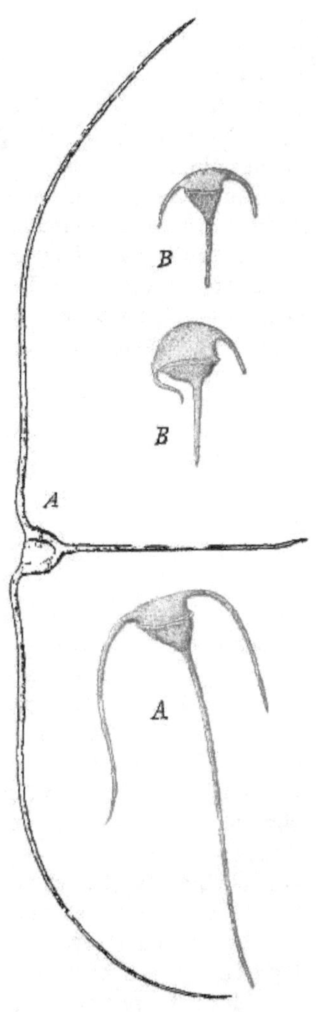

FIG. 131. Peridineæ: species of *Ceratium*. *A*, from the Gulf of Guinea. *B*, from the South Equatorial currents. After Chun.

If the horns of the Peridineæ grow to twelve times the usual length in adaptation to life in sea-water with a salinity increased to the extent of ·002 per cent., then undoubtedly not only the protoplasmic particles of the body which form the horns, but all the rest as well, may be capable of adaptation; and if the *Peridinium* protoplasm has this power of adapting itself to the external conditions, then the capacity for adaptation must be a general character of all unicellular organisms, or rather of all living substance. As will be seen later on, we shall be brought to the same conclusion by different lines of evidence. But a recognition of this must greatly restrict the sphere of operation which we can attribute to saltatory mutations in the sense in which the term is used by De Vries, for adaptations from their very nature cannot arise suddenly, but must originate gradually and step by step, from 'variations' which combine with one another in a definite direction under the influence of the indirect, that is, selective influence of the conditions.

According to the theory of De Vries it seems as if 'variations,' augmented by selection, could never become constant, and that even the degree to which they can be augmented is very limited. As far as this last point is concerned, De Vries seems to me to overlook the fact that every increase in a character must have limits set by the harmony of the parts, which cannot be exceeded unless other parts are being varied at the same time. Artificial selection, in fact, in many cases reaches a limit which it cannot pass, because it has no control over the unknown other parts which ought to be varied, in order that the character desired may be increased still further. Natural selection would in many cases be able to accomplish this, provided that the variation is useful. But of what use is it to the beetroot when its sugar-content is doubled, or to the Anderbeck oats to be highly prized by man? And yet many individual characters have been very considerably increased in domesticated animals by selection: of these we need only call to mind the Japanese cock with tail-feathers twelve feet long.

But undoubtedly these artificial variations do not usually 'breed true' in the sense that De Vries's mutations of *Œnothera lamarckiana* did, that is to say, they only transmit their characters in purity with the continual co-operation of artificial selection. This at least appears to be the case, according to De Vries, in the ennobled cereal races, which, if cultivated in quantities, rapidly degenerate. In many animal breeds, however, this is not the case to the same degree; many, indeed the majority, of the most distinct races of pigeon breed true, and only degenerate when they are crossed with others.

De Vries regards it as a mistake to believe that artificial selection, persevered in for a long time, will succeed in producing a breed which will—as he expresses it—be independent of further selection and will maintain itself in purity. Experience cannot decide this, as we have not command over the unlimited time necessary for selection, but theoretically it is quite intelligible that a variation which had arisen through selection would be more apt to breed true the longer selection was practised, and there is nothing to prevent it becoming ultimately quite as constant as a natural species. For, at the beginning of breeding, we must assume that the variation is contained in only a small number of ids; as the number of generations mounts up, more and more numerous ids with this variation will go to make up the germ-plasm, and the more the breed-ids preponderate the less likelihood will there be that a reversion to the parent-form will be brought about by the chances of reducing-division and amphimixis. That most if not all breeds of pigeon still contain ids of the ancestral form in the germ-plasm, although probably only a small number of them, we see from the occasional reversion to the rock-dove which occurs when species are repeatedly crossed, but that ancestral ids may also be contained in the germ-plasm of long-established natural species is shown by the occurrence of zebra-striping in horse-hybrids. We can understand why these ancestral ids should not have been removed long ago from the germ-plasm by natural selection, since they are not injurious and may remain, so to speak, undetected. It is only when they have an injurious effect by endangering the purity of the new species-type that they can and must be eliminated by natural selection, and this does not cease to operate, as the human breeder does, but continues without pause or break.

I therefore regard it as a mistake on the part of De Vries to exclude fluctuating variation from a share in the transformation of organisms. Indeed, I believe that it plays the largest part, because adaptations cannot arise from mutations, or can only do so exceptionally, and because whole families, orders, and even classes are based on adaptations, especially as regards their chief characters. I need only recall the various families of parasitic Crustaceans, the Cetaceans, the birds, and the bats. None of these groups can have arisen through saltatory, perhaps even retrogressive, 'mutation'; they can only have arisen through variation in a definite direction, which we can think of only as due to the selection of the fluctuations of the determinants of the germ-plasm which are continually presenting themselves.

The difference between 'fluctuating' variability and 'mutation' seems to me to lie in this: that the former has always its basis only in a small majority of the ids of the germ-plasm, while the mutation must be present in most of the ids if it is to be stably transmitted from the very first. How that comes about we cannot tell, but we may suppose that similar influences causing variation within the germ-plasm may bring about variation of many ids in the same direction. I need only recall what I have already said as to the origin of saltatory variations, such as the copper-beech and similar cases. The experiments made by De Vries seem to me to give a weighty support to my interpretation of these phenomena. De Vries himself distinguishes a 'pre-mutation period,' just as I have assumed that the variations which spring suddenly into expression have been in course of preparation within the germ-plasm by means of germinal selection for a long time beforehand. At first perhaps only in a few ids, but afterwards in many, a new state of equilibrium of the determinant-system would be established, which would remain invisible until the chance of reducing division and amphimixis gave predominance to a decided majority of the 'mutation-ids.' In the experiments made by De Vries the same seven new 'species' were produced repeatedly and independently of one another in different generations of *Œnothera lamarckiana*, and we thus see that the same constellations (states of equilibrium) had developed in many specimens of the parent plant, and that it depended on the proportion in which the ids containing these were represented in the seed whether one or another of the new 'species' was produced.

My interpretation, according to which a larger or smaller number of ids were the bearers of the new forms, receives further support from the experiments, for the new species did not always breed true. Thus De Vries found one species, *Œnothera scintillans*, which only yielded 35–40 per cent. of heirs, or in another group about 70 per cent.; the other descendants belonged to the forms *lamarckiana* or *oblonga*, but the number of pure heirs could be increased by selection!

I cannot devote sufficient space to go fully into these very interesting experiments; but one point must still be referred to: the parent form, *Œnothera lamarckiana*, was very variable from the beginning, that is, it exhibited a high degree of fluctuating variability. This tells in favour, on the one hand, of a deep-rooted connexion between 'variation' and 'mutation,' and, on the other hand, it indicates that saltatory variation may be excited by transference to changed conditions of life—as Darwin in his day supposed, and as I have endeavoured to show in the foregoing discussion. De Vries assumes mutation-periods, I believe rightly; but they are not periods prescribed, so to speak, from within, as those who believe in a 'phyletic force' must suppose; they are caused by the influences of the environment which affect the nutritive stream within the germ-plasm, and which, increasing latently, bring about in part mere variability, in part mutations, just as I have indicated in the section on Isolation (vol. ii. p. 280), and indeed, in one of my earliest contributions to the theory of descent[1]. In that essay I suggested the conclusion that periods of constancy alternate with periods of variability, basing my opinion on general considerations, and on Hilgendorf's study of the Steinheim snail-shells. According to De Vries's *Œnothera* experiments we may assume that periods of increased variability may lead to the marked variations sometimes affecting several characters simultaneously, and occurring in many ids, which have hitherto been called 'saltatory' variations, and which we should perhaps do well to call in future, with De Vries, *mutations*.

We cannot yet determine how far the influence of such mutations reaches. I think it is plain that De Vries himself overestimated it, but how many of the species-types which we find to-day depend upon mere mutation can only be decided with any certainty after further investigations. For the present it is well to be clear as to the validity of the general conclusion, that all 'complex,' and especially all 'harmonious,' adaptation, must depend, not upon 'mutation,' but only upon 'variation' guided by selection. As species are essentially complexes of adaptation, originating from a basis of previous complexes of adaptation, there remains, as far as I can see, only the small field of indifferent characters to be determined by mutations, unless indeed we are to include under the term 'mutation' all variations which gain stability, but this would be merely a play upon words. In my opinion *there is no definable boundary line between variation and mutation, and the difference between these two phenomena depends solely on the number—larger or smaller—of ids which have varied in the same direction.*

[1] *Ueber den Einfluss der Isolirung auf die Artbildung*, Leipzig, 1872, p. 51.

LECTURE XXXIV

ORIGIN OF THE SPECIFIC TYPE (*continued*)

Illustration of phyletic evolution by an analogy—Reconciliation of Nägeli and Darwin—Unity of the specific type furthered by climatic variation—By natural selection: illustration from aquatic animals—Direct path of evolution—Natural selection works in association with amphigony—Influence of isolation in defining the specific type—Duration of the periods of constancy—The Siberian pine-jays—Species are, so to speak, 'variable crystals'—Gradual increase of constancy and decrease of reversions—Physiological segregation of species through mutual sterility—Romanes's physiological selection—Breeds of domestic animals mutually fertile, presumably therefore 'amiktic' species also—Mutual fertility in plant species—Mutual sterility certainly not a condition of the splitting up of species—Splitting up of species without amphigony—Lichens—Splitting up of species apart from isolation and mutual sterility, *Lepus variabilis*.

OUR train of thought in the last lecture brought us back again to the so-called 'indifferent' characters, whose occurrence is so often used as evidence against natural selection, as a proof that evolution is guided essentially by internal forces alone. But this objection was based on a fallacy, for the fact that the first small variations are due to internal processes in the germ-plasm does not imply that the whole further course of evolution is determined by these alone, any more than the fact that a sleigh requires a push to start it on its descent down an inclined plane would imply that its rapid descent is due only to the force of the push, and not at the same time to the attraction of gravity. But the analogy is not quite sound, for the processes within the germ-plasm which condition and direct variation do not merely give them the first shove off: they are associated with every onward step in the evolutionary path of the species, they impel it further and further, and without these continual impulses the progressive movement would cease altogether. We have seen that, for internal reasons, germinal selection continues to impel the varying determinants further along the path on which they have started, and thus gives them cumulative strength, and that it is in this way that adaptations to the conditions of life are brought about. The evolution of the character of a species may thus be compared to the course of a sleigh upon a level snow-surface which it could traverse in any direction, but it is moved only by the impulses received through germinal selection. The conditions of life to which the varying parts have to adapt themselves may be thought of as the distant goal, and the processes in the germ-plasm which give rise to variation in a definite direction may be compared to numerous human beings scattered irregularly over the surface of the snow. If the sleigh receives from one of these a push which chances to be in the direction of the goal, it rushes on towards this and ultimately reaches it if the person pushing continues to push in the same direction. So far, then, it seems as if the transformation of the part concerned depended upon germinal selection alone, but we must not forget that the germ-plasm does not contain only one determinant for every part of the body, but as many determinants as there are ids. We must therefore increase the number of our sleighs, and now it is obvious that the pushers of the sleighs, that is, germinal selection, may push one sleigh on toward the goal, but others in the opposite or in any other direction. If we assume that all the sleighs which have taken a wrong direction must reach dangerous ground, and ultimately plunge into an abyss, but that from a neighbouring point sleighs were being dispatched to replace all that came to grief, that these in their turn might attempt to reach the goal, it would ultimately come about that the requisite number of sleighs would arrive at the goal—that is to say, that the new adaptation would be attained.

The abysses represent the elimination of the less favourable variational tendencies, and the constant replacing of sleighs represents the intermingling of fresh ids through amphimixis. If all the sleighs run in the wrong direction they all come to grief, that is, the individual concerned is eliminated with all the ids of its germ-plasm—it disappears altogether from the ranks of the species. But if only a portion of them run in the right direction, care is taken that in following generations, that is, in the continuation of the sleigh-race, this portion combines with those of another group which are also running in the right direction—that is, with the half number of ids from another germ-plasm in amphimixis.

It is not possible to follow the analogy further, but perhaps it may serve to illustrate how germinal selection may be the only impelling force in the organisms, and yet only a small part of its results are determined by itself, and by far the larger part by external conditions. We understand how a variation in a definite direction can exist, and yet it is not that which creates species, genera, orders, and classes; it is the selection and combination of the variational tendencies by the conditions of life, which occurs at every step. There was no variational tendency leading from terrestrial mammals to Cetaceans, but there was a variational tendency moving the nostrils upwards towards the forehead, the hind-limbs towards diminution, the lungs towards lengthening, the tail towards broadening out. But each of these variational tendencies was always only one of several possibilities, and that the particular path which led towards the 'goal' was followed was due to the fact that the others plunged into the abyss to which the wrong paths led, that is to say, they were weeded out by selection. Thus germinal selection offers a possibility of reconciliation between Nägeli's and Darwin's interpretations, which seem so directly contradictory; for the former referred everything to the hypothesis of an internal evolutionary force, the latter rejected this, and regarded natural selection as the main, if not the exclusive factor in evolution. The internal struggles for food, which we have assumed as occurring in the germ-plasm, represent an internal force, though not in the sense of Nägeli, who thought of determining influence operative from first to last, but still an impelling force, which determines the direction of variation for the individual determinants, and must therefore do the same for the whole evolution up to a certain point; for it is only the *possible* variations of the determinants in a germ-plasm which can be chosen, selected, combined, and increased by natural selection, and every germ-plasm cannot give rise to all sorts of variations; the determinants contained in it condition what is possible and what is not, and this is an important limitation to the efficacy of natural selection, and to a certain extent also implies a guiding and determining power on the part of the internal mainspring, to wit, *germinal selection.*

The essential difference between Darwin's view of the transformation of forms and my own lies in the fact that Darwin conceived of natural selection as working only with variations which are not only due to chance themselves, but the intensification of which also depends in its turn solely upon natural selection, while, according to my view, natural selection works with variational tendencies which become intensified through internal causes, and are simply accumulated by natural selection in an ever-growing majority of ids in a germ-plasm through the selection of individuals.

This affects our view of the establishment of a specific type in so far that my intra-germinal variational tendencies are not necessarily, and not always due to chance, though they are so in most cases. If certain determinants are impelled to vary in a particular direction through climatic or any other influences, as we have seen to be the case, for instance, with the climatic varieties of many Lepidoptera, then the corresponding determinants in all the individuals must vary in the same direction, and thus all the individuals of the species which are subject to the same influence must undergo the same variation. Transformations of this kind have exactly the appearance of resulting from 'an internal evolutionary force,' such as Nägeli assumed, and the unity of the specific type will not be disturbed by them.

Nor will this occur, as far as I can see, if the transformation of a species depends solely upon new adaptations and their internal consequences, for if a particular organism has to adapt itself to special new conditions, it will usually be able to do so only in *one* way, and thus natural selection will always allow *the same* suitable variational tendencies to survive and reproduce, so that the unity of the specific type will not be permanently disturbed in this way either. The more advantageous the new conditions of life prove, and the more diverse the ways in which they can be utilized, the more rapidly will the species first adapted to them multiply, and the more will their descendants be impelled to adapt themselves specially to the *different* possibilities of utilizing the new situation, and thus, from a parent species adapted in general to the new conditions, there arise forms adapted to its more detailed possibilities. I must refer again to the previous instance of the Cetaceans which originated from vegetarian littoral, or fluviatile mammals, and have evolved since the Triassic period into a very considerable number of species-groups. All are alike in their *general* adaptation, and these adaptations to the conditions of life of aquatic animals—the fish-like form, the flippers, the peculiarities of the respiratory organs and the organs of hearing—when once acquired would not and could not be lost again: but each of the modern groups of whales has its particular sphere of life, which it effectively exploits by means of subordinate adaptations. Thus there are the dolphins with their bill-like jaws and the two rows of conical teeth, their active temperament, rapid movements, and diet of fish; and the whalebone whales with their enormous gape, the sieve-apparatus of whalebone-plates, and a diet of small molluscs and the like. But each of these groups has split up into species, and if we again regard the principle of adaptation as determining and directing evolution, we are no nearer being able to prove the assumption in regard to individual cases, for we know too little about the conditions of life to be able to demonstrate that the peculiarities of structure are actually adaptations to these. Theoretically, however, it is quite easy to suppose that adaptation to a particular sphere of life was the guiding factor in their evolution, and if this be so—as we have already proved that it is in regard to the two chief groups and the whole class—then the harmony of the structure must be due solely to the continued selection of the fittest. We require no further principle of explanation for the establishment of a specific type.

This 'type' is thus not reached by any indefinite varying of the parent form in all directions, but in general it is reached by the most direct and shortest way. The parent form must indeed have become to some extent fluctuating, since not only the variational tendencies 'aiming at the goal,' but others as well, must have emerged in the germ-plasm; but gradually these others would occur less and less frequently, being always weeded out afresh by selection, until the great majority of the individuals would follow the same path of evolution, under the guidance of germinal selection, which continues to work in the direction that has once been taken. After a short period of variation, which need not, of course, involve the whole organism, but may refer only to certain parts of it, a steady direct progress in the direction of the 'goal,' that is, of perfect adaptation, will set in, as we have seen in the case of the *Planorbis* snails of Steinheim.

We must not forget, however, that natural selection works essentially upon a basis of sexual reproduction, which with its reduction of the ids and its continually repeated mingling of germ-plasms, combines the existing variational tendencies, and thus diffuses them more and more uniformly among the individuals of a whole area of occupation. Sexual reproduction, continual intermingling of the individuals selected for breeding, is thus a very effective and important, if not an indispensable, factor in the evolution of the specific type.

But it is not only in the case of species transformations due to new adaptations that sexual mingling operates; it does so also in the case of variations due to purely intra-germinal causes. We have already seen in discussing Isolation that isolated colonies may come to have a peculiar character somewhat different from that of the parent form, because they were dominated by some germinal variational tendency which occurred only rarely in the home of the parent form, and therefore never found expression there. On the isolated area this would indeed be mingled with the rest of the existing germinal variational tendencies, but the result of this mingling would be different, and the further development of the tendency in question would probably not be suppressed.

We need not wonder, therefore, that specific types occur in such varying degrees of definiteness. If a species is distributed over a wide connected territory, sporadically, not uniformly, it will depend partly upon the mutual degree of isolation of the sporadic areas whether the individual colonies will exhibit the same specific type or will diverge from one another. If the animal in question is a slow-moving one like a snail, the intermingling from neighbouring sporadic colonies will be much slower than in the case of a resident bird such as a woodpecker. Many interesting results would undoubtedly be gained if the numerous careful investigations into the geographical distributions of species and their local races were studied with special reference to this point, and much light would undoubtedly be thrown upon the evolution of the specific type. But it would be absolutely necessary to study carefully all the biological relations of the animals concerned, to trace back the history of the species as far as possible, and to decide the period of immigration, the mode and direction of distribution, and so on.

Nothing shows more plainly the enormous duration of the period of constancy in species than the wide distribution of the same specific type on scattered areas or even over different areas absolutely isolated from one another. If, as we saw, the same diurnal butterflies live in the Alps and the far North, they must have remained unvaried since the Glacial period, for it was the close of that period that brought them to their present habitats, and while other diurnal butterflies now living on the Alps differ from their relatives in the Arctic zone (Lapland, Siberia, and Labrador) in some unimportant spot or line, and must therefore have diverged from one another in the course of the long period since the Glacial epoch, they have done so only to a minimal degree, and in characters which possibly depend solely upon germinal selection and can hardly be regarded as adaptations.

I should like, however, to cite one of the few cases known to me in which a slight deviation from the specific type undoubtedly depending upon adaptation has occurred on an isolated region. The nut-jay (*Caryocatactes nucifraga*) lives not only upon our Alps and in the Black Forest, but also in the forests of Siberia, and the birds there differ from those with us in small peculiarities of the bill, which is longer and thinner in them, shorter and more powerful in ours. Ornithologists associate this difference with the fact that in this country the birds feed chiefly on hard hazel nuts, which they break open with their bill, and on acorns, beechmast, and, in the Alps, on cembra-cones, while in Siberia, where there are no hazel nuts, they feed chiefly upon the seeds of the Siberian cedar, which are concealed deep down in the cones. Thus we find that in Siberia the bill is slender, and that the upper jaw protrudes awl-like beyond the lower, for about 2·5 mm., and probably serves chiefly to pick out the cedar nuts from behind the cone-scales. In the Alps the birds (var. *pachyrhynchus*) break up the whole cone of the cembra-pine with their thick, hard bill, and in the Upper

Engadine, where the nut-jay is abundant, I have often seen the ground underneath the cembra-pines covered with the débris of its meal. In addition to these differences between the two races, the Alpine form is stronger in build, the Siberian form is daintier; in the former the white terminal band on the tail is narrow (about 18 mm.), in the Siberian form it is broader (about 27 mm.).

Such cases of variation of individual parts in different areas seem to me very important theoretically, because they furnish us with an answer to the view which represents the species as a 'life-crystal,' which must be as it is or not at all, and which therefore cannot vary as regards its individual parts. The case of the nut-jay has the further interest that it is one of the few in which we find the new adaptation of a single character without variation of most of the other characters.

It is only in an essentially different sense that we can compare the species, like any other vital unit, to a crystal, in so far as its parts are harmoniously related one to another, or, as I expressed myself years ago, are in a state of equilibrium, which must be brought about by means of intra-selection. This analogy, however, only applies to the actual adjustment of the parts to a whole, and not to their casual adjustment. Species are variable crystals; the constancy of a species in all its parts must be regarded as something quite relative, which may vary at any time, and which is sure to vary at some time in the course of a long period. But the longer the adaptation of a species to new conditions persists the more constant, *ceteris paribus*, and the more slowly variable will it become, and this for two reasons: first, because the determinants which are varying in a suitable direction are being more and more strictly selected, more and more precisely adapted, and are thus becoming more like each other; and secondly, because, according to our theory, the homologous determinants of all the ids do not vary in the required direction, and a portion of the unvaried ancestral ids is always carried on through the course of the phylogeny, and only gradually set aside by the chances of reducing division. But the more completely these unvaried ids are eliminated from the germ-plasm the less likely will they be to find expression in reversions or in impurities of the new specific characters. I may recall the reversions of the various breeds of pigeons to the rock-dove, those of the white species of *Datura* to the blue form, and the *Hipparion*-like three-toed horse of Julius Cæsar, and so on. The unvaried ancestral ids, which in these cases find only quite exceptional expression, will make the new 'specific character' fluctuating, as long as they are contained in the germ-plasm in considerable numbers, but they must become more and more infrequent in the germ-plasm as successive generations are passed through the sieve of natural selection, and the oftener these germ-plasms, to which the chances of reducing division and amphimixis have assigned a majority of the old determinants, are expelled from the ranks of the species by personal selection. The oftener this has occurred in a species the less frequently will it recur, and the more constant, *ceteris paribus*, will the 'type' of the species become.

If we add to this idea the fact that adaptations take place very slowly, and that every variation of the germ-plasm in an appropriate direction has time to spread over countless hosts of individuals, we gain some idea of the way in which new adaptations gradually bring about the evolution of a more and more sharply-defined specific type.

So far, however, we have only explained the morphological aspect of the problem of the nature of species, but there is also a physiological side, and for a long time this played an important part in the definition of the conception of species. Until the time of Darwin it was regarded as certain that species do not intermingle in the natural state, and that, though they could be crossed in rare cases, the progeny would be infertile.

Although we now know that these statements are only relatively correct, and that in particular there are many higher plants which yield perfectly fertile hybrids, it is nevertheless a striking phenomenon that among the higher animals, mammals, and birds the old law holds good, and hybrids between two species are very rarely fertile. The two products of crossing between the horse and the ass, the mule and the hinny, are never fertile *inter se*, and very rarely with a member of the parent stock.

We have to ask, therefore, what is the reason of this mutual sterility of species; whether it is a necessary outcome of the morphological differences between the species, or only a chance accessory phenomenon, or perhaps an absolutely necessary preliminary condition to the establishment of species.

The last was the view held by Romanes. He believed that a species could only divide into two when it was separated into isolated groups either geographically or physiologically, that is, when sexual segregation in some form is established within the species, so that all the individuals can no longer pair with one another, but groups arise which are mutually sterile. It is only subsequently, he maintained, that these groups come to differ from one another in structure. To this hypothetical process he gave the name of 'physiological selection.' This view depends—it seems to me—upon an underestimate of the power of natural selection. Romanes believed that when a species began to split up, even the adaptive variations would always disappear again because of the continual crossing, and that only geographical isolation or sexual alienation, that is, physiological selection, would be able to prevent this. But even the fact that there are dimorphic and polymorphic species proves sufficiently that adaptation to two or even several sets of conditions can go on on the same area. In many ants we find many kinds of individuals—the two sexual forms, the workers, and the soldiers, and these last are undoubtedly distinguished by adaptive characters which must be referred to selection. The same is true of the caterpillars, whose coloration is adapted to their surroundings in two different ways. If the individuals of one and the same species can be broken up into two or more different forms and combinations of adaptations, while they are mingling uninterruptedly with one another, natural selection must undoubtedly be able, notwithstanding the continual intermingling of divergent types, to discriminate between them and to separate them sharply from one another. Assuredly then a species can not only exhibit uniform variation on a single area, but may also split up into two without the aid of physiological selection. Theoretically it is indisputable that of two varieties which are both equally well suited to the struggle for existence, a mixed form arising through crossing may not be able to survive. Let us recall, for instance, the caterpillars, of which some individuals are green and some brown, and let us assume that the brown colour is as effective a protection as the green, then the two forms would occur with equal frequency; but though a mixed hybrid form which was adapted neither to the green leaves nor to the brown might occasionally crop up, it would always be eliminated. It would occur because the butterflies themselves are alike, whether they owe their origin to green caterpillars or to brown, and thus at first, at least, all sexual combinations would be equally probable.

I do not believe therefore in a 'physiological selection,' in Romanes's sense, as an indispensable preliminary condition to the splitting of species, but it is a different question whether the mutual sterility so frequently observable between species has not conversely been produced by natural selection in order to facilitate the separation of incipient species. For there can be no doubt that the process of separating two new forms, or even of separating one new form from an old one, would be rendered materially easier if sexual antipathy or diminished fertility of the crossings could be established simultaneously with the other variations. This would be useful, since pure and well-defined variations would be better adapted to their life-conditions than hybrids, and would become increasingly so in the course of generations. But as soon as it is useful it must actually come about, if that is possible at all. It may be, however, as we have said before, that the two divergent forms depend merely upon quantitative variations of the already existing characters; sexual attraction, whether it depends upon very delicate chemical substances, or on odours, or on mutual complementary tensions unknown to us, will always fluctuate upwards and downwards, and plus or minus determinants, which lie at the root of these unknown characters in the germ-plasm, must continually present themselves and form the starting-point for selection-processes of a germinal and personal kind, which may bring about sexual antipathy and mutual sterility between the varieties. I therefore consider Romanes's idea correct in so far that separation between species is in many cases accompanied by increasing sexual antipathy and mutual sterility. While Romanes supposed that 'natural selection could in no case have been the cause' of the sterility, I believe, on the contrary, that it could only have been produced by natural selection; it arises simply, as all adaptations do, through personal selection on a basis of germinal selection, and it is not a preliminary condition of the separation of species, but an adaptation for the purpose of making as pure and clean a separation as possible. It is obviously an advantage for both the divergent tendencies of variation that they should intermingle as little as possible. This is corroborated by the fact that by no means all the marked divergences of species are accompanied by sexual alienation, and that the mutual sterility so frequently seen is not an inevitable accompaniment of differences in the rest of the organism.

That this is not the case is very clearly proved by our domesticated animals. The differences in structure between the various breeds of pigeon and poultry are very great, and breeds of dog also diverge from one another very markedly, especially in shape and size of body. Yet all these are fertile with one another, and they yield fertile offspring. But they are products of artificial selection by man, and he has no interest in making them mutually sterile, so that they have not been selected with a view to sexual alienation, but in reference to the other characters. The segregation of animal species into several sub-species on the same area is probably usually accompanied by sexual antipathy, since in this case it would be useful although not indispensable. But the matter is different in the case of the transformation of a colony upon a geographically isolated region. 'Amiktic' forms, such as *Vanessa ichnusa* of Corsica, are hardly likely to be sexually alienated from the parent form; we have here to do only with the preponderance of a fortuitous and biologically valueless variation and its consequent elevation to the rank of a variety. The new form was not an adaptation, but only a variation, and as it was of no use, it was not in a position to incite any process of selection favouring its advancement.

But even adaptive transformations on isolated regions from which the parent species is excluded are not likely to develop rapidly any sexual antipathy as regards the parent stock, and I should not be surprised if experiments showed that there is perfect mutual fertility between, for instance, many of the species of *Achatinella* on the Sandwich Islands or of *Nanina* on Celebes, or between the species of thrushes on the different islands of the Galapagos Archipelago, or between these and the ancestral species on the adjacent continent, if that species is still in existence. For there was no reason why sexual antipathy to the parent form should have developed in any of these adaptation forms which have arisen in isolation, and therefore it has probably not been evolved.

That our view of the mutual sterility between species, as an adaptation to the utility of precise species-limitation, is the correct one is evidenced not only by our domesticated races, but even more clearly by plants, in regard to which it is particularly plain that the sexual relations between two species are adaptational. We have already seen in what a striking way the sensitiveness of the stigma of a flower is regulated in reference to pollen from the same plant, that some species are not fertilizable by their own pollen at all, that others yield very little seed when self-fertilization is effected, and that others again are quite fertile—as much so as with the pollen of another plant of the same species. We regarded these gradations of sexual sensitiveness as adaptations to the perfectly or only moderately well-assured visits of insects, or to their entire absence. I wish to cite these cases as well as the heterostylism of some flowers as evidence in support of the conception of the mutual sterility of species which I have just outlined. But this only in passing. The point to which I chiefly wish to direct attention is the mutual fertility of many plant-species. In lower as well as in higher plants fertile hybrids occur not infrequently under natural conditions, and cultivated hybrids, such as the new *Medicago media*, a form made by mingling two species of clover, may go on reproducing with its own kind for a considerable time. A number of Phanerogams yield fertile hybrids, and in Orchids even species of different genera have been crossed and have yielded offspring which was in some cases successfully crossed with a third genus.

If these facts prove anything it is that the factors which determine the mutual sterility of species are quite distinct from their morphological differences, in other words, from the diagnostic characters of the specific type. For a long time the verdict on this matter was too entirely based on observations made on animals, among which mutual sterility arises relatively easily, even where it was not intended (*sit venia verbo!*). Even the pairing, but still more the period of maturity, the relations of maturity in ovum and sperm, and even the most minute details in the structure of the sperm-cell, the egg-shell, envelope, &c., have to be taken into account, and these may bring about mutual or, as Born has shown, one-sided sterility. We know, through the researches of Strasburger, that a great many Phanerogams, when pollinated artificially from widely separated species of different genera and families, will at least allow the pollen-tube to penetrate down to the ovule, and that in many cases amphimixis actually results. It follows that we must not lay too great stress upon the mutual sterility which occurs almost without exception among the higher animals, but must turn to the plants with greater confidence.

Among plants there is very widely distributed mutual fertility between species. I doubt, however, whether the observations on this point are sufficient to warrant any certain conclusion in regard to the importance of the phenomena in the formation of species. At least it is not easy to see why the mutual sterility of many species of plants should not have been necessary or useful in separating species, and why it was not therefore evolved. We may point to the fact that animals can move from place to place as the chief reason, and this factor does undoubtedly play a part, but the widespread crossing of plants by insects makes up to some extent, as far as sexual intermingling is concerned, for their inability to move from place to place. I do not know whether the species of orchid which are fertile with one another belong to different countries, so that we may assume that they originated in isolation, or whether fertile orchids from the same area are fertilized by different insects and are thus sexually isolated. This and many other things must be taken into consideration. Probably these relations have not yet been adequately investigated; probably what is known by some experts has not yet been made available to all. Future investigations and studies must throw more light upon the problem.

In any case, however, we can see from the frequency of mutual fertility among plants that mutual sterility is not a *conditio sine qua non* of the splitting up of species, and we must beware of laying too great stress upon it even among animals. Germinal selection is a process which not only forms the basis of all personal selection, but which is also able to give rise of itself, without the usual aid of sexual intermingling, to a new specific type. And we cannot with any confidence dispute that, even without amphigony, a certain degree of personal selection may not ensue solely on the basis of the favourable variational departures originating in the germ-plasm. It would be premature to express any definite views on this point as yet, but the diverse cases of purely asexual or parthenogenetic reproduction in groups of plants rich in species make this hypothesis seem probable.

The most remarkable example of this is probably to be found in the Lichens, the symbiotic nature of which we have already discussed, in which—now at least—neither the Fungus nor the Alga associated with it is known to exhibit sexual reproduction. If this is really the case, then the existence of numerous and well-marked species of lichens leads us to the hypothesis just expressed, and we must suppose that the unity of the specific type is attained in this case solely by a continual sifting of the useful from the useless variations of the determinants, and through purely germinal intensification of the surviving variational tendencies.

Of course it is possible that the mutual adaptation of the Algæ and Fungi in the evolution of species of Lichens took place very long ago, at a time when sexual reproduction still existed, at least in one of the associated organisms, the Fungus. The Ascomycetes, to which most of the Lichens belong, do not at present usually exhibit the process of amphimixis, as I have already noted; but it may perhaps be still possible to decide whether they must have exhibited it, or at least could have exhibited it at an earlier stage in their evolution. As the group of Thallophytes is a very ancient one, it is not inconceivable that the modern species of Lichens have existed for a long time, and that they had their origin in the remote past with the assistance of amphimixis.

Nor need it be objected to this supposition that it has been found possible to *make new Lichens* by bringing together Fungi and Algæ which had not previously been associated with one another; for in the first place both were already adapted to partnership with other species, and, moreover, so far no one has succeeded in rearing these artificial lichens for any length of time, still less in seeing them evolve into specific forms persistent in natural conditions.

But if this supposition should prove to be not only improbable, but actually erroneous, then the existence of Lichens would afford a clear proof that the 'type' of the species does not depend essentially upon the constant intermingling of individuals, but upon a process which we may best designate *uniformity of adaptation.* We have simply to suppose that under similar external influences similar variational tendencies were started by germinal selection in all the individuals of the two parent species of a lichen, and set a-going by germinal selection, just as a warmer climate gives rise to a black variety in the butterfly *Polyommatus phlaeas*, because similar determinants of the germ-plasm of all the individuals were impelled to vary in the same manner and direction. This would then give rise to quite definite variations, and since only the suitable variational tendencies could survive, primitive though never complicated adaptations would arise. But we cannot assume that the lichens are not adapted to the conditions of their life as well as all other organisms. We cannot judge how far even their shape is to be regarded as an adaptation, whether the formation of encrusting growths, of tree-like forms, of cup or bush-lichens, may not be regarded as adaptations towards a full utilization of the conditions of their life—but even if this is not the case, the formation of soredia remains an undoubted adaptation to the symbiosis of those lichens which exhibit them. The soredia cannot depend upon the direct effect of the conditions of life, for they are reproductive bodies which did not exist before the existence of the lichen, and only originated to facilitate their distribution.

Thus there is still a great deal that is doubtful in our theories as to the transformations of organisms, and much remains still to be done. But even though we may doubt whether adaptations could come about in multicellular organisms without amphigony, we may be quite certain of the converse, that is, that the specific type can be changed in every individual feature by natural selection on the basis of amphigony, even as regards invisible features which only express themselves in altered periods of growth. Even when there is no isolation whatever and no mutual sterility, and when a mobile species is uniformly distributed over a large area, a splitting up into races in regard to one particular character may occur, *simply through adaptation* to the spatially different climatic conditions of the area inhabited.

Early in these lectures we discussed the twofold protective value of the coloration of the 'variable hare' (*Lepus variabilis*), which is distributed over the Arctic zone of the Old and New World, and also occurs in the higher regions of the Alps. Wherever there is a sharp contrast between winter and summer the variable hare exhibits the same specific type, being brown in summer and white in winter, but in regard to this very character of colour-change it forms races to some extent, for it is white for a longer or shorter time according to the length of the winter—in Greenland for the whole twelve months of the year, in Northern Norway only for eight or nine months, in the Alps for six or seven months, but in the south of Sweden and in Ireland not at all. There it remains brown in winter like our common hare (*Lepus timidus*). This is not a question of the direct effect of cold; if it were the species would become white in Southern Sweden also, for there is no lack of severe cold there, but the ground is not so uninterruptedly covered with snow, and so the white colour of the hare would be as often, probably oftener, a danger than a safeguard, and the more primitive double coloration has therefore been done away with by natural selection. The change of colour is thus hereditarily fixed, as is proved by the fact that the Alpine hare, if caught and kept in the valleys below, puts on a white dress at the usual time, which the common hare never does.

As in Southern Sweden the winter coloration has been wholly eliminated, so, conversely, from there to the Arctic zone the summer colouring has been more and more crowded out, and in the Farthest North it has totally disappeared from the characters of the species. We thus see that wherever the species lives the double colouring is regulated, as regards the duration of the winter coat, in exact harmony with the external conditions. There is a pure white, a pure brown, and a colour-changing race, and the latter is subdivided into two—one wearing the winter dress for six, the other for eight months. Probably these could be still further subdivided, if the different regions of the Scandinavian Peninsula were investigated individually from south to north. That the duration of the winter dress has its roots in the germ-plasm, and does not depend solely on the earlier or later period at which the cold sets in, is made clear by the two extreme forms, the white and the brown *Lepus variabilis*, as well as by the behaviour of captive animals. The familiar case of Ross's lemming, which remained brown in the warm cabin, and then suddenly became white when it was exposed to the cold of winter, only shows that the cold acts as a liberating stimulus. The preparatory changes in the pellage are already present, and the stimulus of cold brings them rapidly to a climax. Here, therefore, the necessary variations of the relevant germinal parts must have continually presented themselves for selection, which is intelligible enough, since it is merely a question of plus- or minus-variations. The fact that the six-months' dress can be transformed into an eight-months' dress must have its cause in some minute biological units of the germ-plasm; the determinants of the fur must be able to vary in such a way that a longer or shorter duration of the winter's coat is the result. The possibility of the whole variation depends upon the continual fluctuations of all determinants, now towards plus, now towards minus, and the necessity and inevitableness of each adaptation to the duration of the winter lies in the unceasing personal selection—the inexorable preferring of the better adapted.

LECTURE XXXV

THE ORIGIN AND THE EXTINCTION OF SPECIES

Adaptation does not depend upon chance—The case of eyes—Of leaf-mimicry—All persistent change depends ultimately on selection—Mutual sterility without great significance—Relative isolation (*Lepus variabilis*)—Influence of hybridization—Decadence of species—Differences in the duration of decadence—Natural death of individuals—Extinction due to excessive variability (Emery)?—*Machairodus* as interpreted by Brandes—Lower types more capable of adaptation than higher—Flightless birds—Disturbance of insular fauna and flora by cultivation—The big game of Central Europe.

In the polar hare we have a case in which the adaptations to the life conditions both of time and space are recognizable as the effect of definite causes, and thus as a necessity; but the same must be true everywhere even in regard to the most complex adaptations which seem to depend entirely upon chance; everywhere adaptation results of necessity—if it is possible at all with the given organization of the species—as certainly as the adaptation dress of the hare depends on the length of the winter, and in point of fact not less certainly than the blue colour of starch on the addition of iodine. The most delicate adaptations of the vertebrate eye to the task set for it by life in various groups have been gradually brought about as the necessary results of definite causes, just in the same way as the complex protective markings and colouring on the wing of the *Kallima* and other leaf-mimicking butterflies.

That adaptations can be regarded as mechanically necessitated is due to the fact that in every process of adaptation the same direction of variation on the part of the determinants concerned is guaranteed, since personal selection eliminates those which vary in a wrong direction, so that only those varying in a suitable direction survive, and they then continue to vary in the same direction. But the greatest difference between our conception of natural selection and that of Darwin lies in this: that Darwin regarded its intervention as dependent upon chance, while we consider it as necessary and conditioned by the upward and downward intra-germinal fluctuation of the determinants. Appropriate variational tendencies not only *may* present themselves, they *must* do so, if the germ-plasm contains determinants at all by whose fluctuations in a plus or minus direction the appropriate variation is attainable.

That a horse should grow wings is beyond the limits of the possibilities of equine variation—there are no determinants which could present variations directed towards this goal; but that any multicellular animal which lives in the light should develop eyes lies within the variational possibilities of its ectoderm determinants, and in point of fact almost all such animals do possess eyes, and eyes, too, whose functional capacity may be increased in any direction, and which are adaptable and modifiable in any manner in accordance with the requirements of the case. As soon as the determinants of the most primitive eye came into existence, they formed the fundamental material by whose plus- or minus-variations all the marvellous eye structures might be brought about, which we find in the different groups of the Metazoa, from a mere spot sensitive to light to a shadowy perception of a moving body, and from that again to the distinct recognition of a clear image, which we are aware of in our own eyes. And what wonderful special adaptations of the eye to near and to distant vision, to vision in the dusk and at night, or in the great ocean-depths, to recognition of mere movement or the focussing of a clear image, have been interpolated in the course of this evolution!

All such adaptations are possible, because they can proceed from variations of determinants which are in existence; and in the same way it is possible, at every stage of the evolution of organisms, for eyes to degenerate again, whether they have been high up or low down in the scale of gradations of this perhaps the most delicate of all our sense-organs. As soon as a species migrated permanently from the light into perfect darkness its eyes began to degenerate. We know blind flat worms, blind water-fleas and Isopods, also blind insects and higher Crustaceans, and even blind fishes and amphibians, the eyes of which are now to be found at very different levels of degeneration, as Eigenmann has recently shown in regard to several species of cave-dwelling salamanders of the State of Ohio. In all these cases it is only necessary for the determinants of the eye to continue to vary in the minus direction, and the disappearance of the eye must be gradually brought about.

We must picture upward development in quite a similar way. The forest butterflies of the Tropics could not possibly all have their under surfaces coloured like a leaf if the protective pattern depended solely upon the chance of a useful variation presenting itself. It always presented itself through the fluctuations of the determinants, and thus the appropriate colourings were not merely able to develop, but of necessity did so in gradually increasing perfection. If chance played any part in the matter, it would be quite unintelligible why the protective colouring should occur only where it acts as a protection, and why, for instance, it should not appear sometimes upon the upper surface of the butterfly wing, or upon the posterior wings which are covered when the butterfly is at rest. We have already studied in detail the precision with which the coloration is localized on minute points and corners of the wing: this can only be understood if natural selection works with the certainty of a perfect mechanism. Chance only comes into the matter in so far as it depends upon chance whether the relevant determinants in one id or another are to vary in the direction of plus or minus; but as the germ-plasm contains many ids, and chance may decide it differently in each of these, the presence of a majority of determinants varying in a desirable direction does not depend upon chance, for if they are not contained in one individual they are in another. It is only necessary that they should be present in some, and that these should be selected for reproduction.

We must therefore regard natural selection, that is to say, *personal selection*, as a mechanical process of development, which begins with the same certainty and works 'in a straight line' towards its 'goal,' just as any principle of development might be supposed to do. Fundamentally it is after all a purely internal force which gives rise to evolution, the power of the most minute vital units to vary under changing influences, and it is only the guidance of evolution along particular paths that is essentially left to personal selection, which brings together what is useful and thus determines the direction of further evolution. If we bear in mind that even the minutest variations of the biophors and determinants express nothing more or less than reactions to changed external conditions in the direction of adaptation, and that the same is true of each of the higher categories of vital units, whether they be called cell, tissue, organ, person, or corm, we see that the whole evolution of the forms of life upon the earth depends upon adaptations following each other in unbroken succession, and fitting into each other in the most complex way. The whole evolution is made possible by the power of variation of the living units of every grade, and called forth and directed by the ceaseless changes of the external influences. I said years ago that *everything* in organic evolution depended upon selection, for every lasting change in a vital unit means adaptation to changed external influences, and implies a preference in favour of the parts of the unit concerned, which are thereby more fitly disposed.

In this sense we can also say that the species is a complex of adaptations, for we have seen that it depends upon the co-operation of different grades of selective processes, that in many cases it is produced solely by germinal selection, but that in very many more personal selection plays the chief part, whether in bringing about sexual adaptations, or adaptations to the conditions of existence.

When we have thus recognized that the origin of a variation in a definite direction results as inevitably when it is called forth by the indirect influence of conditions, that is, through the need for a new adaptation, as when it is induced in the germ-plasm by direct causes such as those of climate, we shall not be disposed to estimate very highly the part played by mutual sterility in the origin of species. We shall rather be inclined to assign it a rôle at a later stage, after the separation of the forms has taken place, and this view is supported by the fact of the mutual sterility of most nearly related species, and by the theoretical consideration that the frequency of hybrids, even if these are always eliminated in the struggle for existence, must signify a loss for both the parent species. But no certain conclusion can be based upon either of these arguments—not upon the theoretical one, because here again we are unable to estimate the extent of this loss; and not upon the argument from fact, because the results of experiments in crossing animals have generally been overestimated, since we are apt to regard the most nearly related animals that are at our disposal as being very closely related. Thus, for instance, horse and ass, horse and zebra are undoubtedly rightly included within the same genus, but the fact that there are several species of zebra in Africa gives us an idea of the number of transition stages that may have existed between the horse and the zebra. Entomologists have sometimes reared hybrids between the most nearly related indigenous species of hawk-moth of the genus *Smerinthus*—hybrids of *Smerinthus ocellata*, the eyed hawk-moth, and *Smerinthus populi*, the poplar hawk-moth. I have myself made many experiments of this kind, and have often succeeded in getting the two species to pair and even to deposit eggs, but I have never seen a caterpillar emerge from them. The hybrids do occur, however, and they have been repeatedly obtained by Standfuss. In external appearance they are intermediate between the parent forms, but with marked divergences, thus, for instance, the beautiful blue eye on the posterior wing of *S. ocellata* (Fig. 5, vol. i. p. 69) may have almost disappeared or be only indicated. They are sterile. But we know three species of *Smerinthus* in North America, which are all much nearer to *S. ocellata* than *S. populi* is, for they all possess the eye-spot referred to, although it is less well developed. The proof that the most nearly related species do not yield fertile descendants should be sought for by crossing *Smerinthus ocellata* with one of these American species if it is to have any decisive value.

Experiments of the same kind have been made by Standfuss with different species of indigenous *Saturnia*, and these have shown not only that crossing is possible, but that the hybrids are fertile in their turn. These results are to be valued the more highly because it is well known that Lepidoptera, and even the usually prolific silk-moths, do not readily reproduce in captivity, even within the same species. We have in *Saturnia pyri, spini,* and *carpini* three well-marked distinct species with no intermediate forms in nature, and with quite different colouring in the caterpillars. That these should have been successfully combined in a triple hybrid proves at least that sexual alienation cannot have advanced far in this case.

We must beware, however, of attributing too much to the constant mutual crossing which occurs in a species living on a connected area and of regarding its influence as irresistible. Undoubtedly it must go far towards securing the uniformity of individuals, but not only is it unable to achieve this, but it cannot successfully resist the stronger influences making for variation which may be exerted upon a part of the area of the species. We have already seen that it is quite erroneous to suppose that every new adaptation must be lost sight of again because of the continual crossing with other members of the species upon the same area. Other things being equal, this depends entirely upon the importance of the adaptation in question. Just as climatic influences may be so strong that they entirely overcome the influence of crossing, and give rise to a local race notwithstanding imperfect geographical isolation, so the same may happen in the case of adaptations. It is quite conceivable that the polar hare of Scandinavia may have evolved a whole series of races, each of which is adapted to the duration of the snow in its geographical range, although a crossing of these quick-footed animals must frequently occur in the course of time, even as regards forms from widely separated areas, and although the whole region is inhabited without a break by the species, so that a 'mingling' of the hares of all regions from south to north, and conversely, may take place, and indeed *must* be continually taking place, though of course very slowly.

It is precisely this extreme slowness with which the intermingling of racial characters take place that seems to me essential for the production of local or, as in this case, regional races. It is not difficult to calculate the rate of 'blood-distribution' if we assume that the conditions for a rapid dissemination are as favourable as possible.

Let us assume that it takes place along a certain line—in this case from south to north—and that the numerical strength of the species remains constant, each pair of hares yielding a pair of surviving offspring, which will attain to reproduction. Let us suppose that one of these hares moves his home northwards to the extent of his range, that is, as far as a hare is accustomed to range from his head quarters, and that he pairs with one of the descendants on the next stretch.

Let us further suppose that this stretch is ten kilometres in extent, and that the change of quarters take place once in each year, then the blood of a South Scandinavian hare would have extended ten kilometres further north in ten years, and in a hundred years 100 kilometres; it would not, however, be quite pure, but mixed and thinned by crossing with a hundred mates of different individual bloods, that is, thinned to the extent of 2 to the 100th power, that is, to less than a millionth part. Thus even with these much too favourable assumptions the influence of a region of hares 100 kilometres distant would be actually *nil* upon the inhabitants of a region which was in process of new adaptation. That the assumptions are too favourable is quite obvious, since every surviving hare would not be likely to move his home, and probably the majority would remain in the old quarters and find mates there. The blood-mingling would therefore take place much more rarely, perhaps only once in ten years, and the wandering descendants of the second generation might move southward, and so neutralize the previous blood-mingling, and so on. But let us keep to our favourable assumptions, and attempt to determine how strong the assimilating influence of the blood-mingling from south to north would be upon a point *A*. The blood of the nearest stretch diluted to a half would affect the inhabitants of *A* once in each year; the second stretch would only contribute blood of $\frac{1}{4}$ strength, the third of $\frac{1}{8}$, the fourth of $\frac{1}{16}$, and the blood of the tenth would be diluted to $\frac{1}{1024}$. A region *B*, extending over twenty such stretches, or 200 kilometres, would thus shelter within it a hare population of which the centre would only be influenced from the periphery in vanishing proportions. If the winter were of equal length over the whole area of *B*, all the inhabitants would be tending to vary the period for which the winter dress was worn in correspondence with the length of the winter, and the centre of the region would be the less impeded in this process because the more peripheral areas would also be approximating to the same adaptation. But since even the admixture of $\frac{1}{32}$ of strange blood could have no hindering influence upon a variation, there would remain a region of $2 \times 5 = 10$ stretches upon which the influence of the non-varying regions would be without effect. There would therefore arise a new race in relation to the duration of the winter dress, and this would not cease abruptly, but would gradually pass over into the neighbouring regions, which however would be pure at their centre, just as is probably the case in reality, if we regard *B* as any point in the line of distribution from south to north.

The harmony of the individuals within a species will therefore depend in part upon the mingling of hereditary primary constituents associated with reproduction, but in greater part upon adaptation to the same conditions; it is *a similarity of adaptation*, and the strongest influence which sexual reproduction exerts lies not in the mingling of these hereditary constituents alone, but above all in the reduction in the germ-plasm of the two parental hereditary contributions—a reduction which results from and through the sexual intermingling. It is only this that prevents these primary constituents from varying at too unequal a rate in the transformations of species, and causes them ultimately to resemble each other closely again.

But while mutual sterility is not an absolutely necessary condition in the separation of species, it would be going too far in the opposite direction to regard mutual fertility as something general, or to attribute to it a rôle in the origination of new species.

Certain botanists, like Kerner von Marilaun, regard the mingling of species as a means of forming new species with better adaptations; they suppose that fertile hybrids may, in certain circumstances, crowd out the parent species, and themselves become new species. It will be admitted that such cases do occur, that, for instance, in the north of Europe the hybrid between the large and the small water-lily, *Nuphar luteum* and *Nuphar pumilum*, to which the name *Nuphar intermedium* has been given, has driven both the parent species from the field, because its seeds mature earlier, and it is therefore better adapted to the short vegetative period of the north, but nevertheless we must maintain that the evolution of species on the whole does not take place through hybridization. Such cases are probably nothing more than rare exceptions. This is corroborated by the entire insignificance of hybridization in animals, among which species appear in the same way as they do in plants, and where the mingling of two species occurs only sporadically and in a few species, never to any very great extent.

If species are complexes of adaptations, based in each case on the given physical constitution of the parent species, then we can readily understand the fact that they are in our experience not fixed or eternal, but that they change in the course of the earth's history. The numerous fossil remains in the various strata of the earth's crust prove that this is true in a high degree, that in almost every one of the more important geological strata new species occur, and that not only species and genera, but families, orders, indeed whole classes of animals, which lived at one time, have now completely disappeared from the face of the earth. We can understand this phenomenon when we reflect that the conditions of life have also been slowly changing through the course of the earth's history, so that the old species had only the alternative of dying out, or of becoming transformed into new species.

But simple as this conclusion is, it can hardly be deduced with certainty from the occurrence and succession of the fossil species alone. For instance, we should strive in vain to recognize the cause which led one of those regularly arranged snail-species of the Steinheim lake basin to become transformed into one or two new species at a particular time, or to find the cause which moved those curious tripartite Crustaceans of primitive times, the Trilobites, which peopled the Silurian seas with such a wealth of forms, to become suddenly scarce towards the end of the Silurian period, and to disappear altogether in the succeeding period, the Devonian. The famous geologist Neumayr sought to refer this striking phenomenon to the fact that just at that time the Cephalopods, 'the most formidable and savage marauders among the invertebrate marine fauna,' gained the ascendancy, and it is quite possible that he was right in his surmise, but who is to prove it? Can we decide even in the case of animals now living whether the losses inflicted on a much persecuted species by an abundant and greedy persecutor exceed the numbers of progeny, and are therefore driving the species gradually towards extermination? Probable as such a supposition appears, it cannot be accepted as proven.

Since in many cases of the extinction of great animal-groups we cannot even prove that there was a simultaneous ascendancy of powerful enemies, other factors must be discovered to which the apparently sudden disappearance may be attributed. Many naturalists have tried to guess at internal reasons for extinction, and have adopted the theory—associated with the tendency to assume mystical principles of evolution—that species in dying out are obeying an internal necessity, as if their birth and death were predestined, as it is in the case of multicellular individuals, as if there were a *physiological death of the species* as there is of the multicellular individual.

Neumayr showed, however, that the facts of palæontology afford no support for this view. I need not repeat his arguments, but will simply refer to his clear and concise exposition of the problem. It is obvious that our theory of the extinction of species as due to external causes cannot be rejected on the ground that our knowledge of the struggle that species had to maintain for their existence in past times is even more imperfect than our knowledge of the struggle nowadays, and that we are frequently unable to judge of it at all. But the facts of geology are of value in another, quite different way. They reveal such an extraordinary dissimilarity in the duration of species, and also of the great groups of organisms, that the dissimilarity of itself is sufficient to prevent our regarding the extinction of species as regulated by *internal* causes. Certain genera of Echinoderms, such as starfish (*Astropecten*), lived in the Silurian times, and they are represented nowadays in our seas by a number of species; and in the same way the Cephalopod genus *Nautilus* has maintained itself among the living all through the enormous period from the Silurian sea to our own day. Formerly the Nautilids formed a predatory horde that peopled the seas, and, as we have seen, we may perhaps attribute to their dominance the disappearance of an order of Crustaceans, the Trilobites, which were equally abundant at that period. Now only a single species of nautilus (*Nautilus pompilius*) lives on the coral reefs of the southern seas. Similarly, the genus *Lingula* of the nearly extinct class of Brachiopods, somewhat mussel-like sessile marine animals, has been preserved from the grey dawn of primitive times, with its records in the oldest deposits, and is represented in the living world of to-day by the so-called 'barnacle-goose' mussel, *Lingula anatina*.

On the other hand, we know of numerous species which lasted for quite a short time, such as, for instance, the individual members of the series of Steinheim *Planorbis* species, or of the Slavonic *Paludina* species. Not infrequently, too, genera make their appearance and disappear again within the period of one and the same geological stratum.

These facts not only tell against an unknown vitalistic principle of evolution, but in general against the idea of the determination of the great paths of evolution by purely internal causes. If there were a principle of evolution the dissimilarity in the duration of life could not be so excessive; if there were a 'senile stage' of species and a natural death of species comparable to the natural death of individuals, it would not have been possible for most of the Nautilidæ to have been restricted to the Silurian epoch, and yet for one species to have continued to live till now; and if there were a 'tendency' of species to vary persistently onwards, and to 'become further and further removed from the primitive type,' as has been maintained, then such ancient and primitive Cephalopod forms like the *Nautilus*-species could not have persisted until now, but must long ago have been transmuted into higher forms. The converse, however, is conceivable enough, namely, that the great mass of the species of a group such as the Nautilidæ were crowded out by superior rivals in the struggle for existence, but that certain species were able to survive on specially protected or otherwise favoured areas. We have a fine example of this in the few still living species of the otherwise extinct class of Ganoid fishes. During the Primary and Secondary epochs these Ganoids peopled all the seas, but at the boundary between the Cretaceous and the Tertiary period they retrograded considerably, simultaneously with the great development of bony fishes or Teleosteans, and now they are only represented by a dozen species distributed over the earth, and most of these are purely river forms, while the others at least ascend the rivers during the spawning season to secure the safety of their progeny. For the rivers are sheltered areas as compared with the seas, and large fishes like the Ganoids will be able there to hold their own in the struggle better than they could in the incomparably more abundantly peopled sea.

Thus I can only regard it as playing with ideas to speak of birth, blossoming, standstill, decay, and death of species in any other than a figurative sense. Undoubtedly the life of the species may be compared with that of the individual, and if the comparison be used only to make clear the difference between the causes of the two kinds of phenomena, there can be no objection to it, only we must beware of thinking we have explained anything we do not know by comparing it with something else that is also unknown.

We have already shown that the natural death of multicellular organisms is a phenomenon which first made its appearance with the separation of the organism into somatic or body cells and reproductive or germ cells, and that death is not an inevitable Nemesis of every life, for unicellular organisms do not necessarily die, though they may be killed by violence. These unicellular organisms have thus no natural death, and we have to explain its occurrence among multicellular organisms as an adaptation to the cellular differentiation, which makes the unlimited continuance of the life of the whole organism unnecessary and purposeless, and even prejudicial to the continuance of the species. For the species it is enough if the germ-cells alone retain the potential immortality of the unicellulars, while, on the other hand, the high differentiation of the somatic cells necessarily involves that they should wear themselves away in the performance of their functions, and so become subject to death, or at least that they should undergo such changes that they are no longer capable of functioning properly, so that thus the organism as a whole loses the power of life.

There can be no doubt whatever that death is virtually implied in the very constitution of a multicellular organism, and is thus, so to speak, a foreseen occurrence, the inevitable end of a development which begins with the egg-cell and reaches its highest point with the liberation of the germ-cells, that is, with reproduction, and then enters on a longer or shorter period of decadence, leading to the natural death of the individual.

It is only by straining the analogy that this course of development can be compared with the origin and transformation or extinction of species. Not even the entirely external analogy of the blossoming from a small beginning and the subsequent decay is always correct: for in the fresh-water snails of Steinheim, at any rate, almost the whole of the members of the species underwent a transformation at a particular time, and became a new species, which was after a long time retransformed without any appreciable decrease in the number of individuals being observable. To speak of a 'senile stage' of the species, of a stiffening of its form, of an incapacity for further transformation, is to indulge in a play of fancy quite inadmissible in the domain of natural science.

It is admitted, however, that there is a correct idea at the base of all this, for many species have not passed over into new forms, but have simply died out because they were unable to adapt themselves to changed conditions. This did not happen because they had become incapable of variation, but because they could not produce variations of sufficient magnitude, or variations of the kind required to enable the species to remain an active competitor in the struggle for existence.

It obviously depends upon the coincidence of manifold circumstances, whether an adaptation can be successfully effected or not. Above all, it must be able to keep pace with the changes in the conditions of life, for if these advance at a more rapid rate the organisms will succumb in the midst of the attempt at adaptation. It is probably in this way that the striking disappearance of the Trilobites is to be explained, as Neumayr has pointed out, for the Nautilidæ, a new group of enemies, multiplied so quickly at their expense that they had not time to evolve any effective means of protection. It cannot be maintained for a moment that every species is able to protect itself against extermination by any other; the increased fertility, the increased rapidity of locomotion, the increased intelligence and similar qualities, may all be insufficient, and then extinction follows; not, however, because the species has become 'senile,' but because the variations possible to its organization do not suffice to maintain it in the struggle.

In discussing germinal selection I mentioned the view expressed by Emery, that excessive variation in the same direction from intra-germinal causes has not rarely been the cause of the extinction of species. I also mentioned the very similar view of Döderlein, who could not refer at that time to germinal selection, but assumed internal compelling forces, which pressed a variation irresistibly forward in the direction in which it had started, even beyond the bounds of what is useful for the desired end, and which might thus bring about the extinction of the species. I cannot entirely agree with these views, as I have already indicated, because I do not believe that the impulse to variation can ever become irresistible and uncontrollable. If it could, then we should not see, as we do, innumerable cases in which the augmentation or diminution of a part has gone on precisely to the point at which it ceases to be purposeful. Even the degeneration of organs only proceeds as far as is necessary to accomplish a particular end, as we see plainly from the parasitic Crustaceans of different orders. In many of these parasitic forms the swimming legs degenerate, but in the female only, because these attach themselves by suckers or in some other manner to their host, so that they cannot let go again. But the males need their swimming legs to seek out the females. The females too require them in their youth, in order to seek out the fish from which they are to obtain their food-supply, and thus the degeneration of the swimming legs has come to a full stop exactly at the point where they cease to be of use; they develop in early youth and degenerate later, when the animal becomes sessile. In accordance with the law of biogenesis we may say that while the degeneration is complete in the final stages of ontogeny, its retrogression was not continued back to the germ, but only to the young stages. From this it follows that the progress of a variation may at any time have a goal fixed for it, and we have seen that this is possible by means of personal selection, which accumulates the never-failing fluctuations of the variation in the direction of plus or of minus. In the individual id a determinant X may perhaps decrease and possibly also increase without limit, although we have no certain knowledge in regard to the latter point, but as this determinant is contained in all the ids, there are always plus and minus fluctuations by means of which personal selection can operate.

But of course it requires a certain amount of time for this, and in the fact that this time is often not available lies, I think, the reason why excessive differentiations have often led to the extinction of a species, not because the increase of the excessive organ must go on irresistibly, but because changes in the conditions have made the exuberant organ inappropriate, and it could not degenerate quickly enough to save the species from extinction.

Brandes has recently given a beautiful illustration of this by associating the existence of the remarkable sabre-toothed tigers (*Machairodus*) with enormously long canine teeth, which lived in the Diluvial period in South America, with the gigantic Armadillos which lived there at the same time, whose bony armature two yards in height now excites our admiration. He rightly points out that the dentition of *Machairodus neogaeus* is by no means a typically perfect dentition for a beast of prey, like that of the Indian tiger or the lion: as far as incisors and molars are concerned it was much less effective than that of these predatory animals, and the great length of the dagger-like flattened canines, which protruded far beyond the mouth, entirely prevented the bringing together of the teeth of the upper and lower jaw after the fashion of a pair of pincers. He rightly infers from this that this dentition was adapted to a specialized mode of nutrition, and he regards the great mailed Armadillos, such as the three-yards-long heavy Glyptodont of the Pampas, as the victims into which they were wont to thrust their sabre-teeth in the region of the unprotected neck, and thus to master the almost invulnerable creature, which was invincible as far as all other predatory animals were concerned. Thus the remarkable dentition is explained on the one hand, and on the other the amazing extent and hardness of the victim's coat of mail. Thus, too, we can understand why there should have been at that time a whole series of cat-like animals with sabre-like teeth, in which the length and sharpness of the teeth increased with the bodily size, for these predatory animals corresponded to a whole series of Armadillos, whose size was increasing, as was also the strength of their armour.

Of course this interpretation is hypothetical, but it contains much internal probability, so that it may be taken as a good illustration of the reciprocal increase of adaptations between two animal groups. We understand now why, on the one hand, this colossal tortoise-like armour should have developed in a mammal, and, on the other hand, why these enormously long sabre-teeth should have been evolved; we also understand—and this is the point with which we are here chiefly concerned—why these two 'excessive' developments should ultimately lead to the destruction of their possessors. For a long period the Armadillos were able to save themselves from extermination by increasing their bodily size and the strength of their armour, and they thus saved themselves from persecution on the part of beasts of prey with smaller and weaker teeth. But the predatory animals followed suit and lengthened their teeth and increased their bodily size, until ultimately even the strongest armour of the victim afforded no efficient protection, and the mighty Glyptodonts were by degrees utterly exterminated. But then the death-knell of the *Machairodus* had also sounded, for he was so exactly adapted to this one kind of diet that he could no longer overpower other victims and feed on their flesh; the sabre-teeth prevented him from tearing his prey like other predatory animals, he could probably only suck them.

Even if this is a supposititious case, it serves to show that it was not an internal principle of variation that caused the teeth of these carnivores and the armour of their victims to increase so unlimitedly; it was the necessity of adaptation. They did not perish because armour and teeth increased so excessively, but because neither of these adaptations could be neutralized all at once, and small variations were of no use to them in their final struggle for survival.

In a certain sense we may say that simpler, more lowly organisms are more capable of adaptation than those which are highly differentiated and adapted to specialized conditions in all parts of their bodies, since from the former much that is new may arise in the course of time, while very little and nothing very novel can spring from the latter. From the simplest Protozoan the whole world of unicellular organisms could arise, and also the much more diverse Metazoa; from the lower marine worms there could arise not only many kinds of higher marine worms—the segmented worms or Annelids—but also quite new groups of animals, the Arthropods and the Vertebrates. It is hardly likely that a new class of animals will evolve from our modern birds, because these are already so perfectly adapted to their aerial life that they could hardly adapt themselves to life on land or in the water sufficiently well to be able to hold their own in regard to all the possibilities of life with the rest of the dwellers on land or in water. We do indeed know of birds which have returned entirely to a purely terrestrial life—the ostriches, for instance—and of others which have adapted themselves to a purely aquatic life, such as the penguins, but these are small groups of species, and are hardly likely to increase. On the contrary, we can prove that many have already succumbed in the struggle with man, and we anticipate the extermination of others. But the reason why they are so readily exterminated obviously lies in the fact that they have surrendered the advantage given to them by their bird-nature, by adapting themselves to terrestrial life, and that they are not able to regain it, at least not in the short time that is at their disposal if they are to be saved from extermination. The best example of this is the Dodo (*Didus ineptus*). This remarkable-looking bird, of about the size of a swan, lived in flocks upon the island of Mauritius until about the end of the seventeenth century. It had small wings with short quills which were useless for flight. As it could neither escape by flight nor through the water, and could only move clumsily and awkwardly upon land with its short legs and heavy body, it was hopelessly doomed as soon as a stronger enemy made his appearance. It fell a victim to the sailors who first landed on the island and clubbed it with sticks in huge numbers. Until that event it was without doubt excellently adapted to life on that fertile island, for on a volcanic island in the middle of the ocean there were no large enemies, and it was therefore not dependent on the power of flight for safety, and could pick up abundant food from the ground. But when man suddenly appeared on the scene and began to persecute it, it was not the 'senile rigidity' of its organization that prevented it from making use of its wings again; it was the slowness of variation and consequently of selection, which is common to all species, which impelled it to extinction. The same fate will probably overtake the Kiwi of New Zealand (*Apteryx australis*) in the near future, for though it has so far escaped the arrows of the aborigines, it is not likely in its wingless condition to be able to hold out long against European guns, unless close times and preserved forests are instituted for it, as they have been for our chamois.

Even sadder from the biologist's point of view than such extermination of individual species through the vandalism and greed of our own race is the disturbance of whole societies of animals and plants by man that is going on or has been accomplished on most of the oceanic islands, and we must briefly notice these cases while we are dealing with the decadence of species. I refer to the crowding out of the usually endemic animal and plant population on such islands through cultivation. The first step in this work of 'cultivation' is always the cutting down of the forests which for thousands of years have clothed these islands as with a mantle of green, have regulated their rainfall, secured their fertility, and allowed a medley of indigenous animals, usually peculiar to the spot, to arise. We have already spoken of

St. Helena. The original and remarkable fauna and flora of this island had for the most part disappeared 200 years ago, through the cutting down of trees in the forests, and these were later wholly destroyed by the introduction of goats, which devoured all the young trees as they grew. But with the forests most of the indigenous insects and birds were doomed to destruction, so that now there is not an indigenous bird or butterfly to be found there: only a few terrestrial snails and beetles of the original fauna still survive.

But it is not only on islands that a large number of species have been decimated or entirely exterminated by deforestation, by the introduction of plants cultivated by man and of the 'weeds' associated with these, and by the importation of domesticated animals. In Central Europe not only have all the larger beasts of prey, like the bear, the lynx, and the wolf, almost completely disappeared, but the reindeer, the bison, the wild ox (Aurochs), and the elk have been exterminated as wild animals, and in North America the buffalo will soon only exist in preserved herds, if that is not already the case. Here, of course, the direct interference of the all-too-powerful enemy, man, has played the largest part in causing the disappearance of the species referred to, but the process may give us an idea of the way in which a superior animal enemy may be able gradually to exterminate a weaker species where there is no attainable or even conceivable variation which might preserve them from such a fate. Several of the mammals which I have mentioned are not yet entirely exterminated; even the Aurochs perhaps still exists in the pure white herds preserved in some British parks; but there are more instances than that of the Dodo of the utter extermination of a species through human agency within historic times. It may be doubtful whether the sea-otter (*Enhydris marina*) has not been already quite exterminated because of its precious fur, but it is quite certain that the huge sea-cow (*Rhytina stelleri*), which lived in large numbers in the Behring Straits at the end of the eighteenth and the beginning of the nineteenth centuries, was completely exterminated by sailors within a few decades.

We may therefore gain from what is going on before our eyes, so to speak, some sort of idea of the way in which the extermination of species may go on even independently of man at the present time, and how it must have gone on also in past ages of the earth's history. Migrations of species have taken place ceaselessly, although very slowly, for every species is endeavouring slowly to extend its range and to take possession of new territories, and thus the fauna and flora of any region must have changed in the course of time, new species must have settled in it from time to time, and the conditions of life must have changed, and in many cases this must have led to the extermination of species, in the same way, though not so quickly, as human interference now brings about their doom.

This is true for plants as for animals. A good example, not indeed of complete extermination, but of very considerable diminution in the numbers of individuals of a plant-species by the advent of a species of mammal, is communicated to us by Chun in regard to Kerguelen Land. A flowering plant, the Kerguelen cabbage (*Pringlea antiscorbutica*), has been greatly reduced in numbers since the thoughtless introduction of rabbits to this uninhabited island (1874). While, in 1840, Captain Ross used this plant in great quantities as a preventative against scurvy in his crew, and even carried away stores to last for months, the Valdivia Expedition in 1898 found rabbits in abundance, but the Kerguelen cabbage had been entirely exterminated at every spot accessible to these prolific and voracious rodents. It was only found growing upon perpendicular cliffs or upon the islands lying out in the fiords.

An avoidance of the threatened destruction of a species by its adaptation to the new circumstances can only be possible when the changes occur very slowly, and will therefore be more likely to be achieved in the case of physical changes in the conditions of life, such as climatic changes, a change in the mutual relations of land and sea, and so on. But it appears that even climatic changes do not evoke any variation and new adaptation as long as the species can avoid the changes by migrating. The often quoted case of Alpine and Arctic plants proves this at any rate, that those species which inhabited the plateaus and highlands of Europe did not all vary to suit the change when a warmer climate prevailed, but that in part at least they followed the climate to which they were already adapted, that is, that they migrated towards the north on the one hand and higher up the Alps on the other. It cannot be denied that many of the insects and plants did adapt themselves at that time to the warmer climate, and became the modern species which now inhabit the plains, for many related species occur on the Alps and in the plains, but apparently many others simply made their escape from a climate which no longer suited their requirements. Thus, as far as I am aware, there is no species of *Primula* in South or Central Germany which could be derived from the beautiful red *Primula farinosa* of the Alps, but this species occurs also upon the old glacier-soil at the northern base of the Alps, and in similar soil again in the north of Germany and on the meadows of Holstein.

Similar examples might be cited in regard to the Alpine-Arctic butterflies.

It is intelligible enough that we are still very far from being able to give a precise account of the main changes in the plant and animal world during the history of the earth in regard to the special causes which have produced them. Possibly the future will throw more light upon this subject by extending our knowledge of the fossil remains of all countries. But so much at least we can say at present, that there is no reason to refer the dying out of the earlier forms to anything else than the changes in the conditions of life, the struggle for existence, and the limitation of the power of transformation and adaptation due to the organization which the species has already attained; there is no trace of any such thing as a phyletic principle of life in the vitalistic sense, as far as the decadence of species is concerned.

LECTURE XXXVI

SPONTANEOUS GENERATION AND EVOLUTION: CONCLUSION

Spontaneous generation—Experimental tests impossible—Only the lowest and smallest forms of life can be referred to spontaneous generation—Chemical postulates for spontaneous generation—Empedocles modernized—The locality of spontaneous generation—Progress of organization—Direct and indirect influences causing variation—The various modes of selection—Everything depends upon selection—Sinking from heights of organization already attained—Paths of evolution—The forces effecting it—Plasticity of living matter—Predetermination of the animate world—Many-sided adaptation of each group—Aquatic mammals and insects, parasites—Nägeli's variation in a definite direction—Analogy of the traveller—Genealogical trees—The diversity of forms of life is unlimited—The origin of the purposeful apart from purposive forces working towards an end—The limits of knowledge—Limitation of the human intelligence by selection—Human genius—Conclusion.

We have now reached the end of our studies, and they have given us satisfaction, at least in so far that they have brought us certainty in regard to the chief and fundamental question which can be asked in reference to the origin of the modern animate world of organisms. There remains no doubt in our minds that the theory of descent is justified; we know, just as surely as that the earth goes round the sun, that the living world upon our earth was not created all at once and in the state in which we know it, but that it has gradually evolved through what, to our human estimate, seem enormously long periods of time. This conclusion is now firmly established and will never again become doubtful. The assumption, too, that the more lowly organisms formed the beginnings of life, and that an ascent has taken place from the lowest to the higher and highest, has become to our minds a probability verging upon certainty. But there remains one point which we have not yet touched upon—the problem of the origin of these first organisms.

There are only two possibilities: either that they have been borne to our earth from outside, from somewhere else in the universe, or that they have originated upon our earth itself through what is called 'spontaneous generation'—*generatio spontanea*.

The idea that very lowly living organisms might have been concealed within the clefts and crevices of meteorites, and might thus have fallen upon our earth and so have formed the first germs of life, was first formulated by that chemical genius, Justus Liebig. It seems certain that the state of glowing heat in which meteorites are, when they come into our atmosphere, only affects the outer crust of these cosmic fragments, and that living germs, which might be concealed in the depths of their crevices and fissures, might therefore remain alive, but nevertheless it is undoubtedly impossible that any germ should reach us alive in this way, because it could neither endure the excessive cold nor the absolute desiccation to which it would be exposed in cosmic space, which contains absolutely no water. This could not be endured even for a few days, much less for immeasurable periods of time.

But we have to take account, too, of an entirely general reason, which lies in the fact that all life is transient, that it can be annihilated, and is not merely mortal! Everything that is distinctively organic may be destroyed to the extent of becoming inorganic. Not only may the phenomena of life disappear, and the living body as such cease to be, but the organic compounds which form the physical basis of all life are ceaselessly breaking up, and they fall back by stages to the level of the inorganic. It seems to me that we must necessarily conclude from this that the basis of Liebig's idea was incorrect, that is, the assumption that 'organic substances are everlasting and have existed from the first just in the same way as inorganic substances.' This is obviously not the case, for a thing that has an end cannot be everlasting; it must have had a beginning too, and consequently organic combinations are not everlasting, but are transitory; they come and go, they arise wherever the conditions suitable for them occur, and they break up into simpler combinations when these conditions cease to be present. It is only the elements which are eternal, not their combinations, for these are subject to more or less rapid continual change, whether they have arisen outside of organisms or within them.

It seems to me that these considerations destroy the foundations of the hypothesis of the cosmic origin of life on our earth: in any case they leave the hypothesis without great significance: for if we could even admit the possibility of a transference of living organisms from space, the question would only be pushed a little further back by the assumption, and not solved, for the organisms thus brought in must have had their origin on some other planet, since they are, *ex hypothesi*, not everlasting.

Thus we are directed to our earth itself as the place of the origin of the tellurian world of life, and I see no possibility of avoiding the assumption of *spontaneous generation*. It is for me a logical necessity.

Even about the middle of the nineteenth century there was acute discussion in regard to the occurrence of spontaneous generation. In the French Academy especially Pouchet brought forward arguments in favour of it, and Pasteur against it. Pouchet observed that living organisms made their appearance in infusions of hay and other vegetable material in which any possible living germs had presumably been destroyed by prolonged boiling. Living organisms, Algæ, and Infusorians appeared, notwithstanding the fact that the glass bottles in which they were kept were hermetically sealed. But Pasteur showed that the air contains numerous living germs of lowly organisms in its so-called motes, and that, if these were first removed, Pouchet's infusion would not exhibit any signs of life. He caused the air, which was continually passed through the tubes, to stream first along the heated barrel of a gun, and so destroyed these germs, and no organisms were obtained in the infusions. He showed that the air is teeming with germs by an experiment with boiled infusions which were allowed to lie undisturbed for a considerable time in bottles with open necks, one on the roof of the Institute at Paris, the other on the top of the Puy de Dôme in Auvergne, which was at that time still the highest mountain in France. In the Parisian experiment, organisms appeared in the bottles in a very few days, while in those exposed to the pure air at the mountain-top none were seen, even after months had elapsed.

Strangely enough, these and similar experiments were at the time regarded as conclusive proof against the existence of spontaneous generation, though it is obvious enough that the first living being on this earth cannot have sprung from hay, or from any other organic substance, since that would presuppose what we are attempting to explain. After the fiery earth had so far cooled that its outermost layer had hardened to a firm crust, and after water had condensed to a liquid form, there could at first only have been inorganic substances in existence. In order to prove spontaneous generation, therefore, it would be necessary to try to find out from what mingling of inorganic combinations organisms could arise; to prove that spontaneous generation could never have been possible is out of the question.

It would be impossible to prove by experiment that spontaneous generation could *never* have taken place; because each negative experiment would only prove that life does not arise *under the conditions of the experiment*. But this by no means excludes the possibility that it might arise under other conditions.

Up till now all attempts to discover these conditions have been futile, and I do not believe that they will ever be successful, not because the conditions must be so peculiar in nature that we cannot reproduce them, but, above all, because we should not be able to perceive the results of a successful experiment. I shall be able to prove this convincingly without difficulty.

If we ask ourselves the question how the living beings which might have arisen through spontaneous generation must be constituted, and on the other hand, in regard to what kinds of living forms we can maintain with certainty that they *could not* have arisen thus, it is obvious that we must place on the latter list all organisms which presuppose the existence of others, from which they have been derived. But to this category belong all the organisms which possess a germ-plasm, an idioplasm that we conceive of as composed of primary constituents (*Anlagen*) which have gradually been evolved and accumulated through a long series of ancestors. Thus not only all multicellular animals and plants which reproduce by means of germ-cells, buds, and so forth, but also all unicellular organisms, must be placed in this class. For these last—as we have seen—possess in their nucleus a substance made up of primary constituents, without which the mutilated body is unable to make good its loss, in short, an idioplasm. That this plays the same rôle in unicellular as in multicellular organisms we can infer with the greatest certainty from the process of amphimixis, which runs its course in an analogous way in both cases.

Thus, even though we did not know what Ehrenberg demonstrated in the third decade of last century, that Infusorians in an encapsuled state can be blown about everywhere, and can even be carried across the ocean in the dust of the trade-winds, to re-awaken to life wherever they fall into fresh water, we should still not have remained at the standpoint of Leuwenhoek, who regarded Infusorians as having arisen through spontaneous generation. They cannot arise in this way, nor can they have done so at any time, because they contain a substance made up of primary constituents, which can only be of historic origin, and cannot therefore have arisen suddenly after the manner of a chemical combination.

The same is true of all the unicellular organisms, even of those which are much more simple in structure than the Infusorians, whose differentiation into cortical and medullary substances, oral and anal openings, complex arrangements of cilia and much else, betokens a high degree of differentiation in the cell. But even the Amœba is only apparently simple, for otherwise it could not send out processes and retract them again, creep in a particular direction, encyst itself, and so on, for all this presupposes a differentiation of its particles in different directions, and a definite arrangement of them; and there is in addition the marvellous dividing-apparatus of the nucleus which is not wanting even in the Amœba. All this again points to a historic evolution, a gradual acquiring and an orderly arrangement of differentiations, and such an organism cannot have arisen suddenly like a crystal or a chemical combination.

Thus we are driven back to the lowest known organisms, and the question now before us is whether these smallest living organisms, which are only visible under the highest powers of the microscope, may be referred to spontaneous generation. But here too the answer is, No; for although there is no nucleus to be found, and no substance which we can affirm with any certainty to be composed of primary constituents or idioplasm, we do find distinct traces of a previous history, and not the absolutely simple structure of homogeneous living particles, unarranged in any orderly way, which is all that could be derived from spontaneous generation. It has been shown quite recently that the typhus bacillus possesses an extremely delicate much-branched tuft of flagella, which gives it a tremulous motion, and in the cholera bacillus cortical and medullary substances can be distinguished. Thus even here there is differentiation according to the principle of division of labour, and how numerous must be the minute vital particles of which a substance consists when it can form such fine threads as the flagella just mentioned! Nägeli, who elaborated an analogous train of thought in regard to spontaneous generation, calculated the number of these smallest vital particles (his 'micellæ') which must be contained in a 'moneron' of 0·6 mm. diameter, if we take its dry substance at 10 per cent., and he arrived at the amazing figure of 100 billions of vital particles. Even if we suppose the diameter of such an organism to be 0·0006 mm., it would still be composed, according to this calculation, of a million of these vital particles.

We have reached, in the course of these lectures, the conviction that minute living units form the basis of all organisms, namely, our 'life-bearers' or 'biophors.' These must be present in countless multitudes, and in a great number of varieties in the different forms of life, but all agree in this, that they are simple, that is, they are not composed in their turn of living particles, but only of molecules, whose chemical constitution, combination, and arrangement are such as to give rise to the phenomena of life. But they may vary, and on this power depends the possibility of their differentiation, which has taken place in more and more diverse ways in the course of phylogeny. They, too, arise in the existing organism, like all vital units, only by multiplication of the biophors already present, but they do not necessarily presuppose a historic origin; it is conceivable of them, at least as far as their first and simplest forms are concerned, that they may have arisen some time or other through spontaneous generation. In regard to them alone is the possibility of origin through purely chemico-physical causes, without the co-operation of life already existing, admissible. It is only in regard to them that spontaneous generation is not inconceivable.

We must, therefore, assume that, at some time or other in the history of the earth, the conditions necessary to the development of these invisible little living particles must have existed, and that the whole subsequent development of the organic world must have depended upon an aggregation of these biophors into larger complexes, and upon their differentiation within these complexes.

We shall never be able, then, directly to observe spontaneous generation, for the simple reason that the smallest and lowest living particles which could arise through it, the Biophoridæ, are so extremely far below the limits of visibility, that there is no hope of our ever being able to perceive them, even if we should succeed in producing them by spontaneous generation.

I do not propose to discuss the chemical problem raised by the possible occurrence of spontaneous generation. We have already seen that dead protoplasm, in addition to water, salts, phosphorus, sulphur, and some other elements, chiefly and invariably contains albumen; an albuminoid substance must, therefore, have arisen from inorganic combinations. No one will maintain that this is impossible, for we continually see albuminoid substances produced in plants from inorganic substances, compounds of carbon and nitrogen; but under what conditions this would be possible in free nature, that is, outside of organisms, cannot as yet be determined. Possibly we may some time succeed in procuring albumen from inorganic substances in the laboratory, and if that happens the theory of spontaneous generation will rest upon a firmer basis, but it will not have been experimentally proved even then. For while dead albumen is certainly nearly allied to living matter, it is precisely *life* that it lacks, and as yet we do not know what kinds of chemical difference prevail between the dead proteid and the living; indeed we must honestly confess that it is a mere assumption when we take for granted that there are only chemico-physical differences between the two. It cannot be proved, in the meantime, that there is not another unknown power in the living protoplasm, a 'vitalistic principle,' a 'life-force,' on the activity of which these specific phenomena of life, and particularly the continually repeated alternation of disruption and reconstruction of the living substance, dissimilation and assimilation, growth and multiplication, depend. It is just as difficult to prove the converse, that it is impossible that chemico-physical forces alone should have called forth life in a chemical substance of very special composition. Although no one has ever succeeded, in spite of many attempts, in thinking out a combination of chemical substances which—as this wonderful living substance does—on the one hand undergoes combustion with oxygen and, on the other hand, renews itself again with 'nutritive' material, yet we cannot infer from this the impossibility of a purely chemico-physical basis of life, but must rather hold fast to it until it is shown that it is not sufficient to explain the facts, thus following the fundamental rule that natural science must not assume unknown forces until the known ones are *proved* insufficient. If we were to do otherwise we should have to renounce all hope of ever penetrating deeper into the phenomena. And we have no need to do this, for in a general way we can quite well believe that an organic substance of exactly proportioned composition exists, in which the fundamental phenomena of all life—combustion with simultaneous renewal—must take place under certain conditions by virtue of its composition.

How, and under what external conditions, such a substance first arose upon the earth, from and of what materials it was formed, cannot be answered with any certainty in the meantime. Who knows whether the fantastic ideas of Empedocles in an altered form would not be justified here? I mean that, at the time of the first origin of life, the conditions necessary for many kinds of complex chemical combinations may have been present simultaneously on the earth, and that, out of a manifold variety of such substances, only those survived which possessed that marvellous composition which conditioned their continual combustion, but also their ceaseless reconstruction by multiplication. According to Empedocles, there arose from chaos only parts of animals—heads without bodies, arms without trunks, eyes without faces, and so on—and these whirled about in wild confusion and flew together as chance directed them. But those only survived which had united rightly with others so as to form a whole, capable of life. Translated into the language of our time, that would mean what I have just said—that, of a large number of organic combinations which arose, only a few, perhaps one, would possess the marvellously adjusted composition which resulted in life, and with it self-maintenance and multiplication; and that would be the first instance of selection!

But let us leave these imaginings, and wait to see whether the chemists will not possibly be able to furnish us with a starting-point for a more concrete picture of the first origin of life. In the meantime, we must confess that we find ourselves confronted with deep darkness.

The question as to the 'Where' of spontaneous generation must also be left without any definite answer. Some have supposed that life began in the depths of the sea, others on the shore, and others in the air. But who is to divine this, when we cannot even name theoretically the conditions and the materials out of which albuminoid-like substances might be built up in the laboratory? Nägeli's hypothesis still seems to me to have the greatest probability. According to his theory, the first living particles originated not in a free mass of water, but in the reticulated superficial layer of a fine porous substance (clay or sand), where the molecular forces of solid, fluid, and gaseous bodies were able to co-operate.

Only so much is certain, that wherever life may first have arisen upon this earth, it can have done so only in the form of the very simple and very minute vital units, which even now we only infer to be parts of the living body, but which must first have arisen as independent organisms, the 'Biophoridæ.' As these, according to our theory, possessed the character of life, they must have possessed above all the capacity of assimilating in the sense in which the plants assimilate, that is, of renewing their bodily substance continually from inorganic substances, of growing, and of reproducing. They need not on that account have possessed the chemical constitution of chlorophyll, although the capacity of assimilation in green plants depends upon this substance, for we know colourless fungi, which, notwithstanding the absence of chlorophyll, are able to build up the substance of their body from compounds of carbon and nitrogen.

The first advance to a higher stage of life must have been brought about by multiplication, since accumulations of Biophoridæ, unintegrated but connected masses, would be formed.

In this way the threshold of microscopical visibility would gradually be reached and crossed, but--to argue from the modern Baccilli--long before that time a differentiation of the biophors on the principle of division of labour would have taken place within a colony of Biophoridæ. This first step towards higher organization must probably have taken enormous periods of time, for before any differentiation could occur and bring any advantage the unintegrated aggregates of Biophors must first have become orderly, and have formed themselves into a stable association with definite form and definite structure, somewhat analogous to the spherical cell-colonies of *Magosphæra* or *Pandorina*. Only then was the further step made of a differentiation of the individual biophors forming the colony, and this is comparable to the species of *Volvox* among the lower Algæ. The gradual ascent of these colonies of biophors must, then, be referred to the principles to which we attribute the ascent of the higher forms of life to ever-higher and ever-new differentiations; the principles of division of labour and selection.

These differentiated colonies of biophors have brought us nearer to the lowest known organisms, among which there are some whose existence we can only infer from their pathological effects, since we have not been able to make them visible. The bacillus of measles has never yet been seen, but we cannot doubt its existence, and we must assume that there are bacilli of such exceeding smallness that we shall never be able to see them, even with the most improved methods of staining and the strongest lenses.

These non-nucleated Monera lead on to the stage of nucleus-formation, and this at once implies the cell. As, on our view, the nucleus is primarily a storehouse of 'primary constituents' (*Anlagen*), its origin must have begun at the moment at which the differentiation of the cell-body reached such a degree of differentiation of its parts that a mechanical division into two halves was no longer possible, and that the two products of division, if they were each to develop to a new and intact whole, required a reserve of primordia (*Anlagen*) to give rise to the missing parts. As this higher differentiation would bring about a superiority over the lower forms of life, in that they would make possible the utilization of new conditions of life, but on the other hand could only survive if the differentiation of a reserve of primary constituents, that is, a nucleus, were introduced at the same time, the development of the nucleus can be ranged under the principle of utility to which we traced back the evolution of all higher and more differentiated forms of life. But it would scarcely be profitable to try to follow out in detail the first steps in the progress of organization under the control of selective processes, since we know far too little about the life of the simplest organisms to be able to judge how far their differentiations are of use in improving their capacity for life.

That would be a bold undertaking even in regard to unicellular organisms, and it is only in the case of multicellular organisms that we can speak with greater certainty and really recognize the changing of the external conditions, in the most general and comprehensive sense, as the fundamental cause of the lasting variations of organic forms. We can here distinguish with certainty between the direct and the indirect effect of external influences, and we see how these sources of variation interact upon each other. The lowest and deepest root of variation is without doubt the direct effect of changed conditions. Without this the indirect effect would have had no lever with which to work, for the primitive beginnings of variation would be absent, and an accumulation of theso through personal selection could not take place. It is a primitive character of living substance to be variable, that is, to be able to respond to some extent to changed external conditions, and to vary in accordance with them, or—as we might also say—to be able to exist in many very similar but not identical combinations of substances, and we must imagine that even the first biophors which arose through spontaneous generation were different according to the conditions under which, and the substances from which, they originated. And from each of these slightly different beginnings there must, in the course of multiplication by fission, have been produced a whole genealogical tree of divergent variations of the primitive Biophoridæ, since it is inconceivable that all the descendants would remain constantly under the same conditions of life under which they originated. For every persistent change in the conditions of existence, and especially of nutrition, must have involved a variation in the constitution of the organism, whose vital processes, and especially the repair of its body, depended on these conditions.

But the external influences to which the descendants of a particular form of life were subject never remained permanently the same. Not only did the surface of the earth and its climatic conditions change in the course of time with the cooling of the earth, but mountains arose and were levelled again, old land-surfaces sank out of sight or emerged again, and so on; all that, of course, played its part in the transformation of the forms of life, but did so to any considerable extent only at a later stage, when there were already highly differentiated organisms. These unknown primitive beginnings of life must have been forced to diverge into different variations through the different conditions of the same place in which they lived.

Let us think of the simplest microscopic Monera on the mud of the sea-coast, equipped with the faculty of plant-like assimilation, and we shall see that their unlimited multiplication would cause differences in nutrition, for those lying uppermost would be in a stronger light than those below, and would, therefore, be better nourished, and, consequently, would transmit the variations thus induced to their progeny which arose by fission. Thus it is conceivable that even the more or less favourable position as regards light would bring about the origin of two different races from the same parent form, and as it is conceivable in the case of light, so is it also in regard to all the influences which cause variation in the organism.

We have already seen that variations in the lowest (non-nucleated) forms of life caused by the direct influence of the vital processes may be directly transmitted to the descendants, but that in all those whose bodies have already differentiated into a germ- or idioplasmic-substance, in contrast to a somatic substance in the more restricted sense, this hereditary transmission is only possible in the case of the variations of the germ-plasm, and *hereditary* variations of the species can only arise by the circuitous route of influencing the germ-plasm. The body (soma) can be caused to change by external influences, by the use or disuse of an organ, but variations of this kind are not transmitted; they do not become a lasting possession of the species, but cease with the individual; they are transient changes.

Thus it was only through those external influences—including those from the soma of the organism itself—which affected the germ-substance, either as a whole or in certain of its primary constituents, that hereditarily transmissible variations of the organism arose, and we have already discussed in detail how particular variational tendencies may arise through the struggle of the parts within the germ-plasm, which may give an advantage to certain groups of primary constituents. And these tendencies are of themselves sufficient to cause the specific type to vary further and further in given directions.

Nevertheless, the infinite diversity of the forms of life could never have been brought about in this way alone, if there had not been another—the *indirect*—effect of the changeful external influences.

This is due to the fact that the variations of direct origin sooner or later obtain an influence in determining the viability of their possessors, either increasing or diminishing it. It is this, in association with the unlimited multiplication of individuals, which gives a basis to the principle of transformation, which it is the immortal merit of Charles Darwin and Alfred Russel Wallace to have introduced into science: *the principle of selection*. We have seen that this principle may have a much more comprehensive meaning than was attributed to it by either of these two naturalists; that there is not merely a struggle between individuals which brings about their adaptation to their environment, by preserving those which vary in the most favourable way and rejecting those which vary unfavourably, but that there is an analogous struggle between the parts of these individuals, which, as Wilhelm Roux showed, effects the adaptation of the parts to their functions, and that this struggle must be assumed to occur even between the determinants and biophors of the germ-plasm. There is thus a germinal selection, a competition between the smaller and larger particles of the germ-plasm for space and food, and that it is through this struggle that there arise those definitely and purposefully directed variations of the individual, which are transmissible because they have their seat in the immortal germ-plasm, and without which an adaptation of individuals in the sense and to the extent in which we actually observe it would be altogether inconceivable. I have endeavoured to show that the whole evolution of the living world is guided essentially by processes of selection, in as far as adaptations of the parts to one another, and of the whole to the conditions of life, cannot be conceived of as possible except through these, and that all fluctuations of the organism, from the very lowest up to the highest, are forced into particular paths by this principle, by 'the survival of the fittest.' This ends the whole dispute as to whether there are indifferent 'characters' which have no influence on the existence of the species, for even the characters most indifferent for the 'person' would not exist unless the germinal constituents (determinants) which condition them had been victorious in the struggle for existence over others of their kind, and even the 'indifferent' characters, which depend solely upon climatic or other external influences, owe their existence to processes of germinal selection, for those elements of the determinants concerned were victorious which throve best under such influences. But should variations thus produced by external influence increase so far that they become prejudicial to the survival of their bearers, then they are either set aside by personal selection or, if that be no longer possible, they lead to the extinction of the species. Thus the multitude of small individual variations, which probably occur in every species, but which strike us most in Man—the differences in the development of mouth, nose, and eyes, in the hair, in the colour of skin, &c., as far as they are without significance in the struggle for existence—depend upon processes of germinal selection, which permitted the greater development of one group of determinants, or of one kind of biophor in one case, of another in another. The proportionate strength of the elements of the germ-plasm is not readily lost at once, but is handed on to successive generations, and thus even these 'indifferent' characters are transmitted.

It is obvious that, if the principle of selection operates in nature at all, it must do so wherever living units struggle together for the same requirements of life, for space and food, and these units need not be persons, but may represent every category of vital units, from the smallest invisible units up to the largest. For in all these cases the conditions of the selection-process are given: individual variability, nutrition, and multiplication, transmission of the advantage attained, and, on the other hand, limitation of the conditions of existence—especially food and space. The resulting struggle for existence must, in every category of vital units, be most acute between the individual members of each category, as Darwin emphasized in the case of species from the very first, and persistent variations of a species of living units can only be brought about by this kind of struggle. Strictly speaking, therefore, we should distinguish as many kinds of selection-processes as there are categories of living units, and these could not be sharply separated from one another, apart from the fact that we have to infer many of them, and cannot recognize their gradations. Here, as everywhere else, we must break up the continuity of nature into artificial groups, and it seems best to assume and distinguish between four main grades of selective processes corresponding to the most outstanding and significant categories of vital units, namely: Germinal, Histonal, Personal, and Cormal Selection.

Histonal Selection includes all the processes of selection which take place between the elements of the body (soma), as distinguished from the germ-plasm, of the Metazoa and Metaphyta, not only between the 'tissues' in the stricter sense, but also between the parts of the tissues, that is, the lower vital units of which they are composed, and which Wilhelm Roux, when he published his *Kampf der Teile* ('Struggle of the Parts'), called 'molecules.' It occurs between all the parts of the tissues down to the lowest vital units, the biophors. We must also reckon under histonal selection the processes of selection which take place between the elements of the simplest organisms, and through which these have gradually attained to greater complexity of structure and increased functional capacity. As long as no special hereditary substance had been differentiated, variations which arose in the simplest organisms through selection-processes of this kind were necessarily transmitted to the descendants, but after this differentiation had taken place this could no longer occur—'acquired' modifications of the soma were no longer transmitted, and the importance of histonal selection was limited to the individual. But this form of selection must be of the greatest importance in regard to the adaptations of the parts which develop from the ovum, especially during the course of development, and it is also indispensable all through life in maintaining the equilibrium of the parts, and their adaptation to the varying degree of function required from them (use and disuse). But its influence does not reach directly beyond the life of the individual, since it can only give rise to 'transient' modifications, that is, to changes which cease with the individual life.

In contrast to this is Germinal Selection, which depends upon the struggle of the parts of the germ-plasm, and thus only occurs in organisms with differentiation of somatoplasm and germ-plasm, especially in all Metazoa and Metaphyta — forming in these the basis of all hereditary variations. But not every individual variation to which germinal selection gives rise persists and spreads gradually over the whole species, for, apart from the cases we have already mentioned, in which indifferent variations favoured by external circumstances gain the victory, this happens only if the variations in question are of use to their bearer, the individual. Any variation whatever may arise in a particular individual purely through germinal selection, but it is only the higher form of selection—Personal Selection—that decides whether the variation is to persist and to spread to many descendants so that it ultimately becomes the common property of the species. Germinal and personal selection are thus continually interacting, so that germinal selection continually presents hereditary variations, and personal selection rejects those that are detrimental and accepts those that are useful. I will not repeat any exposition of the marvellous way in which personal selection reacts upon germinal selection, and prevents it from continuing to offer unfavourable variations, and compels it to give rise to what is favourable in ever-increasing potency. Although it apparently selects only the best-adapted *persons* for breeding, it really selects the favourable id-combinations of the germ-plasm, that is, those which contain the greatest number of favourably varying determinants. We saw that this depends upon the multiplicity of ids in the germ-plasm, since every primary constituent of the body is represented in the germ-plasm, not once only, but many times, and it is always half of the homologous determinants contained in the germ-plasm of an individual which reach each of its germ-cells, always, moreover, in a different combination. Thus, with the rejection of an individual by personal selection, a particular combination of ids, a particular kind of germ-plasm is in reality removed, and thus prevented from having any further influence upon the evolution of the species. By this means germinal selection itself is ultimately influenced, because only those ids remain unrejected in the germ-plasm whose determinants are varying in directions useful to the species. Thus there comes about what until recently was believed to be impossible: the conditions of life give rise to useful directions of variation, not directly, certainly, but indirectly.

We may distinguish as a fourth grade of selection Cormal Selection, that is, the process of selection which effects the adaptation of animal and plant stocks or corms, and which depends on the struggle of the colonies among themselves. This differs from personal selection only in that it decides, not the fitness of the individual person, but that of the stock as a whole. It is a matter of indifference whether the stocks concerned are stocks in the actual material sense, or only in the metaphorical sense of sharing the common life of a large family separated by division of labour. In both cases, in the polyp-stock as well as in the termite or ant-colony, the collective germ-plasm, with all its different personal forms, is what is rejected or accepted. The distinction between this cormal selection and personal selection is, therefore, no very deep one, because here too it is in the long run the two sexual animals which are selected, not indeed only in reference to their visible features, but also in reference to their invisible characters, those, namely, which determine in their germ-plasm the constitution of their neuter progeny or, in the case of polyps, their asexually reproducing descendants.

We venture to maintain that everything in the world of organisms that has permanence and significance depends upon adaptation, and has arisen through a sifting of the variations which presented themselves, that is, through selection. Everything is adaptation, from the smallest and simplest up to the largest and most complex, for if it were not it could not endure, but would perish. The principle which Empedocles announced, in his own peculiar and fantastic way, is the dominating one, and I must insist upon what has so often been objected to as an exaggeration—that everything depends upon adaptation and is governed by processes of selection. From the first beginnings of life, up to its highest point, only what is purposeful has arisen, because the living units at every grade are continually being sifted according to their utility, and the ceaseless struggle for existence is continually producing and favouring the fittest. Upon this depends not only the infinite diversity of the forms of life, but also, and chiefly, the closely associated progress of organization.

It cannot be proved in regard to each individual case, but it can be shown in the main that attaining a higher stage in organization also implies a predominance in the struggle for existence, because it opens up new possibilities of life, adaptations to situations not previously utilizable, sources of food, or places of refuge. Thus a number of the lower vertebrates ascended from the water to the land, and adapted themselves to life on dry land or in the air, first as clumsily moving salamanders, but later as actively leaping frogs; thus, too, other descendants of the fishes gained a sufficient carrying power of limbs to raise the lightened body from the ground, and so attained to the rapid walk of the lizards, the lightning-like leaps of the arboreal agamas, the brief swooping of the flying-dragons, and ultimately the continuous flight which we find in the flying Saurians and the primitive birds of the Jurassic period, and in the birds and bats of our own day.

It is obvious that each of these groups, as it originated, conquered a new domain of life, and in many cases this was such a vast one, and contained so many special possibilities, that numerous subordinate adaptations took place, and the group broke up into many species and genera, even into families and orders. All this did not come about because of some definitely directed principle of evolution of a mysterious nature, which impelled them to vary in this direction and in no other, but solely through the rivalry of all the forms of life and living units, with their enormous and ceaseless multiplication, in the struggle for existence. They were, and they are still, forced to adapt themselves to every new possibility of life attainable to them; they are able to do this because of the power of the lowest vital units of the germ to develop numerous variations; and they are obliged to do it because, of the endless number of descendants from every grade of vital unit, it is only the fittest which survive.

Thus higher types branched off from the lower from time to time, although the parent type did not necessarily disappear; indeed it could not have disappeared as long as the conditions of its life endured; it was only the superfluous members of the parent form that adapted themselves to new conditions, and as, in many cases, these required a higher organization, there arose a semblance of general upward development which simulated a principle of evolution always upwards. But we know that, at many points on this long road, there were stations where individual groups stopped short and dropped back again to lower stages of organization. This kind of retreat was almost invariably caused by a parasitic habit of life, and in many cases this degeneration has gone so far that it is difficult to recognize the relationship of the parasite to the free-living ancestors and nearest relatives. Many parasitic Crustaceans, such as the Rhizocephalids, lack almost all the typical characteristics of the crustacean body, and dispense not only with segmentation, with head and limbs, but also with stomach and intestine. As we have seen, they feed like the lower fungi, by sucking up the juices of their hosts, by means of root-like outgrowths from the place where the mouth used to be. Nevertheless, their relationship to the Cirrhipedes can be proved from their larval stages. There are, however, parasites in the kidneys of cuttlefish—the Dicyemidæ—in regard to which naturalists are even now undecided whether they ought to form a lowly class by themselves between unicellular animals and Metazoa, or whether they have degenerated, by reason of their parasitism, from the flat worms to a simplicity of structure elsewhere unknown. They consist only of a few external cells, which enclose a single large internal cell, possess no organs of any kind, neither mouth nor intestine, neither nervous system nor special reproductive organs. But although degeneration cannot be proved in this case, it can be in hundreds of other cases with absolute certainty, as, for instance, in the Crustacea belonging to the order of Copepods, which are parasitic upon fishes, in which we find all possible stages of degeneration, according to the degree of parasitism, that is, to the greater or less degree of dependence upon the host; for organs degenerate and disappear in exact proportion to the need for them, and they thus show us that degeneration also is under the domination of adaptation.

Thus retrogressive evolution also is based upon the power of the living units to respond to changing influences by variation, and upon the survival of the fittest.

The roots of all the transformations of organisms, then, lie in changes of external conditions. Let us suppose for a moment that these might have remained absolutely alike from the epoch of spontaneous generation onwards, then no variation of any kind and no evolution would have taken place. But as this is inconceivable, since even the mere growth of the first living substance must have exposed the different kinds of biophors composing it to different influences, variation was inevitable, and so also was its result—the evolution of an animate world of organisms.

External influences had a twofold effect at every stage upon every grade of vital unit, namely, that of directly causing variation and that of selecting or eliminating. Not only the biophors, but every stage of their combinations, the histological elements, chlorophyll bodies, muscle-disks, cells, organs, individuals, and colonies, can not only be caused to vary by the external influences to which they are subjected, but can be guided by these along particular paths of variation, so that among the variations which crop up some are better adapted to the conditions than others, and these thrive better, and thus alone form the basis of further evolution. In this way definite tendencies of evolution are produced, which do not move blindly and rigidly onwards like a locomotive which is bound once for all to the railroad, but rather in exact response to the external conditions, like an untrammelled pedestrian who makes his way, over hill and dale, wherever it suits him best.

The ultimate forces operative in bringing about this many-sided evolution are the known—and although we do not recognize it as yet, perhaps the unknown—chemico-physical forces which certainly work only according to laws; and that they are able to accomplish such marvellous results is due to the fact that they are associated in peculiar and often very complex different kinds of combinations, and thus conform to the same sort of regulated arrangements as those which condition the operations of any machine made by man. All complex effects depend upon a co-operation of forces. This is seen, to begin with, in the chemical combinations whose characters depend entirely upon the number and arrangement of the elementary substances of which they consist; the atoms of carbon, hydrogen, and oxygen, which compose sugar, can also combine to form carbonic acid gas and water, or alcohol and carbonic acid gas; and the same thing is true if we ascend from the most complex but still inanimate organic molecules to those chemical combinations which, in a still higher form, condition the phenomena of life, to the lowest living units, the biophors. Not only do these last differ in having life, but they themselves may appear in numerous combinations, and can combine among themselves to form higher units, whose characters and effectiveness will depend upon these combinations. Just as man may adjust various metallic structures, such as wheels, plates, cylinders, and mainsprings in the combination which we call a watch, and which measures time for us, so the biophors of different kinds in the living body may form combinations of a second, third, &c., degree, which perform the different functions essential to life, and by virtue of their specific, definite combination of elementary forces.

But if it be asked, what replaces human intelligence in these purposeful combinations of primary forces, we can only answer that there is here a self-regulation depending upon the characters of the primary vital parts, and this means that these last are caused to vary by external influences and are selected by external influences, that is, are chosen for survival or excluded from it Thus combinations of living units must always result which are appropriate to the situation at the moment, for no others can survive, although, as we have seen, they must arise. This is our view of the causes of the evolution of the world of organisms; the living substance may be compared to a plastic mass which is poured out over a wide plain, and in its ceaseless flowing adapts itself to every unevenness, flows into every hole, covers every stone or post, leaving an exact model of it, and all this simply by virtue of its constitution, which is at first fluid and then becomes solid, and of the form of the surface over which it flows.

But it is not merely the surface in our analogy which determines the form of the organic world; we must take account not only of the external conditions of existence, but also of the constitution of the flowing mass, the living substance itself, at every stage of its evolution. The combination of living units which forms the organism is different at each stage, and it is upon this that its further evolution depends; this difference determines what its further evolution *may* be, but the conditions of life determine what it *must* be in a particular case. Thus, in a certain sense, it was with the first biophors, originating through spontaneous generation, that the whole of the organic world was determined, for their origin involved not only the physical constitution by which the variations of the organism were limited, but also the external conditions, with their changes up till now, to which organisms had to adapt themselves. There can be no doubt that on another planet with other conditions of life other organisms would have arisen, and would have succeeded each other in diverse series. On the planet Mars, for instance, with its entirely different conditions as regards the proportions in weight and volume of the chemical elements and their combinations, living substance, if it could arise at all, would occur in a different chemical composition, and thus be equipped with different characters, and without doubt also with quite different possibilities of further development and transformation. The highly evolved world of organisms which we may suppose to exist upon Mars, chiefly on the ground of the presence of the remarkable straight canals discovered by Schiaparelli, must therefore be thought of as very different from the terrestrial living world.

But upon the earth things could not have been very different from what they actually are, even if we allow a good deal to chance and assume that the form of seas and continents might have been quite different, the folding of the surface into mountains and valleys, and the formation of rents and fissures, with the volcanoes that burst from them, need not have turned out exactly as it has done. In that case many species would never have arisen, but others would have taken their place; on the whole, the same types of species-groups would have succeeded each other in the history of the earth. Let us suppose that the Sandwich Islands, like many other submarine volcanoes, had never risen above the surface of the sea, then the endemic species of snails, birds, and plants which now live there could not have arisen, and if the volcanic group of the Galapagos Islands had arisen from the sea not in their actual situation, but forty degrees further south or north, or 1,000 kilometres further west, then it would have received other colonists, and probably fewer of them, and a different company of endemic species would be found there now. But there would be terrestrial snails and land-birds none the less, and on the whole we may say that both the extinct and the living groups of organisms would have arisen even with different formations of land and sea, of heights and depths, of climatic changes, of elevations and depressions of the earth's crust, at least in so far as they are adaptations to the more general conditions of life and not to specialized ones. The great adaptation to swimming in the sea, for instance, must have taken place in any case; swimming worms, swimming polyps (Medusæ), swimming vertebrates would have arisen; terrestrial animals would have evolved also, on the one hand from an ancestry of worms in the form of jointed animals and land or freshwater worms, and again from an ancestry of fishes. Aerial animals would also undoubtedly have evolved even if the lands had been quite differently formed and bounded, and I know of no reason why the adaptation to flight should not have been attempted in as many different ways as it has actually been by so many different groups—the insects, the reptiles (the flying Saurians of the Jurassic period), the extinct *Archæopteryx*, the birds, and the bats among mammals.

We can trace plainly in every group the attempt not only to spread itself out as far as possible over as much of the surface of the earth as is accessible to it, but also to adapt itself to all possible conditions of life, as far as the capacity for adaptation suffices. This is very obvious from the fact that such varied groups have striven to rise from life on the earth to life in the air, and have succeeded more or less perfectly, and we can see the same thing in all manner of groups. Almost everywhere we find species and groups of species which emancipate themselves from the general conditions of life in their class, and adapt themselves to very different conditions, to which the structure of the class as a whole does not seem in the least suited. Thus the mammals are lung-breathers, and their extremities are obviously adapted for locomotion on the solid earth, yet several groups have returned to aquatic life, as, for instance, the family of otters and the orders of seals and whales. Thus among insects which are adapted for direct air-breathing, certain families and stages of development have returned to aquatic life, and have developed breathing-tubes by means of which they can suck in air from the surface of the water into their tracheal system, or so-called tracheal gills, into which the air from the water diffuses. But the most convincing proof of the organism's power of adaptation is to be found in the fact that the possibility of living parasitically within other animals is taken advantage of in the fullest manner, and by the most diverse groups, and that their bodies exhibit the most marvellous and far-reaching adaptations to the special conditions prevailing within the bodies of other animals. We have already referred to the high degree reached by these adaptive changes, how the parasite may depart entirely from the type of its family or order, so that its relationship is difficult to recognize. Not only have numerous species of flat worms and round worms done this, but we find numerous parasites among the great class of Crustaceans; there are some among spiders, insects, medusoids, and snails, and there are even isolated cases among fishes.

If we consider the number of obstacles that have to be overcome in existence within other animals, and how difficult and how much a matter of chance it must be even to reach to such a place as, for instance, the intestine, the liver, the lungs, or even the brain or the blood of another animal, and when, on the other hand, we know how exactly things are now regulated for every parasitic species so that its existence is secured notwithstanding its dependence upon chance, we must undoubtedly form a high estimate of the plasticity of the forms of life and their adaptability. And this impression will only be strengthened when we remember that the majority of internal parasites do not pass directly from one host to another, but do so only through their descendants, and that these descendants, too, must undergo the most far-reaching and often unexpected adaptations in relation to their distribution, their penetration into a new host, and their migrations and change of form within it, if the existence of the species is to be secured.

We are tempted to study these relations more closely; but it is now time to sum up, and we must no longer lose ourselves in wealth of detail. Moreover, the life-history of many parasites, and of the tape-worm in particular, is widely known, and any one can easily fill up the story, of which we have given a mere outline. I simply wish to point out that in parasitic animals there is a vast range of forms of life in which the most precise adaptation to the conditions occurs in almost every organ, and certainly at every stage of life, in the most conspicuous and distinct manner. In the earlier part of these lectures we gained from the study of the diverse protective means by which plants and animals secure their existence the impression that whatever is suited to its end (*Das Zweckmässige*) does not depend upon chance for its origin, but that every adaptation which lies at all within the possibilities of a species will arise if there is any occasion for it. This impression is notably strengthened when we think of the life-history of parasites, and we shall find that our view of adaptations as arising, not through the selection of indefinite variations, but through that of variations in a definite direction, will be confirmed. Adaptations so diverse, and succeeding one another in such an unfailing order as those in the life-history of a tape-worm, a liver-fluke, or a *Sacculina*, cannot possibly depend upon pure chance.

Nevertheless, chance does play a part in adaptations and species-transformations, and that not only in relation to the fundamental processes within the germ-plasm, but also in connexion with the higher stages of the processes of selection, as I have already briefly indicated. After the publication of my hypothesis of germinal selection it was triumphantly pointed out that I had at last been obliged to admit a phyletic evolutionary force, the 'definitely directed' variation of Nägeli and Askenazy. This reproach—if to allow oneself to be convinced be a reproach—is based upon a serious misunderstanding. My 'variation in a definite direction' does not refer to the evolution of the organic world as a whole. I do not suppose, as Nägeli did, that this would have turned out essentially as it has actually done, even although the conditions of life or their succession upon the earth had been totally different; I believe that the organic world, its classes and orders, its families and species, would have differed from those that have actually existed, both in succession and appearance, in proportion as the conditions of life were different. My 'variation in a definite direction' is not predetermined from the beginning, is not, so to speak, exclusive, but is many-sided: each determinant of a germ-plasm may vary in a plus or minus direction, and may continue under certain circumstances in the direction once begun, but its components, the different biophors, may do the same, and so likewise may the groups, larger and smaller, of biophors which form the primordia (*Anlagen*) of the organs within the germ-plasm. Thus an enormously large number of variational tendencies is available for every part of the complete organism, and as soon as a variation would be of advantage it arises—given that it is within the possibilities of the physical constitution of the species. It occurs because its potentialities are already present, but it persists and follows a definite course because this is the one that is favoured. In other words, it is primarily fixed by germinal selection alone, but is then preferred by personal selection above the variants running parallel with it. In my opinion the definite direction of the chance germinal variations is determined only by the advantage which it affords to the species with regard to its capacity for existence. But according to Nägeli the direction of a variation is quite independent of its utility, which may or may not exist. From Nägeli's point of view we could never understand the all-prevailing adaptation, but if the utility of a variant is itself sufficient to raise it to the level of a persistent variational tendency, then we understand it.

Years ago (1883) I compared the species to a wanderer who has before him a vast immeasurable land, through which he is at liberty to choose whatever path he prefers, and in which he may sojourn wherever and for as long as he pleases. But although he may go or stay entirely of his own free will, yet at all times his going or staying will be determined—it must be so and cannot be otherwise—by two factors: first, by the paths available at each place—the variations which crop up—and secondly, by the prospects each of these available paths open up to him. He is striving after a restful place of abode which shall afford him comfortable subsistence, his former home having been spoilt for him by increasing expensiveness or too great competition. Even the direction of his first journey will not depend upon chance, since of the many paths available he will, and must, choose that which leads to a habitable and not too crowded spot. If this has been reached—that is to say, if the species has adapted itself to the new conditions—the colonist sets up his abode there, and remains as long as a comfortable existence and a competence are secure; but if these fail him, if grain becomes scarce, or if prices rise, or if a dangerous epidemic breaks out, then he makes up his mind to wander anew, and once more he will choose, among the many available paths, that which offers him the prospect of the speediest and most certain exit from the threatened region, and leads him to another where he may live without risk. There, too, he will remain as long as he is comfortable and not exposed to want or danger, for the species as a whole only becomes transformed when it must. And so it will go on *ad infinitum*; the traveller will, when he is scared away from one dwelling-place, be able to continue his journey in many directions, but he will always select the one path which offers him the best prospects of a comfortable settlement, and will follow it only to the nearest suitable place of abode, and never further. The transformation of a species only goes on until it has again completely adapted itself. In this way he will in the course of years have traversed a large number of different places which, taken together, may lie in a strange and unintelligible course, but this course has nevertheless not arisen through a mere whim, but through the twofold necessity of starting from a given spot—that in which he had previously lived—the constitution of the species, and secondly of choosing the most promising among the many available paths.

But chance does play a part in determining the route of the traveller, for on it depends the nature of the conditions in the surroundings of his previous dwelling-place, when he is forced to make another move; for these conditions change, colonies are extended or depopulated, a town previously cheap becomes dear, competition increases or decreases, disease breaks out or disappears; in short, the chances of a pleasureable sojourn in a particular place may alter and determine the wanderer who is on the point of leaving his place of abode to take a different direction from that which he would probably have chosen, say, ten years earlier.

The analogy might be carried further, as, for instance, to illustrate the possibility of a splitting up of the species; we may suppose that instead of one wanderer there is a pair, who found a family at their first halting-place. Children and grandchildren grow up in numbers and food becomes scarce. One part of the descendants still finds enough to live upon, but the rest set out to look for a new habitation. In this case, too, many paths, sidewards or backwards, stand open to the wanderers, but only those paths will be actually and successfully followed by any company of them which will lead to a habitable place where settlement is possible. If some of the descendants follow paths with no such prospect they will soon turn back or will succumb to the perils of the journey.

It seems to me that the contrast between this and Nägeli's view of the transmutation of species is obvious enough. According to him the wanderer is not free to choose his path, but goes on and on along a definite railway-line that only diverges here and there, and it cannot be foreseen whether the track leads to paradisaic dwellings or to barren wastes—the travellers must just make the best of what they find. They carry a marvellous travelling outfit with them—a sort of *Tischlein, deck' dich*—the Lamarckian principle, but the magic power of this is very doubtful, and it will hardly suffice to guard them against the heat of the deserts, the frost of the Arctic regions, or the malaria of the marshes into which their locomotive blindly carries them.

According to my view, the traveller—that is, the species—has always a large choice of paths, and is able, even while he is on the way, to discern whether he has chosen a right or a wrong one; moreover, in most cases, one or, it may be, a number of the paths lead to the desired dwelling-place. But it also undoubtedly happens that, after long wandering and when many regions have been traversed, a company may finally arrive at a place which is quite habitable and inviting at first sight, but which is surrounded on several sides by the sea or by a rushing stream. As long as the soil remains fertile and the climate healthy all goes well, but when matters change in this respect, and perhaps the only way back lies through marshes and desert land and is therefore impassable, then the colony will gradually die out—that is the death of the species.

But let us now leave our parable and inquire what paths the organic world has actually taken in its transformations, in what succession the individual forms of life have evolved from one another: in short, how the actual genealogical tree of this earth's animate population is really constructed in detail. To this I can only reply that we have many well-grounded suppositions, but only real certainty in regard to isolated cases. Thus the genealogical tree of the horse has been traced far back, and a great deal is known of the phylogeny of several Gastropods and Cephalopods, but in regard to the genealogical tree of organisms as a whole we can only make guesses, many of which are probable, but are never quite certain. The palæontological records which the earth's crust has preserved for us for all the ages are much too incomplete to admit of any certainty. Many naturalists, notably Ernst Haeckel, have done good service in this direction, for from what we know of palæontology, embryology, and morphology, they have constructed genealogical trees of the different groups of organisms, which are intended to show us the actual succession of animal and plant forms. But, interesting as these attempts are, they cannot for the most part be anything more than guesswork, and I need not, therefore, state or discuss them here in any detail, since they can afford us no aid in regard to the problem of the origin of species with which these lectures are concerned. In regard to the animal world at least—and the case of plants is probably very similar—the record of fossil forms fails us at an early stage. Thus the oldest and deepest strata in which fossils can be demonstrated, the Cambrian formation, already contains Crustaceans, animals at a relatively high stage of organization, which must have been preceded by a very long series of ancestors of which no trace has been preserved. The whole basal portion of the animal genealogical tree, from the lowest forms of life at least up to these primitive Crustaceans, the Trilobites, lies buried in the deepest sedimentary rocks raised from the sea-floor, the crystalline schists, in which it is unrecognizable. Enormous pressure and, probably also, high temperature have destroyed the solid parts as far as there were any, and the soft parts have only left an occasional impression even in the higher strata.

Thus enormous periods of time must have elapsed from the beginning of life to the laying down of that deepest 'Palæozoic' formation, the Cambrian, for not only does the whole chain which leads from the Biophoridæ to the origin of the first unicellulars fall within this period, as well as the evolution of these unicellulars themselves into their different classes, and their integration into the first multicellulars, but also the evolution of these last into all the main branches of the animal kingdom as it is now, into Sponges, Starfishes, and their allies, Molluscs, Brachiopods, and Crustaceans, for all these branches appear even in the Cambrian formation, and we may conclude that the worms also, most of which are soft and not likely to be preserved, were abundantly present at that time, since jointed animals like the Crustaceans can only have arisen from worms. Moreover, we have every reason for the assumption that Cœlenterates also, that is to say polyps and medusoids, lived in the Cambrian seas, because their near relatives with a solid skeleton, the corals, are represented in the formation next above, the Silurian. The same is true of the fishes, of which the first undoubtedly recognizable remains, the spines of sharks, have been found in the Silurian. These two presuppose a long preparatory history, and thus we come to the conclusion already stated, that all the branches of the animal kingdom were already in existence when the earth's crust shut up within itself the first records available for us of the ancestors of our modern world of organisms.

Of course at that time the higher branches had only been represented by their lower classes, and this is true especially of vertebrates, so that, from the laying down of the Cambrian strata to the modern world of organisms, a very considerable increase of complexity in structure and an infinite diversifying of new groups must have taken place. Amphibians do not appear to have been present in Cambrian times; reptiles are represented in the Carboniferous strata, but only appear in abundance in Secondary times;

birds appear first in the Jurassic, but in a very different guise (*Archæopteryx*) from the modern forms, covered indeed with feathers, but still possessing a reptilian tail; later they occur as toothed birds in the Cretaceous, and in Tertiary times they have their present form. The development of mammals must have run almost parallel with that of birds, that is, from the beginning of Secondary times onwards, and their highest and last member appears, as far as is known to research, only in post-Glacial times, in the Diluvial deposits.

To the types which have arisen since the Cambrian period belongs the class of Insects with its twelve orders and its enormous wealth of known species, now reckoned at 200,000. They are demonstrable first in the Devonian, and then in the Carboniferous period, in forms, just as our theory requires, with *biting* mouth-organs; it is not until the Cretaceous strata that insects with purely suctorial mouth-organs—bees and butterflies—occur, as it was also at that time that the flowers, which have evolved in mutual adaptation with insects, first appeared.

The number of fossil species hitherto described is reckoned at about 80,000—certainly only a mere fragment of the wealth of forms of life which have arisen on our earth throughout this long period, and which must have passed away again; for very few *species* outlive a geological epoch, and even genera appear only for a longer or shorter time, and then disappear for ever. But even of many of the older classes, such, for instance, as the Cystoids among the Echinoderms of the Silurian seas, no living representative remains; and in the same way, the Ichthyosaurs or fish-lizards of the Secondary times have completely disappeared from our modern fauna, and many other animal types, like the class of Brachiopods and the hard-scaled Ganoid fishes, have almost died out and are represented only by a few species in specially sheltered places, such as the great depths of the sea, or in rivers.

Thus an incredible wealth of animal and plant species was potentially contained in these simplest and lowest 'Biophorids' which lay far below the limits of microscopic visibility—an indefinitely greater wealth than has actually arisen, for that is only a small part of what was possible, and of what would have arisen had the changes of life-conditions and life-possibilities followed a different course. The greater the complexity of the structure of an organism is, the more numerous are the parts of it which are capable of variation, and the different directions in which it can adapt itself to new conditions; and it will hardly be disputed that *potentially* the first Biophorids contained an absolutely inexhaustible wealth of forms of life, and not merely those which have actually been evolved. If this were not so, Man could not still call forth new animal and plant forms, as he is continually doing among our domesticated animals and cultivated plants, just as the chemist is continually 'creating' new combinations in the laboratory which have probably never yet occurred or been formed on the earth. But just as the chemist does not really 'create' these combinations, but only brings the necessary elements and their forces together in such a combination that they must unite to form the desired new body, so the breeder only guides the variational tendencies contained in the germ-plasm, and consciously combines them to procure a new race. And what the breeder does within the narrow limits of human power is being accomplished in free nature, through the conditions which allow only what is fit to survive and reproduce, and thus bring about the wonderful result --as though it were guided by a superior intelligence—the adaptation of species to their environment.

Thus in our time the great riddle has been solved—the riddle of the origin of what is suited to its purpose, without the co-operation of purposive forces. Although we cannot demonstrate and follow out the particular processes of transformation and adaptation in all their phases with mathematical certainty, we can understand the principle, and we see the factors through the co-operation of which the result must be brought about. It has lately become the fashion, at least among the younger school of biologists, to attach small value to natural selection, if not, indeed, to regard it as a superseded formula; mathematical proofs are demanded or, at any rate, desired. I do not believe that we shall ever arrive at giving such proofs, but we shall undoubtedly succeed in clearing up much that now remains obscure, and in essentially modifying and correcting many of the theories we have formed in regard to this question. But what has been already gained must certainly be regarded as an enormous advance on the knowledge of fifty years ago. We now *know* that the modern world of organisms has been evolved, and we can form an idea, though still only an imperfect one, how and through the co-operation of what factors it could and must have evolved.

When I say *must*, this refers only to the course of evolution from a given beginning; but as to this beginning itself, the spontaneous generation of the lowest Biophorids from inorganic material, we are far from having understood it as a necessary outcome of its causes. And if we have assumed it as a reasonable postulate, we by no means seek to conceal that this assumption is far from implying an understanding of what the process of biogenesis was. I do not merely mean that we do not know under what external conditions the origin of living matter, even in the smallest quantity, can take place; I mean, especially, that we do not understand how this one substance should suddenly reveal qualities which have never been detected in any other chemical combination whatever—the circulation of matter, metabolism, growth, sensation, will, and movement. But we may confidently say that we shall never be able fully to understand these specific phenomena of life, as indeed how should we, since nothing analogous to them is known to us, and since understanding always presupposes a comparison with something known. Even although we assume that we might succeed in understanding the mere chemistry of life, as is not inconceivable, I mean the *perpetuum mobile* of dissimilation and assimilation, the so-called 'animal' functions of the living substance would remain uncomprehended: Sensation, Will, Thought. We understand in some measure how the kidneys secrete urine, or the liver bile; we can also—given the sensitiveness to stimulus of the living substance—understand how a sense-impression may be conveyed by the nerves to the brain, carried along certain reflex paths to motor nerves and give rise to movement of the muscles, but how the activity of certain brain-elements can give rise to a thought *which cannot be compared with anything material*, which is nevertheless able to react upon the material parts of our body, and, as Will, to give rise to movement—that we attempt in vain to understand. Of course the dependence of thinking and willing upon a material substratum is clear enough, and it can be demonstrated with certainty in many directions, and thus materialism is so far justified in drawing parallels between the brain and thought on the one hand, and the kidneys and urine on the other, but this is by no means to say that we have understood how Thought and Will have come to be. In recent times it has often been pointed out that the physical functions of the body increase very gradually with the successive stages of the organization, and from the lowest beginnings ascend slowly to the intelligence of Man, in exact correspondence with the height of organization that has been reached by the species; that they begin so imperceptibly among the lower animal forms that we cannot tell exactly where the beginning is; and it has been rightly concluded from this that the elements of the Psyche do not originate in the histological parts of the nervous system, but are peculiar to all living matter, and it has further been inferred that even inorganic material may contain them, although in an unrecognizable expression, and that their emergence in living matter is, so to speak, only a phenomenon of summation. If we are right in our assumption of a spontaneous generation it can hardly be otherwise, but saying this does not mean that we have understood Spirit, but at most secures us the advantage and the right of looking at this world, as far as we know it, as a unity. This is the standpoint of Monism.

The psychical phenomena, which we know from ourselves, and can assume among animals with greater certainty the nearer they stand to us, occupy a domain by themselves, and such a vast and complex one that there can be no question of bringing it within the scope of our present studies, and the same is true of the phyletic development of Man. But we must at least take up a position in regard to these problems, and there can be no question that Man has evolved from animal ancestors, whose nearest relatives were the Anthropoid Apes. Not many years ago bony remains of a human skeleton, or at least of some form very near to modern Man, were found in the Diluvial deposits of Java, and this has been designated *Pithecanthropus erectus*, and perhaps rightly regarded as a transition form between Apes and Man. It is possible that more may yet be discovered: but even if that is not so, the conclusion that Man had his origin from animal forefathers must be regarded as inevitable and fully established. We do not draw conclusions with our eyes, but with our reasoning powers, and if the whole of the rest of living nature proclaims with one accord from all sides the evolution of the world of organisms, we cannot assume that the process stopped short of Man. But it follows also that the *factors* which brought about the development of Man from his Simian ancestry must be the same as those which have brought about the whole of evolution: change of external influences in its direct and indirect effects, and, besides this, germinal variational tendencies and their selection. And in this connexion I should like to draw attention to a point which has, perhaps, as yet received too little attention.

Selection only gives rise to what is suited to its end; *beyond that it can call forth nothing*, as we have already emphasized on several occasions. I need only recall the protective leaf-marking of butterflies, which is never a botanically exact copy of a leaf, with all its lateral veins, but is comparable rather to an impressionist painting, in which it is not the reproduction of every detail that is of importance, but the total impression which it makes at a certain distance. If we apply this to the organs and capacities of Man, we shall only expect to find these developed as far as their development is of value for the preservation of his existence and no further. But this may perhaps seem a contradiction of what observation teaches us, that, for instance, our eyes can see to the infinite distance of the fixed stars, although this can be of no importance in relation to the struggle for existence. But this intensity of the power of vision has obviously not been acquired for the investigation of the starry heavens, but was of the greatest value in securing the existence of many of our animal ancestors, and was not less important for our own. In the same way our finely evolved musical ear might be regarded as a perfecting of the hearing apparatus far beyond the degree necessary to existence, but this is not really the case: our musical ear, too, has been inherited from our animal ancestors, and to them, as to primitive Man, it was a necessity of existence. It was quite necessary for the animals to distinguish the higher and lower notes of a long scale, sharply and certainly, in order to be able to evade an approaching enemy, or to recognize prey from afar. That we are able to make music is, so to speak, only an unintentional accessory power of the hearing organs, which were originally developed only for the preservation of existence, just as the human hand did not become what it is *in order to play the piano*, but to touch and seize, to make tools, and so on.

Must this, then, be true also of the human mind? Can it, too, only be developed as far as its development is of advantage to Man's power of survival? I believe that this is certainly the case in a general way; the intellectual powers which are the common property of the human race will never rise beyond these limits, but this is not to say that certain individuals may not be more highly endowed. The possibility of a higher development of certain mental powers or of their combinations—whether it be intelligence, will, feeling, inventive power, or a talent for mathematics, music or painting—may be inferred with certainty from our own principles; for not only may the variational tendencies of individual groups of determinants in the germ-plasm be continued for a series of generations without becoming injurious, that is to say, without being put a stop to by personal selection, but sexual intermingling always opens up the possibility that some predominantly developed intellectual tendencies (*Anlagen*) may combine in one way or another, and so give rise to individuals of great mental superiority, in whatever direction. In this way, it seems to me, the geniuses of humanity have arisen—a Plato, a Shakespeare, a Goethe, a Beethoven. But they do not last; they do not transmit their greatness; if they leave descendants at all, these never inherit the *whole* greatness of their father, and we can easily understand this, since the greatness does not depend upon a single character, but upon a particular combination of many high mental qualities (*Anlagen*). Geniuses, therefore, probably never raise the average of the race through their descendants; they raise the intellectual average only through their own performances, by increasing the knowledge and power handed on by tradition from generation to generation. But the raising of the average of mental capacity, which has undoubtedly taken place to a considerable degree from the Australasian aborigines to the civilized peoples of antiquity and of our own day, can only depend on the struggle for existence between individuals and races.

But if the human mind has been raised to its present level through the same slow process of selection by means of which all evolution has been directed and raised to the height necessary for the 'desired end,' we must see in this a definite indication that even the greatest mind among us can never see beyond the conditions which limit our capacity for existence, and that now and for all time we cannot hope to understand what is supernatural. We can recognize the stars in the heavens, it is true, and after thousands of years of work we have succeeded in determining their distance, their size, and gravity, as well as their movements and the materials of which they are composed, but we have been able to do all this with a thinking power created for the conditions of human existence upon the earth, that is to say, developed by them, just as we do not only grasp with our hands, but may also play the piano with them. But all that involves a higher thinking power that would enable us to recognize the pseudo-ideas of everlastingness and infinity, the limits of causality, in short, all that we do not know but regard as at best a riddle, will always remain sealed to us, because our intelligence did not, and does not, require this power to maintain our capacity for existence.

I say this in particular to those who imagine they have summed up the whole situation when they admit that much is still lacking to complete knowledge, say, to a true understanding of the powers of Nature or of the Psyche, but who do not feel that in spite of all our very considerably increased knowledge we stand before the world as a whole as before a great riddle. But I say it also to those who fear that the doctrine of evolution will be the overthrow of their faith. Let them not forget that truth can only be harmful, and may even be destructive, when we have only half grasped it, or when we try to evade it. If we follow it unafraid, we shall come now and in the future to the conclusion that a limit is set to our knowledge by our own minds, and that beyond this limit begins the region of faith, and this each must fashion for himself as suits his nature. In regard to ultimate things Goethe has given us the true formula, when the 'Nature-spirit' calls to Faust, 'Du gleichst dem Geist, den Du begreifst, nicht mir!' For all time Man must repeat this to himself, but the need for an ethical view of the world, a religion, will remain, though even this must change in its expression according to the advance of our knowledge of the world.

But we must not conclude these lectures in a spirit of mere resignation. Although we must content ourselves without being able to penetrate the arcana of this wonderful world, we must remain conscious, at the same time, that these unfathomable depths exist, and that we may 'still verehren was unerforschlich ist' (Goethe). But the other half of the world, I mean the part which is accessible to us, discloses to us such an inexhaustible wealth of phenomena, and such a deep and unfailing enjoyment in its beauty and the harmonious interaction of the innumerable wheels of its marvellous mechanism, that the investigation of it is quite worthy to fill our lives. And we need have no fear that there will ever be any lack of new questions and new problems to solve. Even if Mankind could continue for centuries quietly working on in the manifold and restless manner that has, for the first time in the history of human thought, characterized the century just gone, each new solution would raise new questions above and below, in the immeasurable space of the firmament, as in the world of microscopical or ultramicroscopical minuteness, new insight would be gained, new satisfaction won, and our enthusiasm over the marvel of this world-mechanism, so extraordinarily complex yet so beautifully simple in its operation, will never be extinguished, but will always flame up anew to warm and illumine our lives.

INDEX

[References to vol. ii have the volume prefixed.]

OXFORD: HORACE HART

PRINTER TO THE UNIVERSITY

STANDARD SCIENTIFIC WORKS.

HABIT AND INSTINCT:

A STUDY IN HEREDITY.

BY PROFESSOR C. LLOYD MORGAN, LL.D., F.R.S.,
Principal of University College, Bristol.

Demy 8vo. With Photogravure Frontispiece. 16s.

ANIMAL BEHAVIOUR.

BY PROFESSOR C. LLOYD MORGAN, LL.D., F.R.S.,

Large Crown 8vo. With numerous Illustrations. 10s. 6d.

THE CHANCES OF DEATH,

AND OTHER STUDIES IN EVOLUTION.

BY KARL PEARSON, F.R.S.,
Professor of Applied Mathematics in University College, London, and formerly Fellow of King's College, Cambridge.

Two volumes, Demy 8vo. With Illustrations. 25s. net.

CONTENTS.

STUDIES IN EVOLUTION.

BY CHARLES EMERSON BEECHER, PH.D.,
Professor of Historical Theology at Yale University.

Demy 8vo. With Illustrations. 21s. net.

A TEXTBOOK OF ZOOLOGY.

BY G. P. MUDGE, A.R.C.SC. LOND., F.Z.S.,
Lecturer on Biology at the London School of Medicine for Women, and on Zoology and Botany at the Polytechnic Institute, Regent Street; and Demonstrator on Biology at the London Hospital Medical College.

With Two Coloured Plates and about 200 Original Illustrations.
Crown 8vo. 7s. 6d.

LONDON: EDWARD ARNOLD, 41 & 43 MADDOX ST., W.

STANDARD SCIENTIFIC WORKS.

THE CHEMICAL SYNTHESIS OF VITAL PRODUCTS

AND THE INTER-RELATIONS BETWEEN ORGANIC COMPOUNDS.

BY RAPHAEL MELDOLA, F.R.S.,

Professor of Chemistry in the City and Guilds of London Technical College, Finsbury.

Vol. I. Super royal 8vo. 21*s.* net.

THE ELECTRIC FURNACE.

BY HENRI MOISSAN,

Membre de l'Institut; Professor of Chemistry at the Sorbonne.

AUTHORIZED ENGLISH EDITION.

TRANSLATED BY A. T. DE MOUILPIED, B.SC., M.SC., PH.D.,

Assistant Lecturer in Chemistry in the Liverpool University.

Demy 8vo. With Illustrations. 10*s.* 6*d.* net.

AN INTRODUCTION TO THE THEORY OF OPTICS.

BY ARTHUR SCHUSTER, PH.D. (HEID.), SC.D. (CANTAB.), F.R.S.,

Professor of Physics at the University of Manchester.

Demy 8vo. 15*s.* net.

THE BECQUEREL RAYS AND THE PROPERTIES OF RADIUM.

BY THE HON. R. J. STRUTT,

Fellow of Trinity College, Cambridge.

Demy 8vo. 8*s.* 6*d.* net.

FOOD AND THE PRINCIPLES OF DIETETICS.

BY ROBERT HUTCHISON, M.D. EDIN., F.R.C.P.,

Assistant Physician to the London Hospital and to the Hospital for Sick Children, Great Ormond Street, London.

Demy 8vo. With three Plates in Colour and thirty-four Illustrations in the Text. 16*s.* net.

LONDON: EDWARD ARNOLD, 41 & 43 MADDOX ST., W.

MR. EDWARD ARNOLD'S

LIST OF

Scientific and Technical Books.

LECTURES ON DISEASES OF CHILDREN. By ROBERT HUTCHISON, M.D. (Edin.), F.R.C.P., Assistant Physician to the London Hospital and to the Hospital for Sick Children, Great Ormond Street, London. With numerous Illustrations. Crown 8vo., 8s. 6d. net.

PRACTICAL PHYSIOLOGY. By A. P. BEDDARD, M.A., M.D., Demonstrator of Physiology, Guy's Hospital; J. S. EDKINS, M.A., M.B., Lecturer in Physiology and Demonstrator of Physiology, St. Bartholomew's Hospital; LEONARD HILL, M.B., F.R.S., Lecturer on Physiology, London Hospital Medical School; J. J. R. MACLEOD, M.B.; and M. S. PEMBREY, M.A., M.D., Lecturer on Physiology in Guy's Hospital Medical School. Copiously Illustrated. Demy 8vo., 15s. net.

HUMAN EMBRYOLOGY AND MORPHOLOGY. By A. KEITH, M.D., F.R.C.S. Eng., Lecturer on Anatomy at the London Hospital Medical College. With 300 Illustrations. New, Revised, and Enlarged Edition. Demy 8vo., 12s. 6d. net.

FOOD AND THE PRINCIPLES OF DIETETICS. By ROBERT HUTCHISON, M.D. Edin., F.R.C.P., Assistant Physician to the London Hospital. Fifth Impression. Illustrated. Demy 8vo., 16s. net.

THE PHYSIOLOGICAL ACTION OF DRUGS. An Introduction to Practical Pharmacology. By M. S. PEMBREY, M.A., M.D., Lecturer on Physiology in Guy's Hospital Medical School; and C. D. F. PHILLIPS, M.D., LL.D. Fully Illustrated. Demy 8vo., 4s. 6d. net.

PHOTOTHERAPY. By N. R. FINSEN. Translated by J. H. SEQUÉIRA, M.D. With Illustrations. Demy 8vo., 4s. 6d. net.

CONTENTS.—I. The Chemical Rays of Light and Small-pox—II. Light as an Irritant—III. Treatment of Lupus Vulgaris by concentrated Chemical Rays.

A MANUAL OF HUMAN PHYSIOLOGY. By LEONARD HILL, M.B., F.R.S. With 173 Illustrations. xii + 484 pages. Crown 8vo., cloth, 6s.

A PRIMER OF PHYSIOLOGY. By LEONARD HILL, M.B. 1s.

LECTURES ON THEORETICAL AND PHYSICAL CHEMISTRY. By Dr. J. H. VAN 'T HOFF, Professor of Chemistry at the University of Berlin. Translated by Dr. R. A. LEHFELDT. In three volumes. Illustrated. Demy 8vo., 28s. net; or obtainable separately, as follows:

Vol. I.—**Chemical Dynamics.** 12s. net. Vol. II.—**Chemical Statics.** 8s. 6d. net.
Vol. III.—**Relations between Properties and Composition.** 7s. 6d. net.

THE ELEMENTS OF INORGANIC CHEMISTRY. For use in Schools and Colleges. By W. A. SHENSTONE, Lecturer in Chemistry at Clifton College. xii + 506 pages. With nearly 150 Illustrations. 4s. 6d.

A COURSE OF PRACTICAL CHEMISTRY. Being a Revised Edition of 'A Laboratory Companion for Use with Shenstone's Inorganic Chemistry.' By W. A. SHENSTONE. 144 pages. Crown 8vo., 1s. 6d.

LONDON: EDWARD ARNOLD, 41 & 43 MADDOX STREET, W.

A TEXT-BOOK OF PHYSICAL CHEMISTRY. By Dr. R. A. LEHFELDT, Professor of Physics at the East London Technical College. With 40 Illustrations. Crown 8vo., cloth, 7s. 6d.

THE CHEMICAL SYNTHESIS OF VITAL PRODUCTS AND THE INTER-RELATIONS BETWEEN ORGANIC COMPOUNDS. By Professor RAPHAEL MELDOLA, F.R.S., of the City and Guilds of London Technical College, Finsbury. Two vols. Vol. I. now ready. Super Royal 8vo., 21s. net.

A TEXT-BOOK OF PHYSICS. With Sections on the Applications of Physics to Physiology and Medicine. By Dr. R. A. LEHFELDT. Fully Illustrated. Crown 8vo., cloth, 6s.

PHYSICAL CHEMISTRY FOR BEGINNERS. By Dr. Ch. M. VAN DEVENTER. With a Preface by J. H. VAN 'T HOFF. Translated by Dr. R. A. LEHFELDT, Professor of Physics at the East London Technical College. 2s. 6d.

A FIRST YEAR'S COURSE OF EXPERIMENTAL WORK IN CHEMISTRY. By ERNEST H. COOK, D.Sc., F.I.C., Principal of the Clifton Laboratory, Bristol. With 26 Illustrations. Crown 8vo., cloth, 1s. 6d.

AN EXPERIMENTAL COURSE OF CHEMISTRY FOR AGRICULTURAL STUDENTS. By T. S. DYMOND, F.I.C., Lecturer on Agricultural Chemistry in the County Technical Laboratories, Chelmsford. With 50 Illustrations. 192 pages. Crown 8vo., cloth, 2s. 6d.

THE STANDARD COURSE OF ELEMENTARY CHEMISTRY. By E. J. COX, F.C.S. With 90 Illustrations. 350 pages. Crown 8vo., cloth, 3s. Also obtainable in five parts, limp cloth. Parts I.-IV., 7d. each; Part V., 1s.

A PRELIMINARY COURSE OF PRACTICAL PHYSICS. By C. E. ASHFORD, M.A., Headmaster of the Royal Naval College, Osborne. Fcap. 4to., 1s. 6d.

PHYSICAL DETERMINATIONS. A Manual of Laboratory Instructions for the Determination of Physical Quantities. By W. R. KELSEY, B.Sc., A.I.E.E., Lecturer in Physics to the Bradford Municipal Technical College. 4s. 6d.

ELECTROLYTIC PREPARATIONS. Exercises for use in the laboratory by chemists and electro-chemists. By Dr. KARL ELBS, Professor of Chemistry at the University of Giessen. Translated by R. S. HUTTON, M.Sc. Demy 8vo., 4s. 6d. net.

THE ELECTRIC FURNACE. By HENRI MOISSAN, Professor of Chemistry at the Sorbonne. Authorized English Edition. Translated by A. T. DE MOUILPIED, M.Sc., Ph.D. With Illustrations. Demy 8vo., 10s. 6d. net.

ELECTRICAL TRACTION. By ERNEST WILSON, Wh.Sc., M.I.E.E., Professor of Electrical Engineering in the Siemens Laboratory, King's College, London. Crown 8vo., 5s.

ELECTRICITY AND MAGNETISM. By C. E. ASHFORD, M.A., Headmaster of the Osborne Royal Naval College, late Senior Science Master at Harrow School. With over 200 Diagrams. Crown 8vo., 3s. 6d.

MAGNETISM AND ELECTRICITY. An Elementary Treatise for Junior Students, Descriptive and Experimental. By J. PALEY YORKE, of the Northern Polytechnic Institute, London. With nearly 150 Illustrations. 3s. 6d.

THE BALANCING OF ENGINES. By W. E. DALBY, M.A., B.Sc., M.Inst.C.E., M.I.M.E., Professor of Mechanical Engineering and Applied Mathematics in the City and Guilds of London Technical College, Finsbury. With 173 Illustrations. Demy 8vo., 10s. 6d. net.

THE STRENGTH AND ELASTICITY OF STRUCTURAL MEMBERS. By R. J. WOODS, Master of Engineering, Royal University of Ireland, Fellow of the Royal Indian Engineering College, and Assistant Professor of Engineering Cooper's Hill College. Demy 8vo. 10s. 6d. net.

TRAVERSE TABLES. With an Introductory Chapter on Co-ordinate Surveying. By HENRY LOUIS, M.A., A.R.S.M., F.I.C., F.G.S., etc., Professor of Mining and Lecturer on Surveying, Durham College of Science, Newcastle-on-Tyne; and G. W. CAUNT, M.A. Demy 8vo., 4s. 6d. net.

THE CALCULUS FOR ENGINEERS. By JOHN PERRY, M.E., D.Sc., F.R.S., Professor of Mechanics and Mathematics in the Royal College of Science, etc. Crown 8vo., cloth, 7s. 6d.

ELECTRIC AND MAGNETIC CIRCUITS. By ELLIS H. CRAPPER, M.I.E.E., Head of the Electrical Engineering Department in the University College, Sheffield. viii + 380 pages. Demy 8vo., 10s. 6d. net.

AN INTRODUCTION TO THE THEORY OF OPTICS. By Professor ARTHUR SCHUSTER, Ph.D., F.R.S., Professor of Physics at the University of Manchester. With numerous Diagrams. Demy 8vo., 15s. net.

ASTRONOMICAL DISCOVERY. By H. H. TURNER, Savilian Professor of Astronomy in the University of Oxford. With Diagrams. Demy 8vo., 10s. 6d. net.

VECTORS AND ROTORS. With Applications. Being Lectures delivered at the Central Technical College By Professor O. HENRICI, F.R.S. Edited by G. C. TURNER, Goldsmith Institute. Crown 8vo., cloth. 4s. 6d.

THE PRINCIPLES OF MECHANISM. By H. A. GARRATT, A.M.I.C.E., Head of the Engineering Department of the Northern Polytechnic Institute, Holloway. Crown 8vo., cloth, 3s. 6d.

ELEMENTARY PLANE AND SOLID MENSURATION. By R. W. K. EDWARDS, M.A., Lecturer on Mathematics at King's College, London. For use in Schools, Colleges, and Technical Classes. 304 pages. Crown 8vo., 3s. 6d.

FIVE-FIGURE TABLES OF MATHEMATICAL FUNCTIONS. By J. B. DALE, M.A. Camb., B.A. Lond., late Scholar St. John's College, Cambridge, Lecturer on Pure and Applied Mathematics, King's College, University of London. Demy 8vo., 3s. 6d. net.

AN ELEMENTARY TREATISE ON PRACTICAL MATHEMATICS. By JOHN GRAHAM, B.A., Demonstrator of Mechanical Engineering and Applied Mathematics in the Technical College, Finsbury. Crown 8vo., cloth, 3s. 6d.

PRELIMINARY PRACTICAL MATHEMATICS. By S. G. STARLING, A.R.C.Sc., B.Sc., Head of the Mathematics and Physics Department of the West Ham Municipal Technical Institute; and F. C. CLARKE, A.R.C.Sc., B.Sc.

THE EVOLUTION THEORY. By AUGUST WEISMANN, Professor of Zoology in the University of Freiburg-im-Breisgau. Translated by Professor J. ARTHUR THOMSON. With numerous Illustrations and Coloured Plates. Two Vols. Royal 8vo., 32s. net.

The importance of this work is twofold. In the first place, it sums up the teaching of one of Darwin's greatest successors, who has been for many years a leader in biological progress. As Professor Weismann has from time to time during the last quarter of a century frankly altered some of his positions, this deliberate summing up of his mature conclusions is very valuable. In the second place, as the volumes discuss all the chief problems of organic evolution, they form a reliable guide to the whole subject, and may be regarded as furnishing—what is much needed—a Text-book of Evolution Theory.

ANIMAL BEHAVIOUR. By C. LLOYD MORGAN, LL.D., F.R.S., Principal of University College Bristol, author of 'Animal Life and Intelligence,' etc. With numerous Illustrations. Large crown 8vo., 10s. 6d.

HABIT AND INSTINCT. By C. LLOYD MORGAN, LL.D., F.R.S. With Photogravure Frontispiece. viii + 352 pages. Demy 8vo., cloth, 16s.

A TEXT-BOOK OF ZOOLOGY. By G. P. MUDGE, A.R.C.Sc. Lond., Lecturer on Biology at the London School of Medicine for Women, and the Polytechnic Institute, Regent Street. With about 200 original Illustrations. Crown 8vo., cloth, 7s. 6d.

ELEMENTARY NATURAL PHILOSOPHY. By ALFRED EARL, M.A., Assistant Master at Tonbridge School. With numerous Illustrations and Diagrams. Crown 8vo., cloth, 4s. 6d.

A CLASS-BOOK OF BOTANY. By G. P. MUDGE, A.R.C.Sc. Lond., F.Z.S., and A. J. MASLEN, F.L.S., Lecturer on Botany at the Woolwich Polytechnic. With over 200 Illustrations. Crown 8vo., 7s. 6d.

THE BECQUEREL RAYS AND THE PROPERTIES OF RADIO-ACTIVE SUBSTANCES. By the Hon. R. J. STRUTT, Fellow of Trinity College, Cambridge. With Diagrams. Demy 8vo. 8s. 6d. net.

A MANUAL OF ALCOHOLIC FERMENTATION AND THE ALLIED INDUSTRIES. By CHARLES G. MATTHEWS, F.I.C., F.C.S., etc Fully Illustrated. Crown 8vo., cloth, 7s. 6d. net.

WOOD. A Manual of the Natural History and Industrial Applications of the Timbers of Commerce. By G. S. BOULGER, F.L.S., F.G.S. Fully Illustrated. Crown 8vo., 7s. 6d. net.

PSYCHOLOGY FOR TEACHERS. By C. LLOYD MORGAN, LL.D., F.R.S. xii + 251 pages. Crown 8vo., 3s. 6d.

ANIMAL SKETCHES. By C. LLOYD MORGAN, LL.D., F.R.S. viii + 312 pages, with 52 Illustrations (many of them full-page). Crown 8vo., cloth, 3s. 6d.

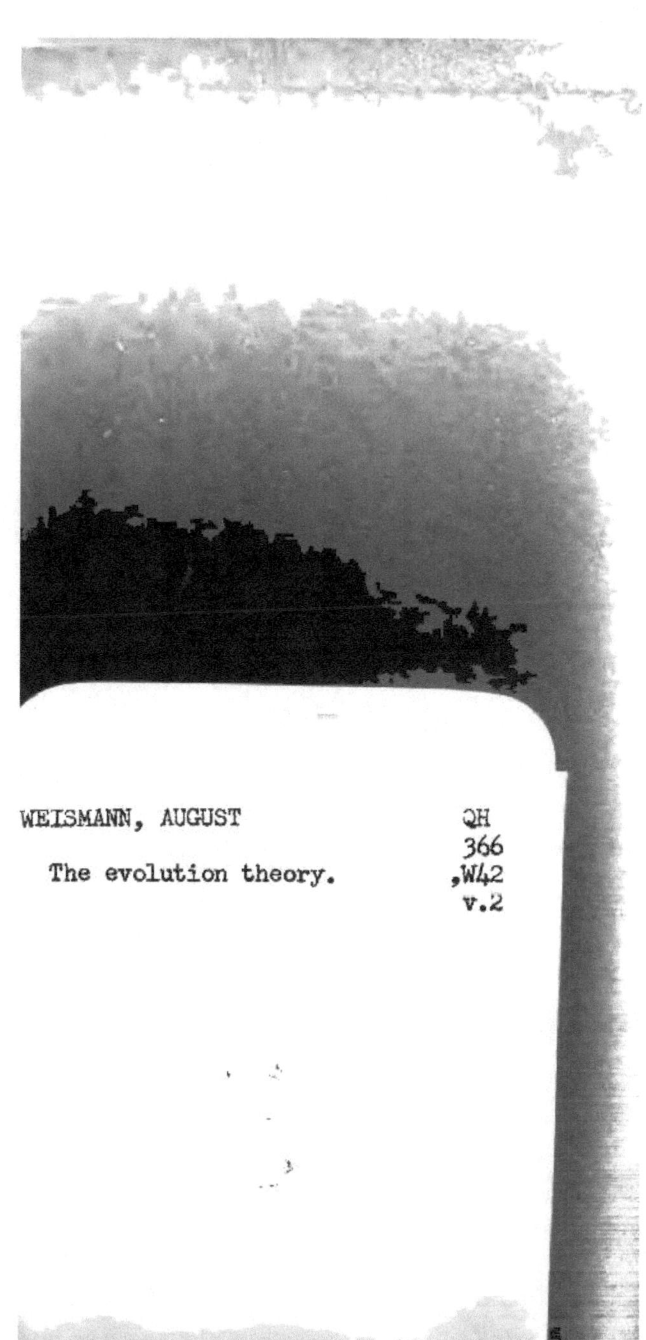

WEISMANN, AUGUST

The evolution theory.

Zeitfracht Medien GmbH
Ferdinand-Jühlke-Straße 7
99095 Erfurt, Deutschland
produktsicherheit@kolibri360.de